MANAGING MICROCOMPUTER SECURITY

MANAGING MICROCOMPUTER SECURITY

Chantico Publishing Company, Inc.

Edited by

Dr. Robert S. Snoyer

Glenn A. Fischer

Business One Irwin
Homewood, IL   60430

This publication is designed to provide accurate and
authoritative information in regard to the subject matter
covered. It is sold with the understanding that neither the
author nor the publisher is engaged in rendering legal, accounting,
or other professional service. If legal advice or other expert
assistance is required, the services of a competent
professional person should be sought.

*From a Declaration of Principles jointly adopted by a Committee
of the American Bar Association and a Committee of Publishers.*

Sponsoring editor: Susan Stevens, Ph.D.
Project editor: Susan Trentacosti
Production manager: Bette K. Ittersagen
Jacket designer: Annette Vogt
Compositor: Carlisle Communications, Ltd.
Typeface: 10/12 Palatino
Printer: Book Press, Inc.

Library of Congress Cataloging-in-Publication Data
Managing microcomputer security / Chantico Publishing Company; edited
   by Robert S. Snoyer, Glenn A. Fischer
      p.   cm.
   Includes index.
   ISBN 1-55623-875-4
   1. Computer security.   2. Business—Data processing—Security
measures.   I. Snoyer, Robert S.   II. Fischer, Glenn A.
III. Chantico Publishing Co.
HF5548.37.M37   1993
658.4'78—dc20   92–12293

Printed in the United States of America
1 2 3 4 5 6 7 8 9 0 BP 9 8 7 6 5 4 3 2

Foreword

This book is a must for companies or individuals who own or utilize a microcomputer. Microcomputers are often called by other names, such as personal computer, PC, workstation, personal workstation, engineering workstation, smart terminal, desktop computer, notebook computer, laptop computer, and no telling what else.

This book tells you how to protect your microcomputer system and preserve the many hours of work that typically go into the writing of programs, the building of databases, the generation of reports, and the other activities involved with managing and using microcomputers.

The potential for loss, misuse, and/or corruption of information contained in the microcomputer files and transmitted over telecommunications links is unlimited. This book contains many actual cases that you would probably never imagine could happen.

A couple of age-old sayings come to mind; they are extremely applicable to the microcomputer security issue:

1. An ounce of prevention is worth a pound of cure.

2. It's too late to close the gate once the horse is out.

This book contains many pieces of advice and numerous checklists, which, if followed, will significantly reduce the risk of loss. In many cases it takes no more effort to implement and utilize good security techniques than it does to ignore the issue until disaster strikes. Everyone who uses microcomputers on an ongoing basis is susceptible to many of the adverse happenings described in this book. It is not a question of *if*, only *when!* Forewarned is forearmed. Be prepared. The microcomputer system you save may be your own.

This book represents the thinking, experience, and input of many of the foremost experts in computer security today. It is quite detailed but is organized so you can quickly and easily find the areas applicable to your situation. The many real-life case studies make it interesting reading as well. This book is designed to become the foremost textbook and reference book on the topic today.

By using the tips and techniques you will learn from this book, you can expect it to pay for itself many times over, and in the extreme case, it could save a fortune or keep a company from going out of business.

One tip that saves one or two hours will typically cover the price of this book. Microcomputer users cannot afford to be without this book.

Dr. Robert S. Snoyer
Glenn A. Fischer

Acknowledgments

This book is one of a series developed through the efforts of the Profit Oriented Systems Planning Program Organization (POSPP). POSPP is a peer-networking organization whose members are senior-level executives responsible for the profitable application of information technology in support of organization goals. The members are executives for vital information systems and services representing a significant number of different organizations worldwide, ranging from Fortune 1000 companies to various government agencies. Multiple industry segments are represented, including firms in banking, insurance, energy, manufacturing, transportation, utilities, consumer products, and various other lines of business. The book represents the experiences of these organizations and the specialized expertise of the outstanding professionals who manage them.

The materials provided by the membership have been compiled and edited by Chantico Publishing Company.

R.S.S.
G.A.F.

Contents

Chapter One

Introduction

MICROCOMPUTER SECURITY

The electronic desktop has made its appearance. As rudimentary as its capabilities appear to be now in comparison with what is promised for the future, today's microcomputer presents many new opportunities— and challenges. The opportunities, increased productivity and creativity, are often cited. Not nearly as visible, yet, is one of the new challenges: providing security. And that is the focus of this book. Gone is the day when "computer" security was the sole domain of the information services/data processing department. In the age of the microcomputer, the managers of every functional area must participate. The spread of microcomputer networks and data repositories accessible by electronic means has made functional line management a full partner. There will be more microcomputers, more networks, and more file-servers. The risks are there. The need for an active and appropriately comprehensive microcomputer security program will only grow.

Microcomputers have proliferated rapidly into the general business environment. They help workers throughout a company to do their jobs better. Microcomputers come in many varieties, and may be called personal computers (PCs), workstations, desktop computers, word processors, portable computers, or terminals. They have become a key factor in processing information in most organizations, and their proper management, control, and security is a necessity.

Microcomputers ("micros") frequently have access to, or produce, large amounts of sensitive information within an organization. The output from these micros is frequently used in making management, sales, and other important decisions. Therefore, the security and management of the information that microcomputers contain and manipulate must be given urgent consideration. The planning and implementation of a microcomputer security program involves many complex organizational and technical factors, and these factors should be systematically analyzed as to their role or effect in specific situations.

1

One of the most basic, and urgent, data security problems presented by microcomputers is that the disks and other memory devices that they use are readily portable. They can easily be loaded with sensitive information, and then be taken elsewhere. Data can be altered. Sensitive information can be compromised. Secrets can be stolen. The fact that large amounts of data can be removed from the premises in a small briefcase or envelope is a problem that must be addressed.

Another urgent security problem is that the computers themselves can be taken out the door, either by permission or not, and they can be connected to other computers, or the contents can be transferred to home computers. Many organizations encourage employees to use computers at home, but the security aspect of such work must be carefully analyzed.

A third urgent security problem is the commonly seen arrangement in which microcomputers are connected to the larger computers of an organization, so that the user of a micro can readily access large amounts of data appropriate to the user's job. The security issue lies in the control of the access method or the electronic link. The security implications are determined by the sensitivity of the data accessed and the ability to control data file changes.

Microcomputer technology is changing rapidly. The machines are now very powerful, as compared with mainframe computers of just a few years ago, and they are handling complex applications and communications connections. Almost all the security considerations that were formerly applied to mainframes now must be applied to the micros.

Microcomputers now do duty as file servers. As such, they are repositories for departmental work, so their security takes on a broader perspective. They are nodes on decentralized and distributed data processing networks. Companies have found that it is more efficient to design, program, enter data, and operate smaller systems at the departmental level using their own personnel, outside the normally controlled "information services" environment. The concept of "demand processing" is becoming increasingly important in today's business environment. There is an insatiable requirement for interactive processing composed of unstructured, ad hoc queries for data that may be in either the company database or in external databases. Complex systems, such as those that provide financial modeling or business graphics, may be used. The security problems are truly enormous and can only be handled if the issue is looked on as a whole, but the analysis is subdivided. That is the approach of this book.

Companies of all sizes are now using the micro system for applications such as electronic mail, message switching, "in-box memos," word processing, testing, computer-aided instruction, accounting and financial applications, analog monitoring, and many other standard and custom applications. As the cost of the microcomputer hardware and software decreases and the power of these systems increases, more and more people will be able to purchase these units for business or pleasure. Portable micros are now available and are adding a new dimension to information processing and customer service. Yet, in many cases microcomputers are acquired and used with little thought given to how they collectively affect the integrity of an organization's information base. In many organizations, the proliferation of microcomputers can best be described as an uncontrolled process. Some organizations have more than 10 different brands of micros being used by employees.

Consequently, not only do corporations lack control over the type of micro hardware and software being purchased (usually under miscellaneous office machine or supply budgets), but they also lack control over the data being processed and stored on these systems. The audit, security, and disaster-planning considerations that are so well established in a large data processing environment must be extended to the micro environment. These considerations are just as important for micros, and are becoming increasingly important, in the home and in business, as computers become more and more a part of our daily lives.

CATEGORIES OF COMPUTERS

Microcomputer is a label that covers a broad range of computer types and powers. It is difficult, and not absolutely necessary, to define precisely the limits of a microcomputer. Capabilities of differently classified types of computers change rapidly. It is helpful, however, to clarify such terms as *microcomputer, minicomputer,* and *mainframe computer,* and to give some broad distinctions between them. There is ambiguity and overlap in reference to processing power, storage capabilities, and peripherals that are interfaced. A microcomputer at the low end may have one CRT (cathode-ray tube) display, a keyboard, and a cassette unit. At the high end, the microcomputer may have multiprocessing capability, multiple printers and other peripherals, and several hundred megabytes of hard-disk storage.

Generally, the main divisions between micro, mini, and mainframe computers are made on the basis of the following:

- Processing speed.
- Multiprocessing capabilities (running more than one program at a time).
- Memory storage capacity.
- The number of peripherals that can be attached and used at the same time.
- Cost.

The industry divides computer systems into several basic categories.

Mainframe computers are also called *central computers.* They tend to be large systems with many peripherals, although smaller organizations will have a much smaller view of "large." Large computers will normally be at a central node of the overall organization, and may control or use networks of terminals and other computers throughout the organization. They will be general-purpose machines (unless they are massive number crunchers designed for a special set of applications). To an outsider, they can be identified as being housed in a separate "computer room" with separate environmental and security controls. To the insiders, they will be identified by the exceedingly rich system functionality available. There is little practical limit on their system expandability, except cost, and their performance can be beyond the average capability of use. Of course, there will be times when the systems are full, and the users are not getting adequate service, but the large computers can always be expanded.

Minicomputer is a common classification for a large number of smaller computers that span a wide range of capability. Their price can vary by a factor of four or more for the same power, applied to a specific application. Minicomputer configurations include stand-alone data processors, small business computers, large intelligent terminals in computer networks, and specialized technical and scientific computers.

Minicomputers are normally located at the user or problem (single purpose) site and operate in both detached and distributed data processing modes. They are frequently connected to mainframes for sharing information. There is no sharp distinction between minicomputers and microcomputers, and their work size and memory size overlap considerably. Minis are larger computers and tend to have larger instruction sets and more registers. Many have a 16-bit word size and can address a 64K memory. They, therefore, contain more program and random access memory (RAM) data space and have more complex input/output (I/O) capabilities.

Minicomputers are low-cost and have an attractive cost-performance ratio compared with mainframes. Therefore, they are excellent for smaller, defined sets of programs, and as nodes in a distributed data processing network. It is to be noted, however, that minicomputers are giving way to supermicros.

Superminicomputer is a currently favored designation for the largest of the minicomputers, although there is no sharp distinction between them and the others. They are somewhat larger, with more memory and more peripherals, than minicomputers. Most of them are produced by manufacturers with a range of computers that are upwardly compatible. Some of the systems advertised as superminicomputers are larger than the smallest of the mainframe, or large computer, category. Thus there is little practical distinction between them. From a usage point of view, the two categories are not different.

Microcomputers are the smallest computers, packaged as systems, that are available. They have two principal areas of use:

1. As small, stand-alone systems at the user site, operating in a detached mode and under local control.

2. As nodes in a network, operating in a distributed client-server or peer-to-peer mode. Local area networks are common. The joining of local area networks with a wide area network now gives the microcomputer another arena, one that is fraught with potential security problems.

Microcomputers are considered to be user-friendly and easy to use, principally because they have limited performance and a limited instruction set and most commonly are used with packaged programs. Most systems are set up to support a limited number of users, even though some chained networks already support up to 255 users. The advent of the supermicros will change this considerably, particularly in their use as departmental file servers and important nodes on a communications network. The enhanced power and storage capabilities have formed a new niche for the supermicro, which is quite capable of competing with minicomputers (particularly at the lower end). The downsizing of applications has been a boon to the microcomputer industry, with applications being taken off the mainframe and spread across microcomputers.

Personal computers, or PCs, are usually microcomputer-based, and have come into common use, displacing calculators of all types, as well as terminals that have limited access to central computers. Some of the names applied to microcomputers are: personal computers, small business systems, word processors, workstations, file servers, intelligent terminals, programmable calculators, desktop computers, dumb terminals, home computers, and hobby computers.

There are other names and types, since microcomputers are used in industrial automation, process control, automatic systems of all types, and word processing. In general, when compared with minicomputers, they tend to support fewer, and smaller, items of peripheral equipment, have less processing power, and, usually, use small tape devices or floppy disks.

Microcomputers usually have their central processing unit (CPU), memory, and I/O circuits integrated into one or more large-scale integrated circuit (LSI) chips. This chip is called a microprocessor. Microcomputers may contain more than one microprocessor and extra memory on other large-capacity semiconductor chips. And, of course, microprocessors are used in parallel processing.

Microprocessors are truly "computer systems" when they are the principal part of the control system in which they are imbedded. They are the central processing element of all levels of equipment, from the microcomputer to the mainframe. They are the "computer on a chip," meaning a CPU, memory, and I/O circuits in a single, LSI chip. Microprocessors may be considered as computer systems when they are used in many control applications. A microprocessor may not handle all normal data processing functions, but it can handle all types of manipulation functions.

Microcomputers are used in business organizations under some managerial direction, and they handle applications that are not, or are not completely, under the control of the larger central computer. From a security standpoint, if a microcomputer is used in an organizational application, and there is some freedom of use of the system at the local level, then it should be analyzed for security control. Many personal computers will thus be included if they are used for organizational applications and have some data interaction with other computers. Some personal computers are simply used as powerful desk calculators by workers.

Dumb terminals may have powerful logic imbedded in them. They are an integral part of the central computer system to which they are attached and are not used for any applications that are not completely controlled by the central computer. Personal computers are, more and more, being linked on peer-to-peer networks where the business application process they are performing runs independent of a mainframe. The mainframe on a network may not be the central focal and control point. Implementation of a network in which the mainframe serves only as a data repository will become more popular. Home computers and hobby computers have proliferated in the millions, and many are used within organizations. Guidelines for their corporate acquisition and secure use may be appropriate if they are funded by the organization and handle sensitive data.

MICROCOMPUTER APPLICATIONS

Applications that once were reserved for minicomputers or mainframes are now appearing on microcomputers. Increased processing capabilities, added features such as graphics and work stations dedicated to serving a related functionality (such as the Information Engineering Facility from Texas Instruments or the Information Engineering Workbench from KnowledgeWare), or a particular image-processing workstation with increased storage and communications features have made the micro an attractive, low-cost addition to the work environment.

Not only are micros used to perform typical accounting applications such as accounts payable, accounts receivable, general ledger, inventory control, invoice/billing, order entry, and payroll, but they are also now being used in broad, more technically advanced applications. These applications include computer-aided software engineering (CASE), design analysis, modeling, and presentation graphics.

Some of the more common applications are defined on the following pages and include:

- Business graphics.
- Database search/retrieval.
- Distributed data processing and networking.
- Electronic mail.
- Financial modeling.
- Word processing.

Portable Microcomputers

A portable microcomputer contains all of the hardware components and software for the desktop model. Currently, systems with 40 and more megabytes of hard-disk capacity, a keyboard, display screen, and 80-column printer are being offered. Obviously, they present a security problem.

Accounting firms, faced with rising audit costs and client resistance to higher fees, are moving into the desktop and portable micro area so their auditors can expedite the audit process. The U.S. Department of Transportation has given its internal auditors portable microcomputers to use in audits designed to ferret out fraud, waste, abuse, and bid-rigging on government contracts. Spreadsheet software has been used to document bid-rigging in the awarding of paving contracts at airports.

Portables add an additional degree of flexibility for micro users. It will become quite common to see a businessperson with a briefcase in one hand and a portable micro in the other. Portable computers also, however, add a new dimension to the problem of securing the hardware, software, and information contained on the portfolio's hard disk or the accompanying diskettes.

Sales people and service representatives are being armed with their own versions of portable computers that tap into transaction and information systems at the central base of operations.

Use of Service Bureaus

Firms that typically have used service bureaus because they could not afford their own system or because they needed additional processing capabilities have found that they can cost-justify doing their own processing on an in-house mini- or microcomputer.

Because of declining revenue in the service bureau market, most major service bureaus have announced moves to exploit the local power of the microcomputer. One service bureau firm has purchased $10 million worth of IBM PCs. Micro tie-in services imitate the intelligent-terminal batch-processing concepts started over a decade ago. The user enters and stores information on the micro during the day and then transmits the data to the service bureau at night. The service bureau processes the information and sends the results via delivery service or telecommunications back to the user the next morning. New security problems are introduced.

Business Graphics

Businesses have long used visual presentations to highlight sales figures, productivity trends, and revenue and earnings comparisons, and to present project-planning schedules. Microcomputer graphics applications can produce all the displays mentioned above. Micros also provide ease of manipulation of graph data and overlay capabilities that help to analyze "what if" situations. Some vendors also offer data-transfer capabilities between applications, such as with financial spreadsheets and the graphics processor. The control of the data in graphics may be more difficult than when the same numbers are clearly listed in columns.

Graphics in the form of bar charts, line charts, and pie charts are being used to process and compare business data. Analytical graphics are being used by organizations to help identify areas of unusual activity. For example, a telephone company is using analytical graphics (comparing one graph, via overlay, with another) to identify the possible fraudulent use of telephones.

The most recent additions in the area of computer graphics are computer-aided drafting (CAD) and design systems. General-purpose CAD systems are used to produce almost any type of drawing, including mechanical, architectural, and electrical drawings, schematics and flowcharts, technical illustrations, office layouts, forms design, organizational charts, and specialized data, such as archeological site documentation or stained glass layouts.

Database Search and Retrieval

Firms such as Compuserve, Westlaw, Dow Jones, Data Courier, The Source, and Mead offer database/library research services to their subscribers. Many of these services provide teleprocessing dial-in service so that an organization can use its terminals or micros to access the central database. One specific inquiry by a user may involve the searching of hundreds of data banks around the world. Once the information is accessed, it can be stored on the micro for further processing. There, it may become mixed with controlled internal data.

Micro-to-Mainframe Connection

People who are using the micro in business are demanding more information. They want to use information from the corporate database in addition to their "own information" on their personal micro. This tie-in to the main database ensures that the same up-to-date data is being used. It also eliminates rekeying of the same data from many sources.

Micro-to-mainframe links generally include file transfer between the micro and the host. Security control on "downloaded" information is simpler than the control of "uploaded" information, which may alter controlled databases.

Networking

Networking involves the connecting of terminals, micros, minis, and/or mainframes to each other in order to have expanded information and processing capabilities. Networks can be formed locally over a cable connected directly to each module of the network and globally by telecommunication systems that link more distant modules. The various network technologies include twisted pair networks, baseband systems and broadband systems.

Devices such as printers or networks modules can be connected in a local area network (LAN) or ring configuration. In this configuration, if one device fails, the ring will break. For this reason, rings are usually "braided" or "woven" to provide backups in case of equipment failures. The most common LAN configuration is called a *databus*, which can be described as a cable strung like a highway with entrance ramps. Any device that is to be connected is simply attached to a ramp. Databus is used by Wangnet and Ethernet.

The security considerations of distributed data processing (DDP), departmental computing, micro-to-mainframe connection, and LANs are included in Chapter Seven, "Database Security and Records Management."

Electronic Mail

Electronic mail is a system that allows a sender to enter a message or document into a computer. The computer stores that message or document until the receiver is ready. The receiver then can answer, forward, file, or delete the message/document.

Through use of the micro, electronic mail can be sent interdepartmentally, interstate, office to household, or by the postal service or by private concern. Executives can mail memos or letters throughout an organization to hundreds of locations, or to just one person two offices down the corridor. Some electronic mail packages even offer the capability of correcting spelling errors.

Electronic mail applications are also being interfaced with other business applications, such as purchasing. Purchase orders can be entered on the micro, routed for approval, then forwarded electronically to the purchasing system.

An application by-product of electronic mail is known as the *electronic bulletin board*. This is a message-sharing system in which a computer's user allows public access to the computer via phone line and terminal. Individuals can access the messages, which may include sales information on new products or common-interest information. Clearly, this can present a security problem.

Estimates place the number of U.S. electronic bulletin boards in the thousands. Two boards alone netted more than 10,000 calls over a recent eight-month period. Large organizations such as Compuserve and The Source are using the electronic bulletin boards to announce new products and services.

Unfortunately, as the use of electronic bulletin boards grows, so does the incidence of abuse. Saboteurs have erased programs and files, and programs have been stolen by people who have accessed the boards.

Financial Modeling

Special software packages, in conjunction with micrographic capabilities, allow managers to perform financial modeling. "What if" situations can be entered, processed, displayed, and printed, in a spreadsheet format or in a graph. Some micro hardware/software also allows graph overlay so that financial modeling results can be visually compared. Usually the data used in such applications is very sensitive.

Word Processing

Word processing involves the input, manipulation, storing, and printing of data. This application has been around for some time and was one of the first applications to appear on the microcomputer. Micros are now used to produce books, letters, and documentation.

Mailing-list applications are an extension of word processing and allow the user to select a group of names from the micro's database for mailing or advertising purposes. Micrographic capabilities now allow the user to select the type font and to vary the character size. Unique security problems are presented.

MICROCOMPUTER SECURITY CONSIDERATIONS

The degree of security to be applied to a microcomputer system will depend on the importance and sensitivity of the applications involved. The security aspects of a microcomputer system operation should be reviewed before the system is developed and installed. The primary objectives of a security review are to ensure that adequate protection is provided and to make security recommendations. Any individual charged with the responsibility of reviewing the adequacy of data processing security must consider the microcomputers.

Developing a good plan is essential to conducting an effective, efficient, and economical security review. The identification of security risks becomes the basis of determining the adequacy of security. Competent data processing systems personnel and the internal audit staff should be asked for their opinions as to what security measures to install and what policies and procedures should be followed. If the microcomputer system is already operating and little thought has been given to security considerations, then a review of the operation should be conducted from the viewpoint of the adequacy of the security methods. This is reviewed in Chapter Nine, "Audit and Control."

Checklists are included for probing the critical areas associated with microcomputer security planning, management, and control. They will help determine the actual security condition, rather than the perceived circumstances. These checklists can be used either in the planning stage or after the installed equipment has been operating. They cover the principal points of management concern relative to security.

The two primary objectives of an electronic data processing (EDP) security review of a microcomputer system are:

1. *To ensure that adequate protection is provided.* This consists of identifying resources requiring protection, determining the types of potential hazards, assessing the adequacy of protective controls and devices, and continually testing the security measures. The computer system may supply and control operating data critical to the success of the rest of the organization. A review of the protection provided assures that the security measures are adequate.

2. *To make security recommendations.* It is impossible to foresee and prevent all potential dangers; therefore, it is necessary periodically to review the security of an operation and to recommend control improvements. These recommendations may include methods and procedures for the operation, creation of a disaster recovery and backup plan, establishment of various physical measures, and so on.

The checklists that are included in some chapters direct the reviewer quickly to key concerns and sensitive areas. They provide a good fact-gathering procedure to spotlight critical areas that may have been overlooked or that are outside the technical experience of the security officer or review team. The checklist approach minimizes the time required by the reviewers in gathering basic data, and by the personnel within the data processing organization in answering. The checklists also provide *action-oriented* direction toward the most significant problems and requirements.

OVERVIEW OF THE BOOK

Managing Microcomputer Security provides detailed information and checklists for planning, implementing, and reviewing microcomputer security. The book's chapters are as follows.

Chapter One: Introduction

Chapter Two: Security Management Considerations

The elements of managing the security function in a microcomputer environment are addressed. Particular attention is paid to positive security awareness training, since security training is a fundamental necessity for the end users, who have little formal background in EDP or security.

A number of threats and vulnerabilities are defined, as well as personnel and documentation considerations.

Chapter Three: Computer-Related Crime

After a brief discussion regarding computer-related crime statistics and the elements of computer crime, a number of computer-related crimes are explored. The crimes are classified by type, including collusion, counterfeiting, espionage, fraud, sabotage, etc. Also included are descriptions of computer-related crime techniques and methods, such as asynchronous attack, browsing, data aggregation, logic bombs, spoofing, and viral attack techniques.

The primary purpose of this section is to familiarize readers with the techniques that have been used to commit computer-related crimes with a microcomputer, so that they may pay particular attention to those vulnerabilities.

Chapter Four: Hardware Security

Equipment and methods for hardware control are described. Control of the organization's microcomputer hardware is an important element in the overall microcomputer security plan. Controls include establishing policies and procedures that govern equipment inventory, equipment identification and marketing, and access control.

Chapter Five: Physical Security and Environmental Considerations

The particular problems of microcomputer security management are discussed, and the concept of multilevel security is described. There are many workplace hazards for microcomputers and their associated magnetic media. Typical examples of problems are given. Information on threats to magnetic media is provided. Checklists are included, covering the physical security of microcomputers, the handling of supplies, and the environmental considerations in micro operation.

Chapter Six: Software Security

Software security involves the protection of an organization's operating system and application programs from intentional or unintentional use, alteration, or deletion. Protection for software is offered in the form of hardware/software protection devices, control of sensitive programs and program changes, adequate and proper backup, and legal protection. Software-protection devices, sensitive-program control, and backup are addressed in this section. A checklist is provided for the review of software security considerations.

Chapter Seven: Database Security and Records Management

Microcomputer-based data files and records usually receive little attention from users, but they are important to consider, particularly for sensitive or critical programs. Databases and records usually are under the control of specialized management groups, and access to them must be understood by microcomputer users. The requirements of file backup, though familiar to data processing people, must also be understood by micro users. These points are outlined, and a checklist is provided to review the key elements. The security problems associated with micro-to-mainframe connections are also addressed.

Chapter Eight: Telecommunications Security

Because the problems and threats in communications and teleprocessing are specialized, an illustration is provided that explains the elements of teleprocessing and the threats involved. The particular concerns of management with communications networks are listed and discussed. Checklists are provided relative to communications access control and communications backup.

Chapter Nine: Audit and Control

As the utilization of microcomputers increases, the need for control and audit of these computers also increases. This chapter addresses the audit and control considerations of microcomputers used in a stand-alone environment, in a distributed data processing environment, and as "dumb" terminals utilizing a terminal emulation mode.

Chapter Ten: Microcomputer Insurance

Some of the elements of microcomputer insurance policies are discussed, and a sample policy is included. Checklists are provided for reviewing the insurance coverage that is described. They are applicable for both microcomputer and mainframe operations.

A number of insurance companies are now offering specific policies for microcomputers. Note, however, that organizations that already have an existing policy for their mainframe operations may be covered for any micros used in their business.

Chapter Eleven: Legal Issues and Legislation

Some of the legal issues involved in software protection are briefly outlined. These include piracy, copyrights, trade secrets, patents, and employee contracts. State and federal computer-related crime laws and legislation are also described.

Chapter Twelve: Disaster Preparedness and Recovery

Disaster recovery planning and arrangements for contingency backup operation are important. This chapter provides information and procedures for developing the required contingency plans. A checklist is provided to aid in the analysis of the priority of concerns to management.

A useful approach relates the cost of different levels of security and disaster recovery measures to need. Mandatory, necessary, and desirable measures are discussed as a relative scale for initial management analysis.

Chapter Thirteen: Baseline Security

This chapter introduces the *baseline security* concept for use with microcomputer systems. Baseline checklists are provided to guide the user through the various control objectives and respective control elements as presented in the sections of this manual.

The baseline security concept is the result of many years of experience in the field of computer security. Over the years many security checklists, worksheets, and audit guidelines have been established and updated by specialists and practitioners who have researched and implemented computer security in larger organizations. This combined knowledge is now at the level where a standard of security, or baseline, can be developed. This baseline can be helpful to all organizations using computers. Security needs specific to an organization should be added to the baseline for that organization.

Chapter Fourteen: Securing the Microcomputer-to-Mainframe Link

The microcomputer-to-mainframe link has had a significant impact on the data processing function. As information processing extends from the central site to remote sites, the challenge of providing security for information and its processing becomes more difficult. This chapter provides security guidelines for the microcomputer-to-mainframe link, and a program to review the adequacy of current security. The security review program is oriented toward the four microcomputer-to-mainframe approaches: terminal emulators; database extract and download; link utilities; and embedded links. A fully developed microcomputer-to-mainframe link security program that is based on the practices of several leading corporations is also included in this chapter. On-line system security considerations are reviewed in-depth.

Chapter Fifteen: Some Final Thoughts

In this concluding chapter some final thoughts are presented on where industry stands in the implementation of a microcomputer security strategy. A brief look is taken at industry trends in regard to the most important microcomputer security elements. Also presented, briefly, is "How to Proceed from Where You Are Now."

Chapter Two

Security Management Considerations

The problems of managing security in a microcomputer environment are outlined briefly, with emphasis on the accuracy of information, privacy requirements, and business continuity. Information security is the protection of data against accidental or intentional destruction, modification, or disclosure. Positive security awareness training is particularly important; security training is a fundamental necessity for the end users who have little formal background in data processing.

The various vulnerabilities, or fault groups, are also outlined, with emphasis on human vulnerabilities and personnel considerations. Documentation and document classification are a necessity for security.

The U.S. Department of Defense (DOD) security classification standards are listed, as they show criteria for varying levels of security. Four checklists cover security management considerations.

ANALYZING SECURITY NEEDS

How do you manage security in the microcomputer environment? Risk management policy indicates that it is the job of the owner (not necessarily the user) of the system and its data to decide what has to be protected and what does not, and to what degree it has to be protected. To determine the level of security required, a *threat analysis* should be made. The kinds of problems that your organization may encounter may be determined by the following:

- Products or services offered by your organization.
- Location (the level of criminal activity in the area).
- Environment (flood area, earthquake, volcano, etc.).

Many other threat elements and security areas should also be considered, and they are listed later in this chapter for your review. It is important

17

to remember that any security hardware or software options or physical-site security should be cost-justified. Many smaller businesses and micro owners cannot afford the cost of electronic data processing (EDP) security devices or the costs and time associated with EDP audit procedures that are available to the larger organizations. It would not be cost-effective to install $30,000 worth of physical security to protect a $4,000 microcomputer that does not contain highly sensitive, valuable data.

A common-sense approach to your security needs is the best approach. Adequate security can be achieved through the proper mix of security administration, risk analysis, disaster contingency planning, and psychological security (people and security awareness). Physical security, hardware and software security, communications security, and good auditing techniques are elements that, if integrated into a sound security plan, will provide a level of protection that will meet the needs of any business.

ACCURACY OF INFORMATION

Today's businesses strive to maintain the accuracy and integrity of their computerized information. However, despite all of the modern, sophisticated auditing techniques and computerized controls, a major problem facing our nation's businesses is that of erroneous data. In dollar terms, problems caused by inaccurate data cost our nation's businesses more than all the white-collar crimes combined.

Many people tend to blame "the computer" for errors, but it is usually not the computer that errs. Instead, information is either entered incorrectly or the computer program processing the data has been designed incorrectly. Particularly in the age of the electronic desktop, with its connections to other corporate computer resources, accuracy of information is essential.

The importance of accuracy is demonstrated by some recent incidents involving computers:

• Colorado River floods occurred after erroneous data was fed into the Bureau of Reclamation computers, which, subsequently, kept too much water behind the dams in the spring.

• Doctors who were administering microwave radiation therapy to a 62-year-old man accidentally reprogrammed the man's pacemaker to work at 214 beats per minute, causing his death.

• Because of a computer-based error, the Vancouver stock index lost one point a day for more than a year. The index had lost 574 points by the time the error was discovered.

- The British destroyer *Sheffield* was sunk during the Falkland islands war when the ship's defense system mistakenly recognized an incoming Exocet missile as a friendly weapon and failed to have it shot down.
- An unarmed Soviet cruise missile crashed in Finland in 1984 because it had been inaccurately programmed with a war-plan flight path. As soon as the programming error was discovered, Moscow was warned and within seconds, the United States was informed via military hot line to the Pentagon. Two Soviet MiG-25 interceptors, with pilots specially trained to shoot down cruise missiles, were scrambled to chase the missile. One of the jets did shoot it down.

Although these are some of the more sensational incidents involving accuracy problems, a minor programming error in a small-business environment could produce devastating results for that business.

PRIVACY

Privacy refers to the rights of individuals and organizations to determine for themselves when, how, and to what extent information about them is to be transmitted to others.[1]

Information privacy is a growing concern and a growing problem for society. Data about our businesses and about ourselves are stored in manual and computerized files in hundreds of government, law enforcement, and public and private business entities. Credit unions, banks, employment agencies, private associations, credit card companies, health and life insurance companies, hospitals and medical offices, police agencies, and state and federal agencies are among the repositories of personal and business information.[2]

SECURITY

Information security is the protection of data against accidental or intentional destruction, modification, or disclosure. Security of information is a solution to information accuracy and privacy, but not a total solution. There is no such thing as a 100 percent secure system.

---

[1]James Martin, *Security, Accuracy, and Privacy in Computer Systems* (Englewood Cliffs, N.J.: Prentice Hall, 1973), p. 5.

[2]John M. Carroll, *Confidential Information Sources: Public and Private* (Los Angeles: Security World Publishing Co., 1977), pp. 21–27.

A security program is best achieved by consent. Get your employees involved in the security program design. Ask for their comments and ideas. Let them "own" the security plan and be responsible for making security happen within the organization.

The philosophy of a security program must be tailored to the philosophy of a particular business. The small-business owner who uses the microcomputer for standard accounting applications is unlikely to require the same level of security as the Federal Reserve Bank.

DISASTER

The loss of data to disaster is another constant threat. Floods, fires, earthquakes, and tornadoes have had devastating effects on businesses and their customers. It is the responsibility of an organization to plan for operational continuity in the event of a disaster, to be prepared for it when it does occur, and to be able to respond to the needs of customers or clients as soon as possible after a disaster. Continuance of operations is essential in today's competitive environment.

SECURITY AWARENESS TRAINING

The following is taken from a bulletin written by Jack Bologna, president of Computer Protection Systems, Inc.:

> The current literature in the fields of security and risk management is filled with references to the need for employee "security awareness." But what is security awareness? Is it campaign posters and slogans, or the telling of "horror stories" or "war stories," or something more? How is security awareness different than security indoctrination, orientation, education, training, or security information dissemination, intelligence dissemination, or policy dissemination? And, how is security awareness different than risk analysis, loss prevention, risk reduction, loss reduction, and security controls, safeguards, defenses, and countermeasures? How does security awareness differ from security policies, procedures, and security planning?
>
> A secure state (security awareness) is a state of mind which derives from a *feeling* of security, that is, a feeling that we are free from danger or risk of loss, a feeling that we are reasonably free from doubt, anxiety, or fear. Notice we said *"feeling."* Security is not necessarily a rational thing. We can *feel* secure and yet be in great danger, and feel *insecure* and yet be in no danger. Fears, doubts, anxieties, and uncertainties can even exist in "secure" environments—that is, environments which are relatively free of risks. Our

minds can sometimes play tricks on us. And, our minds can be manipulated by others who may wish to exacerbate or exploit our fears and doubts for their purposes. Advertisers have been known to try that ploy to win sales for their products. The media sometimes also exploits fears to draw attention to an issue or to help shape public opinion. It is called "news slanting." Politicians play the game, too. And candidly, we in security have not been above exploiting fear to win attention or action.

One problem with exploiting fear as a strategy to win attention or action is that when it gets overdone or to a point of saturation, we lose credibility. The public then turns a deaf ear to the message. Stridency becomes a turn-off. We can not psychologically handle a steady diet of bad news. So our minds provide us with psychological escapes like denial (it can not happen to me), rationalization (sour grapes and sweet lemons), distortion (that ain't the way I heard it), repression (forget about it), projection (it is your problem), and fantasy (everything is beautiful). These are the more positive responses to a steady diet of bad news. The negative responses are panic, depression, despair, resignation, and feeling forlorn.[3]

Security training, if effective, has positive impacts on three areas of learning domain:

1. Knowledge is improved.
2. Skills are developed or enhanced.
3. Attitudes are changed for the better.

The major objectives of security awareness training are:

- To alert personnel to the specific security threats and risks they and the company face, both current and long range.
- To get personnel committed to taking cooperative and constructive action should breaches of security occur.
- To identify and implement opportunities for improvement.

The word *peril* in the Chinese system of writing is formed by joining the characters for two other words: *risk* and *opportunity*. Security training too often focuses on the risk side of the coin. Security training should also focus on the opportunity side. How can we make our company safer, healthier, and a better place to work? Security is not just a job role or function. It is a commitment to excellence. It does not involve just one

---

[3]Jack Bologna, "Strategic Security Planning for Awareness: An Educational Design for Security Training Programs" (Plymouth, Mich.: Computer Protection Systems, Inc., 1981).

person or one department. It involves the whole organization. Without the whole organization's commitment to security, there is likely to be very little security in the organization. Commitment to security (or to any principle) can only come from involvement in its design and participation in its execution. We call this concept "Asking for Security," because it draws on employee attitudes, skills, and knowledge and because it involves employees' participation. They must tell management what they desire and need to know about security and what they would like to be able to do better. For management to predesign their education and training without their input may diminish their commitment. So we cannot just tell them about security, we must ask them to participate in it.

Security awareness is, therefore, a state of mind, based on feeling that we are relatively safe from danger or risk of loss, because we have taken all necessary and reasonable precautions to protect ourselves and the organization against predictable risks through a process of strategic and operational security planning and education. Figure 2–1 illustrates these relationships.

Security awareness training is an educational and developmental strategy designed to enlist the aid, cooperation, and support of all employees toward the creation of a company work environment that is relatively free of security hazards, threats, and risks. The major educational impact of security awareness training is on individual attitudes toward security. A constructive attitude is fostered by an appreciation of the value of security to both the company's and the individual's well-being and long-term growth. Such an appreciation can be cultivated if all employees are involved in the design and execution of a strategic and comprehensive security plan for their own protection and for the protection and preservation of the organization's other assets.

An integrated approach for the creation of security awareness should, therefore, incorporate planning and educational strategies: planning, to identify security risks and opportunities for improvement; and education, to develop commitment to the plan so that constructive action will follow.

VULNERABILITY ASSESSMENT

Data and system vulnerabilities and other elements that can either partially or totally destroy data stored on a microcomputer system, or that can render the system and its components partially or totally inoperable, are outlined in this chapter. Chapter Five, "Physical Security and Environmental Considerations," contains additional information.

FIGURE 2–1
A Security Awareness System

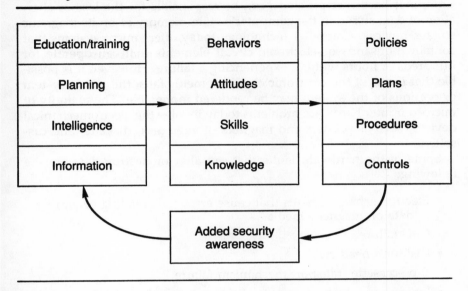

Vulnerabilities

There are two classifications used to categorize data processing elements in this book: *hardware* and *software*. Hardware pertains to the computer itself and all of its components and peripheral devices. Also included in the hardware category is support equipment, such as unit record devices and off-line optical character reader (OCR) and communications equipment. The software category encompasses everything else: data, programs, and documentation.

For purposes of discussion here, vulnerabilities are arranged in six categories:

- Hardware vulnerabilities.
- Software vulnerabilities.
- Database vulnerabilities.
- Communications vulnerabilities.
- Human vulnerabilities.
- Natural and man-made disasters.

Hardware Vulnerabilities

Computer hardware problems can be responsible for the loss or alteration of data stored in the computer's main memory or on its magnetic storage devices. Computer technology today offers micro systems that contain thousands of electronic circuit elements that can operate for hundreds of hours without experiencing a failure. However, it is possible that if one of the electronic circuit elements fails, the whole system or portions of the system may be rendered inoperable. The majority of microcomputer hardware problems today involve the electromechanical devices, such as printers and magnetic-storage disk, diskette, and cassette units.

Some of the hardware faults that can alter or destroy data are the following:

- Electromechanical faults that cause erroneous reading or writing of data on magnetic media.
- CPU failure.
- Disk-unit head crash.
- Tape-cassette transport mechanism failure.
- Buildup of lubricating oils or dirt that is transferred from the read/write mechanism to the magnetic media.
- Bad circuit board or chip.

Software Vulnerabilities

Software faults, including programming errors and algorithmic errors, are a major cause of data loss or data contamination. Some of these faults are listed below by category.

Operating system. Operating system software and its revisions (new releases) have been marketed without being fully tested and debugged.

Vendor-supplied software packages and in-house programming. Possible faults are:

- Logic errors, programming errors.
- Poor or inaccurate documentation.
- Faulty design.
- Insufficient testing.

Algorithmic errors. These include:

- Round-off errors.
- Truncation.

Documentation. Possible faults are:

- Errant procedures, file layouts, specifications, etc.
- No documentation or insufficient documentation.

Database Vulnerabilities

A useful definition of *database* is presented by James Martin in his book *Principles of Database Management:*

> A database is a collection of interrelated data stored together with controlled redundancy to serve one or more applications in an optimal fashion; the data are stored so that they are independent of programs which use the data; a common and controlled approach is used in adding new data and modifying and retrieving existing data within the database. One system is said to contain a collection of databases if they are each entirely separate in structure.[4]

To be classified as a database in today's terms, data must be stored in some form on a mass-storage device. Although significant advances have been made in laser technology and optical disk recording, magnetic media are universally used for the storage of data. Microcomputer-related mass-storage media include disk, diskette, and cassette.

Database contamination occurs when data stored on a mass-storage device become unusable because the data are inaccessible or inaccurate. Database contamination may involve inaccurate field data as well as inaccessible or inaccurate record (or record segment) or file (or file segment) data. File directory and header label information may also be contaminated to an extent that would prohibit file access, unless recovery of the necessary data was possible.

One form of database contamination is that of data loss associated with magnetic media problems. A discussion of potential problems and magnetic media handling is addressed in Chapter Five.

Database contamination or data loss associated with magnetic media may be caused by physical damage of the recording medium, equipment malfunction, software problems or errors, operator error, erasure, overwrite, criminal act, intentional act, or disaster.

---

[4]James Martin, *Principles of Database Management* (Englewood Cliffs, N.J.: Prentice Hall, 1983).

Communications Vulnerabilities

Communication faults stem primarily from equipment failure or transmission problems as outlined below.

Equipment failures

- Hardware faults.
- Power problems (spikes, transient errors, etc.).
- Wrong switch settings (baud rates, parity, full/half duplex, etc.).
- Noncompatible equipment (EBCDIC vs. ASCII).
- Poor maintenance.
- Transmission cable damage due to water damage or toxic vapors (from backup power batteries, etc.).

Transmission problems

- "Noise" on-line causes data to be modified, added, or dropped. Noise can be caused by line quality (grade) problems, cross talk, a person accidentally picking up an extension line, and atmospheric interference (related to wind, rain, lightning, ice, etc.).

Human Vulnerabilities

Human error causes more damage and results in loss of more money and time than all the other vulnerability elements combined. Improper training or just plain carelessness has resulted in exorbitant amounts of data loss and computer rerun time. Data can also be lost, modified, or used for criminal purposes.

Unintentional/Accidental Errors

- Data entry keying errors.
- Omissions.
- Playful malignancy.
- Operator deletion of a file.
- Update of wrong file—or same file twice.
- Use of wrong version of programs or data files.
- Use of wrong job/file parameters, which destroys information.
- Pressing of wrong button.
- Design or coding errors in programming.
- Improper procedures.
- Negligence.
- Spilling of liquids on equipment.
- Careless handling of magnetic media.
- Careless handling of equipment.
- Misplaced diskettes/cassettes.
- Mislabeled diskettes/cassettes.

Intentional/Criminal Acts

- Arson.
- Bombs (bomb threats).
- Civil disorders.
- Espionage.
- Extortion.
- Fraud.

- Malicious damage.
- Sabotage.
- Terrorism.
- Theft.
- War.

Natural and Man-Made Disasters

The history of data processing reveals that many man-made and natural disasters have struck companies that were unprepared and unable to cope with the emergency. These companies suffered considerable damage and losses to equipment, facilities and data. In some cases, there was also loss of life.

Natural disasters or "acts of God" include cold weather, dust storms, earthquakes, flood, hot weather, humidity, hurricanes, ice storms, sand storms, snow storms, tidal waves, tornadoes, volcanic activity, and wind storms. Man-made disasters include boiler explosions, chemical accidents, fire, explosions, corrosive liquids or materials, dust, explosions, falling objects, fire, floor/roof/wall collapse, heat and air conditioning failures, nuclear attack, radar, terrorist attack, utility failures (power blackout or brownouts, power surges, spikes, drops, gas or water problems), and static electricity

PERSONNEL CONSIDERATIONS

To ensure adequate safeguards in the micro environment, especially in a small business or in the distributed approach of larger organizations, the following control measures related to personnel should be considered.

Divide responsibilities. This involves the separation of duties. For example, the individual who runs the micro to produce accounts payable checks should not also be the person who signs and distributes the checks.

Bond critical personnel. Protect the organization by bonding personnel who are in critical or sensitive positions.

Cross-train. Cross-train employees in computer applications. This allows for coverage during vacation or sick leave or termination of an employee.

Maintain a clean-desk policy. Do not allow employees to leave important documents, computer reports, or magnetic media on their desks.

Establish a security awareness program. Provide information (policies and procedures) and training on security. Answer the following questions:

- *Who* is to be involved and what are their responsibilities?
- *What* is to be secured?
- *Why* is it to be secured?
- *Where* are important items to be secured?
- *When* are they to be secured? During work hours? After hours?
- *How* is the information, magnetic media, etc., to be secured? (desk, locked file cabinet, fireproof safe, etc.)

The object of security awareness training is to achieve security by consent.

Make sure that security is taken seriously.

Make sure security rules are followed. Make sure that employees and outsiders follow your security rules. Security, being negative by nature, will be forgotten if left alone.

Know your employees. When morale is low, risk is high. The greatest threat to any data processing environment is a disgruntled employee. Also, do any employees have addictions that require extra money to support?

Terminate properly. Take care when firing an employee. If he is in a critical job position, help him clean out his desk, collect his ID card and any office keys, and walk him to the door or to the personnel department. (Counseling and severance pay should be provided. It will make both of you feel better!)

Control outsiders. Control outsiders, check identification, restrict access to certain areas, especially your computer site for unescorted visitors.

Control contract/outside computer specialists.

- Control access; what areas are off-limits, if any?
- Keep a visitor log (name, organization, date, time in/out, purpose of visit).
- Log in/out programs and documentation.
- Restrict/control copying of files and programs. (It is easy for someone to copy your preferred customer list onto a diskette and to conceal and walk away with that information.)

- Control program changes.
  - Do you allow changes without your consent?
  - Do you review/test changes that are made?
- Are the program and user documentation kept up to date?
- Is testing done with live data?

DOCUMENTATION AND DOCUMENT CLASSIFICATION

Documentation

Documentation manuals provided by microcomputer manufacturers are generally quite well written and organized. Manuals include instructions for operating the micro and procedures for running application packages, such as payroll, accounts receivable, and graphics. Additional manuals are available on programming languages. Many of the vendors' manuals, however, do not adequately cover security, file backup, or audit controls. A multitude of books are published on proprietary packages such as Lotus, dBase, and so on. Oftentimes these supplement and clarify the vendors' instructions on password protection already written into the software.

The area of documentation that is often lax or nonexistent is documentation of custom programming. Many microcomputer users do their own programming and operate their own system. Therefore, the need to write documentation concerning their programs does not seem necessary to them. This nondocumentation approach plays havoc with the auditor who is trying to substantiate the accounting practices of a small-business micro user or of a self-developed micro application system that is part of a larger distributed data processing micro network. Also, the nondocumentation approach usually catches up with the programmers when they try to run their package months later. They usually end up looking at the program source code to determine input and operating criteria.

Document Classification

A number of documentation classification schemes are used by private business and government. In many businesses there will be no need to classify or secure documentation. Some, however, will find it prudent to establish controls for their micros' application operating manuals and possibly for the design specifications and program documentation.

Output reports may also need to be classified, because of the sensitivity of the information contained in the reports. If output reports are classified, they should be marked on each page with the appropriate classification level designation, such as "for internal use only." This can be done by the computer, with a rubber stamp, or by hand-printing in ink. Each page of the report should also contain the date and page number. The last page of the report should be marked as the last page. The first page of the report should contain only the security classification designation, date and page number. The report name or ID may also be printed, or it may be suppressed in order to further secure the report. A second cover page can be generated; it can contain the above information in addition to the report name.

A document classification scheme that is used by many private business organizations is presented below and involves the classification levels of:

- Unclassified.
- For Internal Use Only (or Classified).
- Confidential (or Company Confidential).
- Registered Confidential.

Unclassified. This classification is for general documentation, which may include documentation that would not pose a threat to a company's security operations if improperly disclosed.

For Internal Use Only or Classified. This classification level restricts documents to use within the corporation. Such documentation would include sensitive micro application operating instructions, design information, and computer security policies and procedures.

Confidential or Company Confidential. This level of classification refers to information that could be detrimental to an individual or to the company if it were improperly disclosed. Policies, procedures, and other documentation that fall within this category would be made available to those individuals with a need to know, based on their job position or function. This level of documentation must be secured under lock and key. Reproduction would be closely controlled or prohibited altogether. Confidential documents may be written on special colored paper, which deters xerographic reproduction.

Registered Confidential. This designation would only be used in the most highly confidential situations. Strict document control and security standards must be followed. This classification requires that the confidential classification security procedures be followed in addition to requiring the signature or initials of the person receiving the report on the report itself. Each report is assigned a unique control number, which is printed or written on each page of the report.

This classification also requires that a list of the people who can see and possess registered confidential material be maintained by someone authorized by the control function. A control log listing the material by control number, the location of the document, date/time of a check-in and check-out, and signature of recipient must be maintained and secured.

SECURITY CLASSIFICATION STANDARDS

Security classification standards have been established by the Department of Defense Computer Security Center (CSC) since its establishment in 1981. The primary goal of the CSC is to encourage the widespread availability of trusted security systems—that is, systems that employ hardware and software integrity measures that are sufficiently effective and flexible to be used for processing a range of sensitive or classified information. Such encouragement is brought about by evaluating the technical protection capabilities of industry- and government-developed systems, advising systems developers and managers of their systems' suitability for use in processing sensitive information, and assisting in the incorporation of the corresponding technical requirements in the systems' acquisition process.

They have developed a number of evaluation criteria as yardsticks against which systems are evaluated. The criteria classify systems into four broad hierarchical divisions (D, C, B, and A) of increased security protection and provide a basis for evaluation of the effectiveness of security controls built into automatic data processing system products. The criteria are as follows:

Division D	(D)	Systems without passwords.
Division C	(C1)	Class 1: Provides identification and authorization
	(C2)	Class 2: Provides identification and authorization and audit trails
Division B	(B1)	Class 1: Provides labels and marking of data
	(B2)	Class 2: Class 1 plus mandatory controls, including labels, a "trusted path" in which the user communicates

with the operating system and is able to know it is the operating system and not a spoofing program, hardware and software that implement a computer security policy, configuration management, and intention to convert channels.

(B3) Class 3: Based on a mathematical model, has trusted facility management and recovery so that if the computer crashes, it does not compromise information.

Division A   (A) Based on a formal model with structures, specifications, and information-flow confinement.

Under this classification system, all higher-level classifications must meet the qualifications of the lower-level divisions, (i.e., B2 classifications must also meet C1, C2, and B1 requirements).

Although this classification scheme and the controls that have been studied apply principally to larger computer systems, in which the DOD is primarily concerned, they may also be applied within the micro environment, especially when client-server processing is present.

Copies of the criteria, and further information about the evaluations of systems that have been performed, may be obtained by contacting:

Department of Defense Computer Security Center
Office of Technical Support
9800 Savage Road
Fort Meade, MD 20755-6000

Information may be obtained on:

- CSC Vulnerability Reporting Program.
- Formal product evaluations: reports on specific products.
- Endorsed Tools List (ETL): the tools and versions currently supported.
- Evaluated Products List (EPL): a compilation of the ratings.

SECURITY MANAGEMENT CONSIDERATIONS CHECKLISTS

The following checklists are useful for reviewing the management considerations and vulnerabilities that were outlined in this chapter. They may be used in planning security measures or in reviewing security measures that are already in place.

FIGURE 2–2
Management Considerations

No.	Item	Response			
		Yes	No	N/A	Comments
1.	Is the selection and purchase of micro-computers in your organization controlled?	—	—	—	
2.	Has a specific individual been assigned to the selection, purchase, and control of micros (centralized control)?	—	—	—	
3.	Is there micro equipment accountability and control organizationally and departmentally?	—	—	—	
4.	Are micro users given training in the security risks and vulnerabilities of the use of such equipment?	—	—	—	
5.	Are microcomputer courses conducted that instruct users on proper system operation and magnetic media handling?	—	—	—	
6.	Are the micro users informed of their security and control responsibilities?	—	—	—	
7.	Have written policies and procedures been implemented that govern the security and control of micro equipment and applications?	—	—	—	
8.	Are these policies supported by top management?	—	—	—	
9.	Has a physical inventory been made of all micro equipment?	—	—	—	
10.	Are stringent controls placed on any micro use that could affect the accounting records of the company?	—	—	—	
11.	Are there adequate controls to protect against the invasion of privacy of personnel records, etc.?	—	—	—	
12.	Are your internal and external auditors aware of your micro systems?	—	—	—	
13.	If your micros are used to perform work for other organizations, is the work carefully controlled?	—	—	—	
14.	If outsiders have access to your micros, is their use controlled?	—	—	—	
15.	Does top management approve of and support the use of micros?	—	—	—	

FIGURE 2–2 *(concluded)*

No.	Item	Yes	No	N/A	Comments
16.	Has someone been assigned responsibility for disaster planning for the micro equipment?	___	___	___	
17.	Have emergency procedures been established to follow for each type of possible disaster or criminal act?	___	___	___	
18.	Has the amount of possible financial loss been determined in case of disaster, criminal act, accident, etc.?	___	___	___	
19.	Does the disaster-recovery plan take into consideration multilocation micro operations?	___	___	___	
20.	Has a "test" disaster been conducted?	___	___	___	
21.	Have arrangements been made to replace the micro hardware and software in case of a disaster?	___	___	___	
22.	Has the effect of short-term and long-term downtime of your micro been analyzed?	___	___	___	
23.	Could downtime result in loss of business, customer dissatisfaction, or loss of revenue?	___	___	___	

FIGURE 2–3
Vulnerability Assessment

		Response			
No.	Item	Yes	No	N/A	Comments
	Note: Have you fully analyzed your company's exposure to the vulnerabilities listed below?	___	___	___	
1.	*Hardware*				
a.	Electromechanical device failure?	___	___	___	
b.	CPU failure?	___	___	___	
c.	Disk unit head crash?	___	___	___	
d.	Cassette transport mechanism failure?	___	___	___	
e.	Dirt/dust, unclean environmental problems?	___	___	___	

FIGURE 2–3 *(continued)*

No.	Item	Yes	No	N/A	Comments
f.	Circuit failure?	——	——	——	
g.	Power problems?	——	——	——	
2.	*Software*				
a.	Operating system problems?	——	——	——	
b.	Logic errors?	——	——	——	
c.	Programming errors?	——	——	——	
d.	Faulty design?	——	——	——	
e.	Insufficient testing?	——	——	——	
f.	Algorithmic errors:				
	—rounding?	——	——	——	
	—truncation?	——	——	——	
g.	Poor or errant documentation?	——	——	——	
3.	*Database and Magnetic Media*				
a.	Physical damage of recording medium?	——	——	——	
b.	Equipment malfunction?	——	——	——	
c.	Software problems?	——	——	——	
d.	Operator error?	——	——	——	
e.	Operator mishandling?	——	——	——	
f.	Erasure?	——	——	——	
g.	Overwrite?	——	——	——	
h.	Criminal act?	——	——	——	
i.	Intentional act?	——	——	——	
j.	Disaster?	——	——	——	
k.	Magnetic media unreadable?	——	——	——	
4.	*Communications Equipment*				
a.	Hardware?	——	——	——	
b.	Power problems (spikes, transient errors, etc.)?	——	——	——	
c.	Improper switch settings?	——	——	——	
d.	Noncompatible equipment?	——	——	——	
e.	Poor maintenance?	——	——	——	
5.	*Communications Transmission*				
a.	Transmission line/cable problems?	——	——	——	
b.	Noise problems?	——	——	——	
c.	Wiretapping/eavesdropping?	——	——	——	

FIGURE 2–3   *(concluded)*

No.	Item	Yes	No	N/A	Comments
6.	*Human Problems—Unintentional/Accidental*				
a.	Data entry keying errors?	___	___	___	
b.	Omissions?	___	___	___	
c.	Playful malignancy?	___	___	___	
d.	Operator deletes a file?	___	___	___	
e.	Operator updates wrong file, or same file twice?	___	___	___	
f.	Operator uses wrong version of programs or data files?	___	___	___	
g.	Operator specifies wrong job/file parameters which destroys information?	___	___	___	
h.	Operator presses wrong button?	___	___	___	
i.	Programming/design or coding errors?	___	___	___	
j.	Improper procedures?	___	___	___	
k.	Negligence?	___	___	___	
l.	Spilling of liquids on equipment?	___	___	___	
m.	Careless handling of magnetic media?	___	___	___	
n.	Careless handling of equipment?	___	___	___	
o.	Misplaced diskettes/cassettes?	___	___	___	
p.	Mislabeled diskettes/cassettes?	___	___	___	
7.	*Human Problems—Intentional/Criminal*				
a.	Malicious mischief?	___	___	___	
b.	Disgruntled employees?	___	___	___	
c.	Criminal acts?	___	___	___	
8.	*Man-Made Disasters*				
a.	Contiguous operations—fire/explosions?	___	___	___	
b.	Dust?	___	___	___	
c.	Fire?	___	___	___	
d.	Utility failures?				
	—power blackout/brownouts?	___	___	___	
	—power surges, spikes, drops?	___	___	___	

FIGURE 2-4
Personnel Considerations

No.	Item	Yes	No	N/A	Comments
			Response		
1.	Is there adequate separation of duties for the operation of sensitive programs?	___	___	___	
2.	Are critical personnel bonded?	___	___	___	
3.	Are your microcomputer operators cross-trained?	___	___	___	
4.	Do you maintain a clean-desk policy? (This includes clearing blackboards and flip charts of sensitive information.)	___	___	___	
5.	Has a security awareness program been established and implemented?	___	___	___	
6.	Is security taken seriously?	___	___	___	
7.	Are security rules followed?	___	___	___	
8.	Do the managers "know" their employees?	___	___	___	
9.	Have procedures been established for employee termination?	___	___	___	
10.	Have controls been placed on outsiders?	___	___	___	
11.	Do the managers follow the security rules?	___	___	___	
12.	Have background employment checks been made on new hires?	___	___	___	
13.	Are employees given regular performance appraisals and encouraged to discuss their feelings?	___	___	___	
14.	If there appear to be any disgruntled employees, is the situation discussed?	___	___	___	
15.	If employees constitute a threat, can they be transferred or dismissed immediately?	___	___	___	
16.	During an emergency situation, are only specific employees allowed access to:				
	a. the building?	___	___	___	
	b. the microcomputers?	___	___	___	
	c. the disk/diskette storage safe?	___	___	___	

FIGURE 2–4   *(continued)*

No.	Item	Yes	No	N/A	Comments
17.	Are these employees supplied with special passes and identification cards that include their picture and signature?	——	——	——	
18.	Are these specific employees furnished with special company letters and/or passes to authorize access to the place of work? (Employees may have to travel through restricted geographic areas or during curfew time periods. Special passes should be acquired beforehand, if possible, from the proper civil authorities.)	——	——	——	
19.	Do you have someone assigned the responsibility of restarting production?	——	——	——	
20.	Do your plans include the scheduling of the following personnel in case of disaster?				
	a. Microcomputer operators.	——	——	——	
	b. Programmers.	——	——	——	
	c. Systems analysts.	——	——	——	
	d. User/customer personnel.	——	——	——	
	e. Vendor support.	——	——	——	
	f. Maintenance staff.	——	——	——	
	g. Management.	——	——	——	
	h. Clerical support.	——	——	——	
	i. Auditing personnel.	——	——	——	
	j. Security personnel.	——	——	——	
	k. Utility personnel.	——	——	——	
21.	Has a phone directory been prepared that lists the critical personnel in priority sequence?	——	——	——	
22.	Is the phone directory in an easily accessible location (taking into consideration privacy and document security)?	——	——	——	
23.	Are backup personnel available for emergency situations?	——	——	——	
24.	Are management personnel able to run the microcomputer operation in an emergency?	——	——	——	
25.	Are your personnel cross-trained on each other's duties and equipment?	——	——	——	

FIGURE 2–4 *(concluded)*

No.	Item	Yes	No	N/A	Comments
26.	Are all backup personnel properly trained in their respective duties?	—	—	—	
27.	Have employees been trained in the following?				
	a. All types of emergency procedures as identified by your threat analysis.	—	—	—	
	b. Use of fire equipment.	—	—	—	
	c. Security procedures.	—	—	—	
	d. Orderly shutdown of equipment and utilities.	—	—	—	
28.	*For Programmers and Outside Consultants*				
	a. Is there access control with certain areas off-limits?	—	—	—	
	b. Is there a visitor log (name, organization, date, time in/out, purpose of visit)?	—	—	—	
	c. Are programs and documentation logged in/out?	—	—	—	
	d. Is there restriction and control of the copying of files and programs? (It's easy for someone to copy your preferred customer list onto a diskette and to conceal and walk away with that information.)	—	—	—	
	e. Are program changes controlled?	—	—	—	
	f. Are changes allowed only with proper consent?	—	—	—	
	g. Do you review and test changes that are made?	—	—	—	
	h. Is the program and user documentation kept up-to-date?	—	—	—	
	i. Is testing never done with live data?	—	—	—	
29.	*Service Personnel and Others*				
	a. Are maintenance/custodial personnel controlled when servicing the areas where microcomputers are located?	—	—	—	
	b. Are unauthorized personnel not allowed in areas where micros are located?	—	—	—	
	c. Are personnel instructed to challenge unidentified visitors?	—	—	—	

FIGURE 2–5
Documentation

No.	Item	Yes	No	N/A	Comments
		Response			
1.	Is a copy of all vital documentation stored in a secure place at a backup site?	___	___	___	
2.	Does the backup program documentation include:				
	a. program design specifications?	___	___	___	
	b. program narrative?	___	___	___	
	c. listings of source code?	___	___	___	
	d. flowcharts?	___	___	___	
	e. record layouts?	___	___	___	
	f. vendor technical manuals?	___	___	___	
3.	Do the backup microcomputer-run instructions include:				
	a. applications-run instructions?	___	___	___	
	b. operation flowcharts?	___	___	___	
	c. data control information?	___	___	___	
	d. quality-control requirements?	___	___	___	
	e. data recovery and restart procedures?	___	___	___	
	f. switch settings?	___	___	___	
	g. printer forms alignment information?	___	___	___	
	h. identification of forms to be used?	___	___	___	
4.	Do you record documentation with ballpoint pen, pencil, or typewriter? (Felt-tip pens are usually water soluble and writing becomes unreadable if exposed to water.)	___	___	___	
5.	Are the program and run instructions/ documentation complete enough so that a person who is not familiar with the operation can run the application?	___	___	___	
6.	Does the documentation include:				
	a. application description?	___	___	___	
	b. file layouts?	___	___	___	
	c. input instructions?	___	___	___	
	d. output instructions?	___	___	___	
	e. formatting (report) information?	___	___	___	
	f. file?	___	___	___	

FIGURE 2–5 *(concluded)*

No.	Item	Yes	No	N/A	Comments
	g. run frequency/scheduling?	——	——	——	
	h. field definitions and names?	——	——	——	
	i. sample printouts?	——	——	——	
	j. control total/verification procedure?	——	——	——	
	k. audit trail requirements?	——	——	——	
	l. information pertaining to interface with other systems?	——	——	——	
7.	Is someone responsible for the control and security of documentation:				
	a. at the on-site location?	——	——	——	
	b. at the off-site location?	——	——	——	
8.	Has a document classification system been established?	——	——	——	
9.	Is it followed?	——	——	——	
10.	Is there a regular printout of a diskette/disk directory listing all of the files?	——	——	——	

Chapter Three

Computer-Related Crime

Computer-related crime is crime that involves a computer system as a means or as a target in the perpetration of a crime. Statistics are given to show the pervasiveness of computer-related crime. The elements and categories of computer-related crime compared with traditional crime are given.

A computer criminal's motives are discussed. The many varieties of methods of operation are noted, including collusion, counterfeiting, embezzlement, espionage, extortion, false pretenses, forgery, fraud, larceny, malicious mischief, sabotage, terrorism, vandalism, and wire fraud, together with some techniques and methods. The vulnerability of microcomputers is emphasized because of their wide use in businesses.

THE SCOPE OF THE PROBLEM

Computer-related crime can be defined as a crime that either directly or indirectly involves a computer system as a means or as a target in the perpetration of the crime.[1] Computer-related crime can be committed by employees inside the organization, by outsiders, or by both internal and external criminals acting in collusion. Computer criminals generally net more money per incident than non-computer-related white-collar criminals, generally because of the high concentration of assets controlled by and contained in computers.

Micro and minicomputers are widely used in businesses of all sizes throughout the world. Because of the lack of controls that is usually found in smaller organizations that use computers, along with a typical lack of segregation of duties, the micro and minicomputer installation in a small business is a prime target for both internal and external criminals.

---

[1] Timothy A. Schabeck, *Computer Crime Investigation Manual* (Madison, Wisc.: Assets Protection, 1979). Information extracted from chapters 3 and 9. Used with permission.

Many of the computer crime examples presented in this section straddle the line between unethical and illegal practices. Many data processing professionals have advanced through their EDP career with the feeling that it is all right to copy or use other organizations' programs under certain circumstances. These programs may be acquired through friends at another company, through a terminal or microcomputer connected to a computer center in a communications environment, or simply by the copying of software that is on an unattended stand-alone personal computer or workstation. The individual may feel that he is doing nothing wrong; he is only trying to save time by not having to "reinvent the wheel," that is, not having to write similar programs that other organizations have already developed (such as payroll). As innocent as this individual may think that he is, his unethical and illegal acts can be prosecuted under a multitude of federal or state laws, which include those specifically written for computer crime along with the felonies of larceny and wire fraud.

COMPUTER–RELATED CRIME STATISTICS

The actual number of computer crime cases is unknown, and much of the data used to assemble the current crime statistics is inaccurate. However, it is quite evident that most computer crimes, as is the case with all white-collar crimes, are not reported to the police. Most organizations, unless required by law to do so, are reluctant to prosecute white-collar criminals, because of the detrimental publicity that an organization may receive. It has been estimated that only approximately 15 percent of known white-collar crimes are reported to the police.

Recent FBI computer-related crime statistics indicate the following:

- 1 percent of all computer-related crime is detected.
- 7 percent of those detected are reported to police.
- One out of every thirty perpetrators receives a jail sentence.

August Bequai, a Washington, D.C., attorney specializing in computer-related crime and hi-tech legal matters, has made the following observations:

- Computer-related crime costs industry more than $200 million annually.
- Embezzlement and stock frauds account for $3 billion.
- There have been 1,400 electronic fund transfer scams.

- The FBI has put 400 agents through its four-week training course in computer crime investigation, but has a two-year waiting list.
- The Secret Service has trained about 200 of its agents in computer crime investigation.
- Computer crime investigation training generally consists of one- or two-day seminars, and "that is it," Bequai says. In New York City, he says, there is *no* computer crime training for investigators.
- Law enforcement is hobbled by a lack of funding for training in computer crime.

The results of a special random survey of Data Processing Management Association (DPMA) members concerning computer security was recently published in *COMP-U-FAX*, a DPMA newsletter. Some of the survey findings are given below.

• Company executives are aware of the importance of data security, but often fail to provide actual support and assistance to their desktop management.

• A survey of DPMA members indicated that an accumulative average of 2.7 percent of their corporate budget is allocated toward data security.

• DPMA members also said that their organizations would each lose $142,676.58 per day in the event of a system failure.

• The areas of greatest vulnerability were ranked as follows: (1) DP/MIS staff, (2) clerical users, (3) outsiders, (4) management users.

• Computer safeguards suggested by members were physical security, software security packages, user education and training, management awareness, and better auditing procedures.

Another survey was undertaken in an attempt to pinpoint the methods, causes, and commonality of computer-related crime. Detmar Straub of the Management Information Services Program at Indiana University also surveyed DPMA members. Here is a summary of the findings from 170 survey responses:

• 21 percent reported that one-on-one system abuses had occurred in the past three years—with the perpetrator known. Outsiders committed 2 percent of the crimes. Insiders included programmers, analysts, machine operators, and data entry clerks.

• A "significant" number of suspected abuses were reported; some companies reported hundreds of suspected abuses.

Categories of abuse included:

- Misuse of computer services (49 percent: 42 percent unauthorized use, 7 percent disruption of services).

- Program abuse (24 percent).
- Data abuse (22 percent).
- Hardware abuse (5 percent).

Respondents described 56 abuses:

- Just 2 percent of the abuses were reported to police.
- "Tapeworm" programs (viruses) were reported to be found by several of the respondents.
- 45 percent employ a data security staff.
- Most abuses were detected by accident.

As for the perpetrators:

- 27 percent acted out of ignorance or improper professional conduct.
- 26 percent out of playfulness.
- 25 percent for personal gain.
- 22 percent out of maliciousness or revenge.

ELEMENTS OF COMPUTER CRIME

A study for the Law Enforcement Assistance Administration, titled "The Investigation of White-Collar Crime: A Manual for Law Enforcement Agencies,"[2] defines the five elements of white-collar crime. In general, these five elements can also apply to computer crime. However, it is important to recognize at the outset that the elements discussed below apply more to the "white-collar" types of computer crime than to the types of "common" computer crime such as arson or burglary.

As stated in the manual, it is important that the investigator and prosecutor of white-collar crime, vis-à-vis computer crime, recognize that these crimes invariably display certain characteristics. It is possible to analyze the execution of these schemes and note that the offenders have certain common objectives. Familiarity with these five elements can provide a general framework for planning and undertaking action to combat computer crime.

---

[2] Battelle Law and Justice Center, *The Investigation of White-Collar Crime: A Manual for Law Enforcement Agencies*. Available from U.S. Government Printing Office, Washington, D.C. 20402, Stock No. 027–000–0057–1.

Before the individual elements are reviewed, it is important to note the possible cyclical or recidivist nature of computer crime. The majority of computer crimes that are responsible for large monetary losses take place over a period of time and usually require the repeated commission and cover-up of an illegal act. Usually, only small amounts of money are embezzled from an organization at one time. However, over a period of time the amount usually grows.

As Figure 3–1 shows, computer crime involves five elements.

1. Intent to Commit a Wrongful Act

As mentioned earlier, many of the computer abuse incidents border between the unethical and the illegal. However, most personnel know the essence of the laws that apply to their conduct in their work environment and can be held responsible for their acts. These people usually know when they are involved in a wrongful act, although they may not have an awareness that a particular statute is being violated. Intent involves the presence of some wrongful purpose or objective.

2. Disguise of Purpose of Intent

Disguise of purpose involves the character of the offender's conduct or activity in the implementation of his plan. He uses disguise to cover up the actions he undertakes to implement his scheme. Disguise can take the form of forged source documents, altered computer input or output, or hidden program routines. Verbal disguise is also usually employed in combination with the items above.

3. Reliance by Offender on Ignorance or Carelessness of the Victim

"The Investigation of White-Collar Crime" manual states, "While intent and disguise, the first two elements, are clearly elements which originate with and are controlled by the white-collar offender—involving the offender's own objective and chosen method of execution—reliance . . . on ignorance and carelessness of the victim is a victim-related element, since it is based upon the offender's perception of victim susceptibility. The offender will not go forward unless he feels he can depend upon the inability of the victim to perceive deception."[3]

---

[3] Ibid., pp. 21–26.

FIGURE 3–1
Elements of Computer Crime

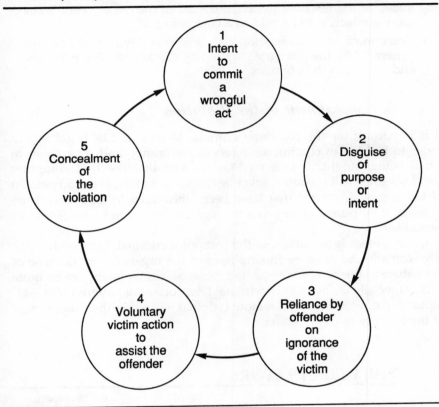

One of the biggest fears that a computer criminal has is the fear of being caught. In order to avoid this situation, he carefully plans and executes the crime, taking great care in covering up his trail to avoid being apprehended.

4. Voluntary Victim Action to Assist the Offender

The offender must usually induce the victim to voluntarily undertake some act in order to successfully complete his illegal scheme.

In computer crime instances, this may include the following:

- The obtaining of management approval to run a test on the organization's accounts receivable system. The "test" is really a disguise for the offender to produce a list of the organization's customers which is to be sold to a competitor.
- Creation of fictitious medical claims so that payment checks are generated by the computer, signed by the authorizing personnel, and mailed to the offender.

5. Concealment of the Violation

It is important for the computer criminal to conceal his illegal acts in order to be able to continuously repeat his crime—and, of course, to avoid being caught. It is a well-known fact that the best computer fraud schemes will probably never be detected. In fact, about 95 percent of the computer crimes that have been uncovered to date have been uncovered by pure accident, not through investigation by investigators or auditors.

Concealment is important to the computer criminal, because he usually works in the open as an employee of the organization. Because of the nature of the computer and its processes, concealment can be quite easy, especially in the remote terminal teleprocessing environment. Manipulation of accounts via a remote terminal will aid in the concealment of the identity of the offender.

THE PERPETRATORS

This section analyzes and identifies potential computer criminals. Motives are addressed as well as methods of operation (modi operandi).

Motives

Many of the factors that motivate a person to commit a computer-related crime are addressed below. The motives listed have been given by a criminologist—and by the criminals themselves. Psychologists warn that the studying and classifying of motives is not a very helpful means of identifying potential perpetrators. However, the reader may find review of the following list to be beneficial, in that some of the motives listed may be applicable to individual suspects in a computer-crime investigation. Possible motives should always be immediately identified. The knowledge of possible motives may aid in the identification of the primary and/or principal suspect (see Figure 3–2).

FIGURE 3–2
Motives

1. Personal gain.
2. Organization's gain over a competitor.
3. "Robin Hood syndrome": Take from the rich (organization) and keep it.
4. "Game playing": Trying to break the security of a computer system or access confidential data to see if it can be done. Test of skills. Technical ingenuity.
5. So easy to embezzle—management and computer controls are lax.
6. The department is crooked—criminal skills taught by peer group.
7. Hatred of organization—felt that the organization had cheated them. Revenge.
8. Individual gets into financial trouble:
   • Gambling.
   • Drugs.
   • Social exposure (most common).
9. The computer is an ideal target for attack; it has no feelings, and great damage can be inflicted on an organization.
10. If it is known that a supervisor is involved in a criminal activity, the subordinates may feel that it is also right for them to be involved.
11. Group expectations: social norms, bravery, source of income.
12. May want to feel important. Ego trips.
13. Differential association and group behavior: The computer criminal in his act deviates from the accepted practices of his associates only in small ways. For hackers, there is a very fine line between hacking for adventure and hacking with criminal intent. Groups of hackers form, like the "4-1-4 Gang," who work in complicity with each other to achieve a set of tasks such as the unauthorized access to a computer system. The need to "out-do" the other person is strong and when a new task is achieved, it is usually shared with other group members and/or placed on an electronic bulletin board.
14. An individual has financial problems and is ashamed to ask anyone for help.
15. An individual can overcome protests of his conscience by means of rationalization.
16. Mentally disturbed: psychotics, psychopaths, and other unbalanced persons.

Modus Operandi (Method of Operation)

A summary of the habits, techniques, and peculiarities of a computer criminal's behavior is often referred to as the *modus operandi*, or M.O., which means *method of operation*. The M.O. often serves to reveal a criminal's identity as if it were a fingerprint impression of his character and personality.

In the traditional M.O. arrangement system, the following are considered the significant elements in the detection of offenders: property,

description, observations at scene, motive, time, peculiarities, and observed peculiarities.[4] Because of the nature of computer crime, this type
of M.O. breakdown is usually not applicable to computer criminals.
Individual computer criminals are usually not repeaters, or recidivists,
after they have been apprehended, and therefore do not develop a
definite M.O. that could be used as a unique personal identifier. However, some basic M.O. patterns can be developed for computer criminals
in general. These M.O.s are listed in Figure 3–3.

CATEGORIES OF CRIME

This section identifies the various computer-related crime methods and
techniques and legal classifications. Some of the legal descriptions are
based on a general consensus of state and federal laws. Definitions of
crime and their elements tend to vary from state to state. The state and
federal computer-related crime laws are listed in Chapter Eleven, "Legal
Issues and Legislation."

Collusion

Collusion occurs when more than one person is involved in cooperation
for a fraudulent purpose. Collusion among members of a data processing staff such as an operator, programmer, and analyst could result
in large undetected losses. User departments may also be involved.
Likewise, collusion may occur between employees outside of data
processing—for example, between warehouse personnel and order-
entry or inventory personnel. Also, hackers in collusion with each other
have caused large amounts of damage.

Several other points can be made about collusion:

- Many collusion schemes include management personnel.
- In computer-related bank fraud and embezzlement, there is usually a high degree of collusion.
- Collusion schemes have been known to involve more than 60
  people in a single case.

---

[4] Charles E. O'Hara, *Fundamentals of Criminal Investigation*, 2d ed. (Springfield, Ill.:
Charles C. Thomas), pp. 597–98.

FIGURE 3–3

Modus Operandi: Characteristics of Computer Criminals

Personal Profile Category	*Patterns and Traits*
Age	10–46 years old
Sex	Male (usually)
Skill level	A wide range has been involved in computer-related crime.
	Management.
	Highly experienced professionals.
	Technical specialist.
	Clerical personnel.
	Students.
Occupation (partial list only)	Students.
	Presidents of firms.
	Senior executives.
	Management personnel.
	Accountants.
	Programmers.
	Clerks.
	Terrorists.
	Military/intelligence personnel.
	Organized crime.
Personal characteristics	Bright.
	Eager.
	Highly motivated.
	Adventuresome.
	Qualified.
	Willing to accept technical challenge.
	Highly desirable employee/student.
	Hard worker.
	First person to trust—last person you would suspect of doing wrong.
	Once involved in fraud, seldom suggests new methods of running systems for fear that a radical change in procedures would result in his exposure.
	Greatest fears: exposure, ridicule, loss of status.
	Always on guard:
	First in office.
	Last to leave.
	Eats lunch at desk.
	No vacation.
	After caught:
	Tries to minimize the criminal aspects of his activity.

FIGURE 3-3 *(concluded)*

Personal Profile Category	Patterns and Traits
Collusion	Varies. One-man operation—solves his own personal problems in his own personal way. Controls can force collusion. Interdepartmental collusion. Intradepartmental collusion. Collusion between outsiders (hackers—electronic bulletin boards). Collusion: Insiders/outsiders.
Relation between occupation and crime	*Most* computer crimes are committed by individuals employed in a position of trust within the company.
Criminal record	Usually no criminal record. Not a professional criminal.
Perpetration	Unauthorized data manipulation during authorized computer use (legitimate tools). Unauthorized computer use (illegitimate tools).

Case Examples

U.S. Secret Service. The U.S. Secret Service arrested six high school students in Milwaukee for taking part in a nationwide caper by computer hackers to obtain thousands of dollars worth of computer goods and services. More than three dozen computer hobbyists were involved; most were juveniles. It was anticipated that more arrests would take place in Detroit, Seattle, Los Angeles, Chicago, and Memphis. The students used the hacking scheme to buy thousands of dollars worth of computer and related equipment with the use of stolen credit card numbers. The equipment was sent to a mailbox rental service in Waukesha, Wisconsin. The Secret Service installed a surveillance camera at the site to monitor pickups from the mailbox.

Operational procedures on how to perpetrate the scam were contained on an electronic bulletin board. The procedures were written by someone known as "Iceman, Leader of the Black Triangle." The stolen credit card numbers were obtained from computer databases the hackers had illegally accessed, and by foraging for carbon receipts of credit card purchases. The electronic bulletin board that operated out of Milwaukee was "The World of Cryton." It also contained a list of stolen credit card numbers. The numbers were used to establish accounts with

CompuServe and The Source, which allow users to exchange electronic messages and to buy goods and services from their homes or offices.

NASA—Marshall Space Flight Center. The youths who broke into the system used techniques shown in the film *War Games*. The techniques utilized the automatic dialing system and password bypass techniques depicted in that film. The hackers attempted to thwart investigation attempts by erasing password access records stored on NASA's system.

Members of the "4-1-4" gang have also used techniques for illegal entry shown in *War Games*. The movie, as well as various episodes from the TV series "Whiz Kids," shows the procedure used to access systems. A micro, equipped with an automatic dialing system and a modem, is programmed to systematically dial all of the telephone numbers within a specified area—by area code, exchange, etc. Any numbers that are answered with a modem carrier tone are written to a file. These numbers are then used by the hackers to access the systems.

Counterfeiting

The process of imitating or copying especially with intent to deceive is counterfeiting. It may involve, for example, duplicate computer print runs of checks or other negotiables. In another case, magnetic tape tickets used in a West Coast and a foreign country's toll-collecting system were counterfeited in order to raise the value of the tickets from 5 cents to 20 dollars. This alteration was done with a steam iron and 2 or 3 cents worth of magnetic material.

Some consideration is being given to enacting laws covering counterfeiting of electronic computer impulses.

Embezzlement

Embezzlement is the fraudulent conversion of the property of another by a person to whom it is entrusted (larceny after trust). *Defalcation* is a term used at times to describe an embezzlement. Statutes define embezzlement as either a felony or a misdemeanor, depending on the value of the property.

Computer-related banking embezzlement methods include:

- Kiting: writing a check against uncollected funds in a bank account to cover a check.
- Lapping: a circle of kited checks where the last one in the circle covers the first.

- Fictitious float: abusing the "float" to cover a check.
- Check and cash manipulation.
- Manipulation of accounts.

Embezzlements have been committed through the manipulation of computer input (data diddling). Such manipulation includes modification/ forgery of source documents and adding, deleting, or modifying punched cards prior to running the job on the computer. Many customers, after receiving erroneous bills, etc., have been told that the computer had made a mistake when in fact an embezzlement scheme was being perpetrated.

Programmers have been charged with embezzlement for "round-down" schemes (salami slicing). Round-down is a process that deletes the least significant digit or digits of a number and adjusts the part retained in accordance with some rule. Programmers have deposited the remainder of each adjustment into their own accounts.

Espionage

Espionage is generally divided into two categories: industrial and foreign. *Industrial* espionage is the unethical and/or illegal collection of information and data that contributes to an evaluation for a commercial enterprise and that may be used to the detriment of the organization by competitors. *Foreign* espionage includes the same elements as industrial espionage with the exception that the information is to be used by a foreign government and not an industrial concern. Computer diskettes, tapes, and microfilm containing business information and defense secrets have been sold to or stolen by foreign agents.

In the realm of industrial espionage, competitors have used many of the following techniques to gain information about an organization:

- Bought or stole copies of computer data files in the form of diskettes, magnetic tape, or printed reports. Information included mailing/customer lists, research data, and marketing data.
- Accessed, through teleprocessing time-sharing methods, an organization's computer files.
- Hired and/or interviewed current or former employees of an organization to gain information.
- Purchased their competitors' products for analysis.

In addition, pictures have been taken through data center windows of documents, printouts, or of information displayed on CRT screens. Discarded waste paper, punched cards, and computer reports have been analyzed to obtain valuable information about an organization and its systems.

In the foreign arena, U.S. computer companies employees have sold data about their company's computer to the former Soviet Union. Information that was sold included magnetic tapes, photographs, electronic components, micro programs, and engineering maintenance manuals.

Also, hidden wireless transmitters were found inside a CPU at a U.S. security agency and in computers used in Vietnam.

Extortion

A broad legal definition of extortion is to obtain money or valuables from a person by violence, threat, or abuse of authority. Most state statutes require the following elements of cause be shown:

1. Oral or written communication.
2. That the communication maliciously threatens to accuse another of any crime of offense, or threaten any injury to the person or property of another.
3. The intent to extort money or any pecuniary advantage or to do or not to do some act.

Usually, there need be no intent of ill will against the victim. Vague threats, however, are insufficient to meet statutory requirements, as are those threats that are not terrifying to the ordinary person. Also, the threat is not dependent on the state of mind of the victim.

The Hobbs Act, Title 18, Section 1951, mandates that it is a violation for anyone to obstruct, delay, or affect commerce by robbery, extortion, or to attempt or conspire to do so, or to commit or to threaten physical violence to persons or property in furtherance of a plan or preparations to do anything in violation of this section.

Types of extortion

- *Bomb threats.* Threat against the company in general or the data center for money or because of the type of data being processed, by a disgruntled employee or by outsider
- *Kidnapping.* Kidnapping of strategic employee(s) for ransom or other reason
- *Theft.* Theft of important programs, data (files), or documentation. Sometimes theft is done for ransom.
- *Blackmail.* Extortion by threat—especially of public exposure.

Examples

- Extortion can be used to damage the economic welfare of a business or of an individual either through the use of the computer system or by directing threats at the system itself.
- Through the use of on-line systems, electronic fund transfers, etc., information about an individual or an organization is usually readily accessible for use in legitimate business operations. However, these systems could be manipulated in order to access information about an individual's private life for blackmail or other extortion purposes.
- Computer centers have been taken over by dissidents and kept out of operation until their demands were met.

False Pretenses

False pretenses is a statutory crime in which there must be a false representation of a material fact (past or present) which causes the victim to pass title of his property to a wrongdoer who knows his representations are false and who intends to defraud the victim.[5] This includes:

- Falsification of an organization's computer records to create a false view of that company's financial strength.
- Falsification of computer reports to substantiate false financial sales, statistical, research, and inventory figures.

The criminal must obtain possession of the property to be guilty of this crime.

Forgery

Forgery, under common law, was defined as the "fraudulent making or alteration of a writing to the prejudice of another's rights." Forgery is usually classified as a felony and is defined by statutes which confirm common law and extend its scope.[6]

The elements of forgery are the following:

- There must be a false writing or alteration of a document.
- The document must be apparently capable of defrauding.
- There must be an intent to defraud another.

---

[5] August Bequai, *Computer Crime* (Lexington, Mass.: Lexington Books 1977), pp. 31–33.

[6] Harold F. Russell, *Foozles and Frauds* (Altamonte Springs, Fla.: The Institute of Internal Auditors, 1977), pp. 104–105.

In many jurisdictions, it is quite probable that the utilization of a false entry code, a symbol of right, privilege, and identification, which prints out on any machine and is used to defraud or injure, is forgery.

Forgeries may involve the following:

• Negotiable instruments and other documents such as computer-printed stocks, bonds, checks, coupons, bills, bills of lading, shipping invoices, receipts, and government documents.

• Source documents which serve as a basis for computer input have been forged. Information being processed and/or information stored on computer files could be modified with the use of forged documents. Forged documents can also result in the generation of fraudulent computer output in the form of checks and reports that can be used to defraud.

• *Computer output.* Checks generated by the computer based on false data fed into the computer are considered forgeries, since the computer acted as the agent of the felons.

• *Blank forms.* Blank payroll and accounts payable checks may be found in most computer rooms.

Fraud—General

Fraud involves the intentional misrepresentation of the truth to deceive the owner. In computer crime the fraud occurs:

• When a wrongdoer attempts to conceal his actions through incorrect entries or changes in the organization's records or files.

• When the wrongdoer is not entrusted with the assets that he actually steals.

One of the basic tenets of the law of fraud is that fraud may be committed by a suppression of the truth as well as by the suggestion of falsehood.

Types of fraud. For purpose of clarity and discussion, computer fraud has been classified into the following categories:

1. Bank fraud.
2. Deceit.
3. Float fraud.
4. Mail fraud.
5. Wire fraud.

A corporation may be held liable for the fraud and deceit of its officers and agents acting within the scope of their corporate authority or employment, even though the corporation did not authorize, concur in, or know of the fraud.

Programs have been modified to suppress or alter computer output reports.

Larceny: Grand and Petit

Larceny is the wrongful or fraudulent taking and carrying away of personal property from another person with the intent to deprive the owner of his property. The offense is committed once the personal property is moved any distance, even though it is not successfully carried off. The offense is committed without regard to whether the victim is aware that the larceny is being committed.[7]

- *Grand larceny* usually involves property valued at $100 or more (felony).
- *Petit larceny* involves property valued at less than $100 (misdemeanor in most jurisdictions).

Elements

1. The accused wrongfully took, obtained, or withheld the property.
2. The property must belong to another.
3. The property must be taken away (need only be a few inches).
4. Intent to deprive the owner of his property must be present.

For example:
- Theft of computer time or services is considered by some jurisdictions as larceny.
- Taking of the following items would constitute larceny:
  - Hardware (Theft of terminals is common, especially in universities).
  - Software (programs).
  - Computer printouts.
  - Magnetic files.
  - Punched cards.
  - Computer supplies.
  - Documentation.

---

[7] Bequai, *Computer Crime*, pp. 28–31.

- Trade secrets.
- Credit cards.
- In some jurisdictions, to take the property with the intent of selling it back to the owner for ransom is larceny.
- Individuals have been charged with grand larceny when, because of key punching or programming errors, large amounts of money were deposited to their bank accounts, and they took advantage of the error and spent large amounts of the money before being apprehended.
- In some jurisdictions a person using a stolen credit card number for use in accessing a computer system and its services could be found guilty of theft of services or labor under false pretenses.
- Under federal law (in a general interpretation) any misappropriations of software (such as theft or conversion) that is subject to some measure of government control, custody, or ownership could be charged with embezzlement or theft of public money, property or records (18 U.S.C. section 641).
- The head of a computer payroll firm was charged with larceny when it was discovered that bad checks totaling over a million dollars had been issued by his firm. Several hundred thousand dollars in income tax withholdings and social security payments were also missing.
- Programs have been stolen from organizations by competitors to help reduce their system/program development time and cost (theft of trade secrets.)

Two case examples follow.

In Columbia, Maryland, a 13-year-old boy was arrested for allegedly stealing thousands of dollars worth of computer programs and equipment and rare comic books with his micro. The boy said he did it for the "challenge." He used his micro to purchase computer equipment and programs by using credit-card numbers supplied by hackers in the Midwest. He ordered $3,000 to $4,000 worth of goods (including rare comic books) over the telephone and had them delivered to unoccupied model homes in his neighborhood. A search of the boy's house produced programs that let him illegally access AT&T, Sprint, MCI, and other long-distance telephone services. The access programs simulated the tones used by the phone service companies' own computers. One of the programs simulated the beep tones that a pay phone makes when coins are inserted. The tones were recorded on a portable recorder and used to gain access to long distance lines from any pay phone.

The boy, who learned his computer skills in less than a year, has been charged with credit-card fraud. The investigation of his activities was based on information supplied by an informant.

In Marlboro, Massachusetts, an 18-year-old high school student has pleaded not guilty to larceny charges for allegedly gaining illegal access to his high school's computer system. The illegal access was discovered by a school employee who noticed that someone had attempted to gain access to the school's DEC PDP-11. Telephone-call traces were made to the student's house, and he was charged with stealing electronically processed or stored data with a value of more than $100. If found guilty, he could be sentenced to a maximum of five years in prison.

Malicious Mischief/Destruction

Malicious mischief applies to the malicious damage to or destruction of the property of another. This offense is usually a misdemeanor.[8]

Elements

1. There must be some physical injury to the property of another.
2. The injury must impair the utility or diminish the value of the property.
3. The property must either be destroyed or have suffered some substantial injury.
4. The damage must be inflicted with malice. *Malicious destruction* is the term used by federal statutes and applies to the malicious damage to or destruction of federal property.

For example, governmental and nongovernmental computers and data centers have been attacked and either damaged or destroyed. Some malicious mischief/destruction cases have involved shooting the computer or computer terminals and pouring liquids into the central processing unit.

If files or programs contained on a disk or tape unit are damaged or destroyed, although no physical harm has come to the tape or disk drive or media, malicious mischief can still be charged. This charge would have to be substantiated through careful description of the damage by the prosecutor.

Sabotage

Sabotage can be defined as the damage to or destruction of the property of a governmental or business organization. Sabotage may be directed toward a computer or its components and may be used to hinder normal computer operations.

---

[8] Ibid., pp. 33–34.

Sabotage can take many forms and may be perpetrated by disgruntled employees, competitors, terrorists, or foreign agents.

Forms of sabotage

• *Bombs.* Bombings of data centers by terrorist or extremist groups are quite common. Foreign countries are currently experiencing an increase in the number of computer facility bombings.

• *Arson.* Fire has been used to destroy computers and data stores on magnetic and paper files. In one case, gasoline was poured directly on the computer and peripheral equipment and then ignited.

• *Water.* Intentional activation of fire sprinkler systems by disgruntled employees can cause extensive damage to computer equipment.

• *Firearms.* Disgruntled employees have used high-powered rifles, shotguns, and handguns to attempt to disable computers. Air conditioning units that support data processing operations have been disabled by high-powered rifles. Without air conditioning most large computers must be shut down, to prevent overheating.

• *Utilities.* The electric power supply to the computer can be sabotaged in order to suspend processing.

• *Program.* People have modified existing programs or written new programs for the purpose of sabotaging their organization's computer system. Files can be erased, account status can be changed, report information can be modified, or programs can be erased. Programs have been entered via remote devices that caused a computer system to go down, or "crash."

• *Magnets.* Magnets have been used to destroy magnetic files. In order for a magnet to be effective in erasing data, it must be of sufficient size (power) to do so. An extremist group used magnets to erase the front portions of magnetic tape reels. Tests have been conducted with a magnet that had the power to lift 40 pounds. When placed directly against the edge flange of the tape reel, the first 350 feet of the tape were rendered unreadable. The same magnet held one inch from the reel produced no loss of data. However, when this magnet was placed against the side of the reel, all of the data on the tape was erased.

Computer operators can sabotage the system via console or, as in one case, by inserting small metal objects in the circuitry of the computer which cause short circuits and extensive machine down time. In one case, wire cutters and acid were used to destroy a university's computer.

Computer manufacturers such as IBM have felt the brunt of the many bombings and other acts of sabotage by dissidents. EDP employees who have been fired and allowed to remain for a couple of weeks at their job have sabotaged their organizations' data processing systems by scrambling on-line computer files so as to prevent access of information and by removing labels from computer tape reels.

Terrorism

Terrorists can direct physical attacks against an organization's data processing facility in order to cripple the normal operations of the organization. Computer systems, their personnel and/or their facilities could be held as hostage by terrorists.

It is common knowledge that computers are becoming more and more a prime target for terrorist attacks. Terrorist groups know that the best way to cripple a multinational or local organization is by attacking their data processing operations.

Numerous cases of terrorism directed at data processing operations have been documented. Many of those attacks were directed against American companies overseas. Published terrorist attacks against DP systems have taken place in Italy, France, Argentina, the United States, Iran, El Salvador, the United Kingdom, and Germany.

The following is a case example.

Neo-Nazi terrorist group using computers. An investigation of an American Nazi group called the White American Bastion, or *Bruder Schweigen* (Silent Brotherhood) uncovered microcomputers and databases used to carry out its terrorist activities. A computer network is used by group members to keep in contact with each other and to maintain a list of their enemies.

According to the *Detroit Free Press* and the *Chicago Tribune*, "The network, created by an electronics engineer who belongs to the group, allows members to call phone numbers in Idaho and Texas and to call up an 'Aryan Database' on the home micros. The network has seven levels of access, each reached by typing in code words, and it includes hit lists of Jewish groups and individuals."

The group of an estimated 150 members finances itself partially through robbery of armored cars and counterfeiting. One large weapon and munitions cache has been uncovered. The Nazi group also has established a point award system that in order to become an "Aryan warrior," applicants must accumulate a total of one point. Fractions of a point of varying values are awarded for such things as the murder of federal judges, FBI agents, and other federal officials and employees as well as the murders of Jewish people, black people and others. This group is apparently responsible for the machine gun execution of a

Denver radio personality who spoke out against anti-Semites and white supremacists.

Vandalism

Vandalism is the willful or malicious destruction or defacement of public or private property. In the case of computers, vandalism usually would involve some form of damage of the computer and/or its components. Objectives of vandalism are to destroy the computer and/or its components, to make the system inoperable, to cause additional expense, and to cause business interruption. Vandalism usually results in large monetary losses because of the great cost of computer systems.

Wire Fraud

The federal wire fraud statute is identical to the mail fraud statute with the exception of the federal medium abused. The wire fraud statute has two essential elements:

1. A fraud or scheme to obtain money or property under false pretenses.
2. Use of the telecommunications medium for the purpose of executing or attempting to execute the fraud.

For example:
- When a remote terminal or microcomputer is used to perpetrate a fraud, or when the telephone is used to call an accomplice, the wire fraud statute is applicable—so long as the message crosses state lines.
- Wire fraud has been charged in many cases involving the illegal and fraudulent transfer of funds over the Federal Reserve Wire (Fedwire).
- Wire fraud has also been charged when a perpetrator uses a terminal to access information or to steal programs from competitors or other sources.

COMPUTER-RELATED CRIME TECHNIQUES AND METHODS

The various techniques and devices described below illustrate the many different types of computer system vulnerabilities. To date, a relatively insignificant number of computer crimes have been uncovered, which indicates the use of the more sophisticated techniques. This low reporting may be due to the reluctance of organizations to report computer crime or, more probably, because computer criminals utilizing these techniques are difficult to detect.

Many of the techniques listed apply to mainframe computer system processing capabilities. However, micro-to-mainframe linking expands greatly the criminal opportunities of previous terminal-to-mainframe interface.

Asynchronous Attack

Asynchronous attack involves the changing of operational control parameters after the computer's supervisory program checks them. The parameters are changed by the perpetrator so that he or she can circumvent some security protection feature of the computer system. This method of attack is possible because computers are able to process input/output and relinquish control back to the user of concurrent processing. Asynchronous attack is also referred to as the "time-of-check and time-of-use" attack.[9]

Between-Lines Entry

This method employs an extra terminal or micro tapped into the communication channels to affect entry to the computer system. In this scheme the perpetrator does not interrupt the legitimate user, but enters his commands between the commands of the user. Not wanting to interrupt the regular user limits the type of request the perpetrator may make, so to extend his access time he can cancel the user's sign-off signals so as to continue operating in his name.[10]

Browsing

Browsing is the "searching of residue or storage for unauthorized information." It is sometimes used to break into a system and, at other times, after penetration, to discover more unauthorized information. Searching a trash container for log-on password or user identification (sometimes known as the "waste basket threat") is the most basic form of browsing.

---

[9] IBM, "Data Security and Data Processing Volume 5—Study Results," TRW Systems, Inc., Stock No. G320–1375, p. 48.

[10] Bruce J. Walker and Ian F. Blake, *Computer Security and Protection Structures* (Stroudsburg, Pa.: Dowden, Hutchinson & Ross, 1977), p. 12.

It often provides enough information to support the impersonation of a legitimate user. Trash also yields lists, notes, discarded teleprinter ribbons or platens, and data on paper, or magnetic media which can be searched for sensitive information. In short, anything not erased or overwritten before being discarded is of potential use to a penetrator.

In *Assets Protection* James Finch writes, "Other forms of browsing are searching files to which a user has accidentally gained access, the perusal of source listings, and looking over the shoulder of a person using a teleprinter."[11]

Clandestine Code Changes

Clandestine program code changes involve the submission of "patch code," possibly with the pretext of maintaining or updating an operating system, application program, or utility program. This "patch" would allow the perpetrator to concurrently make both legitimate and illegitimate modifications.

Code changes can be initiated by either application or system programmers. Clandestine program code can also be initiated by the computer hardware/software vendor, either before being installed at the user site or as an updated software version.

Data Aggregation

Data aggregation occurs when certain related data stored in separate locations is relatively nonsensitive, but the same data, when combined, becomes significantly more sensitive. Figure 3–4 illustrates data aggregation. Information from files that could be compromised through the use of data aggregation may include information on:

- Health care.
- Defense/security.
- Customer files.
- Research and development.
- Manufacturing processes.
- Insurance.
- Competitive plans and strategies.

---

[11] James H. Finch, "Espionage and Theft Using Computers," *Assets Protection* 2, no. 1 (1976).

FIGURE 3–4
Data Aggregation

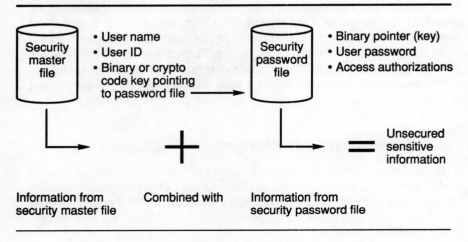

Data Diddling

Data diddling is the most common computer scam. This involves the changing of data before or during the input to the computer; that is, counterfeiting, forging, altering, or fabricating input documents and/or data.

Data Inference

A perpetrator may obtain sensitive information by deducing it from data acquired through a series of inquires. For example, he may inquire into a statistical health file to determine the number of people who have been addicted to a certain type of drug. Through further questioning techniques (age, sex, county, etc.) it may be possible to identify a particular individual, such as a politician or company official, who had been addicted to drugs. This information could then be used for blackmail.

Electronic Bulletin Boards

Electronic bulletin boards are databases stored on micro, mini or mainframe computers. The purpose of the "boards" is to share information with others who have been given access. The boards, however, appear to be a rallying point for hackers, and some boards are even being used for criminal and terrorist activities as noted earlier in this chapter. Efforts are currently under way to draft a model computer crime bill that would penalize operators of electronic bulletin boards for aiding and abetting in a crime or solicitation of a computer-related crime.

What follows are case examples.

Theft of services—Canada. Four Montreal college students, 18 to 20 years of age, used their "blue box" microcomputer program to reach out and touch people and bulletin boards throughout the world—to the tune of $20,000. The fraud was uncovered when the Bell Canada Telephone Co. computerized tracking system showed an unusual number of long-distance calls coming from the homes of the students. The students allegedly had modified software in their modems to dial toll-free numbers automatically and take control of the switching interchange.

Raids of the student's homes by police and Bell Canada computer experts resulted in the seizure of several Apple IIs and Novation Inc. Apple-Cat modems. (The modems apparently were modified to generate the 2,600 Hz tones utilized in Bell Canada's and AT&T's networks.)

The students did not know each other except by aliases. Each possessed 300 to 500 floppy diskettes containing programs that included not only games but also instructions for building napalm grenades.

A hacker in London. The *London Daily Star*, a British newspaper, was so impressed with one of the 16-year-old hackers who was accused of breaking into the NASA computer that it invited him and his parents to London. The newspaper was doing a story about the need for computer security in England. At a local computer store that was used as a demonstration site by the hacker, he showed how to write the sequential dialing program that was used to access the NASA computer system.

Also, during his demonstration he uncovered a very large hacker underground, that is, an electronic bulletin board that contained passwords and access numbers of British computer users, including the University of London and Barclays Bank.

Electronic Surveillance

Electronic surveillance of a computer system can occur in the form of active and passive wiretapping of the system's communication or teleprocessing network. Also, many machines, such as computers, terminals, modems, and cathode ray tubes (CRT), give out powerful electromagnetic radiation that can be picked up by electronic surveillance equipment. A common CRT that employs a 50-times per second screen refresh rate can be monitored at a distance of one-half mile. The radiation from this machine can then be easily converted into the data that is being transmitted.

The most common type of electronic computer surveillance is passive or "listen only" wiretapping. A tape recorder can be used to record the data signals passing over a communication line. With the proper modem, the recorder could be played back to another terminal, which would print or display the characters that were transmitted.

Active wiretapping involves the entering of false messages or the modification of the terminal user's message. Banking and financial institutions employing EFT (electronic funds transfer) are especially susceptible to this type of system penetration.

It is estimated that nearly $70 trillion annually is electronically transferred over unprotected telephone communication lines in the United States.

Computers and their associated equipment, such as terminals, printers, typewriters, teletypes, etc., produce various emanations which can be intercepted by electronic surveillance methods. The emanations may be magnetic, RF or acoustic, or even perturbations of power or noise levels injected into the power lines. The magnetic-field characteristics of printers and typewriters may be received at short range by induction and sent through a radio transmitter to a listening post for interpretation of the typewritten message. Theoretically, a transmitter can be wired directly to the printing system such that specific keying signals are transmitted to the listening post rather than the ambiguous magnetic signature. In either case, the emanation characteristic of each alphabet character is unique. After analysis, these characteristics may be deciphered and further emanations become readable.

Another energy signature that can be read with great difficulty is noise from printing machines, which corresponds to the message being printed. The audio spectrum of these emanations is caused by various shifting gears, striking keys and magnetic solenoids. Some of these signals can be received by a suitable eavesdropping microphone and transmitted to a listening post through direct wire or radio link for processing into meaningful intelligence.[12]

The most common computer crimes involving teleprocessing are theft of timeshare services and malicious mischief. Computer criminals gain

---

[12] J. S. Van Deweker, *The Science of Electronic Surveillance* (Thousand Oaks, Calif.: Ashby & Associates), pp. 116–117.

unauthorized access to the central processing unit via their terminals in order to acquire trade secrets, programs, and confidential data or to cause the computer system to go down, or "crash."

Investigation of computer crimes involving teleprocessing usually requires the use of sophisticated electronic monitoring equipment and/or an in-depth knowledge of the system's programs, operating characteristics, and equipment being penetrated. Some basic forensic investigation techniques that can be used are the analyses of earprints, palmprints, and fingerprints found on a questioned transmission data set phone. Phone-call tracing is a valuable resource for apprehending criminals who use remote terminals in the commission of their crime.[13]

Erasure

Magnetic tape, diskette, or cassette files may be erased either by electronically or magnetically degaussing or by writing (via program) over the magnetic medium with new data. (See "Scavenging" in the latter part of this section.)

Implied Sharing

Generally, computer systems operate in two basic modes: user mode and supervisory mode. The "supervisor" is a series of system programs whose function it is to provide services for, and to supervise and control the running of, a number of "user" programs. Control is turned over to the supervisor any time the normal flow of processing is interrupted by a change of state in the system, such as the input and output of information to and from various devices.

In many of today's computer systems the supervisory and user programs share the same work space in the computer's memory. This could pose problems, as indicated in the following example.

Supervisory information containing a security authorization table is read into a work space (a specific portion) of memory for use in processing security access logic. Upon completion of the security access routine, the security authorization table still resides in that portion of memory. Because the routine has been completed, that portion of memory is not available to other users. If the security authorization information has not been erased, that information could be read by the subse-

---

[13] Tim A. Schabeck, "Computer Crime Investigation: Part 3," *Assets Protection* 2, no. 4 (1977), p. 7.

quent user of that portion of memory. The information could also be read by using computer vendor-supplied "dump" programs that would display or print the contents of that portion of the computer's memory.

Logic Bombs

Instructions inserted in a computer operating system or program which facilitate the perpetration of an unauthorized or malicious act. Two examples follow.

Sabotage—United States. Criminal charges have been filed against Dennis Williams, 30, and Michael Lampert, 22, former employees of Collins Foods International, Inc. The two allegedly programmed "logic bombs" that would erase inventory and payroll information processed by the company for 400 Kentucky Fried Chicken franchises and Sizzler Family Steak Houses. The programmed commands, one of which was set to activate on June 7, would have also shut down the computer system and erased all traces of the destructive commands. The motive is still unknown.

Logic bomb—Los Angeles. The Los Angeles Police Department's computer fraud unit investigated a programmed "logic bomb" which halted operations on the IBM 3081 computer used by the city's Department of Water and Power (DWP). It is thought that an insider was responsible for placing the logic bomb, which caused the system to crash every time it was used.

Masquerading

Masquerading, or impersonation, occurs when an unauthorized user attempts to act as an authorized user. Masquerading can be accomplished by using the following methods:
- Use of someone else's valid password.
- Use of someone else's terminal.
- Use of various phone company "customer service" options, such as call-forwarding.
- Coaxial cables located in transmission control units (TCU) could be switched. Terminals, in many cases, are identified by port addresses in the TCU. A user's terminal could be disconnected at the TCU by a perpetrator. The terminal user would then be informed that his terminal was "down" or broken — and that someone would be sent to fix it. In

the meantime, the perpetrator could hook his terminal into the user's port in the TCU in order to manipulate the system for criminal purposes.

"Piggy-Back" Entry

This is accomplished by "selective interception" of communications between a user and the central processor, and then releasing these with modifications or substituting entirely new messages while returning an error message to the user.[14] Information could be added, modified, or deleted from a system by using this method.

Piracy (Theft of Software)

Piracy involves the unauthorized copying (or duplication) of software. Software theft is out of control, especially in the microcomputer software area. Laws at the state and federal level are currently being enacted to help prevent this widespread criminal abuse.

Salami Slicing

This involves the thefts of small amounts of money from a large number of sources: for example, shaving a penny from each savings account during an interest calculation run or rounding off the mills (one tenth of a cent) and accumulating them for transfer to the perpetrator's account.

Scavenging

Scavenging pertains to the reading of residual information left in the computer memory or on other magnetic files. See also, *implied sharing.*

Information on magnetic tape can sometimes be read even after it has been erased or written over. After a period of time magnetic data can become "embedded" in the backing of the computer magnetic tape. Through electronic means this data can be recovered and read. If an organization uses a program to overwrite master files, it may be possible to subsequently read the master file information by identifying the former timing mark (on the tape) associated with the master file information.

---

[14] Walker and Blake, *Computer Security and Protection Structures,* pp. 11–12.

Spoofing

A communication line user can be tricked into thinking that he is communicating with his computer, when, in reality, he is communicating with an intercepter such as another computer, a mini-computer, intelligent terminal, or micro.

Superzapping

"Superzap" is a name of an IBM utility program that is used to help get a computer system operating after a system malfunction. All computer systems, large and small, have some type of superzap program. These programs usually override all systems security mechanisms and, therefore, are potentially very lethal weapons in the hands of a skilled computer criminal.

Trapdoor

Trapdoors are weak points in the computer system where access can be made while bypassing security controls. These trapdoors can be discovered through detailed study of the systems documentation, through collusion with the systems programmer, or through experimentation.

Trojan Horse

The Trojan horse technique gets its name from the method it employs. A program is introduced to the system that has embedded routines and, based upon a specific signal or condition, the illegal routine is activated.

Example: A retail business computer programmer wrote a credit approval and account balance program. Whenever a sales transaction with his account number was processed through his program, credit was approved, and his account balance would remain unchanged.

Viruses (Worm)

A computer "virus," also known as a "worm," is a small program or program subroutine that "infects" or "eats its way" through other programs, usually by inserting devastating instructions into them. This process continues until all of the programs in a system, or, because of networking, computers throughout an entire organization (or the country), contain one or more infected programs. At a given time, the virus/

worm programs/routines would be triggered to execute the job they were intended to perform.

John Brunner writes about virus-line programs in his book *The Sockware Rider*, where "tapeworm" programs ate their way through a computer network in order to get enough main memory so that the virus could duplicate itself. Computer scientists (and hackers) have been challenging themselves with a game called "Core War," which resembles a controlled viral attack. Each player enters a program into the same computer. The programs are designed to chase each other's programs around memory, trying to infect and kill rivals.

Bill Landreth, in his book *Out of the Inner Circle*, discusses worm programs. Some of his main points are the following:[15]

• Worm programs run along with other programs, usually in a program name that fits right into what the system is running (such as accounts payable programs).

• They are never found. Worm programs destroy themselves.

• Some worm programs only use unused computer resources (memory, peripherals).

• Typically they are low-priority programs using time/memory only when available.

• Worm programs can be run in many different segments, with each segment having the information needed to rebuild (regenerate) preceding and succeeding segments in case one is inadvertently destroyed.

A *Wall Street Journal* article told of the latest in computerological warfare:

> [The] director of development in the engineering department of CBS Inc. and home-computer buff was browsing recently through the offerings of Family Ledger, a computer bulletin board that can be used by anyone with a computer and a telephone to swap advice, games, or programs — or to make mischief. [The director] loaded into his computer a program that was billed as enhancing his IBM program's graphics; instead, it instantly wiped out the 900 accounting, word processing, and game programs he had stored in his computer over the years. All that he was left with was a taunt glowing back at him from the screen: "Arf! Arf! Got You!"

---

[15] Bill Landreth, *Out of the Inner Circle* (Bellevue, Wash.: Microsoft Press, 1985).

Chapter Four

Hardware Security

In this chapter, some of the methods of hardware security control are described, including equipment inventory and control, equipment identification, and personnel access control. Hardware security devices are briefly outlined, including electrical power access control. The need for backup equipment is emphasized. A hardware security checklist is provided.

HARDWARE CONTROL

Control of the organization's microcomputer hardware is an important element of the total microcomputer security environment. Controls include establishing policies and procedures that govern equipment inventory, equipment identification and marking, personnel access to a micro, and control of the applications being processed.

Equipment Inventory and Control

Equipment inventory. Inventory control logs should be maintained that list the microcomputer's CPU and peripheral devices. The following information should be recorded:

- Description of hardware device, including add-on cards.
- Model number.
- Memory storage size (Ks or Ms).
- Manufacturer's serial number.
- Warranty number.
- Warranty date.
- Name, address, and phone number of where the item was purchased.
- Date purchased.
- Company identification number.

Equipment control. A second log should be maintained to keep track of the location of each microcomputer and peripheral device. The equipment control log should have the following information:

- Description of device, including add-on cards.
- Manufacturer's serial number.
- Company identification number (this is detailed in the next section).
- Current location of this particular piece of equipment.
- Name, ID number, department, and phone number of person using or having responsibility for it.
- (If a peripheral device) Same information as above and/or ID or micro CPU that the equipment is being used with.
- Date (and time, if required) equipment is checked out or assigned.
- Date (and time, if required) equipment is checked in or returned.
- Person's signature.

In smaller organizations, inventory logs may consist of only those entries that record a single microcomputer's CPU and its related peripheral equipment. In the larger organization with many microcomputers, the control log should be maintained by the department or person that controls the use and placement of micros. The inventory and control logs should be stored in a secure location. A copy of the inventory log should be stored in a secure off-site location with the company's other vital records.

Equipment Identification and Marking

In addition to the inventory log of all equipment, which includes the device manufacturer's serial number, a special identification number should be etched or written with special ink on the device. Manufacturer serial numbers are often placed on tags that can be removed from the equipment; this method should be avoided.

Personally owned computers should be etched or engraved (with an electric engraver or scribe) with the owner's driver's license or state identification number. Preceding that number should be the two-digit state code and a slash (/). If the system's owner does not have a driver's license or state ID, the home phone number with area code should be used. The reason for the driver's license, state ID, or phone number is that they could be used to facilitate tracing by the police department in the event the units are stolen. Microcomputers that are owned by an organization should be etched with the company name, telephone number including area code, and the special ID number. It is wise to mark the equipment in at least two places.

Ultraviolet marking pens are also useful for marking equipment. However, if the units are stolen, most police agencies will not think of using a "black light" to check the recovered property for ultraviolet markings.

Personnel Access Control and Operation Control Logs

Personnel access control.   Where appropriate, controls should be established and policies and procedures written to govern access to the microcomputer. It should be made clear to each employee exactly what his or her job is in reference to the microcomputer and the system's applications.

Use of the micros should be restricted to only those people who are authorized access, especially when the micros are used to process critical and sensitive information and when they can tie into a network and mainframe.

Operation control logs.   Where appropriate, operation control logs can be useful for recording which person used the system to process an application. Micro operation control logs should contain the following information:

- System identification.
- Date.
- Name or identification of person using the system.
- Time signed on.
- Time signed off.
- Jobs processed.

HARDWARE SECURITY

Hardware Security Devices

There are a number of devices on the market that can be used to provide security for microcomputer equipment. One such device, an electrical-power access-control device, places access control on the micro by limiting its use to those individuals who have a key or combination to the access-control unit. A number of devices for physically securing microcomputer equipment are available. Among their forms are the following:

- Locking devices that secure the micro to the top of the desk or table surface by bolts or by a special glue substance.
- Work tables that have a protective security cover that can be placed over the micro when it is not in use.
- Secure cases that house the micro and allow access only by a key that unlocks the case.
- Electrical-power access-control devices.

Electrical power access control.   One method of securing a micro against unauthorized use is by securing access to the power source. Power access-control devices may utilize a key and lock or a combination-lock security approach. The micro's power cord cap is secured within the protection device as shown in Figure 4–1. Some of the units are installed with an alarm that will activate if the device is tampered with.

Backup Equipment

Standby replacement redundancy is a hardware backup method that is common in most of the larger organizations. This method makes use of additional hardware components that are usually kept in an off-line storage or parts inventory area. For instance, if a micro's printer fails, a new one is brought from the storage area to replace the faulty unit.

An adequate inventory of spare microcomputer components needs to be maintained. The quantity in inventory should use as a base the mean-time-between-failure (MTBF) rate for a specific component. The spare

FIGURE 4–1
Electrical Power Access Control

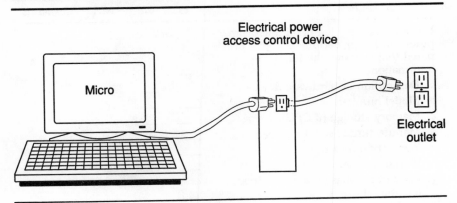

components should be periodically tested. Standby components should also be controlled and secured to prevent their unauthorized use. Organizations having only one microcomputer from a particular vendor may take advantage of the following backup options in the event of a breakdown:

1. Repair or replace the faulty unit.
2. Use another vendor's micros (if compatible) to process information until the unit is operable.

Larger organizations have the following options:

1. Repair or replace the faulty unit.
2. Switch the faulty unit with other like units in the office.
3. Use redundant replacement equipment from the storage area.
4. Use another organization's micro.

HARDWARE SECURITY CHECKLIST

Figure 4-2 is a checklist that can be used for reviewing the security considerations outlined in this chapter.

FIGURE 4-2
Hardware Security

No.	Item	Response			
		Yes	*No*	*N/A*	*Comments*
1.	Has an inventory log of all microcomputers and their peripherals been prepared that contains the following information?				
	a. Description of hardware device.	___	___	___	
	b. Model number.	___	___	___	
	c. Memory storage (if CPU).	___	___	___	
	d. Manufacturer's serial number.	___	___	___	
	e. Warranty number.	___	___	___	
	f. Warranty date.	___	___	___	
	g. Place of purchase (name, address, telephone).	___	___	___	

FIGURE 4–2 *(continued)*

No.	Item	Yes	No	N/A	Comments
	h. Date purchased.	—	—	—	
	i. Your company's identification number (engraved on unit).	—	—	—	
2.	Has a control log for all microcomputers been established that contains the following information?				
	a. Description of device.	—	—	—	
	b. Manufacturer's serial number.	—	—	—	
	c. Company identification number.	—	—	—	
	d. Location of equipment.	—	—	—	
	e. Date/time checked out.	—	—	—	
	f. Date/time checked in.	—	—	—	
	g. Authorized signature.	—	—	—	
3.	Has each component of the peripheral equipment been marked/etched with an identification such as a driver's license number (for personally owned systems) or the company's name and telephone number and internal ID number?	—	—	—	
4.	Are all microcomputers secured with devices that prevent theft of the equipment or removal of circuit boards?	—	—	—	
5.	Have personnel controls been established for the use of each micro, including:				
	a. general authorizations?	—	—	—	
	b. authorizations by application?	—	—	—	
6.	Is an operation's control log kept for each micro that contains the following information?				
	a. Systems identification.	—	—	—	
	b. Date.	—	—	—	
	c. Name or identification of person using the system.	—	—	—	
	d. Time signed on.	—	—	—	
	e. Time signed off.	—	—	—	
	f. Jobs processed.	—	—	—	
7.	Is there backup equipment available for your vital computer hardware equipment?	—	—	—	

FIGURE 4–2 *(concluded)*

No.	Item	Yes	No	N/A	Comments
8.	Is there an accurate and complete inventory kept of your current microcomputer specifications and configurations including number and type of:				
	a. microcomputers?	—	—	—	
	b. cassette drives?	—	—	—	
	c. disk drives?	—	—	—	
	d. printers?	—	—	—	
	e. diskette readers?	—	—	—	
	f. other peripherals and components?	—	—	—	
9.	Has the acceptable amount of downtime been determined for each piece of equipment at your location:				
	a. on a short-term basis?	—	—	—	
	b. on a long-term basis? (The amount of acceptable downtime usually depends on the equipment's workload and the number of hours in use.)	—	—	—	
10.	If hardware failure occurs, is there an alternative method for processing (such as manual systems)?	—	—	—	
11.	Is there a backup system available:				
	a. on site?	—	—	—	
	b. off site?	—	—	—	
	c. through alternative sites (your company or other companies)?	—	—	—	
	d. with loaner equipment?	—	—	—	
12.	Is the off-site location close enough to allow smooth recovery operations?	—	—	—	
13.	If the current microcomputer is outdated or so unique that backup equipment is hard to find, have special arrangements been made?	—	—	—	
14.	Are personnel trained in the procedures for:				
	a. orderly shutdown of hardware?	—	—	—	
	b. orderly power-up of hardware?	—	—	—	
	c. manual processing of applications in case of system failure?	—	—	—	

Chapter Five

Physical Security and Environmental Considerations

The particular problems of microcomputer security management are discussed, with the necessary concept of multilevel security. The principal points of access control and supplies control are noted.

There are many workplace hazards for microcomputers and their associated magnetic media. A number of environmental considerations are addressed, including the microcomputers themselves, magnetic media erasure, static electricity, electrical power problems, fire extinguishers, and water protection, with typical examples of the problems. Preventive maintenance is briefly discussed. Checklists are provided covering the physical security of microcomputers, the handling of supplies, environmental considerations in operations, and preventive maintenance.

PHYSICAL SECURITY AND SITE SECURITY

Most people assume that nothing bad (crime, accident, disaster) is going to happen to them. The common attitude is that "it always happens to the other person—not to me." However, the following considerations are offered:

- The rapid proliferation of microcomputers in both corporations and small businesses has been largely uncontrolled from a security standpoint.
- Micros are smaller and more friendly than their predecessors, and also more of a risk. They are usually housed on a desk in an open environment, rather than in a secure data processing center.
- One micro may be used by several employees and/or outside consultants or programmers. The casual operating environment is the rule, rather than the exception.

- Magnetic storage media are uncontrolled and unaccounted for.
- A single diskette or cassette has the capability of storing large amounts of sensitive business information. These storage mediums are small and readily concealable, and can be removed from the area without notice. A device such as a Bernovilli box provides hundreds of megabytes of storage in an easily concealable medium. CD-ROM and optical disk are other storage media that require special security considerations.
- The micro environment usually is subject to reduced operating controls and audit trails. Separation of duties is often nonexistent.

Policies and procedures that pertain to office equipment and data processing security in most large organizations are often nonexistent in small businesses. Physical security and site security should be built around the multilevel concept of security. In a microcomputer environment, these levels may be identified as follows:

Level 1: Perimeter security

- Security of areas surrounding the building where micros are housed.

Level 2: Building security

- Access control, proper lighting, alarm systems, and environmental control systems.

Level 3: Internal site location

- Access control, hardware security devices, alarm systems, and environmental controls.

Level 4: Procedures

- Hardware, software, and database security, audit controls, and microcomputer security policies and procedures.

A physical security review should be made of the above levels of security.

Physical Security Controls

Locks, guards, badges, sensors, alarms, and administrative measures should be used to protect physical facilities, computer, data communications, and related equipment. These safeguards are required for access monitoring and control, for the physical protection of the computer, and to protect data communications equipment from damage by accident, fire, and environmental hazard, both intentional and unintentional. These safeguards are employed to detect, deter, prevent, and report security exposures. Audit consists of determination of existence of specific physical security measures, effectiveness of their functioning, and testing of reliability.

A number of physical and site security control devices and considerations are addressed below. Additional information is provided in other chapters of this book.

Access control. A primary level of security lies in the locked office. Standard key locks or combination push-button locks offer adequate security in most microcomputer settings. As with any normal home and office access security and key/combination systems, the key or combination should be controlled and changed on a regular basis. Doors should be of durable construction and have an adequate fire rating.

Access-control card systems are also quite effective if used properly. These systems are typically found in larger companies that have mainframe systems and in companies whose products and services dictate the need for the access-control card approach. Companies may secure the microcomputer locations in the main office area through the use of the access-control card systems. However, the cost of securing each micro location normally would be prohibitive. Consideration should be given to installing file servers that contain sensitive and/or large quantities of data in secured areas.

Supplies control. There are a number of security and control considerations that apply to microcomputer forms and supplies. These considerations include:

- Backup forms and supplies.
- Forms handling and security.
- Shipping.
- Receiving.
- Storage.
- Accountability.
- Obsolete forms.
- Alternative methods of report form preparation.

(See the "Supplies" checklist [Figure 5–5] at the end of this chapter).

ENVIRONMENTAL CONSIDERATIONS

Environmental considerations are addressed on the following pages and include:

- Microcomputer and magnetic media.
- Magnetic media erasure.
- Static electricity.
- Electric power problems.
- Fire extinguishers.
- Water alert protection.
- Protective covers.

Microcomputer and Magnetic Media

It usually does not take long for microcomputer users to realize that it is not prudent to leave their micro equipment and magnetic media unprotected against workplace hazards. Over the years, dating back to the first microcomputers or "intelligent terminals" of a decade ago, there have been a number of what might be called "interesting" occurrences. Some of these occurrences and other observations are listed below.

• Diskettes have been used as coasters for coffee cups, pop bottles, etc., so that the desk or table surface would not be damaged. (Magnetic media should be secured in the appropriate storage container. Water and other liquids can damage media and render them unusable.)

• An ashtray is kept next to, or on top of, the diskette. (Cigarette smoke alone can cause diskette read/write problems. Ashes, in addition to the smoke, can cause problems, not only to the magnetic media, but also to the magnetic recording hardware device.)

• To "facilitate" handling and control, diskettes have been stapled or paper clipped to source documents, or secured with a rubber band to the batch of documents. (Protect your media by using approved storage files.)

• Diskettes and cassettes sometimes are inadvertently placed on top of or next to common magnetic office devices, such as paper-clip holders or magnetic clips, which can cause partial or total erasure of data. (Paper clips can assume magnetic qualities while stored on a magnetic holder.)

• Magnetic media have a coercivity (magnetic intensity for removing residual magnetism) of approximately 300 oersteds. Erasure of information stored on the media would occur only if a field approaching that value were to touch or come within a fraction of an inch of the magnetic media. Some magnetic paper-clip holders, as well as magnetic cabinet latches and other magnetic devices common in the office environment, have sufficient magnetic strength (some are over 1500 oersteds) to cause erasure of data on the magnetic media at the area of contact.

- It is common for magnetic media to be placed on top of a radio or on a CRT. (Data problems can occur when the radio, CRT or micro are turned on and off, because of electromagnetic interference.)
- Micro operators have depressed the wrong keys on the keyboard and have inadvertently erased or written over stored information. (Keep your files backed up.)
- The degausser (magnetic media eraser) has been used to clear the wrong diskettes or cassettes. (Control its use.)
- Static electricity buildup has caused numerous problems. (Static electricity is addressed later in this section.)
- Cassettes and diskettes are often stored on window ledges and in cars, where rapid temperature variations and sunlight can cause warping of the media with resultant read/write problems. (Use the proper storage devices.)
- Incorrect external labels have been affixed to cassette cases or diskette jackets, resulting in lost files. Also, glue substance from certain types of labels has leaked through the protective diskette jacket—rendering the diskette and its data unusable. (Establish labeling standards.)
- Liquids have been spilled on the microcomputer, resulting in short circuits, equipment damage, and malfunctioning keyboards. (Keep coffee cups etc. away from your micro equipment.)
- Fingerprints from direct contact of the fingers with the magnetic media can cause read/write problems. (Handle magnetic media carefully, by the diskette jacket or cassette case only.)
- The electromechanical device in a telephone initiates a magnetic field when the telephone rings. (This field can affect data if the magnetic media are placed directly against the phone.)
- Ballpoint pens and sharp pencils are commonly used to write the file information on the external label while the label is on the diskette. (The pressure of the writing can cause scratching or indentations on the magnetic media itself. Labels should be prepared prior to affixing them to the diskette.)
- Power fluctuations are a common problem and disrupt micros. (Use a surge resistor.)
- Cassette tapes become unwound.
- Diskettes make fine "Frisbees," and people have been known to "pass the data, please."
- Peanut butter and jelly sandwiches and diskettes do not mix (as well as potato chips, pretzels, and other snacks found near the micro environment). (Also, brush your hair in an area away from your micro.)

Read/write heads fly over the magnetic storage hard disk surface on an air bearing of only 80 to 135 microinches, depending on the type of disk. As seen in Figure 5–1, contamination in the form of dust, grease particles, smoke, etc., can build up on disk recording surfaces and increase head-to-disk separation. This causes temporary errors, retries, and data checks. At this stage, most data should be recoverable with thorough cleaning of the disk. However, if dirt is allowed to build up, crashes and other permanent damage to heads and disk surfaces are inevitable.

Keeping a clean operating environment is even more critical with the diskette and cassette storage devices used with today's microcomputers. Most of the devices record or erase data via direct contact of the read/write heads with the magnetic media recording surfaces.(Note: Most diskette and cassette devices' read/write heads come in direct contact with the diskette or cassette recording surface.)

Magnetic Media Erasure

Figure 5–2 was published by the 3M Company and addresses magnetic tape/media erasure threats. Specific areas addressed are:

FIGURE 5–1
Common Contaminants and Their Relationship to Hard-Disk Read/Write Head Flying Heights

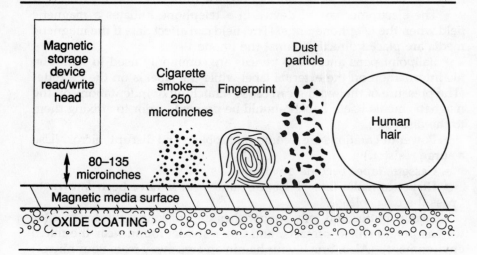

- Magnetic fields.
- Heat.
- Other forms of energy:
  - lightning.
  - radar.
  - microwave.
- Antihijacking devices.
- X-ray inspection equipment.

Although this information was published a number of years ago and was directed at magnetic tape, the information is still very relevant for the magnetic media used in the microcomputer environment of today.

A Special Note About Airport Security Devices

Recently, the Federal Aviation Administration (FAA) reaffirmed that airport security devices, such as metal detectors and X-ray scanners, do not harm microcomputers or magnetic media—with one exception as noted below. An FAA security official has stated that the magnetic field generated by metal detectors at airports is very weak, typically only one gauss. Magnetic storage media, such as tapes and diskettes, will not be damaged unless they are exposed to 200 to 300 gauss. X-ray machines used to examine baggage at airports also generate a weak field, about 1,000 times weaker than levels that would damage solid-state components. These machines pose no threat to magnetic media. However, magnetic media could be erased by magnetic fields generated by motors—such as those used in the luggage and security-device conveyor belts at the airports.

FIGURE 5-2
The 3M Perspective: Magnetic Tape Erasure—How Serious Is the Threat?

It's often difficult to separate fact from rumor, especially when variations of the rumor reappear from different sources and sometimes contain a shred of truth. As part of a continuing program, our laboratory has been investigating the various ways in which stored magnetically recorded data can be maliciously or accidentally destroyed. Simply stated, our findings indicate that while it is, in fact, possible to inadvertently or intentionally destroy magnetic tape records, it is not likely to be as easily accomplished as some magazine and newspaper articles have implied.

FIGURE 5–2 *(continued)*

We have read of a case where tapes containing Internal Revenue Service records were destroyed by a nearby airport radar. While this makes exciting reading, it is interesting to note that as this information, or rather misinformation, was picked up and published by various trade and consumer periodicals, it was amplified and modified to make it even more sensational. This distortion is typified by the fact that at this point in time, nobody is really too sure just where this incident was supposed to have happened. Different authors have credited various cities with this mysterious mishap. At last count, New Orleans, Austin, Texas, and Atlanta seem to be strong contenders.

Just as unique are the reports recently published in several sources that relate the tale of the workman who forgot he had a magnet in his toolbox. It seems that when he walked into the computer center, he just about put a major credit card company out of business. Or, have you heard the one about how a disgruntled employee erased 50,000 reels of computer tape in just minutes by touching a dime store magnet to the metal storage cabinet doors in the tape library?

Since we are in the tape business, maybe we hear more than our share of these stories; or maybe they seem more meaningful to us because we are in a position to more quickly separate fact from fiction. At any rate, it is probably safe to say that we have just about heard them all. The one that we especially like describes how recorded tapes can be made safe from erasure by wrapping them in wet newspaper.

We could go on and on with the humorous and the ridiculous, but information loss is of real concern and is a truly serious matter to the thousands of our friends whose job it is to make sure that everything runs smoothly on the computer and that the data in storage is really in storage and not quietly fading away. With this as a preamble, let's take a good hard look at just what is involved and what could not be involved with the subject of altering or erasing computer tapes.

An Important Fact

One of the greatest advantages of magnetic tape for storage of information is the ease with which old information can be erased to make room for the new.

Magnetic tape can thus be used again and again as new information becomes available. But, this very fact that makes magnetic tape such an ideal and versatile medium for information capture, storage, and retrieval often prompts an important question. If the tape is so easy to erase, what is the probability that it could be erased accidentally?

Aside from physical destruction of a tape, which is an obvious loss of information, only two forms of energy are capable of significantly affecting the recording on magnetic tape. These are heat and magnetic fields. In the following paragraphs, each of these forms of energy will be discussed separately. We will examine just how they affect tape, and to what degree and under what conditions they can cause accidental erasure of information.

Magnetic Fields

All magnetic materials have an intrinsic property called coercivity. This property is measured in units called the oersted, which defines the intensity of a magnetic field that is required to demagnetize or erase the material. For example, a ma-

FIGURE 5–2   *(continued)*

terial with coercivity of 100 will be erased by a magnetic field with a magnitude of 150 oersteds, but a material with a coercivity of 300 would not be erased by the same field. Since magnetic computer tape has a coercivity of approximately 300 oersteds, erasure of information stored on the tape would occur only if a field approaching that value were to penetrate into the reel.

Where might a field of such intensity be found that could cause accidental erasure? The fact is, a field of this magnitude is very rare. The Earth's magnetic field has a strength of approximately 0.6 oersted. The field from an electric hand drill under full load is in the order of 10 oersteds at the surface of the drill case. A reel of magnetic tape pressed against the body of the drill would be in no danger of being erased.

The magnetic fields surrounding heavy power wiring can be intense directly at the surface of the wire, but at the point where contact with the wire can be made (through insulation or conduit), fields will not be capable of erasing tape. If a line cord were laid directly across a reel of tape and then short circuited, the short-circuit field intensity could possibly erase the portion of the tape in the immediate area of the line cord. The electron beam in a television picture tube is deflected magnetically. The fields directly around the deflection yoke of a TV set could erase a tape, the fields outside the TV cabinet are much too low to have any effect.

It can be stated without reservation that magnetic fields surrounding AC-operated equipment and appliances in both the home and in an industrial environment are not capable of erasing magnetic tape. The same, however, is not true of permanent magnets.

Improvements in permanent magnetic materials in recent years have led to increased use in a wide variety of applications ranging from pencil holders to refrigerator door latches. These small magnets have surface field intensities as high as 1,500 oersteds. If, for example, a reel of tape were to touch a magnetic door latch, information might be lost from the portion of the tape that came in direct contact with the magnet. Magnets that are sewn into towels or those that are used to secure notes to metal bulletin boards are also of sufficient strength to cause erasure of recorded material at their area of contact.

Some low-priced sound recorders make use of a magnet of this type to wipe the tape clean of previously recorded information. It is placed just before the record head, and the tape must pass over and be in immediate contact with it on its way to being recorded. In the playback mode, it is mechanically swung out of the tape path and, of course, has no effect.

Other objects in common use would include magnetic key chains and flashlights that have magnets affixed to their cases.

Small permanent magnets could be very troublesome indeed, if it were not for one very helpful factor—the factor of distance. A magnetic field falls off in intensity approximately as the square of the distance from the magnet. In other words, if one doubles the distance at which a field is measured, the intensity will be one-fourth as great as at the shorter distance. From this we see that distance is what really protects a tape from accidental erasure. While the field intensity of a magnet may be sufficient to erase a tape placed in contact with it, a spacing of just an inch can totally protect the tape. In most instances, the spacing provided by the box or canister in which the tape is contained will provide adequate distance.

FIGURE 5–2 *(continued)*

From this it can be seen that the mere presence of a magnet in the same room with the tape would not be the cause of any concern, and would not be capable of doing any harm. If a flashlight with a magnet holder were attached to the outside of a tape storage cabinet, it, too, would not pose any threat of erasing the tape that was stored inside the cabinet.

A magnetic field can be partially shielded by a box made of soft iron, but this would be an expensive and cumbersome way to attempt to protect a tape from accidental erasure. Since a spacing of just about an inch or two will protect a tape from even the strongest commercially available magnet, distance becomes a more certain and more easily applied method of protection.

It seems, then, that accidental erasure by either electrical appliances or permanent magnets is just not likely as many have been led to believe. Of course, if one is concerned about intentional or malicious erasure of magnetic tape, the small permanent magnets which are available in any hardware store can be a real danger. A six-ounce horseshoe magnet passed several times across the flanges of a reel of tape could almost totally erase it.

We hasten to add, however, that only the reel of tape that came into contact with the magnet would be affected. Other tapes in the area, even those next to or under the altered reel, would show no signs of information loss or signal degradation. By now you know the reason. They would be too far away from the magnet. Before leaving this subject, it would be well to add one more important point.

Contrary to what has been seen in print several times, reels of tape do not have the ability to "conduct" the magnetism, applied by a permanent magnet, from one reel to another. There is no chain reaction effect. We think that this rumor must have been started by someone who noticed when a straight pin is picked up by a magnet, a second pin can be attached to the first. Maybe a third one can even be hung on to the second. This may be true with pins and paper clips, but it just does not work that way with magnetic tape. You cannot wipe out a whole library by touching a magnet to the reel of tape on the end of a row.

Heat

Excessive heat, such as that which may be generated by a fire in the tape library or computer room, can damage magnetic tape. In general, however, the damage is purely physical and not magnetic in nature. High temperatures can soften or otherwise change the characteristics of the tape's plastic backing. If the temperature is high enough, actual charring can take place and the embrittled physical condition may make it difficult to extract that information. One might compare this to attempting to read printed information on a blackened and badly burned page of paper. There is a case, however, where the recorded information itself could be lost.

Materials that normally exhibit magnetic properties tend to lose their magnetic abilities when their temperature is increased. The point at which this occurs varies with different substances. Iron oxide, the magnetic material usually used in the manufacture of computer tapes, will lose information recorded upon it, using current digital techniques, at about 850 degrees Fahrenheit. This has never posed a problem because this temperature is far in excess of that which would physically destroy the tape.

FIGURE 5–2   *(continued)*

There is a new type of magnetic material known as chromium dioxide that behaves quite differently. The same degree of loss that would be encountered with iron oxide at 850 degrees Fahrenheit will occur at about 250 degrees Fahrenheit with chromium dioxide. While this temperature will also have an effect upon the plastic backing, it would not be high enough to cause complete destruction.

There have been instances in which information stored on a tape is of such an important or valuable nature that great pains have been taken to recover the information from the tape exposed to a fire. The tape is carefully unwound, treated, repaired, and made as fit as possible to be used for reconstituting the recorded information. In these instances, a tape made with chromium dioxide would have been totally erased by the heat, and any attempt to reconstitute the recorded information would have been futile.

As a practical matter, one does not need to worry about exposing tape to elevated temperatures, as long as those temperatures do not affect the tape physically. The environments in which humans normally function will not harm magnetic tape.

Other Forms of Energy

The world is full of electrical and magnetic phenomena such as lightning discharges, radio transmissions, static electricity, and high-power radar beams. There is a great deal of misinformation and misunderstanding concerning the effects of these phenomena on magnetic tape.

Of all of them, only a lightning discharge could possibly cause accidental tape erasure, and then only if the discharge occurred within a few inches of the tape. Lightning discharges reach current amplitudes of several thousand amperes. If such a discharge were to travel along, say, a water pipe, and if a reel of tape were within a few inches of that pipe, erasure could occur.

As we mentioned earlier in this paper, high-power radar systems have been blamed for the loss of recorded information on magnetic tape. While it is true that a magnetic field of several thousand oersteds may exist directly in front of a radar antenna, the field intensity drops to below the critical level only a few yards away. The burning hazard to humans within this high-intensity area is so great that precautions are taken to keep the immediate area in front of the antenna well clear of personnel and other objects.

We can see just how impossible it would be for a roll of tape to enter this area accidentally. Beyond this danger area, the radar beam is not capable of affecting magnetic tape. This may be hard for some to believe after they have heard of instances of photographic flashbulbs being triggered when only moderately close to a powerful radar installation. We also have read that demolition experts will not work with electrically detonated dynamite caps in the vicinity of a radar antenna or radio broadcasting tower.

The explanation here has to do with the kind of energy that is involved. Dynamite caps and flashbulbs are triggered by the electrical field that is propagated from the antenna, not by the magnetic field that exists only in the immediate area of the antenna itself. The electric field's intensity is intentionally strong, and in the case of a radar antenna, is actually focused to concentrate its energy within its operating range.

FIGURE 5-2 *(continued)*

It would not be possible to get close enough to a high-power radar antenna for it to erase a recorded tape without also doing a physical harm to the person who was carrying it. The tape would also incur very obvious physical damage from the heating produced by the radar beam's electric field.

In our experimentation on this subject, we placed reels of tape in a microwave oven (sometimes called a radar oven). Even at this extremely close range, erasure did not occur before the tape and plastic reel began to melt and actually burn from the induced heat. We have also placed recorded tape in the path of an X-band radar beam with a range of 250 miles. The reels were positioned at intervals from a maximum of 18 feet to a minimum of 16 inches from the antenna. The antenna was made to scan from one reel to the other for 16 minutes. After this exposure period, the tapes were checked for proper signal amplitude. We did not notice a single incident of recording degradation, nor did we see any deterioration of the physical tape structure.

While we hope that these paragraphs will put to rest those rumors concerning the effect of radar on magnetic tape, we do believe that it is possible to lose data recorded on a computer tape as a result of radar energy. Since that may sound like a contradictory statement, a word of explanation is in order.

It is possible for a radar beam to affect the logic circuits of the computer itself. These circuits operate at extreme speed and are activated by extremely small voltages. If the computer is not adequately grounded, the logic can be triggered by radar transmission and cause random noise pulses to be placed on the tape. This, of course, could occur when the tape was being written, but could also happen when the tape was being read. If the grounding of the tape transport were not proper, the radar signal could induce enough energy in the head assemblies to actually place noise pulses on the tape. A similar effect would be possible should static electrical discharge take place between the operator and the equipment as the result of static charge buildup on the operator's body or clothing. This noise would appear as meaningless information to the computer and cause the job to abort. Since these pulses are actually on the tape, subsequent attempts to use the file would also result in an aborted run.

We cannot emphasize strongly enough that the hypothesized radar condition could only happen while a tape was being run on an improperly grounded piece of equipment. The static discharge effects could happen, however, even if equipment grounding were proper.

There are well-established procedures used by industry to eliminate or greatly reduce the incidence of static electricity discharge. Among these are humidity control, the use of conductive footware and grounded flooring, and the avoidance of silk, nylon, and other similar static-accumulating fabric for clothing.

Neither radar beams nor static electricity will have any adverse effect on the tape while it is in storage. It is the electronic equipment upon which the tape is used that could be sensitive to radar energy and static discharge, not the tape itself.

Antihijacking Devices

Considerable work has been conducted recently toward the development of metal detection and antipilferage devices. These devices are used in airline terminals to detect concealed weapons that may be carried aboard aircraft, and in

FIGURE 5–2 (*continued*)

stores and libraries to detect unauthorized removal of merchandise and books. There are two basic types in use. Since one of these could affect magnetic tape, we will discuss each of them individually.

Most of the equipment in use at various airports throughout the nation could be classed as passive devices. They are designed to detect subtle changes in the earth's normal magnetic field. The shape of the earth's fields is distorted by metal objects, and their presence will cause a change that can be sensed by the detection unit. These units do not generate a field of their own, and, therefore, cannot erase or otherwise harm magnetic tapes.

A second type of detector is classified as an active device. Usually a doorway or walkway is surrounded with a moderately intense AC magnetic field. These systems are not yet in widespread use, but will undoubtedly find increased application with time. To date, the most intense field employed in such a system is in the order to 100 oersteds.

While such a field will not totally erase a tape, it would probably reduce the amplitude of the recording on it. Most of the detection systems operate with a field less than 20 oersteds, and one could carry recorded tape through such a field without affecting the recording. It is presumed that as the use of such systems becomes more widespread, notices and warnings of their presence, and of the possibility of their affecting magnetic tape (and other objects such as hearing aids), will be posted.

Unless you are sure that the detection device is of the passive type or a low-power active type, care should be exercised when transporting recorded tape through detection stations. It would be advisable to inform the attendant operating the unit that you are carrying recording tape. If there is any doubt as to how it will be affected, request that it not be passed through the monitor and ask instead that it be visually inspected. The extra few minutes that this might take may be a worthwhile investment to preserve a recording.

X-Ray Inspection

From time to time we hear of packages that have been subjected to X-ray inspection during shipment. Questions often arise concerning what effect this will have on recorded tape.

Despite the conclusion of an impossibility that results from a purely theoretical consideration of such a suggestion, we have, in the laboratory, carefully recorded tape with information of known signal levels. After subjecting these tapes to quantities of X-radiation far in excess of what would be expected for routine package examination, we have not found any incidence of signal decay or erasure. While we are aware of comments from tape users that indicate their tapes were completely erased while in transit, our findings do not support the fact that this was caused by being subjected to X-rays.

Conclusion

It is our hope that between page one of this document and this point, much of the mystery concerning the erasing of magnetic tape has disappeared. We have explained just what is involved in the erasing of tape and the conditions that must be present in order for erasure to take place. We have seen that the factor of distance works in favor of magnetic recording tapes, and that a spacing of

FIGURE 5–2 *(concluded)*

only a few inches is usually all that is necessary to totally protect a tape from even extremely strong magnetic fields.

As a final summation, we can again say that while it is, in fact, possible to inadvertently or intentionally destroy magnetic tape records, it is not likely to be as easily accomplished as some magazine and newspaper articles have implied. Armed with the kind of facts that we have just covered, you will now be better able to judge the credibility of stories on erasure that you come across in the future.

Source: Prepared by Product Communications, Data Recording Products Division, 3M Company, 1990. Reproduced with permission of 3M Company.

Static Electricity

Static electricity (electrical charges caused by friction) is created by a temporary surplus or deficiency of electrons. Problems caused by static electricity are:

- Cassette tape drag or skew.
- Diskette problems.
- Static buildup on tape or diskette, which may attract dust, which can contaminate the magnetic media's magnetic coating, causing read/write errors.
- Microcomputer memory being "zapped" or lost due to static buildup when touched.
- Information on a CRT being erased or altered.

Control of static electricity includes:

- Humidity control.
- Proper grounding of equipment.
- Antistatic spray.
- Static floor mats.
- Static table mats.

The information in Figure 5–3 was published by the 3M Company and addresses static electricity and its effects. Although this was published some time ago, and deals primarily with magnetic tape, the information and concepts are still applicable to the magnetic media used in today's microcomputer environment.

Electrical Power Problems

One of the more common causes of data loss is the sudden loss of power with variations in the line voltage. The quality of available AC power is usually not adequate for microcomputer operations, especially in older buildings and homes. Irregular levels of power are experienced in most office buildings and manufacturing facilities. The quality of power formerly was more than adequate for devices such as motors, typewriters, and light bulbs.

In general, there are five basic electrical phenomena that can adversely affect the microcomputer. These phenomena, which will either erase temporary memory or damage equipment, depending on the type and level of failure, are as follows:

- Voltage spikes/surges.
- Voltage dips/brownouts.
- Power interruptions.
- Noise interference.
- Dangerous conditions.

FIGURE 5–3
Static Electricity and Its Effects

Generally, static electricity is not a major problem today because the magnetic coatings of most computer tapes now available are conductive and the tape transports are equipped with static reduction devices. The effects of static on tape signal output and equipment maintenance merit a review of the conditions which concern static buildup and its neutralization. Static electricity (electrical charges caused by friction) is created by a temporary surplus or deficiency of electrons. Its presence on recording tape is a result of the tape contacting itself when leaving the tape reels and also when passing over the various tape transport components. Static electricity may cause problems at the high tape speeds and rapid start-stop times used in modern tape transports. Tape drag or skew are some of the problems created by static which can affect signal output or promote excessive tape and magnetic head wear. Also, static buildup on the tape or transport may attract dust which can contaminate the tape coating causing write and read errors.

Static Buildup

An excess or deficiency of electrons on the tape surface will create corresponding negatively or positively charged areas. The voltage potential of the static buildup is related to the electrical resistance of the tape coating. A high-resistance coating causes a tape to build up a greater static charge potential

FIGURE 5-3   *(continued)*

than a tape with low coating resistance, which dissipates a static charge easier (see illustration). The increase of tape transport speeds and faster **start**-stop times create additional static buildup on the tape surface because the tape contacts itself when leaving the reels and the transport components at very high speeds.

Static Buildup versus Tape Speed and Tape Resistance

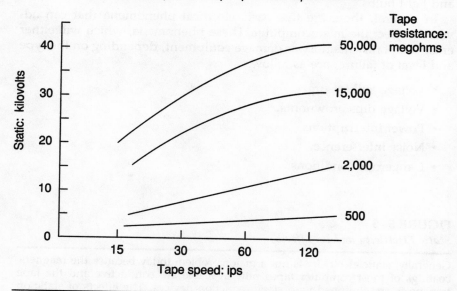

Another major factor concerning static buildup on tape is the relative humidity level in the area where the tape transport is operating. Humidity is important in that the airborne moisture particles provide a path for static dissipation. Very dry air has a relatively high dielectric strength and tends to insulate the tape surfaces, causing very rapid and high-potential static electricity buildup. A temperature of about 70° Fahrenheit and a relative humidity of about 50 percent is considered optimum for maximum operating efficiency. Higher humidity levels are not necessary and may cause hydroscopic adhesion.

Effects of Static Buildup

Because of the polarity of static charges, the tape can be attracted to itself or to the components of the transport. The static attraction that creates "drag" may cause displacement of the time base, which can affect signal output. Static may

FIGURE 5–3   *(continued)*

also be manifested as tape flutter and oscillations in the transport vacuum chambers resulting in tape and speed variations.

Occasionally, when using a tape with relatively high resistance, electrostatic discharges or "arcing" may occur from head to tape or on the tape reels. Although this situation is not dangerous or damaging to the tape or transport, it can result in recorded noise or data errors. This condition is aggravated by the use of high-resistance tape in a low-humidity environment. One of the detrimental effects of static electricity on tape is the attraction of dust and other contaminants. When this debris is wound into a reel of tape, it may adhere to the magnetic-coated surface, which can result in signal losses that cause write or read errors. These errors occur because the debris lifts the tape surface from the magnetic heads and causes reduced signal output. This output loss is especially critical when recording high densities.

Methods of Static Control

The ability to dissipate a static charge is dependent on the electrical properties of the material. Conductive materials, such as metals, have highly mobile electrons and will easily neutralize a static buildup. Nonconductive materials or insulators, such as plastics, cannot easily neutralize static. The dissipation of a static charge may be either through the surrounding air or through a direct transfer, such as when the charged material is brought into physical contact with a grounded material. It might be reasoned that the magnetic material used in magnetic coatings would be a good conductor allowing sufficient drain of static buildup. In many magnetic coatings, however, this is not true.

By carefully controlling the special compounds used in the tape coating, the resistance value of the tape can be maintained at a desirable low level. It is not practical to reduce oxide resistance to near-zero level, as experience has shown that this type of tape exhibits a tendency to cling to itself and stick to adjacent layers after several passes through a transport. As a result, the magnetic coatings used in the manufacture of modern tapes allow uniform static drain characteristics. These coating formulations offer a resistance of less than 500 megohms per square (a square of tape is a tape length that is equal to its width). There are some high-resistance magnetic coatings that are generally unsuitable for computer use and that exhibit tape resistance that may be as high as 100 times greater than the recommended maximum. In comparison, there are computer tapes now available with coating resistance of 100 megohms per square that virtually eliminate tape associated static problems.

An excellent method now in use by most transport manufacturers to reduce static buildup is accomplished by lining the transport vacuum chamber walls and other large surface areas that contact the tape with a material which reduces the surface-to-surface contact. A typical material has a glass-beaded surface such as Scotchlite brand #234, which allows the tape to contact only the outermost points of the minute spherical surfaces (see illustration). The smooth beaded material allows only a minimum of surface contact, which reduces static buildup, attraction, and drag.

FIGURE 5–3   *(concluded)*

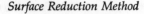

Surface Reduction Method

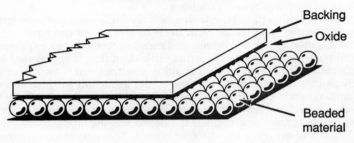

Summary

The consideration of static electricity has influenced the development of magnetic coatings as used in modern tapes. Most coatings now in use provide the low-resistance quality without sacrificing magnetic efficiency or durability. The benefits of controlling the resistance levels of the coating are the substantial reduction in tape drag and flutter resulting from static. A most important factor in static control is the reduction in the attraction of dust particles to the tape surfaces. To properly reduce dust damage, control of the relative humidity and overall cleanliness is essential. Generally speaking, if precautions to maintain cleanliness and atmospheric control of the tape transport operating area are observed, and high-resistance tapes are avoided, the undesirable effects of static electricity will be greatly minimized.

Voltage spikes/surges.   A voltage spike is a voltage impulse that lasts only a few millionths of a second and can reach as high as 6,000 volts. A voltage surge is a voltage impulse of longer duration (a few thousandths of a second), and has lower high-voltage peak values (3,000 volts). Possible causes are:

- Other equipment sharing the same power is turned on or off, affecting the load current (power tools, air conditioners, office equipment, elevators).
- Faulty or arcing switches.
- Load switching by power companies.
- Static discharge.
- Electrical storms.

Possible damage that can result includes:

- Data stored in RAM (random access memory) can be altered or destroyed.
- Circuit melting/burnout.
- Insulation breakdown in memory chips.
- Disk-drive head crash and pitting of drive heads.
- Hazardous shorts and even fire can be caused due to electrical arc-over.
- Premature component failure.
- Equipment downtime.
- False computer output.

Power protection devices, including surge-suppression devices and isolation transformers, can be used.

Voltage dips/brownouts. The level of voltage to the system will also decrease at various times. Momentary dips occur when the local utility service experiences a sudden overload. These drops last from 20 milliseconds to a few seconds. The power company will compensate, but not until the adverse effect hits your system.

Also common in certain areas are intentional and continual reductions in voltage known as "brownouts." This happens when utility companies are forced to reduce power in order to keep going during extended and excessive power demand periods.

Possible causes include:

- Power company experiencing a sudden overload.
- Extreme weather conditions, when air conditioning or heating systems are constantly turning on and off.
- Power company voltage reductions (brownouts).
- Electrical storm.
- Power equipment failure.
- Addition of heavy equipment to power load.

The damage that can occur from these events includes:

- Disruption of computer operations.
- Damage to equipment when power is restored abruptly.

Power protection devices include the following:

- UPS (uninterruptible power source).
- Reserve supply equipment.
- Inverters.
- Motor generators.

Note: When a power failure occurs, turn the system off to protect it against the power surges that can occur when the power is restored.

Power interruptions.   In an interruption, power to the building is completely shut off. This can happen for a fraction of a second or up to several days. Possible causes are power company failure, storms, or a blown fuse.

Possible damage includes disruptions of computer operations and damage to equipment when power is restored abruptly.

Available protection devices include UPS (uninterruptible power supply), reserve supply equipment, and motor generators.

Note: When a power failure occurs, turn off the microcomputer to protect it against the power surges that can occur when the power is restored.

Noise interference.   Noise interference in both transverse and common modes exists as EMI (electromagnetic interference), RFI (radio frequency interference), and EMP (electromagnetic pulse interference), each having its specific causes.

EMI is caused by fluctuating magnetic fields that are present because of:

- Fluorescent light systems.
- Dimmer switches.
- Loose or defective light sockets.
- Automobile ignition systems.
- Sunspot activity.

RFI occurs because the power lines act like antennae and pick up radio, television, two-way, and CB radio signals, transmitting these signals down the line. Intercom systems are also major RFI interference sources.

EMP interference is caused by a collapsing magnetic field brought about by lightning. A nuclear explosion also would instigate EMP interference. Possible damage includes the following:

- RAM memory wipeouts.
- Display fadeouts.
- Scrambled programs.
- Erroneous data output and loss.
- Data transmission interference.
- Glitches.
- Altered memory blocks.

Available protection devices include surge suppressors that provide spike, surge, and noise protection, and low-pass filters. Most computer equipment contains protection features in its power supply circuitry.

Dangerous conditions.   It is a good idea to check the electrical circuit that is going to be used for microcomputer power, especially if you are using more than one electrical wall outlet for the CPU, terminal, printer, or other peripheral devices. If one of the wall outlets has reversed polarity (the positions of ground and hot circuits are reversed at the outlet) and the micro is plugged into a regular outlet and the CRT or other peripheral is plugged into the reversed polarity outlet, *an electrical equipment explosion may occur.*

This reversed-polarity problem does not affect most electrical appliances. However, because the micro and its peripherals are interconnected with exterior power interface cables, and because multiple power cords are used, correct electrical circuits are critical. Polarity testers are available for under $10 from most computer retail stores.

Fire Extinguishers

Although CRT and microcomputer fires are extremely rare, areas where microcomputers are used should have hand-operated extinguishers available for use if necessary. The extinguishers should be clearly marked, possibly with a red painted area on the wall, and the path to them should not be blocked. Extinguishers should be clearly marked as to the type of fire that they can be used for. They should also be periodically checked for correct operation and the correct amount of pressure.

Each class of fire requires a specific type of extinguishing agent. Using the wrong extinguisher could be dangerous and may do more harm than good. The classes of fire and types of extinguishers are addressed below:

• *Fires in ordinary combustible materials* (paper, wood, fabrics, rubber, and many plastics). Quenching by water or insulating by tri-class (ABC) dry chemical is effective.

• *Fires in inflammable liquids* (gasoline, oils, greases, tars, paints, lacquers, and flammable gases). Tri-class (ABC) and regular dry chemical, Halon, and carbon dioxide agents smother these fires.

• *Fires in live electrical equipment* (motors, generators, switches, and appliances). A nonconducting extinguishing agent, tri-class (ABC), regular dry chemical, Halon, or carbon dioxide (CO_2) is required. CO_2 extinguishers are recommended for micro-related fires. Microcomputer vendors suggest that if the micro starts smoking, pull the plug and leave it alone. The problem will probably extinguish itself quickly. If there is evidence of heat, or if a flame is visible, direct the CO_2 extinguisher's contents through the vent openings in the micro's cabinet.

A warning: *Do not apply the CO_2 gas directly to the face of the CRT.* Application of CO_2 to the glass surface can lead to a sudden temperature drop, which could fracture the glass. As a result, there may be an implosion, in which air rushes into the now-ruptured vacuum within the tube and bounces back. This action can propel fragments of the tube's glass more than 18 inches away from its face.

Water-Alert Protection

Water-alert alarm systems are available and can prove very useful in the micro environment, especially in locations where water seepage is possible, such as in basements or on the floor above the microcomputer. Water-sensing devices are normally placed on the floor of the area that needs to be protected. If water comes in contact with the sensors, the alarm is activated. Such sensors are used particularly to protect electrical cables under the floor.

Self-contained water alarm systems are available, as well as those which can tie in to an existing alarm system.

Protective Covers

Protective static-resistant covers for micros and other EDP equipment are available to protect the equipment against dust, cigarette ashes, spillage, water leaks, etc. These covers are to be used only when the equipment is not in use. Use of these covers when the equipment is being used, or covering the equipment when it is still hot from use, can cause heat damage to the equipment.

Preventive Maintenance

A good way to prevent unexpected system downtime is to schedule a regular downtime for preventive maintenance (PM). PM usually only takes a few hours every week or two. During preventive maintenance, diagnostic programs may be used to exercise the system's components, and peripherals may be serviced by lubricating and by cleaning. Maintenance logs should be maintained and can prove to be very useful in the analysis of reoccurring problems.

Microcomputer Cleaning Products

Microcomputers need to be maintained and cleaned the same as the larger minicomputers and mainframe systems. Cleaning can be accomplished by the micro operator and should include the items listed below.

Never directly spray electrical equipment with cleaning solutions. Use a cloth dampened with water or cleaning solution or use the special cleaning cloths and products recommended by the computer vendor.

Microcomputer items that may be cleaned by the user are:

- Screen (CRT).
- Keyboard surface.
- Magnetic media devices—read/write heads and transport rollers.
- Printer; use vacuum to remove paper fibers, lint, and dust.
- Print wheel/print head (if recommended by vendor).

Physical Security and Environmental Considerations Checklists

The following checklists (Figures 5–4 through 5–7) are useful to review the points covered in this section on physical security and environmental considerations. They may be used either for planning purposes or for a review of the situation.

FIGURE 5–4
Physical Security and Site Security

No.	Item	Yes	No	N/A	Comments
				Response	
1.	Is the perimeter security adequate?	___	___	___	
2.	Is the building's security adequate for:				
	a. access control?	___	___	___	
	b. proper lighting?	___	___	___	
	c. alarm systems?	___	___	___	
	d. environmental controls for air conditioning, heat, humidity?	___	___	___	
3.	Is the internal site (microcomputer location) security adequate for:				
	a. access control?	___	___	___	
	b. hardware security devices?	___	___	___	
	c. alarm systems?	___	___	___	
	d. environmental controls?	___	___	___	
4.	Are doors and locks secure?				
	a. Are keys or combinations controlled?	___	___	___	
	b. Are they changed frequently?	___	___	___	
	c. Is a control log kept of people who have key/combination?	___	___	___	
5.	If card access control systems are used, are cards controlled?	___	___	___	
6.	Is the micro area secured during non-working hours? (at night, weekends, lunch, and break times)	___	___	___	
7.	Have policies and procedures been developed for access control?	___	___	___	
8.	Is access to the electrical power supply controlled and secure?	___	___	___	
9.	Are the floors and ceilings watertight?	___	___	___	
10.	Is there sufficient area around the micro to allow for adequate ventilation? (Do not set books, papers, or diskettes next to or on top of the micro, as overheating of the micro may occur.)	___	___	___	

FIGURE 5–4   *(concluded)*

No.	Item	Yes	No	N/A	Comments
11.	Are the microcomputers kept away from windows:				
	a. where people can view the materials that are being processed?	——	——	——	
	b. where the sight of the micro equipment may present an opportunity for theft?	——	——	——	
12.	Are the office furnishings and furniture fire-resistant?	——	——	——	
13.	Does the building's access control:				
	a. assure the control of the general public traffic flow?	——	——	——	
	b. assure that violators pass through control areas?	——	——	——	
14.	Is the micro located in an area away from water and steam pipes in the ceilings, walls, and floors?	——	——	——	
15.	Do contiguous departments or areas such as flammable-liquid storage areas and manufacturing process areas have potential for causing disaster:				
	a. in adjacent rooms?	——	——	——	
	b. on floors above the micro area?	——	——	——	
	c. on floors below the micro area?	——	——	——	

FIGURE 5–5

Supplies

No.	Item	Response			
		Yes	No	N/A	Comments
1.	If the user's forms or supplies are destroyed, is there an adequate backup quantity stored in a readily accessible, safe place? Are there:				
	a. printed forms?	——	——	——	
	b. plain stock (single and multipart)?	——	——	——	
	c. printer ribbons?	——	——	——	
	d. cassettes?	——	——	——	
	e. diskettes?	——	——	——	

FIGURE 5–5 *(continued)*

No.	Item	Yes	No	N/A	Comments
2.	Have emergency order times been established with the vendors?	___	___	___	
3.	Is there an adequate quantity of forms/supplies if the supplier is hit by disaster or union strike? (Note: You may want to use multiple vendors for vital forms and supplies.)	___	___	___	
4.	Are there sufficient supplies to cope with vendor "back orders"?	___	___	___	
5.	Are there complete lists of forms and supplies?				
	a. Do they have specific order numbers?	___	___	___	
	b. Do they have the name, address, and phone number of the vendor?	___	___	___	
	c. If forms, has a sample copy been included (size, color, stock, grade, etc.)?	___	___	___	
	d. If computer input/output media (e.g., diskettes and tapes), have densities, tracks, and model numbers been included?	___	___	___	
6.	Is there off-site secure storage for backup forms?	___	___	___	
7.	Have the necessary quantities of backup forms been determined?	___	___	___	
8.	Does the backup facility have space for the forms?	___	___	___	
9.	Has provision been made for control of vital forms at the backup facility?	___	___	___	

Forms Handling and Security

No.	Item	Yes	No	N/A	Comments
10.	Do orders have beginning and ending consecutive numbers?	___	___	___	
11.	Are any copies of forms attached to the outside of cartons? (They should not be.)	___	___	___	
12.	Are form names omitted from labels and identified by code numbers only?	___	___	___	
13.	Are beginning and ending consecutive numbers shown on label?	___	___	___	
14.	Does the label state "no missing numbers" or have missing numbers listed?	___	___	___	
15.	Is there control of numbered forms and are they issued in correct numerical sequence?	___	___	___	

FIGURE 5–5 *(continued)*

No.	Item	Yes	No	N/A	Comments
	Shipping Forms				
16.	Are shipments of critical/sensitive forms handled by bonded or armored carriers?	——	——	——	
17.	Are shipments insured?	——	——	——	
18.	Are shipments checked and receipted for, at each point handled during shipment?	——	——	——	
	Receiving Forms				
19.	Are deliveries made to a secure receiving area?	——	——	——	
20.	Does receiving check each carton against the order for assurance that no forms are missing?	——	——	——	
21.	Are forms delivered to a responsible person who will give a receipt?	——	——	——	
	Storage of Forms				
22.	Are forms logged in and receipt given for delivery?	——	——	——	
23.	Is a log maintained of all persons entering and leaving the storage area?	——	——	——	
24.	As forms are issued, is a receipt obtained and are they logged out?	——	——	——	
25.	Is a receipt given for spoiled and unused forms returned and are they logged in?	——	——	——	
26.	Does storage protect against extremes of heat, cold, and humidity?	——	——	——	
27.	Is a backup supply stored separately from the main supply?	——	——	——	
	Accountability for Forms				
28.	Are there forms control procedures?	——	——	——	
29.	Are all spoiled and unused forms accounted for?	——	——	——	
30.	Are forms logged in and out?	——	——	——	
31.	Are periodic and/or surprise audits taken of forms in on-site, off-site, and vendor storage?	——	——	——	
32.	Does anyone assume responsibility for control after issue?	——	——	——	

FIGURE 5–5   *(concluded)*

No.	Item	Yes	No	N/A	Comments
	Obsolete Forms				
33.	Are obsolete forms removed from back-up storage and replaced by new forms?	___	___	___	
34.	Are there control procedures for destruction of obsolete vital forms?	___	___	___	
35.	Are there provisions for removal and disposal of other obsolete forms?	___	___	___	
36.	Has an optional print routine for printing form headings on stock forms been considered as an alternative method of report form preparation?	___	___	___	
37.	Has the use of transparent overlays and copiers been considered?	___	___	___	

FIGURE 5–6
Environmental Considerations

			Response		
No.	Item	Yes	No	N/A	Comments
	Housekeeping				
1.	Are the microcomputer area and equipment kept clear of paper and paper residue?	___	___	___	
2.	Are wastebaskets dumped outside of the micro area to reduce dust discharge?	___	___	___	
3.	Are the carpeting and floor wax antistatic?	___	___	___	
4.	Are low-fire-hazard waste containers used?	___	___	___	
5.	Are only small amounts of cleaning solvents allowed in the area?	___	___	___	
6.	Is smoking prohibited in the area of the micro?	___	___	___	
7.	Are drinks prohibited in the area of the micro?	___	___	___	
8.	Is static electricity controlled with appropriate floor coverings and humidity control?	___	___	___	

FIGURE 5–6 *(continued)*

No.	Item	Yes	No	N/A	Comments

Microcomputer and Magnetic Media Handling

9. Are diskettes kept from being used as coasters for coffee cups or as ashtrays? ___ ___ ___

10. Are diskettes kept from being stapled, clipped, or bound with rubber bands? ___ ___ ___

11. Are diskettes/cassettes properly stored and protected? ___ ___ ___

12. Are diskettes/cassettes kept from being placed on top of or next to magnetic devices such as paper-clip holders? ___ ___ ___

13. Are diskettes/cassettes kept form being placed on top of or next to the radio or telephone? ___ ___ ___

14. Is the magnetic media degausser kept in a secure place and used with discretion? ___ ___ ___

15. Are magnetic media kept from being stored on window ledges or in someone's car? ___ ___ ___

16. Are approved external gummed labels used? ___ ___ ___

17. Are labels prepared prior to placing them on the diskette? ___ ___ ___

18. Is magnetic media handled correctly? ___ ___ ___

Electrical Power

19. Have electrical power monitoring and control devices been installed to protect against:
    - voltage spikes/surges? ___ ___ ___
    - voltage dips/brownouts? ___ ___ ___
    - power interruptions? ___ ___ ___
    - noise interference? ___ ___ ___
    - dangerous conditions, such as reverse polarity of plugs? ___ ___ ___

20. Is there a separate electrical circuit for each major microcomputer system? ___ ___ ___

21. Depending on the nature of the information the company processes, is there a need for an uninterruptible power system? ___ ___ ___

22. Are the electrical system and data processing equipment properly grounded? ___ ___ ___

FIGURE 5–6   *(concluded)*

No.	Item	Yes	No	N/A	Comments
	Fire and Water Protection				
23.	Are CO_2 or Halon fire extinguishers strategically located around the building, clearly marked and accessible?	___	___	___	
24.	Are personnel adequately trained regarding use of the extinguishers?	___	___	___	
25.	Have fire and smoke sensors been placed in the area where the microcomputer is located?	___	___	___	
26.	Has the fire extinguisher been inspected recently?	___	___	___	
27.	Have water-alert systems been installed to detect water on the floor above the micro area and/or the floor where the micro is located?	___	___	___	
28.	Are protective covers available for the microcomputer and other electrical equipment (to protect against water damage and dirt)?	___	___	___	

FIGURE 5–7
Preventive Maintenance

No.	Item	Response			
		Yes	No	N/A	Comments
1.	Has regular preventive maintenance (PM) been scheduled and performed?	___	___	___	
2.	Is a maintenance log maintained showing when PM was conducted?	___	___	___	
3.	Does the maintenance log keep track of all hardware problems that have occurred?	___	___	___	
4.	Are the following microcomputer components cleaned and checked on a regular basis?				
	• Screen (CRT).	___	___	___	
	• Keyboard surface. (Also, use vacuum to remove dirt and dust from keyboard.)	___	___	___	

FIGURE 5–7   *(concluded)*

No.	Item	Yes	No	N/A	Comments
	• Magnetic media devices:				
	• read/write heads.	——	——	——	
	• tape transport mechanisms.	——	——	——	
	• Printer:				
	• print wheel/mechnanism.	——	——	——	
	• paper fibers, lint, and dust vacuumed.	——	——	——	
	• Air intake vents and filters.	——	——	——	
	(Note: See Figure 5–6, Environmental Considerations—Housekeeping)				

Chapter Six

Software Security

Software security involves the protection of an organization's operating systems and application programs from intentional or unintentional use, alteration, or deletion. The need for the control of source codes is noted. A number of computer systems protection features are described, including protection devices, protected files, passwords, program-change control, data comparison, self-destructing programs, and encryption. The control of sensitive programs and program changes and the use of backup and security packages are emphasized. A checklist is provided for the review of the software security controls.

SOFTWARE SECURITY

Software security involves the protection of an organization's operating systems and application programs from intentional or unintentional use, alteration, or deletion. Protection for software is offered in the form of hardware/software protection devices, sensitive-program and program-change controls, adequate and proper backup, and legal protection. Software protection devices, sensitive-program control, and backup are addressed in this chapter. Database security is addressed in Chapter Seven. Legal security considerations include protection by copyright, trade secret, patent and/or employee contract. These are discussed in Chapter Eleven.

For protection purposes, it is a good idea to label program source code with two items:

- A statement of ownership.
- A notice of prohibition of copying.

Various other identifying labels can be placed throughout the program code to "fingerprint" or identify the program.

In the micro-to-mainframe environment, software security at both the micro end and the mainframe end becomes even more critical. Programs and data can be downloaded from the mainframe to micro or uploaded from the micro to mainframe. Because of the micro's storage and copying capabilities, stringent mainframe security policies and access controls should be installed and monitored for proper operation. (Refer to Chapter Eight, "Telecommunications Security.")

PROTECTION DEVICES

A few hardware/software devices are available that protect a company's microcomputer software from being copied or run on another's system. One such unit allows software to be copied, but, once copied, to run only on machines with a hardware security device plugged into the game port socket. The device's manufacturer supplies each software company with a series of access keys that are unique to that particular company. A special feature provides for self-destruction of the access-key logic if anyone tries to tamper with the device.

COMPUTER SYSTEM PROTECTION FEATURES

Protected Files

Most microcomputer operating systems provide some means of protecting software programs and data files. Under CP/M-MBASIC, program files can be saved (protected) in an encoded binary format. The programs can be loaded and executed, but any attempts to list or edit the program file would not be allowed by the operating system and basic compiler.

Diskettes, like audio tapes, can be write-protected, which means that the diskette can be read, but not altered. Write-protection instructions are contained on the diskette packaging.

Passwords

Other operating systems have much more elaborate software protection features, such as multilevel password security and multilevel program protection levels. Password control is not available for some micros, so if it was wanted, it would have to be programmed by the user.

Program and data files can be protected on some micros by including a password as part of the file name. Typically, a file would be given a name that includes both the visible portion of a file name and an "invisible" password. This password, in reality, is also part of the file name. Most systems have control-sequence keys and procedures for entering information such as passwords in a nonrepeat or nondisplay mode. Using this technique, a protected file name for a payroll master file would look like the following example:

PAYRLMST.pppp

In this file name, "pppp" is the invisible password (part of file name). A directory or library listing of the file name would only show the "PAYRLMST" and not the password.

Most of the more sophisticated proprietary packages for micros, including word processing programs, have some type of password security capability. Some have multiple levels, at the system level and at file levels. The use of a new program that requires a password to access DOS is another mechanism for protecting programs on micros.

Program Change Control

Most basic program compilers or interpreters will log the date any time a program is executed. In addition, many systems will assign a random number or code to each program as it is saved. A log of the program file name, the date it is changed, and a random identifier code is stored by the operating system on disk. If the program is changed and saved, a new random ID is assigned. A review of logged program ID numbers with those of current program ID numbers would indicate if any changes had been made, or at least, if the program had been saved again.

If it was suspected that a program had been modified, file-compare utilities could be used to compare the current program file against backup copies of the program. Any differences would be displayed by the compare utility.

Data Compression

Data compression (file packing) is commonly used to reduce the amount of unused space in disk and tape files. Unnecessary spaces and zeros are deleted from the file. It is an excellent way not only to compress the data, but also to reorganize it to reduce disk-level movement, with the resulting benefit of lengthening the usable life of the disk.

Example:

Data: DAVIS 00000002654xxxxx123
Compressed version: DAVIS *726543#5123

The *7 indicates seven zeros, and the #5 indicates there are five spaces. There are many techniques of data/file compression and can include encryption techniques as well.

Self-Destructing Programs

One of the latest software protection techniques involves self-destruction of the program being altered. An attempt to modify a protected program would scramble the program file on disk so that it would be rendered useless. At the same time the block of main memory in which the program was located would also be scrambled.

Encryption

Encryption is another means of protecting both data and program files. Various encryption techniques are available that code either the entire file or portions of a file. Processing of encryption files, however, is usually slower, because the data has to be decrypted to its natural form prior to being processed by the computer. Once processed, the data then needs to be reencrypted. Encryption is described in Chapter Eight.

CONTROL OF SENSITIVE PROGRAMS AND PROGRAM CHANGES

If a microcomputer is used to process and store sensitive information, it is recommended that stringent controls be placed on the program, including new programs and program changes. Recommended controls include the following:

- Maintaining a list of sensitive programs including program name and description and the name or ID number of the programmer responsible for the program.
- Separation of programmer responsibilities so that one programmer does not become familiar with the total system. (This is not easy to implement in smaller organizations.)
- Securing sensitive programs and related documentation in a safe place.
- Logging in/out of sensitive program documentation.
- Preventing unauthorized patching of program object code.

- Having a control group or management person review all requests for changes to programs.
- Planning unannounced audits of program changes.
- Reviewing and approving program test results.
- Maintaining a history of new programs and program changes.
- Insuring that analyst/programmer notes and documentation are stored in a secure location or destroyed if no longer required.

BACKUP

Maintaining copies of programs and data in any data processing environment is paramount. Microcomputer owners have been known to spend hours, even days, programming and testing applications, only to have them destroyed in a fraction of a second when the tired programmer enters a wrong command, presses the wrong key, or copies the wrong file.

It is equally important to keep a copy of the microcomputer's operating system software, if copying is allowed by the vendor. Copies of the operating system and application software should be kept in a secure off-site location as well as in a secure on-site location.

SECURITY SOFTWARE PACKAGES

Security software packages or routines for microcomputers are currently very limited and usually only provide access control via menu security or password schemes. These packages or routines are generally provided by the manufacturer of the hardware or operating system. Security in the stand-alone, desktop environment does not have the high priority that security in the network or micro-to-mainframe environment does. Also, microcomputer system overhead, in terms of storage and system resources, usually cannot support any significant security software packages or routines while other applications are being processed.

Security for networks and the micro-to-mainframe interface is addressed in Chapter Eight.

SOFTWARE SECURITY CHECKLIST

Figure 6–1 is a checklist that can be used for reviewing the security considerations outlined in this chapter.

FIGURE 6–1

Software Security

No.	Item	Yes	No	N/A	Comments
			Response		
1.	Is the software protected legally by:				
	a. copyright?	—	—	—	
	b. patent?	—	—	—	
	c. trade secret?	—	—	—	
	d. employee contract?	—	—	—	
2.	Has a company identification and protection statement been embedded in each source program?	—	—	—	
3.	Are protection hardware/software devices being used to protect the company's proprietary software?	—	—	—	
4.	Have the following controls been placed on sensitive programs, including new programs and program changes?				
	a. Control list of sensitive programs:	—	—	—	
	• program name/description.	—	—	—	
	• programmer responsible for program.	—	—	—	
	b. Separation of programmer duties.	—	—	—	
	c. Appropriate storage of sensitive programs and related documentation.	—	—	—	
	d. Documentation check in/out logs.	—	—	—	
	e. Restrictions against program patching.	—	—	—	
	f. Management review of all changes and requests for changes.	—	—	—	
	g. Audits of program changes.	—	—	—	
	h. Review and approval of program test results.	—	—	—	
	i. History log maintained of programs and program changes.	—	—	—	
	j. Documentation.	—	—	—	
5.	Are controls established so that the wrong version of a program will not be processed?	—	—	—	

FIGURE 6-1 *(continued)*

No.	Item	Yes	No	N/A	Comments
6.	Is backup operating system software available that is identical to the:				
	a. operating system version?	___	___	___	
	b. operating system release?	___	___	___	
7.	If the backup operating system is not identical, is it compatible with the present operating system?	___	___	___	
8.	Has there been a test of running the operating system software on the backup computer?	___	___	___	
9.	Have the application programs that are vital to the company's operation been defined and listed?	___	___	___	
10.	Are these programs copied at regular intervals?	___	___	___	
11.	Is a copy of the source code maintained?	___	___	___	
12.	Is a copy of the object code maintained?	___	___	___	
13.	Is a set of test data maintained (including the desired test results) for each application system for testing at the backup location?	___	___	___	
14.	Are the application programs written so as not to depend on any one particular piece of hardware?	___	___	___	
15.	Is adequate security provided for on-site and off-site software storage?	___	___	___	
16.	Are the storage cabinets and safes resistant (depending on the nature/importance of material stored) to:				
	a. burglary?	___	___	___	
	b. fire?	___	___	___	
	c. smoke?	___	___	___	
	d. water?	___	___	___	
17.	If vendor-supplied software is used, is there a clause in the contract that extends the terms of the license to permit use of the software on backup equipment?	___	___	___	
18.	Is there a person assigned specific responsibility for software backup, security, and control?	___	___	___	

FIGURE 6–1 *(concluded)*

No.	Item	Yes	No	N/A	Comments
19.	Are surprise inventories taken of the software maintained at the backup location?	___	___	___	
20.	Have there been copies made, for storage at the backup site, of:				
	a. utility programs (sorts, merges, file, reorganizations, file recreates, etc.)?	___	___	___	
	b. new operating system updates that have not yet been applied?	___	___	___	
21.	Have "waiting periods" been established for routine program operation, requiring that, after a certain length of time, no matter for what reason, certain action is necessary? (A list of approximate run times should be maintained to aid in scheduling as well as a check to determine if a program may be in a loop.)	___	___	___	

Chapter Seven

Database Security and Records Management

Microcomputer-based data files and records usually receive little attention from users, but are important to consider, particularly for sensitive or critical programs. The considerations in micro–mainframe connection security are outlined. There are some security problems that are uniquely important to data access by end users. These include access to applications, downloading of data, uploading of data, and diskette data control.

Usually database and records management are under the control of specialized groups, and the access rules must be understood by micro users. The database risks and the problems of file backup must be understood by the users. The considerations in records management should also be known. A checklist is provided to review the key elements in database and records control.

DATABASE SECURITY

Microcomputer-Based Data Files

Little has been done in the area of securing the software and data stored in the stand-alone, desktop microcomputer. The hierarchical database security structures, including authorization, departmentalization, and compartmentalization schemes, that are used in the mini and mainframe database environments are essentially nonexistent in the microcomputer environment. The reason for this is primarily one of economics. As indicated in earlier sections of this book, it is difficult to justify the cost of the software and the system overhead resources required to run database security software. Also, most micros are limited in the number of programs that can be run at the same time, unless multitasking/multiprogramming is featured. Companies that need to enhance database security beyond the password stage have usually written their own custom software or have modified the software application packages.

One way of controlling micro-based data is by assigning responsibility for it to a specific individual. In essence, that individual may be known as the "owner" of the data and would have complete responsibility for its control, security, and backup.

Because of the frequent interchange of data among micro users, there should be clear distinctions made between owner, user, and custodian of the data. Controlling responsibility can then be assigned to specific individuals. The owner of the data is usually in the department that generates it and has complete responsibility and authority for its control, security, and backup. The user of the data is granted authority to access and use certain files and possibly update them. The user should abide by the procedures, standards, and rules for the use of the data that have been established by the owner or by management. The custodian of the data has the operational control of the database in which the data resides. The custodian may be expected to manipulate and update the data and to exercise security control over it.

MICRO-TO-MAINFRAME
CONNECTION SECURITY

Several security problems are associated with micro–mainframe connections.

Establishing File Protection Systems

Few new solutions to the problems of protecting the central data files, other than the use of passwords and extract-data files, have been developed. As the complexity of data interchange calls for more sophisticated security measures, and as users demand access to more current files, neither passwords nor extract-data files will provide adequate protection. Overly restrictive protection systems, however, may frustrate the end users who have legitimate claims on the data.

Need for Clear Guidelines

The problems of micro–mainframe connection are new and little understood, but they must be studied by the information services staff. Clear guidelines are necessary to give direction to the systems programming group and to put limitations on end users. The problems addressed by such guidelines should include the following:

- Who has access to which applications?
- Where will the extracted data be stored?
- Who will be responsible for updating the extracted files?
- Who will manage the file integrity?
- Who will document the data extractions and changes?

Privacy of Stored Data

A great deal of data in the average system files should remain confidential to selected groups of people. If others have access to confidential data, they may extract it and display it. A number of privacy problems exist with applications and require advice from personnel and legal specialists.

Adequate Security

Assuming that adequate security currently exists on the mainframe, and that simple passwords will control all access requirements, is not sufficient security. Passwords are compromised rapidly in network situations. They are passed out to other people and are left lying on desks. They are a necessity that must be implemented and maintained, but they are not sufficient alone. In addition, intelligent people who have had computer training will be allowed access to data files that were previously confined to the data processing center. The individual and specific problems of security must be examined carefully to ensure that a given product can provide security and the required backup features.

GENERAL MICRO–MAINFRAME SECURITY CONSIDERATIONS

The security problems in the use of data by many end users are based on common law and common sense. When microcomputers are provided, breaking into many networks is easy, but determining if break-ins have occurred is usually not as easy. The idea of "hacking," or simply breaking into data files for the sake of the accomplishment or to see if there is anything interesting there, has become so commonplace that it is accepted in computer literature. However, in many cases, it may pose a threat to an organization. Some actions that are commonly taken by computer users are simply against the law. Business and personal ethics are greatly needed in the workplace, but they are not always present.

Those responsible for the management of data must realize that many people simply do not understand the common law. Therefore, those responsible for maintaining the data files must use common sense to make it difficult for others to destroy, change, or manipulate data for personal satisfaction or for profit.

A number of particular aspects of data security should be analyzed by the Information Services staff or appropriate security personnel. The importance of these aspects may be unique to each organization, but they all should be considered. They are outlined in the following section.

Aspects of Data Security

Use of proprietary software. Most software that is used in business is proprietary: it has copyright protection. This protection is difficult to enforce, but at times, the owners may obtain proof of violations. It is important for an information services department to advertise the copyrights, and not to do any illegal copying itself. This problem is difficult to control except through explicit publication of the laws involved and reliance on the ethics of the employees.

To protect itself in potential legal suits, a company should have a written policy that is widely distributed and that explicitly outlaws software privacy and establishes penalties, up to and including dismissal.

Nonbusiness use of systems. An organization may encourage employees to take microcomputers home and use them for training. However, it should never encourage employees to use them for personal profit.

Respect for privacy. Privacy laws and rules are realistically required to prevent individuals from being hurt. Not only must data regarding private information be controlled, but also the concept of the misuse of private data must be publicized.

Diskette management. Individuals frequently do not have a sense of the importance of the information that they have assembled on their easily transportable diskettes. In most organizations, diskettes simply lie around on desktops. Aspects of diskette management should be part of the initial training of all end users.

Communications security. The problems of security in a communications network are complex, and controls are frequently breached, both inadvertently and intentionally. All end users who are communicating sensitive data should be alerted to the problems involved. In some cases, when security is particularly important, the use of encryption systems should be considered.

Backup and recovery. End users frequently become highly dependent upon the data files that they have created and stored in their microcomputers. They must be alerted to the real possibilities that they can have a local disaster through fire, theft, or electronic problems and can lose their files. The simple actions required to allow for backup and recovery in the event of a disaster should be explained to them.

NECESSARY SECURITY CONTROLS ON DATA

Some security problems are uniquely important to the planned data-access arrangements in end-user computing. These are discussed below.

Access to Applications

User access to microcomputer and mainframe applications systems is usually governed by simple controls. Application programs are given only to approved personnel. Restrictions on the copying of programs are published, and an attempt is made to enforce them. The users are given access to the information they need, but to nothing else. Two types of products help in this control: profiles and passwords. The purpose of the *password* is to give some control over the *initial access*. The purpose of a *profile* is to control the types of search and access that will be carried out for that user *after access has been gained*. In addition to the password, the product may require the user to give other information, such as the serial number on the diskette being used. The password and the profile can be checked, sorted, and then matched against subsequent inquiries. This measure is in addition to any other security systems that may be in place.

Two-level control is necessary because passwords are notoriously difficult to control. If they are not changed, they become well known. If they are changed too frequently, people write them down in obvious places to remember them, and they become useless. Controls can be established so that if someone is missing a diskette or if the password has been changed, the entrance capability can be voided. Then, when the transaction gets to the mainframe, it not only gets turned off, but the void command gets sent to the micro and wipes out the diskette.

Downloading of Data

Clearly, there is a problem with downloading financial or other sensitive data to diskettes, which can then be taken from the premises. There is no viable way of protecting all diskettes. Users must have data from the mainframe, and there must be some sort of data download package in which data from the host becomes a file stored locally on the micro. Mainframe data should generally not be on the diskettes in mainframe form; partly because the great amount of data will fill the micro memory rapidly, and partly because the files need to be structured and formatted specifically for the application on the microcomputer. The download information-extraction package can give the user selection capabilities and can give the administrator control capabilities.

In essence, the end user simply requires a logical view of the data, and need not know what controls or limitations are placed on access to other data. The package should simply limit data access at the database, data segment, field, and value levels. This can be handled by having the database administration group create templates that define the micro user access to mainframe data.

Uploading of Data

Some solutions to the control over the uploading of data exist, but many problems still remain. The uploading of data creates the greatest security exposure of all aspects of micro–mainframe connections. The most common solution at present is to upload into a *buffer* area, or *shadow database*, which allows later incorporation of the data into the main database under control. This is effective, but really only a temporary measure. The products currently available allow only a partial solution to this full-linkage problem, but have to be used until better solutions are devised. The long-term solution will be interfaces with more complex systems so that the micro updating will become part of the standard data processing. This is already being done in several industries where the value of having immediate updates is greater than the cost of the complex system.

Diskette Data Control

The control of data on diskettes is mostly an unsolved problem. Diskette data can be lost, damaged, removed, or altered. End users can take mainframe, controlled data onto a diskette and mix it with their own uncontrolled data. Then they can pass it on to others or write reports from it with no record maintained, much less an audit trail, that confirms the source or integrity of the data.

CONTROLLING CENTRAL DATABASE ACTIVITIES

Database Management System

The introduction of a database management system has a stabilizing effect on the database. It provides a central access point to the data. All requests for and changes in the data are performed by the system. This degree of control facilitates the management of data and promotes integrity and privacy. In addition, the improved integrity promotes more intensive use of the data and increases its value as an asset to the organization.

The numerous features of a database management system are provided to the user through a common interface. A common data definition approach allows multiple users simultaneous access to the same database, and the system provides all of its capabilities to each database defined. The database management system thus facilitates the interaction among people, machines, and data.

The goal of database integrity has a pervasive effect on the database administration functions. Although integrity protection is never completely achievable (neither the technology nor the resources are available), several integrity controls can be invoked by the database administrator to achieve an effective level of integrity. These controls range from the preventive measures of data definition control through the assurance measures of backup and recovery. Among the most prominent procedures that a database administrator uses to achieve database control are the following five.

1. *Control over the data definition* ensures that the data conforms to its definition and that conformance is maintained through the life of the data.

2. *Access control* protects the data from access by unauthorized persons or for unauthorized purposes. Some form of restricted access is usually required for both privacy and integrity assurance. A regulatory mechanism is required in the database management system so that the database administrator can manage access control.

3. *Audit trail* is maintained by the database administrator to demonstrate that the confidentiality of the data has been maintained. Access is controlled by the same access control mechanism, and its incidence can be controlled by a clear separation of the testing and operational environments of the database.

4. *Update control* assures that the user has the appropriate authorization to change data values. There are two levels of concern in update control: data addition, and data modification and deletion. In many situations, the need to monitor the modifications and deletions to the database is greater than the need to monitor the additions.

5. *Concurrency control* provides database integrity by controlling the concurrent programs that perform the update function. Typically, systems employ some form of lockout mechanism at the file or record level in the database to aid the database administrator in this function.

Database Risks

Database technology introduces new activities into an organization. These activities include the database administration function. As activities and job functions change, so do the risks. While there are many advantages to database technology, risks also are associated with the use of that technology.

The database is not a single file, but rather a group of files intertwined into a single organizational structure. This new method of storing data poses the following new or increased risks.

Inaccurate or incomplete data entered into the database.   This is a usage risk, meaning that if inaccurate or incomplete data are entered by a single individual into the database, multiple users will rely on those data and potentially make improper decisions.

Data not entered on a timely basis.   The failure to enter data on a timely basis may not be known to other users who rely on the timeliness of that data to make business decisions, and, thus, they may make improper decisions.

Integrity errors not detected.   The integrity of the database may be lost, and yet that fact may not be known to the users of the database.

Program changes incorrectly performed.   If the programs that process data in a database are incorrect, they may cause errors within the database.

Cause of problems unknown.   Failure to provide adequate documentation or adequate problem definition may make the investigators of that program unable to identify the cause.

Broken pointers/chains. The interconnection between data elements in the subschema may be broken, which results in users not being able to recall the needed data from the database.

Parts of database lost during reorganization. The reorganization process may fail to include all the parts in the reorganized database.

Database technology reduces or eliminates some of the risks associated with nondatabase technology. Some of the risks that are eliminated include the following:

- Redundancy between data in two or more application systems.
- Inconsistency of data between two or more application systems.
- Ability of anyone reading the computer file to view every record and data item on the file.
- Ability of a dedicated application to manipulate data within that application. (This is eliminated if the database administrator assumes responsibility for the integrity of data within the database.)
- Improper decisions made because of untimely or incomplete data. (This assumes that data within the database is more timely and complete than dedicated applications.)
- Lost opportunity due to inability to develop applications on a timely basis. (This assumes systems analysts and programmers are adequately trained in database technology to utilize it effectively in application development.)

To minimize the impact of these new and increased risks, new methods of control will be required. Selection and implementation of the appropriate controls ensure both the continued integrity of the database and the achievement of the stated database objectives.

RECORDS MANAGEMENT

Value of Records

Each organization needs to identify what information is critical to its survival. This includes not only administrative, accounting, and financial records, but also proprietary and trade secret information. In order to determine what information is critical, ask this question: "Can my company/department, etc., adequately function if the microcomputer-based information becomes unavailable for use?"

The National Fire Protection Association (NFPA) has defined four classes of records as follows:

- Vital records (Class I): Essential to operation, irreplaceable, or needed immediately after a disaster. Cannot be quickly reproduced. Examples: master files, programs, company records.
- Important records (Class II): Essential to operation, but can be reproduced without critical delay. Examples: data files, input/output files.
- Useful records (Class III): Inconvenient if lost, but loss would not prevent prompt restoration of operations after a disaster. Examples: historical files and data.
- Nonessential records (Class IV): Not necessary to replace if lost.

Magnetic Media Storage

Adequate, environmentally controlled, secure storage for magnetic media is essential in micro-based operations. As outlined in an earlier section, diskettes and cassettes have suffered many indignities at the hands of micro users who were in too much of a hurry to get the job done, or who used their diskettes as coasters for their coffee cups so they would not damage their desks. (Remember, the diskette that is sitting underneath your coffee cup may be the product of hundreds of hours of your work and may contain your company's total accounting records.) When you are working with cassettes/diskettes, use the proper desktop storage devices.

Magnetic media storage considerations include the following:

- Dust-free environment.
- Fire-rated, smoke- and water-resistant storage cabinet.
- Lockable storage, if necessary.
- Controlled access.
- For off-site backup: extra copies of software, data files.
- For on-site backup: extra copies of software, data files.
- With primary copies: correct handling and storage while in use.
- For sensitive information: files kept separate and controlled.
- For working files: separation from scratch work files.
- Proper labeling: external and internal.
- Periodic inventory of media taken and control logs maintained.
- Environmental controls: safe temperature and humidity levels.
- Storage of media away from window ledges, magnetic devices, etc.

Magnetic Media Erasure Devices

One means of ensuring that diskettes or cassettes containing no-longer-needed sensitive data do not end up in an authorized person's possession is to erase the data via the use of special devices designed for that purpose. Magnetic erasure devices are available for diskette, disk, and cassette.

Backup

The term *backup* has two meanings in the security context:

1. The creation of a copy of a file or documentation for recovery purposes.
2. Pertaining to equipment or procedures that are available for use in the event of failure or overloading of normally used equipment or procedures.

This chapter addresses the copying of files for backup purposes. In general, it is recommended that three copies or "generations" of a database file be kept: the son, the father, and the grandfather generations. This generation concept is illustrated in Figure 7–1.

Backup involves a number of considerations.

Database size.   The size of the database will determine the time it takes to "dump" or copy that database.

Backup schedule.   The scheduling of backup depends on the following factors:

- Database size (volume).
- Criticality of the data (vital or nonvital).
- Processing-time constraints.

Each organization needs to establish a backup plan for each of its files. While daily backups will be required for some files, others may only need to be copied once a week or once a month.

Differential backup.   Differential dumps involve copying only the records that have changed since the last run.

The following points should also be considered:

- Dual updating. This involves the updating of two identical files by the transaction being processed.

FIGURE 7–1
Generations of Files

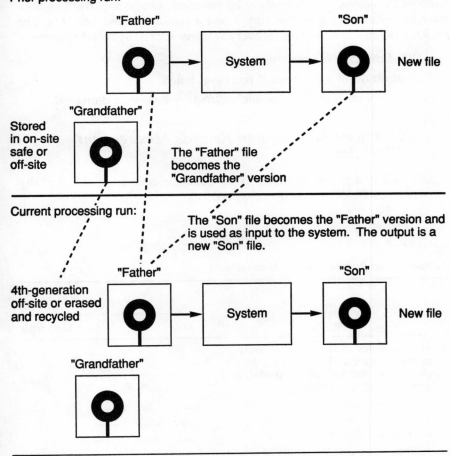

Prior processing run:

"Father"   "Son"

System   New file

"Grandfather"

Stored
in on-site
safe or
off-site

The "Father" file
becomes the
"Grandfather" version

Current processing run:

The "Son" file becomes the "Father" version and
is used as input to the system. The output is a
new "Son" file.

"Father"   "Son"

4th-generation
off-site or erased
and recycled

System   New file

"Grandfather"

- Audit logs/journals. As a database record is updated, the originating transaction record and the database "before" record and the database "after" record are recorded in a log file.
- Some database files never need to be copied because it would be easier to recreate the file.

Magnetic Media Recovery

Data loss associated with magnetic media caused by such occurrences as equipment malfunction, software problems or errors, operator error, erasure, or overwrite, can potentially be reversed. One company, The Software Store, in Michigan, has developed a package called Disk Fix. The package offers the following recovery features for CP/M-based systems:

- CP/M diskette file recovery.
- Restoration of a file after it has been killed.
- Recovery of data after the file's directory has been damaged.

Database Security and Records Management Checklist

Figure 7–2 is a checklist that can be used for reviewing the security considerations outlined in this chapter.

FIGURE 7–2
Database Security and Records Management

No.	Item	Response			
		Yes	No	N/A	Comments
1.	Has the value of the data processing records been classified into the NFPA classes of vital, important, useful, and nonessential, including:				
	a. input records?	___	___	___	
	b. source documents?	___	___	___	
	c. control documents?	___	___	___	
	d. magnetic tape/disk file records?	___	___	___	
	e. programs?	___	___	___	
	f. output data?	___	___	___	
2.	Is there understanding of and compliance with legal-record retention regulations for:				
	a. the Internal Revenue Service (IRS)?	___	___	___	
	b. insurance?	___	___	___	
	c. legal considerations?	___	___	___	
	d. customer/product history information?	___	___	___	

FIGURE 7-2 *(continued)*

No.	Item	Yes	No	N/A	Comments
3.	Have the possible types of threats and vulnerabilities that your records/files may be exposed to been evaluated for:				
a.	data-entry errors?	___	___	___	
b.	data transmission errors?	___	___	___	
c.	mechanical malfunctions?	___	___	___	
d.	program errors?	___	___	___	
e.	updating of wrong file?	___	___	___	
f.	computer operator errors?	___	___	___	
g.	lost files?	___	___	___	
h.	defective magnetic media?	___	___	___	
i.	theft of records?	___	___	___	
j.	criminal activity?	___	___	___	
k.	loss by natural disaster?	___	___	___	
4.	Are duplicate copies of all vital records maintained?	___	___	___	
5.	Is a list of critical vital files maintained?	___	___	___	
6.	Is reconstruction capability maintained for paper and magnetic files? (Possibly in the three-generation, son-father-grandfather approach)	___	___	___	
7.	Are daily file dumps and transaction files maintained for construction purposes?	___	___	___	
8.	When magnetic files are copied for off-site storage, are the copies checked for:				
a.	readability?	___	___	___	
b.	accuracy?	___	___	___	
9.	Are the on-site and off-sight magnetic media storage cabinets:				
a.	fire-resistant?	___	___	___	
b.	smoke-resistant?	___	___	___	
c.	water-resistant?	___	___	___	
d.	movable so that they may be relocated quickly in the event of disaster?	___	___	___	
e.	secure?	___	___	___	
f.	fitted with casters for easy evacuation?	___	___	___	

Note: Make sure the storage cabinets can be moved through the doorways.

FIGURE 7–2 *(continued)*

No.	Item	Yes	No	N/A	Comments
10.	Are critical records microfilmed as an additional means of providing backup?	___	___	___	
11.	Is there a procedure for evacuating the critical files in case of emergency?	___	___	___	
12.	Is a paper shredder or an incinerator used for the disposal of:				
	a. computer and typewriter carbon paper?	___	___	___	
	b. old classified documents?	___	___	___	
	c. program listings and test data?	___	___	___	
	d. old reports?	___	___	___	
	e. worn-out magnetic diskettes?	___	___	___	
	f. microfilm?	___	___	___	
13.	Is access to information on the micro's database strictly controlled?	___	___	___	
14.	Are detailed transaction records kept for a "safe" period of time? (If a micro user is low on diskettes/cassettes, needed files are sometimes accidentally erased.)	___	___	___	
15.	Are there ways of ensuring that the correct version of the database file is being used?	___	___	___	
16.	Are outdated files controlled so they are not processed accidentally?	___	___	___	
17.	Does the software provide for internal label checking?	___	___	___	
18.	Is the magnetic cassette/diskette erasure (degaussing) device stored in a secure place?	___	___	___	
19.	Have these magnetic media storage controls been considered?				
	a. Dust-free environment.	___	___	___	
	b. Fire rating, smoke and water resistance.	___	___	___	
	c. Lockability if necessary.	___	___	___	
	d. Controlled access.	___	___	___	
	e. Off-site backup: extra copies of software, data files.	___	___	___	
	f. On-site backup: extra copies of software, data files.	___	___	___	
	g. Primary copies: handled and stored correctly while in use.	___	___	___	

FIGURE 7–2 *(concluded)*

No.	Item	Yes	No	N/A	Comments
h.	Sensitive information files kept separate and controlled.	——	——	——	
i.	Working files kept separate from scratch files.	——	——	——	
j.	Proper labeling.	——	——	——	
k.	Periodic inventory of media taken.	——	——	——	
l.	Environmental controls, safe temperature and humidity levels.	——	——	——	
m.	Media stored away from window ledges, magnetic devices.	——	——	——	

Chapter Eight

Telecommunications Security

Once the microcomputer is taken out of the realm of stand-alone status and integrated into a communication-based system, new threats and vulnerabilities surface that need additional control and security. Telecommunication network configurations link microcomputers, minicomputers, mainframes, and automated office systems together.

Statistics regarding the growth of telecommunication networks indicate that in 1981 there were about 300 microcomputer networks in the United States and by 1985, more than 90,000 networks were installed. It is estimated that more than 1 million networks will be installed by 1993. Local area networks will connect over 20 million devices, or at least 20 percent of the installed base of eligible devices.

This chapter presents an introduction to telecommunication and network security. Levels of telecommunication system complexities, including open and closed network architecture, are also provided. Microcomputer networking, local area network topologies, transmission media, and access methods are defined. Telecommunication and network security issues are addressed, including local area network security, network security vulnerabilities, system-access control, input/output and network-access control, file-access control, hardware security considerations, and encryption considerations. Telecommunication and network security checklists are provided, including a network security product evaluation. A section on encryption reviews the basics of data encryption and its use for securing computer-based data.

NEW USES, NEW THREATS

Once the microcomputer is taken out of the realm of stand-alone status and integrated into a communication-based system, new threats and vulnerabilities surface that need additional control and security. Communication network configurations link microcomputers, minicomput-

136

ers, and mainframe systems together. Many networks consist of these computers in addition to automated office equipment such as electronic mail, teleconferencing, videotex, video broadcasting, facsimile transmission, telemetry, and word processing.

The communication network concept makes information available so the job can be done in a more effective and efficient manner. This, in turn, produces higher profits for the employer. However, communication networks are becoming a cause of concern among top-level management. These concerns are:

- Preserving data integrity. If more people have direct interface with the company's central database, data could become contaminated. Control of the central database is now more important than it was in the past.

- Preventing the misuse of company data. There is a possibility that data stored not only on the central database, but also on microcomputers, minicomputers, and office automation equipment, could be electronically copied for unethical or criminal purposes.

- Using disaster preparedness and recovery planning to provide for the protection, security, and preservation of data that has become increasingly critical in the day-to-day running of the business.

- Providing a clear definition, through policies and procedures, for the use of microcomputers in the organization, regardless of whether the micros are company-owned or personally owned. Policies and procedures also need to adequately define company data as compared with personal data.

- Using vendor-supplied microcomputer software on multiple systems within an organization without the proper licenses.

- Assessing the threat of manipulation by micro users. Managers can no longer assume that most people do not know about computers and the technical aspects of data processing. Micro users are becoming more sophisticated, and many have programming skills.

Definition of Telecommunications Security

Telecommunications security as used in this text is the sum of four definitions, namely:

Teleprocessing: An information transmission system that combines telecommunication, EDP systems, and man-machine interface equipment to interact and function as an integrated whole.

Data: Any discrete, digital representation of information rather than analog information. Examples of data formats are:

- Binary signal levels.
- Collection (ASCII character set, control characters, etc.).
- Converted analog information; for example, through modem, an analog-to-digital or a voltage-to-frequency conversion process.

Telecommunication: Any transmission, emission, or reception of signs, signals, words, images, sounds, or intelligence of any nature by wire, radio, fiber, visual, microwave, or other electromagnetic system. Included in the above (but not exclusively) are all telephone, telegraph, teletype, facsimile, fiber optics, satellite, data transmission, and closed-circuit television systems.

Security: Any procedure, method, or technique used to achieve or maintain control of the overall data communications process, including the assurance of integrity of the transferred information and verification of the identities (by way of an agreed-upon format) of the sender and receiver involved.

Communications Channels

The most common device used as a dataset to handle data-stream transfers is a modem (MOdulator-DEModulator). (See Figure 8–1.) The most frequently used transmission media for separated facilities is a common-carrier network, usually telephone lines. These lines may be signal-conditioned, especially for faster transmission rates. Among other possible channels of communications are telegraph lines, coaxial cable, laser waveguides, satellites, radio links, fiber optic cable, and microwave links.

TRENDS IN SOFTWARE, HARDWARE, FIRMWARE, AND DESIGN

A problem of planning and managing the security of data communication systems is that it is a constantly developing field. New equipment and techniques are readily available. Some address specific areas of data communication security, while others are ideas applicable to a broad spectrum of possibilities. Major trends in software, hardware, firmware, and design include the following:

- Functional integration. A number of software packages have driven this trend, including spreadsheets, management support systems, telecommunication controls, database management systems, desktop publishing, and word processing. On-chip vertical integration of hardware

FIGURE 8–1
Illustration of Modulation–Demodulation

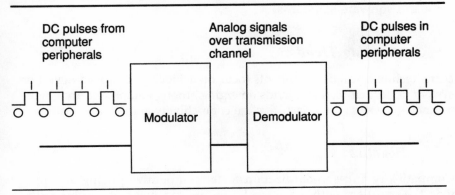

and software is another factor, encompassing operating systems, high-level programming languages, input/output, datacomm, MMU, and the Data Encryption Standard (DES) algorithm.

• Transparency of systems to the users. This trend has yielded operating systems with extended capabilities through the use of protocol converters and translators.

• Transportability of software between computers. The notable elements of this trend are machine-independent software and device-independent application packages.

• Compatibility and standardization in the industry. This trend is advantageous for security managers.

• Use of broadband networks, including voice, data, and video. The notable example is the integrated services digital network (ISDN).

• Use of voice recognition or electronic signatures.

COMPATIBILITY AND STANDARDIZATION IN THE INDUSTRY

Consider the area of fully distributed data processing systems (DDP). Compatibility between the operating system and network software becomes paramount to the realization of an overall, efficient system. For DDP systems or stand-alone systems that must share storage media (e.g., floppy diskettes), there must exist hardware compatibility (e.g., disk sizes, track formatting, equivalent number of sectors per track, number of bytes per sector, skewing of sector reads). The means for achieving compatibility depends on the market acceptance of both hardware and software standards.

Growing Trends

Many technological developments focus on achieving improved device or system performance. Two trends emerging among equipment from high-technology system manufacturers are compatibility and standardization.

Benefits

Compatibility and standardization foster competitive pricing and provide the end user with a system he or she can feel comfortable with. Knowing that second-source vendors are in the marketplace also reassures the end user. By maintaining compatibility or offering upward-compatible systems, devices, or subsystems, product vendors can be confident that their latest product offerings will have a greater likelihood of purchase by present EDP customers and by prospective users.

Peripheral products for a system are more likely to be produced when several manufacturers serve a market segment that still represents a reasonably large account base. Though the evolution of standards takes a considerable amount of time, the resulting benefits to end users and to manufacturers will often expand dramatically once the standard is made official.

Accepted or Emerging Standards

Standards for hardware (bus signals, pinouts, etc.), networks, software, and data communications are proliferating. Examples of standards in these and other areas are provided in Figure 8–2. Standards that are accepted in the system or operation areas can only be of aid to the security manager. They provide advantages in the control and review of systems and cut down on the proliferation of security points.

LEVELS OF SYSTEM COMPLEXITY

A computer system can vary from a single-user system operating in a non-network configuration to a collection of fully distributed, multitasking, concurrent-processing nodes in a large network arrangement.

FIGURE 8-2
Accepted or Emerging Standards

Hardware standards

Bus: IEEE488, IEEE796, IEEE696, Unibus, Q-Bus, VMEbus, Versabus.
Network interfaces: ENP, LANCE, UniLAN.
Rigid disk interfaces: SASI, ST506, ESDI.
Serial interfaces: RS232C, RS449.
Parallel interfaces: Centronics.
Console terminals: Emulation features for DEC's VT-100, VT-52, IBM 3270s, HP-3000.

Encryption/decryption standards

DES algorithm.
Electronic signature methods.
Scrambler/descrambler equipment.

Operating systems

UNIX, XENIX, MP/M, CP/M, MS-DOS, PC-DOS.

Application software

DBMS.
Electronic spreadsheets.
Engineering workstations.
    • CAD/CAM programs.
    • Device-independent graphics such as CORE (SIGGRAPH).
Terminal emulation.
Installation programs (for various terminals).

Storage media formats (for LANs, multiuser environments)

Software: Data interchange format (DIF).
Physical media: Bytes/sector.

Network standards

System network architecture (SNA).
Access methods: Token ring, CSMA/CD, UniLAN.
IEEE802: Multiple approaches to LANs.

Protocol standards

Synchronous vs. asynchronous.
BISYNC, SDLC, HDLC.
Access: UniLINK.

Protocol converters/translators

Asychronous-to-synchronous.
BISYNC-to-SDLC.

In general, teleprocessing systems are classified as *open* or *closed* systems.

An open teleprocessing system is defined as an information network that includes physically dispersed computers connected by communication media and that can be accessed from computers connected to another network: for example, through dial-up or dedicated lines (see Figure 8–3).

The open network system has become more common in today's computer processing environment. Organizations are using common-carrier (telephone company) facilities to promote voice/data communications, distributed processing, and communications at remote locations. They are also using national computer-based electronic mail and informational reference services.

Important functional characteristics of open networks that may be of interest to access control system designers include the following[1]:

- A distributed systems architecture that facilitates database and resource sharing.
- An increasing demand for user friendliness.
- Use of common-carrier facilities that lend themselves to wiretapping or interception of data.
- Increasing implementation of local area networks (LANs) that are also capable of external communication or connection.

A closed teleprocessing system can be defined as an internal network that is not connected to an external system. None of the network elements in a closed environment are accessible by an outsider through public carrier facilities (Figure 8–4).

Closed networks are common, especially in smaller organizations that use minicomputers and microcomputers for data processing. An organization may have an internal network made up of hundreds of terminals, microcomputers, and peripheral devices. Because of the nature of the business, there may be no need to communicate with outside sources.

However, many organizations have a limited-access network. The limited-access network, also referred to as a partially closed network, allows outside communication under certain circumstances. The most common example of limited access is where a hardware/software service organization will dial in to a customer's computer to perform software maintenance or on-line hardware diagnostics. Many organizations

---

[1]Jerome Lobel, *Foiling the System Breakers* (New York: McGraw-Hill, 1986), pp. 131, 213–14.

FIGURE 8–3
Open Teleprocessing System

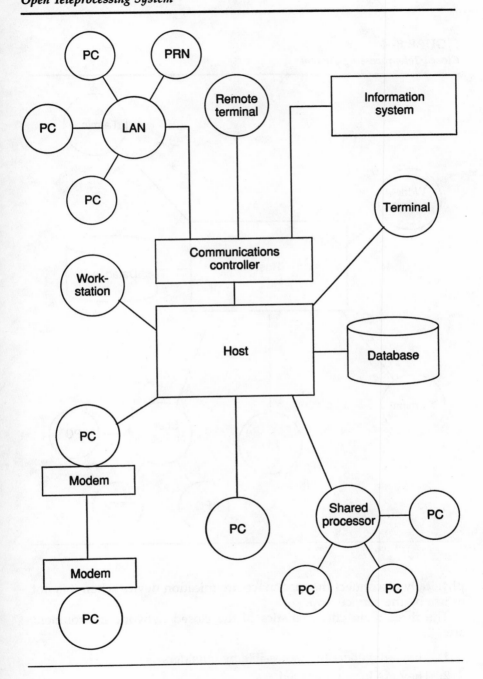

FIGURE 8–4
Closed Teleprocessing System

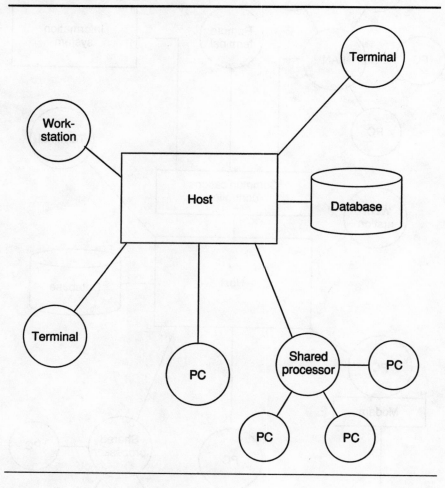

physically disconnect the modem/communication device when it is not in use by the service firm.

The three main characteristics of the closed network environment are:

1. They are generally inaccessible by outsiders.
2. They are locally installed.
3. Most of the user resources tend to be known.

A secure access-control design can be made based on these characteristics. The design would include all of the necessary security and control elements of the open system with the exception of the external access–oriented security nodes.

Communication System Configurations and Networks

Within the open and closed communication architecture, a number of system configurations and networks are possible.

Single-user systems configurations.   These would have the following:

- Dumb terminal or intelligent terminal with modem/acoustic coupler to access telephone dial-up services (CompuServe, The Source, etc.)
- Stand-alone computer with file storage on floppy or hard disks.
- Single-user to single-user system data transfer through a direct wire (null modem) or acoustic coupler/modem.
- Common operating system (resident to computer), which could involve CBBS (computer bulletin board systems) and RCPM (remote control program for microcomputers).

Multi-user configurations.   These would have the following features:

- One central computer with several terminals tied in.
- User areas assigned in operating system with shared files for fundamental operations.

Local area networks (LANs).   These are multi-user systems connected to one another in a bus-connected, star, ring, or other configuration. Types include captive, open, proprietary, and hybrid (any combination of these).

Wide area network (WAN) (expanded LAN).   A WAN is a collection of linked host computers using a common protocol, connecting the systems over long distances. Types of WANs include research networks (ARPA Internet, CSNET); private-company networks (Xerox Internet, DEC Easynet, IBM Vnet); cooperatives (groups having similar interests, especially universities) (BITNET, FIDONET, RAMNET); commercial networks (E-Mail-oriented WANs); and municipalities (city, county, state networks) using municipal area networks (MANs).

Regional networks. These operate by fiber optic and micro-wave links.

MODERN MICROCOMPUTING NETWORKING

Those assigned the responsibility of network security should have an in-depth understanding of network architecture and operations.

Three Types of Microcomputer Networking

Microcomputer networking can be accomplished by three different ap-proaches, none of which is inherently superior to the other. The three types are as follows:

1. Micro-to-mainframe links. These are two-tier networks where the micros are directly connected to the central mainframe computer.

2. Departmental computers. These are three-tier networks where a group of micros are networked with a departmental minicomputer while it is connected to the central mainframe computer.

3. Microcomputer peer networks. These are single-tier networks where a group of micros are interconnected, usually in a LAN. The LAN frequently has gateways to the central computer and to external net-works or other LANs.

Micro-to-mainframe links. In the micro-to-mainframe link (Figure 8–5), the power of the central mainframe computer is used for the management of the internal microcomputer networks, intracom-pany and external networks, and the operation of large central data-bases. Several architectures are available. The general operational con-trol can be strong, but the security of the central files may be difficult to maintain if the microcomputers that are connected are powerful. It is suited to large, transactional applications and to large data files that can be accessed with sufficient control. This approach is usually controlled tightly by the information services department.

The micro-to-mainframe link is a host network that supplies shared processing. The host computer is the most intelligent device in the sys-tem and will store the largest data files. In the cases where the terminals attached to the host are "dumb" terminals, control is relatively easy to

FIGURE 8–5
Micro-to-Mainframe Link

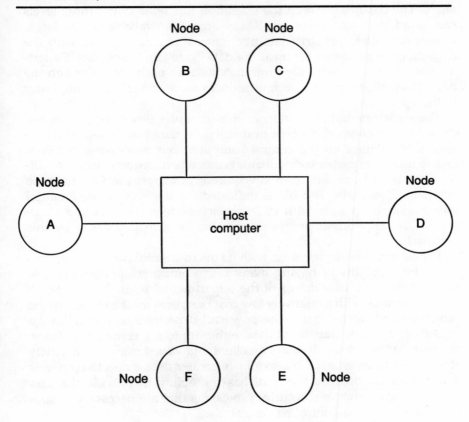

Each node represents a fully operational and independent microcomputer (with necessary data for processing).

maintain. Where there are intelligent microcomputers, control may be complex. The architecture is hierarchical because the communicating components are unequal.

Departmental computers. In the use of departmental computers, three levels of computer power are intertwined and balanced (see

Figure 8–6). A powerful minicomputer is connected between the central mainframe and the microcomputer. The approach has many advantages. The balance between the operation functions of the three levels can be adapted and adjusted. Ready access is available to the large, central data files, yet strict security controls can be imposed with the departmental processor acting as the data "gate" and controller. Departmental micros will normally communicate with each other through the departmental processor, which introduces more control and complexity to the operation.

The departmental computer, or departmental processor, comes the closest to the classical concept of distributed data processing. Connection is maintained to the central computer, but processing power is distributed. It is particularly advantageous when frequent access to different data in large data files is required; however, the files must be maintained securely. The file is indicated for the analysis of financial information by people with different access requirements and clearances. The application programs can also be managed easily by this approach.

The departmental computer, with its micro-to-mini connections, provides the capability of having many microcomputer applications resident on the large disk drives of the departmental mini. This is then a shared resource with a relatively low cost per micro for the storage of the programs and related data. The powerful departmental mini allows a smooth and simple transfer of data, either up to the central mainframe or down to the micros. It offers excellent and varied micro connectivity at the departmental level. It also allows greater user access to corporate data resources, because the mini has the ability to provide the data selection, screening, and security provisions that are necessary in supplying access to the controlled central files.

The most common functions designed into the departmental minicomputer are the following:

- A gateway to information in the mainframe memory.
- Central data files and file backup.
- Shared database and management of the DBMS.
- Central control of office automation functions, such as electronic mail, word processing, and departmental files.
- Software server for the microcomputers.

Some departmental minicomputer arrangements use the minicomputer strictly as a file server for the departmental micros. The mini supplies controls, security, and the access to the central mainframe. It then downloads requested files to the micros on demand. Other depart-

FIGURE 8–6
Departmental Computers

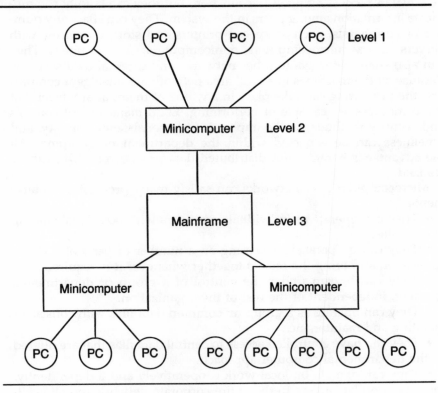

mental minicomputer arrangements put more power in the mini, and reduce the PCs to the position of on-line terminals, which are micro-to-mini and in the same category as the micro-to-mainframe operation method. At the end of the spectrum where the mini is essentially a file server, the typical applications are analyses of the data. At the end of the spectrum where the mini is the departmental controller, the applications are on-line operational systems.

Microcomputer peer networks. These and local area networks are rapidly being introduced into all sizes of organizations. These are networks where micros in departments and buildings are linked for efficient sharing of information and common connection to the central computer or external networks.

Microcomputer peer networks are systems of data communication between a small number of intelligent machines. The machines may not be equal in processing power or function, but they can readily communicate information among peers in the system. They can share any number of peripherals, such as special printers and storage devices, with servers such as microcomputers, minicomputers, or mainframes. They can also share gateways to other networks and external data services. Because all the machines in a local area network are intelligent computers, the processing can take place in any one of them, at any level that the computers are capable of performing. Local management controls and security methods can be imposed. Data consistency, validity, and timeliness can be expected within the department or grouping. All the advantages heralded for distributed data processing (DDP) can be realized.

Microcomputer peer networks can satisfy many processing requirements:

• They can operate as individual computers with occasional sharing of data files.

• They can do parallel processing on a number of parts of a single application and bring the results together whenever it is required.

• They can be run under the control of a group or departmental manager, independent of the rest of the organization.

• They can operate as a group on common data files with consistent updating and maintenance.

• They can have controlled access to central data files that are offered by the departmental computer approach.

• They can operate on local work cooperatively and independently, yet have complete access to the entire corporate network and all available data.

• They can share expensive peripherals and other computing devices.

LANs or microcomputer peer networks can make efficient use of shared resources, and differing levels of group, departmental, and central control that are appropriate can be implemented. They can satisfy the increasing demand for organizational data at the microcomputer level while optimizing the use of hardware and software resources.

Departmental minicomputer-controlled networks and microcomputer peer networks are compatible and may be mixed and matched. First, a LAN grouping of micros, or the micro peer networks, frequently has gateways to external networks. These are often connections to a midrange computer, such as a departmental mini, which provides all the normal functions of a departmental processor to the LAN rather than to separate micros. Second, individual micros are constantly becoming more powerful. Software for the 486-based micros is rapidly being produced and marketed to put them into multiprocessing environments that are more similar to the larger minicomputers than to the microcomputers. Such highly functional micros will be able to sit in the LAN network, yet supply most of the capabilities of the departmental mini.

The categories of departmental processor and LAN should not be considered as separate and distinct ways of computing, but rather as functional types of computing that may be used independently, but that can be used together in the same system.

In most microcomputer LANs, one of the micros is equipped with more memory and more peripherals, and acts as a *file server*, or *print server*. It may also be the point of connection to other networks, and thereby act as a *communication server* and a *database server*. Over time, this micro is built up and extended to the point that it may become a super micro or a small mini. There is no defined boundary to distinguish between such equipment. There will always be departmental minicomputers controlling a number of microcomputers. There will always be peer networks of micros where one or more may be more powerful than the others. There will be more combinations of these two architectural arrangements that defy such simplistic classification. The three types of networking described are simply to show generic approaches. They are in no way limiting or exclusive.

LAN: AN INTRODUCTION

A LAN is a communication facility that usually serves a single building, or group of buildings, and does not use common carriers or public communication services for transmission. LANs may have *gateways* to the telephone network or to wide area networks (WANs). They may also have *bridges* to other LANs.

Most organizations have found that their information systems must be highly interconnected to be effective. As business strategies and operational plans are developed, it becomes evident that success depends directly upon the ability to share costly system elements, and to communicate information rapidly and efficiently. In businesses, the LAN has proven effective in providing such sharing and communication. It can supply instantaneous desk-to-desk communication. It enhances the microcomputer terminal to function as a telephone, typewriter, and copier. The efficiency of handling information in an office can be greatly improved. The LAN has become necessary in distributing the information in laboratories and automated factories. Many previously incompatible systems can be directly linked.

The obvious use of the LAN is its ability to enable a large group of users to share common resources. The LAN's limited range also enhances management's ability to exercise control over it.

In many information system environments the number of terminal users requiring access to the database, use of the processor's computation capacity, or connection with a remote resource not only tests the computer's capacity, but also creates problems with the installation, operation, and maintenance of the terminals. These problems can seriously affect the effectiveness of the computer operation. The addition of devices to the computer configuration entails expensive ports. The restriction on cable lengths forces management to cluster terminals in less-than-desirable operating conditions. Another benefit of the LAN is the reduction in cabling costs each time a cluster of terminals is added to the information system environment.

Advantages of the LAN are as follows:

- Interconnection for hundreds of users.
- Device-to-device distances of thousands of feet.
- Computer access without increased port equipment.
- Extensive cable reduction.
- Utilization of multiple data rates.

One of the advantages of the LAN is the ability of the user organization to exercise control over it. The LAN is a privately owned, user-administrated facility that is free of the constraints of the Federal Communications Commission (FCC) or the public carriers. The LAN is limited in its geographic range from a few hundred feet to 35 miles, with transmission speeds from 2.5 to 50 megabits per second. Potentially, every device on the LAN is able to communicate with every other device, and as the technology develops, the devices of different vendors will be capable of communicating with each other. A major feature of the LAN is its flexibility of structure. The LAN can be structured to facilitate installation in almost any physical plant and integration into many business applications.

The LAN's economic benefits are its most appealing features. Not only can devices be added to the network without acquisition and connection of costly computer ports, but there is also the elimination of cabling charges each time terminals are moved or implemented. Its effect in the computer room, where the mainframe is relieved of the job of arbitrating among users access to storage and communications facilities, is substantial.

The major advantage of the LAN is its ability to enable all connected users to share resources, such as storage devices, program loads, and data files. The cost of hardware disks, printers, and connections to external communications can be split among all of the users. While yielding extensive savings through elimination of hardware duplication, it also will enhance the users' opportunity to benefit from hardware that they might be hard pressed to justify independently. Resource sharing is one of the most beneficial features of the LAN.

LAN Topologies

The topology of the LAN is determined by the physical and logical relationship of its devices to one another. Since all the devices on the network must share the common communications path, a technique is needed that will enable a device to recognize signals addressed to it, and to transmit signals to similar devices in the network. The three basic technologies used in a LAN are: the *ring*, the *linear bus* and the *tree*, and the *star*. Each has a number of variations as efficiency is built into the system and as new requirements are identified and fulfilled.

The ring network. The ring network, which is circular in shape, has information packets that are routed in one direction, and all messages are received by all devices. Each message contains the identification of its origin and the identification of its destination. One method of accessing a ring is to have package transporters of a fixed size constantly circulating around the loop. When a device has a message for transmission on the network, it inspects each of the passing transporters until it finds an empty one; then it loads its message. The data is held in a buffer until the empty transporter is identified. The "empty slot" method of message transmission is the basis of the Cambridge Data Ring, developed at Cambridge University in England.

An alternative form of ring technology is presented by Datapoint's ARCnet (attached resource computer system) token-passing network. Similar to the old single-track railways, the token signals circulate around the devices on the network. A device is able to load a message only if it is in possession of the token. Since there is no slot, as in the Cambridge technology, there is no limit to the size of the packet, so it affords greater flexibility.

Because the ring networks are constructed as a series of point-to-point paths formed into a loop, each device tap breaks the cable. Each device tap then receives data from the tap higher on the cable and regenerates it to the tap lower on the cable. A bypass connection is required to ensure continued operation if a station fails. Figure 8–7 depicts a ring network.

Linear bus and the tree networks. In the bus network, the user devices are attached to the transmission medium by taps along a single length of cable that can be extended at one end. A tree network is a complex linear bus where the cable branches at either or both ends, but offers only one transmission path between any two stations. The bus LANs are usually based on coaxial cable and may utilize dual parallel cables—each handling the traffic in one direction. Figure 8–8 depicts the linear bus network, and Figure 8–9 depicts the tree network.

The star network. In the star network, each device is connected to a central switch, most often a PABX. The connecting medium is usually a twisted pair of telephone lines. The major weakness of this type of network is the reliance on control from a central point that is vulnerable to failure. Transmission speed is also restricted because of the capacity of the twisted pair. Figure 8–10 depicts the star network.

LAN Transmission Media

One of the basic issues in the design of the LAN is the physical medium specified for the network. There are three media that are offered by the vendors: twisted copper pair, coaxial cable, and fiber optic cable. Each is best suited under certain conditions, having its own physical characteristics and supporting its own transmission techniques. Naturally, cost and performance are important considerations in the selection of the transmission media, as in all other aspects of the LAN.

Twisted copper pair. The twisted copper pair is easy to install and fits snugly against baseboard or bends neatly around a pillar.

Along with its reasonable price and convenience, the twisted pair has a number of shortcomings as a data transmission medium. Normal voice traffic on the twisted pair is barely affected by interference caused by other office equipment. However, the same interference raises havoc on data transmitted on the twisted pair. The noise caused by typewriters, copier machines, and air conditioning equipment severely limits the speed of data transmission. A line hit by electronic interference will destroy more bits of data the faster it is transmitted. Another shortcoming of the twisted pair is the distance that the data signal will travel

FIGURE 8–7
A Ring Network

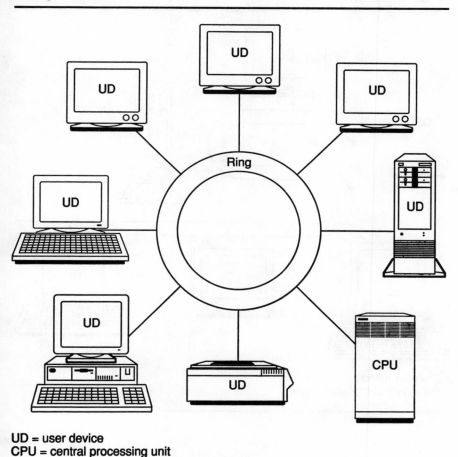

UD = user device
CPU = central processing unit

without protection or regeneration. The farther the signal travels on the twisted pair, the weaker it gets and the more susceptible it becomes to outside interference.

There are measures that can be taken to alleviate the impact of these shortcomings. The twisted pair can be shielded to reduce its exposure to interference. The shielding, however, sharply increases the cost of the medium. In order to increase the distance for the signal to travel effectively, repeaters must be installed on the line. These, too, are expensive.

FIGURE 8–8
The Linear Bus Network

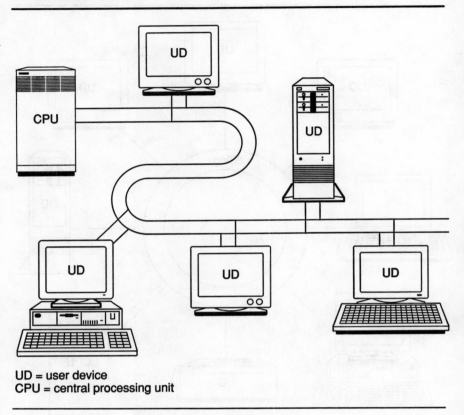

UD = user device
CPU = central processing unit

The twisted pair is most efficiently used in small networks where distances are limited and cost is an uppermost consideration.

Coaxial cable. The most widely used transmission medium in the LAN is the coaxial cable. Though its many forms allow it to adapt to a variety of application requirements, the structure of coaxial cable is the same in all forms. The central conductor, the element that carries the signal, is covered with a non-conducting insulation material, then by a metalized material for shielding. It is then wrapped in a protective coating. Because these layers are concentric around the common axis, the term *coaxial* is used.

FIGURE 8–9
The Tree Network

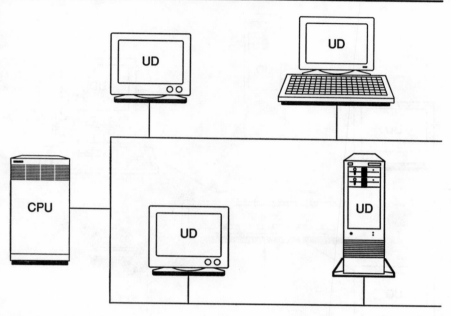

UD = user device
CPU = central processing unit

The two types of coaxial cable in general use for the LAN are named for the transmission techniques they support. Baseband coaxial cable contains a single path where many signals are time-division multiplexed at rates up to 10 million bits per second. In the LAN application, the baseband signal is always digital. The presence of specific voltage represents the "on" condition and the lack of that voltage represents the "off" condition. The broadband coaxial cable is frequency-division multiplexed, providing up to 30 channels on a single cable.

Baseband technology. Baseband transmission is similar to the transmission system used in data communications applications. Information is encoded as a digital signal. It is transmitted directly with only one signal present on the medium that occupies the entire cable bandwidth. The baseband signal is cast onto the cable in both directions, away from the sending device.

FIGURE 8–10
The Star Network

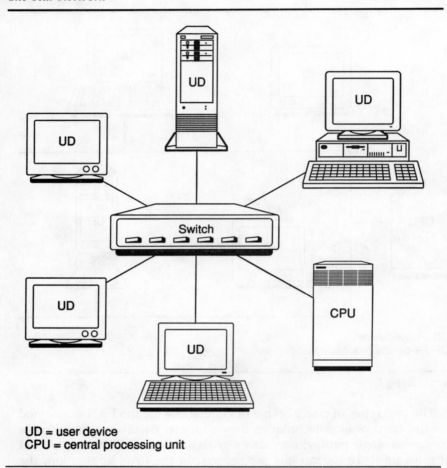

UD = user device
CPU = central processing unit

The baseband cable is more expensive than the broadband, depending on the type of cable used. It may require conduit to comply with fire regulations and cannot extend beyond a few thousand feet without expensive digital repeaters.

Baseband cable is easy to install and requires almost no maintenance. The addition of devices is also an inexpensive task.

Broadband technology. Broadband coaxial cable carries many signals at the same time, each using a different frequency channel on the medium. The signals are always analog: i.e., bits of information are represented by variations in the strength or frequency of a carrier signal. The data channels of a broadband LAN can also share the same cable with other analog signals operating at different frequencies. The broadband signal is transmitted in one direction only, due to the nature of the coupling and amplifying hardware necessary to carry the radio frequency signal. To enable a device to send and to receive unidirectional signals, two techniques are utilized. In the one most commonly used, the originating device sends signals on a specific frequency to a frequency translator at the "head end" of the cable. This frequency translator resends the signal at a higher frequency. In this manner, signals in one direction cannot interfere with signals in the other direction. Broadband cables of this type are *midsplit;* half of the cable is used for traffic in one direction and the other half is used for traffic in the opposite direction. If the system is designed to carry a large load of video traffic, it is *subsplit.*

The other method for handling unidirectional traffic is to install dual parallel cables. The cable is looped at the head end so that it connects with each device twice. In this type of system, each device has a transmitter on one of the cables and a receiver on the other. This enables the devices to send and receive on the same frequency, effectively doubling the number of channels available. On the minus side, the amount of cable required is doubled.

Another feature that increases the cost of the broadband cable is the need for modems to propagate the digital signal on the analog radiofrequency channels. A broadband data network requires careful physical design. Its elements must be accurately tuned to operate on the specific frequencies, and a staff of trained radio frequency technicians is required for design and maintenance. The cable and hardware elements are sensitive to environmental changes.

Broadband networks operate most effectively in large applications where the cost of additional expertise and maintenance can be justified. The networks can be used in large campus configurations and carry voice and video traffic as well as data.

Hybrid technology. One of the more recent innovations of the LAN is the hybrid baseband and broadband system. In this system, a broadband trunk is used to carry data along several local baseband subnetworks. This type of network can also carry local video conferencing along with the data traffic. By limiting the number of elements to be maintained on the broadband portion, the hybrid system takes advantage of the best features of both technologies. It utilizes the baseband's superior data-handling capability and the broadband's flexibility for voice and video handling.

Fiber optic cable. Copper corrodes, glass does not. Copper conducts electricity, glass does not. Copper is expensive, glass (silicon) is one of the earth's most abundant substances. Although fiber optics are costly, they hold the most potential for LANs. As the newest medium in the LAN market, fiber optic cable is the most limited.

Fiber optic transmission is limited to a single band per cable, which means that it is limited to baseband technology. Experimentation indicates that eventually the fiber optic cable will carry a bandwidth many times that of the present community antenna television (CATV) cable. However, it has many known features that make its use in a LAN difficult.

Fiber optic cable is difficult to tap because each fiber must be aligned with hundreds or thousands of others to ensure a continuous connection. New technology is simplifying the connection problem and may simplify it further.

As fiber optic cable experiences extensive use in telephone applications, it will become less expensive, and technology will progress so it will reach its potential.

LAN Access Methods

The *access method* is a feature of the LAN that enables the connected devices to transmit information over the communication facility. Without some form of control, messages would be pumped into the network haphazardly, with little chance of reaching their destination in a readable condition. The access method imposes some form of control over the connected devices, enabling them to transmit their messages and ensuring that a message en route will not be interrupted or garbled.

Historically, access to networks has been controlled by a busy tone when occupied, similar to the telephone busy signal, or control of the network has been vested in some central site. In old computer networks, the central processor or its communication front end polled the on-line devices and requested their transmissions. This method was necessary because the on-line devices were not very bright; they were capable of recognizing their own identification code and little more. With the arrival of more intelligent devices, distributed access methods became possible and enabled each device to participate in controlling the network.

Two classes of distributed access are *contention* (or random) access and *deterministic* access. With the contention access method, any device is able to initiate transmission at any time. The deterministic method of access requires each device to wait its turn.

Contention access. The contention access method is a technique of random access to the LAN where a number of devices transmit and receive traffic on a shared single main channel.

Carrier sense multiple access (CSMA). In a CSMA network, a broadcast technique is used that enables all the connected devices to sense the traffic on the network. When one of the devices desires access to the network, it listens on the main data channel to sense activity, which it recognizes as traffic. If it senses traffic, it delays its transmission for a random interval and then listens again. When the device fails to sense traffic, it accesses the channel and transmits its message.

CSMA/Collision detection (CD). A problem with the CSMA network is the time wasted sending a message into collision (when two devices listen, hear no traffic, and simultaneously generate messages). This time can be recaptured partially by designing the devices to listen for other traffic while they are transmitting. They need to listen for that period of time at the start of transmission equal to the propagation delay of the cable. Collisions can occur only during the time it takes the message to reach to the farthest device. The feature that enables the device to detect the collision supports a network called CSMA/CD, to indicate the addition of collision detection (CD).

CSMA/CA. Another technique used to control the devices on a CSMA network is a feature called collision avoidance (CA). In this scheme, a priority system is engineered into the network and directs a transmitting device that detects other traffic. It continues transmitting if the contending device is of lower priority, or ceases transmission if the contending device is of a higher priority. An example would be a simple system where the device would cease transmission if the contending device was to its left, and continue transmission if the contending device was to its right (left being upstream to the head end). A disadvantage to all CSMA networks is that as the traffic volume increases, the number of potential collisions increases, and access to the network is delayed.

Deterministic access. A ring network, where a physical sequence of devices closes upon itself, is one of the oldest local network topologies. In the ring, a device generating a message transmits the data to the next device in sequence. If this device is not the one to which the message is addressed, it retransmits the data to the next device in sequence. This process continues until the data arrives at the correctly addressed device. That device copies the information into a buffer, marks it as received, and transmits it to the next device in sequence.

Eventually, the message is received by the station that originated it. Upon determining that the message was received in order, it removes the message from the network. The time consumed in the message's trip around the ring, including a 1-bit delay at each device and normal network propagation delay, is called *walk time*.

There are a number of schemes that manage the right to transmit on a ring network. Two of the most popular are the *token ring* and the *slotted ring*.

Token passing access method.   In one of the most widely used access methods, a packet is marked IN USE by one of the leading bits in a section called the token. A device that has traffic to transmit, monitors it on the network until it detects a token that is identified as AVAILABLE FOR USE. It sets the bit in the token to the IN USE state and enters its traffic. A frame-check sequence at the end of the packet of information enables the receiving device to ensure the accuracy of what it has received. Upon retransmission, the destination station inserts one bit at the end of the packet to indicate that the message was received correctly. Upon receipt of the original message, the originating device checks the end of the packet to ensure proper receipt of the destination device. In the event that the message was not received properly, it is repeated. Figure 8–11 depicts the operation of a token passing network.

Slotted access method.   The slotted access method is used exclusively on ring networks. It is a deterministic access method similar to the token passing. However, instead of circulating a token, the devices transmit an empty data frame, which a device may fill upon receipt in its turn. The slotted access method is more deterministic than the token passing access method, because the technique not only dictates which device can have access to the network, but also dictates the size of the message that can be transmitted.

TELECOMMUNICATIONS AND NETWORK SECURITY

Teleprocessing systems comprise the following five basic elements:

1. Personnel.
2. Data and databases.

FIGURE 8–11

The Token Passing Network

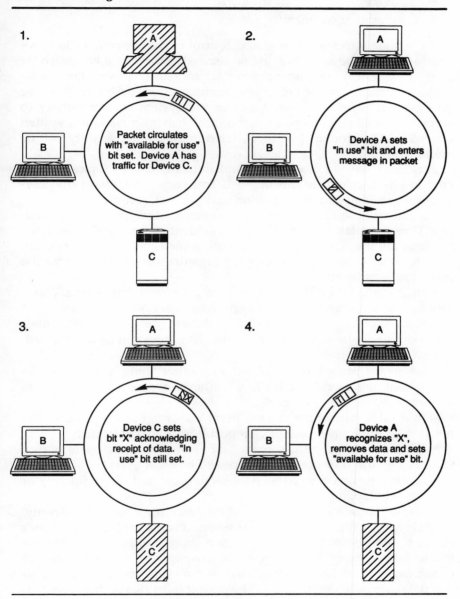

1. Packet circulates with "available for use" bit set. Device A has traffic for Device C.

2. Device A sets "in use" bit and enters message in packet

3. Device C sets bit "X" acknowledging receipt of data. "In use" bit still set.

4. Device A recognizes "X", removes data and sets "available for use" bit.

3. Hardware.

4. Software.

5. Communication links.

To provide effective security and control of the communication process, all of the above areas must be secured. If adequate hardware security is installed, but no software security mechanisms are implemented, security for the entire telecommunications system will not be possible. Likewise, if those who use the system do not adhere to security policies (such as password control, leaving a password written on notes lying around the office), telecommunication security will be ineffective.

Personnel, hardware, database, and software security topics are covered in other sections of this manual. This section addresses considerations regarding telecommunication and network security.

As network use and technology increase, so does the need for security. Threats to data security that were evident in the stand-alone environment are multiplied when a network is installed. LAN systems are used to handle sensitive data in many organizations. LANs present the following security concerns:

• In a number of LAN topologies (configurations), information that is sent by one user can be read by every other user on that network.

• Most LANs transmit through digital messages. These digital messages can easily be read by a computer. Messages can be intercepted, altered, and then forwarded.

• LANs are being interconnected with other "long haul" networks throughout the world. In turn, unauthorized access to the system increases.

• In a LAN environment, new users may forget to sign off of the network or to remove a sensitive report from a shared printer.

• File servers and print servers that service multiple users reduce security because they are readily accessed by most users.

• LANs are subject to passive (observe only) and active (modify or destroy) wiretapping.

Some organizations, because of their concern for network security, have stopped using LANs. Others disconnect some or all of the network access to the system prior to application processing. In many governmental high-security operations, any microcomputer that is attached to a mainframe must have its hard-disk and diskette drives removed so that data cannot be downloaded. The printer must also be disconnected.

The functions and complexity of telecommunication have frequently been understood in detail only by those who specialized in the area and have the responsibility for the operations of the communication network. However, end users are now becoming more familiar with techniques used in the network, and many attempt to reach files or to use functions that are not intended for their use. Therefore, telecommunications is a critical area for an organization, not only to maintain the integrity of the data in the files, but also to limit the possibilities of theft of assets or services, intrusion with intent to defraud, or disastrous damage. Security measures should be taken at all levels, from locks and guards to system and program measures.

Of course, a data network analysis can be handled in technical detail with the appropriate tests and calculations. Management's concern, however, is to determine if such an analysis has been made by the technical personnel, and if the factors have been considered appropriately. Management must be assured that its staff is aware of the data volume and network cost in detail and has considered the reasonable alternatives. The size, usage, and structure of a communication system is critical to the degree of security control that must be used.

Items needed to review telecommunication and network security include the configuration and topology of the telecommunication network, the type of transmission media used, and a detailed list of the communication hardware. Information about usage of the telecommunication network, including origin and destination of locations, frequency and times of calls, and average and peak data rates, is also important. Finally, a security review should assess the applications for which telecommunication facilities are used, the public service used for communication, reports on reliability experience, and the security measures that have been taken.

LAN Security

The first problem associated with security for LANs relates to the nature of the devices networked.[2] Among the devices being networked are general purpose computers. Most people refer to them as microcomputers or personal computers (PCs), but they are, in fact, powerful computers that grow in sophistication every day. A LAN is a collection of these computers that exchange data at high speeds.

---

[2]The information contained in this section has been extracted from "How To Secure Your Department's Local Area Network," by W. Mark Goode, president of Micronyx, Inc. Micronyx specializes in communication and network security products. Micronyx is located at 1901 N. Central Expressway, Richardson, Texas 86080, (214) 690-0595.

Goode used *Trusted Network Interpretation*, also called "The Red Book," by the U.S. Department of Defense, as a basis for his paper.

Each microcomputer is a gateway to that network. As a gateway, it is a point of entry and a point of exit. Users can move information into the network, move it around the network, and move it out of the network. But the microcomputer is a gateway to more than just the LAN. Merely adding a modem and a communication software program like Crosstalk XVI transforms a micro into a gateway to other networks. Many of these networks are unsecured and public, with no protection for information. In almost every case, these micros are electronically unmanageable gateways to a variety of computing networks and systems.

The second problem associated with LAN security relates to the movement of data between the microcomputer and the file server. The data moves unprotected as clear text along the cables and wires. This unprotected information is wide open to interception from unwelcome eavesdroppers. The problem grows worse as LANs are linked together by microwave transmission or inexpensive dial-up facilities. Few organizations use any kind of encryption technology to protect the information.

The third problem relates to the interconnectivity of LANs with existing secure computing systems. In an environment dominated by the quest for interoperability, some departments and agencies are connecting micros and LANs to systems designated as secure. As pointed out in the "Red Book," the interconnectivity of systems with different levels of security presents serious security problems. One of these problems is the cascading problem. For instance, if you connect the LAN to BLACKER (a Department of Defense secure network), then data can migrate from BLACKER's secure network to the unsecured environment of a LAN. Once in the LAN environment, the data can be easily compromised. Worse, any microcomputer on that LAN with a modem added to it can push the classified data out of the secure environment into a public, switched network.

A fourth problem relating to LAN security is that of environment-oriented security systems compared with object-oriented security systems. These are the two basic approaches to securing data. In an object-oriented system, the security information resides in the objects, or files, and travels with them.

Built-in LAN security systems are environment-oriented. In an environment-oriented system, the LAN control program is enhanced to include features that control access to the data. This access control system is effective only if the data never leave the file server. However, data leave continually: they are always processed by the micros' CPU on the network. Once the data are in the CPU, the user can move the data to a location other than the file server.

A practical example will illustrate the problem. Assume that the LAN has a sophisticated control program that can protect a file from being altered (READ-ONLY PERMISSION). On the file server, user X has stored a Lotus worksheet in a subdirectory and allows READ-ONLY PERMISSION to other users. User Y now logs onto the network, brings the Lotus worksheet into his microcomputer's memory and saves it to his local hard or floppy disk. When that Lotus worksheet is stored on his local device, none of the file protection is present. The microcomputers' local storage devices are beyond the control of the LAN protection system because the data has left the environment where it was protected.

Solving the problem.   Solving the LAN security problem is not easy. It requires the use of technology that integrates easily with installed systems and that does not interfere with the user. Network security solutions include: security kernels, environment and object orientations, and encryption.

Security kernels.   As with personal computers, the LAN needs a security kernel. The Department of Defense "Red Book" states that this can be achieved in several ways, but the result is called a Network Trusted Computing Base (NTCB). The NTCB operates the same as a TCB on a computer system: it mediates the attempts by people to get access to information. On a network, this has to be done in a way that includes the microcomputer. The micro is a general-purpose computer in need of the same level of security as the LAN control program. Both the micro and the LAN TCBs must work together to govern access to data. If these TCBs do work together, the result is a NTCB. Or, if the TCBs communicate with one another, kernel-to-kernel communication results.

To illustrate this, go back to the previous example. Suppose there were TCBs on all the micros on the LAN and user Y accesses the Lotus spreadsheet. Depending on how user Y's TCB is configured, he may not be able to use his local disk drives to store anything when he is using the LAN. He would be prevented from modifying or updating the spreadsheet. The Department of Defense calls this resource access control, and it is vital in a networked environment.

Environment and object orientation.   The problem of environment-oriented security systems was mentioned earlier. It was stated that this protection technique was effective only if the data never left the control of the LAN control program. This almost never happened. The only effective alternative is an object-oriented approach to security that places the access control information in a label that travels with the object, in this case, a file.

Because the data is constantly moving in the LAN, the access rules must travel with the file. That concept requires that each data file be labeled at the time of its creation with the access rules stored within the file. Regardless of where the data travels, the rules governing access move with the file. In a LAN environment where data moves from CPU to CPU, the data is fully protected. If the data ever leaves the LAN, it is still protected.

Encryption. Encryption needs to be integrated within a network to secure communication between networked CPUs. In its most elegant form, encryption would occur at the application level of a system, would require no intervention by the user, and would effectively secure the data within the computer and on the network.

Consider a typical LAN installation. As the data leaves a micro and heads back to the file server, it is moving in an unprotected state (clear text). Anyone can monitor the LAN cables and intercept the data.

However, if the data was encrypted as it left the CPU, then monitoring would have no impact on the integrity of confidentiality of the data. Well-designed systems will use a multikey system, manage all the keys, and handle all encryption and decryption with the operating system of the micro. Equally important, none of the encryption will affect the control program of the LAN.

The file-access labels added to every file are not protected against attack. There is no need to purchase separate encryption modems for local or remotely attached micros: the encryption is built into the operating system.

The solution. Look for solutions that are complementary to the LAN system. Any micro security solution that is evaluated should work with the LAN. It should not be an environmentally dependent solution. If the solution does not protect the data as it leaves the micro, duplication of effort will result. Management of the micro's security domain and the LAN's security system has to be done.

Determine if the vendor is working to integrate solutions so that the LAN security system and the micro security solution will converge.

Ultimately, the solutions should migrate into a single, comprehensive strategy. A system that provides central-site administration to all micros secured on the LAN is desired.

Users have little desire to master the complexities of securing micros and LANs. Most would prefer that the security system be invisible to them. They do not want to see it, know about it, or run into it. And, if they do run into it, they want to know why there is a problem and then go about their work.

There is one exception. Many users have a growing concern about the privacy of their work. Most would like a simple tool to keep other people, who have no need to know, out of their files. They want to assert their right to own their information. Their data is a form of intellectual property in need of protection. They want to control *who* can look at the data and *where* it can be examined or used. A well-designed system will provide this facility with as few as one command.

Network Security Vulnerabilities

The network topologies and transmission media are susceptible to a number of threats and vulnerabilities. As illustrated in Figure 8–12 and Figure 8–13, the networks are most vulnerable to active or passive wiretaps.

System Access Control

A careful study of the IBM Personal Computer product family (and compatibles) will show that the products were not designed to meet security concerns now widespread in public and private sectors.[3] Also, these products ignore many of the issues raised by EDP auditors and DP professionals. Microcomputers are now network-attached, compounding these problems. This raises another set of problems. It is not hard to see why many security professionals are concerned about having micros in their organizations.

There are three aspects of access control that can be implemented on the personal computer:

---

[3]Information presented in this section has been extracted from "The Executive's Guide to Workstation Management and Data Security," published by Micronyx Inc., pp. 32–35.

FIGURE 8–12
Network Topology Vulnerabilities

Topology	Vulnerability
Ring network A ring network is circular in shape. Information packets are routed in one direction.	• All messages are received by all devices on the network. • Wiretap.
Linear bus and tree networks User devices are attached to the transmission medium by taps along a single length of cable that can be extended at one end.	• Pulling out the "T" connector causes the network to go down. • Wiretap.
Star network Each device is connected to a central switch.	• The major weakness of this type of network is the reliance upon control from a central point that is vulnerable to failure. • Wiretap.

FIGURE 8–13
Transmission Media Vulnerabilities

Transmission Media	Vulnerability
Twisted copper pair Most common is telephone cable.	• Interface noise from office equipment. • Wiretap.
Coaxial cable Most widely used in the LAN. There are three types: baseband, broadband, and hybrid.	• "T" connector taps are possible.
Fiber optic cable A fiber optic system consists of a transmitter that converts digital signals into light energy, an optical fiber carrier line, and a receiver that converts light back to a digital format.	• Fiber taps. Taps may be inserted at a legitimate splice: for example, one technique is similar to that used to align fiber during splicing. Taps may also be done at bends where signal leakage can be sensed by highly sensitive photodetectors. A signal booster can reinsert the signal at the outgoing bend side of the tap. Because phone companies routinely use devices to tap and monitor fiber lines, the technology exists for secret surveillance.

1. Implementing control of access to the system.
2. Implementing control of access to specific files.
3. Implementing control of access to the specific hardware components and network.

These layers of access control are like nested, concentric layers. Peel
away one layer and another level access control is presented. The central
design challenge on workstations (micros or PCs) is to implement access
control that is unobtrusive but secure. Once the system has verified that
a user should have access to something, there should be no barriers to
his entry. Figure 8–14 illustrates the hallway that allows swift passage to
the data for a valid user.

The first challenge this subsystem faces is controlling access to the
workstation. It is vital that this is done before DOS starts. This is critical
because DOS is a single-state operating system. Once loaded, the user
can command complete control of the computer. In Triad Plus, end-user
identification and authentication occur after power to the system has
been applied, but before the operating system is loaded. (Triad Plus is a
Micronyx network security product. This discussion does not endorse
any specific products.)

Identifying the user and authenticating the identification present
their own challenges. With Triad Plus, two forms of identification are
required before the system can validate a user. The first identification
requires a password. The workstation administrator can require this
password to be a minimum length. He can also specify the lifetime of the
password, so that once it has expired, the user must update the password before proceeding. All password management is automatic and
does not require the intervention of the workstation administrator.

The token plays an important role in end-user identification and
authentication. The token is the repository for the user's password as
well as the password's date of creation and date of expiration. As a
consequence, there is no password database on the system that can be
compromised. The token is a battery-backed storage device that implements a security protocol when communicating with the Triad Plus
token, and only a valid security process can initiate that feature. Should
a user forget his or her password, the workstation administrator is provided a utility allowing him or her to read the token contents. Should a
user lose his or her token, the workstation administrator can create
another one.

The entire process of end-user identification and authentication is a
closed-loop series. The user has three attempts to present the correct
information to the system before a penalty is incurred. After three incorrect attempts, the workstation administrator can force the system to

FIGURE 8–14
Three Levels of Access Control

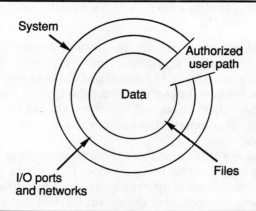

lock up for a preprogrammed period of time. This time period can be from 1 to 99 minutes and is designed to prevent a high-speed hacker attack. The fifth failed attempt produces a similar lockout. The sixth failed attempt invokes an audible alarm that sounds for a preprogrammed duration. All subsequent log-on failures produce the same condition. Turning the micro off will not break the cycle. Rather, Triad Plus stores the last state of the machine and restores it when power is again applied, up to five years later in an extreme case. The only way to defeat this process is to remove the Triad Plus system from the computer, a perilous choice that will be examined later. Figure 8–15 illustrates the lockout and alarm process.

Some may consider this process an unnecessary burden. However, a valid user can pass through this gateway in less than 15 seconds. It is vital that the system knows who is using the computer, because this information is used to make other resource decisions later on. It is also critical that everyone be identified because security professionals have discovered that the insider threat is the most harmful.

Input/Output and Network Access Control

Once the system knows who is using the computer, other resource decisions can be made. One aspect of personal computing that is different from a mainframe work relates to input/output (I/O) and network resources. In a mainframe computer, everything that occurs under pro-

FIGURE 8–15
Closed-Loop Log-on System

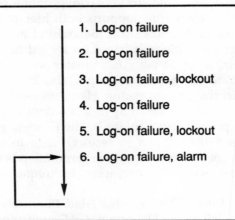

1. Log-on failure
2. Log-on failure
3. Log-on failure, lockout
4. Log-on failure
5. Log-on failure, lockout
6. Log-on failure, alarm

gram control must make use of the operating system. If a user or application wants to make use of a disk drive or communication subsystem, he or she requests it from the operating system. It is easy to see how security controls can be implemented in this environment: secure the operating system, and the entire computer can be secured.

Personal computers, particularly the IBM PC and derivatives, are not as well-behaved. Many application programs, rather than use the operating system to request system resources, simply "grab" the resources without the knowledge of the operating system. As a consequence, these programs can be fast. Securing these computers is more complex. Any security system for the microcomputer that simply watches DOS or monitors operating-system activity will miss important security violations. The security system must watch hardware devices and remove them from the control of DOS as well as applications if a security threat is present.

Triad Plus implements a form of I/O and network gateway control through what is known as the Device Access Permissions and Access State tables. This approach is modeled after the Department of Defense recommendations and allows the workstation administrator to control what I/O and network gateway resources are available to a user. These access states vary by user and allow the workstation administrator to reconfigure the micro's hardware depending on the user's classification. The information on the user's access state is stored in the token and is presented to the system after the user has been validated. All of this occurs before DOS loads, so that after the operating system starts, Triad

Plus tells DOS what resources are and are not available for that user during that session. Figure 8–16 illustrates the Device tables that are used in the workstation administrator's configuration program.

This access-control technique supports both hierarchical and nonhierarchical access methodologies. In a hierarchical access-control environment, access to data objects is based on a rigid hierarchy of access authority. For example, a manager has greater access authority than a clerk. The nonhierarchical access technique (also known as domains of access) is found in the private sector. Here, access to data objects is determined not so much by hierarchy as it is a domain of authority. An example from the private sector might be the following: the vice president of finance is denied access to research data in the engineering department in spite of his rank within the corporation because he has no need to know. These two contrasting access techniques are illustrated in Figure 8–17.

All of this is enforced through the Triad Plus Reference Monitor/Inhibitor (RMI). Modeled after Department of Defense specifications, the RMI checks all system activity to determine whether a process is valid for a particular user and data object. If it is not, the process is stopped. If it

FIGURE 8–16
Device Access Permissions Table and Access State Table

DEVICE ACCESS PERMISSIONS									USER ACCESS PERMISSIONS		
Hierarchy: ON		ACCESS STATES							Access state for:		Hierarchy: ON
	1	2	3	4	5	6	7	8	Unclassified 1		
									Confidential 2		
Diskette Read	Y	Y	Y	Y	Y	Y	Y	Y	Secret 3		
Diskette Write	N	N	Y	Y	Y	Y	Y	Y			
Hard Disk 0 Read	N	Y	Y	Y	Y	Y	Y	Y			
Hard Disk 0 Write	N	Y	Y	Y	Y	Y	Y	Y			
Hard Disk 1 Read	N	Y	Y	Y	Y	Y	Y	Y			
Hard Disk 1 Write	N	Y	Y	Y	Y	Y	Y	Y			
Parallel R/W	N	Y	Y	Y	Y	Y	Y	Y			
Async Comm R/W	Y	Y	Y	Y	Y	Y	Y	Y			
Bisync Comm R/W	N	N	Y	Y	Y	Y	Y	Y			
SDLC R/W	N	N	Y	Y	Y	Y	Y	Y			
Network R/W	N	N	Y	Y	Y	Y	Y	Y			
DCA IRMA Comm R/W	N	N	Y	Y	Y	Y	Y	Y			
ARCNET R/W	N	N	Y	Y	Y	Y	Y	Y			
Exit & Save: Press End & Return									Exit & Save: Press End & Return		
HELP? press F1 Quit? Press Esc									HELP? press F1 Quit? Press Esc		
PGDN to USER ACCESS PERMISSIONS									PGDN to DEVICE ACCESS PERMISSIONS		

© Micronyx, Inc. 1987

FIGURE 8–17
Hierarchical and Nonhierarchical Access Control

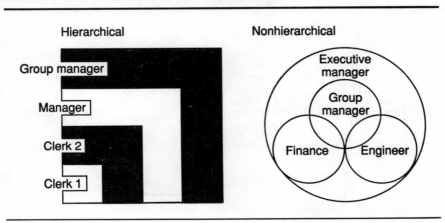

is, the process is allowed to continue. Figure 8–18 illustrates the RMI in action. The only time a user knows that a security system is present is when a violation occurs. Then, a message flashes to the screen notifying him or her that violation has occurred. A record of that violation is also made.

File Access Control

It may be necessary, for higher security-risk applications, to control who has access to database files. This function is usually performed by the workstation or network manager. The analysis of who can have access to which files can be a time-consuming task, especially in network-oriented systems with many users and multiple database files. Each user must be reviewed for every file in the system.

The file access and device access capabilities that should be considered include the following:

- Directory access.
- Subdirectory access.
- File access.
- File open/close.
- File create.
- File delete.
- File search.
- Record modify.
- Record delete.
- Record add.
- Diskette read/write.
- Hard Disk/write.
- Parallel read/write.
- Async comm read/write.
- Bisync comm read/write.
- Network read/write.

FIGURE 8–18
Reference Monitor/Inhibitor

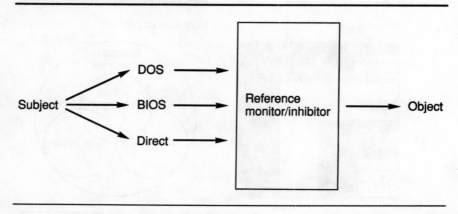

Figure 8–19 is a simplified worksheet that can be used to assist the network security planner in assigning file access permission levels. The first step is to identify all of the applications and files on the system and to assign a risk value to each. The second step is to identify all network users and assign a security level based on job function and need to know, or need to see database information. The reason for access should also be noted.

Hardware Security

Five security considerations regarding network hardware components are given below.

1. Some installations may desire to have the network file server secured in a locked room. The file server should not be used as a workstation. The keyboard should also be disconnected or locked.

2. Use a removable backup storage device that can be removed from the system and secured when not in use.

3. Use a "router" to transmit sensitive information to the correct user. A router is a dedicated microprocessor that transmits messages between workstations. It passes to other LANs only information that is properly addressed.

4. Modems should not be connected to workstations unless they are absolutely necessary.

5. Keep microcomputer start-up diskettes in a secure place.

FIGURE 8-19
File Access Control Worksheet

Name _____

Dept. _____

Dates _____

Security Levels _____

Approved By: _____

Page _____ of _____

Item no.	Application	File	Risk H-High M-Med L-Low	File Read-only	File Read and write	Record Add	Record Update	Record Delete			Reason

Encryption Considerations

Encryption is a viable solution for network systems where high security is required. Before an encryption hardware and/or software package is purchased, however, a full needs-assessment study should be done. Most encryption packages or mechanisms result in system performance degradation because of the encryption algorithm process. Other considerations concerning encryption include the following:

• If any part of the encrypted file is damaged, even a single bit, the file may be unrecoverable.

• Encryption may be beneficial for highly sensitive data on a disk where many users have access.

• Encryption can be used in conjunction with word processing for securing highly sensitive data.

More information on encryption is included later in this chapter.

Communication and Network Security Checklists

Figures 8–20 through 8–26 are checklists that provide an introduction to many of the security analysis aspects of communication and network systems. They can be used as a screening mechanism to review the security measures that are in place or under consideration. Negative responses do not necessarily indicate a security problem; they simply indicate areas that should be investigated further.

ENCRYPTION

Within the last decade, there has been a vast increase in the accumulation and communication of digital computer data in the private and public sectors. Much of this information has a significant value, directly or indirectly, and requires protection. Sensitive information concerning individuals, organizations, and corporate entities is collected by federal agencies in accordance with statutory requirements and is processed in computer systems. This information requires some type of protection, and cryptographic protection may be specified by the authority responsible for the data. The National Bureau of Standards Data Encryption Standard (DES) must be employed when cryptographic protection is required for unclassified federal Automated Data Processing (ADP) data. The DES Modes of Operation Standard defines the methods or modes where the DES may be implemented.

FIGURE 8–20
General Data Communications Security Considerations

No.	Item	Yes	No	N/A	Comments
			Responses		
1.	Is there a configuration chart showing:				
	a. the location of micros?	—	—	—	
	b. the number of lines?	—	—	—	
	c. the types of lines?	—	—	—	
	d. the location of modems?	—	—	—	
	e. the types of modems (by manufacturer/model)?	—	—	—	
	f. the distances of lines?	—	—	—	
	g. the branches of the main lines?	—	—	—	
	h. locally developed software?	—	—	—	
2.	Is there a written procedure for what to do in case of an emergency for:				
	a. lines?	—	—	—	
	b. modems?	—	—	—	
	c. micros?	—	—	—	
3.	Are personnel trained for emergency procedures in information services?	—	—	—	
4.	Are lines switchable in case one or more of them are down?				
	a. Automatically?	—	—	—	
	b. Manually?	—	—	—	
5.	Has the scattering and loss of source documents been discussed with the auditors?	—	—	—	
6.	Has consideration been given to audit trails?	—	—	—	
7.	Are the telecommunication systems critical enough to warrant the use of a multiprocessor environment?	—	—	—	
8.	Are specific micros designated as security computers?	—	—	—	
9.	Do any of the security computers operate in the unattended mode at any time?	—	—	—	

FIGURE 8–20 *(continued)*

No.	Item	Yes	No	N/A	Comments
10.	Is secure teleprocessed information transmitted on leased or dedicated lines?	___	___	___	
11.	If secure teleprocessed information is on dial-up lines, are checks made on access to it?	___	___	___	
12.	Are identification codes, passwords, or key words used, including terminal ID and operator ID?	___	___	___	
13.	Are these codes changed frequently?	___	___	___	
14.	Is there documented control of these codes or other security features in the teleprocessing system?	___	___	___	
15.	Is access to the system restricted to certain levels of employees?	___	___	___	
16.	Are the computers locked when not in use?	___	___	___	
17.	Can master files be updated only from selected microcomputers?	___	___	___	
18.	Is sufficient audit-trail material retained in sensitive programs?	___	___	___	
19.	Is sufficient data retained to assure that nothing is lost during outages?	___	___	___	
20.	Can individual records be reconstructed if they are accidentally lost in sensitive programs?	___	___	___	
21.	Is there a computer response to check the input in systems that update files?	___	___	___	
22.	Are communication junction and terminal boxes locked?	___	___	___	
23.	Are junction and terminal boxes included in the periodic security survey?	___	___	___	
24.	Are security lines within buildings secured by conduit?	___	___	___	
25.	Are the building entrance points for communication lines checked periodically for illegal breaks?	___	___	___	

FIGURE 8–20 *(concluded)*

No.	Item	Yes	No	N/A	Comments
26.	Is the system wiring run clear of known sources of noise (e.g., rectifiers, medical equipment, heavy construction equipment, generators, etc.)?	—	—	—	
27.	Are all lines tested periodically to ascertain that they are good?	—	—	—	
28.	Are all lines tested periodically to ascertain that they are not tapped?	—	—	—	
29.	Are signal-strength tests performed on the lines routinely?	—	—	—	
30.	Are written backup procedures provided at all user sites?	—	—	—	
31.	Are the backup procedures periodically tested?	—	—	—	
32.	Has consideration been given to teleprocessing on a backup machine if the data center goes down?	—	—	—	
33.	Have the programs been tested on the primary and backup computer?	—	—	—	
34.	Is vital master information duplicated (e.g., routing lists)?	—	—	—	
35.	Which of the following techniques are utilized to guard against illegal access to storage or data files?				
	a. Table look-up.	—	—	—	
	b. Special labeling.	—	—	—	
	c. Passwords.	—	—	—	
	d. Program structure.	—	—	—	
	e. Complete memory lockout.	—	—	—	
36.	Is message release not possible without the message being complete?	—	—	—	
37.	Are updates to master files or other critical files controlled?	—	—	—	
38.	Are there programmed checks on the updating of files?	—	—	—	

FIGURE 8–21
Communication Access Control

		Responses			
No.	Item	Yes	No	N/A	Comments
1.	Are one or more of the following access controls provided?				
a.	Passwords (for logging on the micro-computer and to the mainframe).				
	— for sign-on.	___	___	___	
	— for menu system control.	___	___	___	
	— for "in-program\"	___	___	___	
	— for utility programs.	___	___	___	
	— for different applications (accounts receivable, accounts payable, payroll, R&D, etc.).	___	___	___	
	— for question-and-answer sequence (asks specific personal information).	___	___	___	
	— for private/personal.	___	___	___	
	— for a combination of the above (multilevel password schemes).	___	___	___	
b.	card-key access control.	___	___	___	
c.	locking mechanisms (for locking the micro).	___	___	___	
d.	access logs maintained on the micro-computer and on the equipment being accessed.	___	___	___	
2.	Do the access logs have the following information?				
a.	User ID.	___	___	___	
b.	Time/data logged on/off.	___	___	___	
c.	Jobs performed.	___	___	___	
d.	Records accessed.	___	___	___	
e.	Micro ID.	___	___	___	
f.	Record of invalid attempts.	___	___	___	
3.	Is cryptography used?	___	___	___	

FIGURE 8–22
Password, Log-on, and Related Items

No.	Item	Yes	No	N/A	Comments
		Responses			
1.	Are detection and prevention elements incorporated in the software design for data security?	___	___	___	
2.	Is access time provided for a user's response given an upper limit?	___	___	___	
3.	If so, what form of error message occurs?				
	a. A simple message to the user.	___	___	___	
	b. Sounding of an alarm.	___	___	___	
4.	Is such activity logged into the computer system's storage areas?	___	___	___	
5.	Does the log-on herald sequence only appear after proper credentials have been entered by the user?	___	___	___	
6.	Are passwords stored and transmitted in encrypted form only?	___	___	___	
7.	Are passwords optional to any particular local groups?	___	___	___	
8.	Can some groups be specified as INCOMING ONLY status?	___	___	___	
9.	Is there a protection scheme when access to a list of groups is requested by a user?	___	___	___	

FIGURE 8–23
Modems and Communication Links

No.	Item	Yes	No	N/A	Comments
		Responses			
	Does any modem unit or appropriate communication link incorporate the following features?				
1.	Capability for restricting *any* terminal to calling *only* the destinations AND applications you authorize.	___	___	___	
2.	Concealment (to prevent unauthorized use) of:				
	a. telephones.	___	___	___	
	b. passwords.	___	___	___	
	c. account numbers.	___	___	___	
	d. log-on codes.	___	___	___	

FIGURE 8–23 *(concluded)*

No.	Item	Yes	No	N/A	Comments
3.	Is error detection and correction integral to the communication link with selective retransmission of blocks found to contain errors?	—	—	—	
4.	Is scrambler/descrambler circuitry offered?	—	—	—	
5.	If so, is it an integral feature?	—	—	—	
6.	If modems have programmable parameters, can access to these parameters be controlled by a multilevel password scheme?	—	—	—	
7.	Are modems integral to each unit (terminal, workstation, or desktop computer)?	—	—	—	
8.	Can a modem be loaded dynamically with characteristics required by each user's applications, while maintaining the appropriate clearance level?	—	—	—	
9.	Can the modem provide user access to nonlocal application software, programs, or services? (Such gateway functions should be carefully monitored.)	—	—	—	
10.	Is an auto-dial feature present to minimize user-based dialing errors?	—	—	—	
11.	Is there protection circuitry for internal circuitry (e.g., if excessive source voltages and currents should appear on the transmission/telephone lines)?	—	—	—	
12.	Is dial-up/call-back (with dial-up modem) security provided:				
	a. with monitoring on a continual basis?	—	—	—	
	b. with transaction reporting (to printer, terminal, and/or computer), including:				
	— telephone call origination and termination lines?	—	—	—	
	— duration of call?	—	—	—	
	— supervisor access?	—	—	—	
	— other?	—	—	—	

FIGURE 8–24
LAN Security Considerations

No.	Item	Yes	No	N/A	Comments
			Responses		
1.	Are all network users identified and listed?	___	___	___	
2.	Are all network applications and files identified and listed?	___	___	___	
3.	Has it been determined how and what information will be shared?	___	___	___	
4.	Is it necessary to install separate LANs for sensitive data?	___	___	___	
5.	Are access rights based on need?	___	___	___	
6.	Is highly sensitive data stored on removable media?	___	___	___	
7.	Has a menu system been installed to regulate application access?	___	___	___	
8.	Are local drives secured or redirected to limit downloading?	___	___	___	
9.	Do users have access to the microcomputer operating system commands?	___	___	___	
10.	Have operating system commands been renamed (e.g., FORMAT) to prevent inadvertent erasure of files?	___	___	___	
11.	Has full-network access been assigned to:				
	a. network administrator?	___	___	___	
	b. backup network administrator?	___	___	___	
12.	Is encryption software/hardware available to the network users?	___	___	___	
13.	Is the network file server secured?	___	___	___	
14.	Are start-up diskettes secured when not in use?	___	___	___	
15.	Are modems disconnected from the micro and the LAN when not in use?	___	___	___	
16.	Are call-back devices required?	___	___	___	
17.	Are password policies implemented?	___	___	___	
18.	Are they controlled and monitored?	___	___	___	
19.	Does each user understand the importance of network security (security awareness)?	___	___	___	
20.	Does the secured file server have a removable backup storage device that can be removed from the system and secured when not in use?	___	___	___	
21.	Is a "router" used to transmit sensitive information?	___	___	___	

FIGURE 8–25
LAN Security Product Evaluator

No.	Characteristics to Be Considered	Product		
		A	B	C
1.	Is the product protected from being bypassed and disarmed?	—	—	—
2.	Is the product protected from device drivers loaded at power-up that can bypass the authorization check and disarm the security program?	—	—	—
3.	Is the encryption key hidden?	—	—	—
4.	Is the key inaccessible to DEBUG and similar programs?	—	—	—
5.	Do lockout combinations remain even when the system is turned off and back on?	—	—	—
6.	Is the product on the Department of Defense's Evaluated Product List?	—	—	—
7.	Does the maximum-security configuration allow the use of all devices, including diskette drives?	—	—	—
8.	Is the user's data deleted from temporary memory at log off?	—	—	—
9.	When a user deletes a file, is the data in the file automatically zeroed?	—	—	—
10.	Does the product protect against a trespasser's hacking even after log on?	—	—	—
11.	Does the product control I/O devices at all levels?	—	—	—
12.	Do violation alarms remain when the system is turned off and back on?	—	—	—
13.	Can file access be limited to:			
	a. a group?	—	—	—
	b. a machine?	—	—	—
	c. an organization?	—	—	—
	d. a combination of the above?	—	—	—
14.	Does the product have token-access capabilities?	—	—	—
15.	Is the password entered by the user hidden from any memory-resident program that could record it for unauthorized usage later on?	—	—	—
16.	Are files owned by different users protected when stored on floppy disks?	—	—	—
17.	Are hacking attempts recorded even if the hard disk is disabled?	—	—	—
18.	Is the product easy to install?	—	—	—
19.	Is it "transparent" to the user once he logs on?	—	—	—
20.	Can the product run on the LAN even if the micro is not equipped with a hard disk?	—	—	—
21.	Can the user suspend work in progress in a secured mode and return to it later?	—	—	—

FIGURE 8–26

Communications Backup

		Responses			
No.	Item	Yes	No	N/A	Comments
1.	Have the causes of short-term communication failures been determined on:				
	a. batch-processing communication systems?	___	___	___	
	b. on-line "real time" processing?	___	___	___	
	c. local communication networks?	___	___	___	
	d. remote communication networks?	___	___	___	
2.	Have the causes of long-term communication failures been determined on:				
	a. batch-processing communication systems?	___	___	___	
	b. on-line "real-time" processing?	___	___	___	
	c. local communication networks?	___	___	___	
	d. remote communication networks?	___	___	___	
3.	Have backup plans been made and tested in case of total, long-term failure of the communication system?	___	___	___	
4.	Does the backup communication system take into consideration:				
	a. mail?	___	___	___	
	b. radio communications?	___	___	___	
	c. manual procedures?	___	___	___	
	d. alternative networks?	___	___	___	
5.	Does the backup site contain communication capabilities similar to the primary site for:				
	a. hardware?	___	___	___	
	b. software?	___	___	___	
	c. communication utility service?	___	___	___	
	d. proper cables and connectors?	___	___	___	
6.	Is the communication system thoroughly documented?	___	___	___	
7.	Is a copy of the documentation stored at the backup site?	___	___	___	

FIGURE 8–26 *(concluded)*

No.	Item	Yes	No	N/A	Comments
8.	Depending on the critical nature of the communication system, have backups for the following been considered?				
a.	Microcomputers.	___	___	___	
b.	Multidrop lines.	___	___	___	
c.	Concentrators.	___	___	___	
d.	Modems.	___	___	___	
e.	Transmission control units.	___	___	___	
f.	Data sets.	___	___	___	
g.	Terminals.	___	___	___	
9.	Depending on the sensitivity of the information, have the following been taken into consideration?				
a.	Communication hardware security features.	___	___	___	
b.	Means of identifying the micro user.	___	___	___	
c.	Cryptographic devices.	___	___	___	
d.	Data scramblers.	___	___	___	
10.	Has the communication hardware at the backup site been tested?	___	___	___	
11.	Are there extra terminals, microcomputers, cables, etc., available for immediate replacement of bad equipment (hardware redundancy)?	___	___	___	
12.	Is the vendor support adequate?	___	___	___	
13.	Can the vendor supply extra hardware during an emergency?	___	___	___	
14.	Are the communication system's programs backed up?	___	___	___	
15.	Is a copy of the communication system's programs stored at the backup site?	___	___	___	
16.	Are the program copies current?	___	___	___	
17.	Have the program copies been tested?	___	___	___	
18.	Does the communication system's software:				
a.	recognize failures?	___	___	___	
b.	provide diagnostic messages?	___	___	___	
c.	allow for reassignment of terminals?	___	___	___	
d.	provide for message sending/ receiving capabilities?	___	___	___	
e.	provide adequate security?	___	___	___	
f.	monitor unauthorized access attempts?	___	___	___	
19.	Has permission been received to use the system's software on another company's computer for emergency backup?	___	___	___	

The rapid growth of computer data banks increases threats to personal privacy. Since data banks are often accessible from remote computer terminals, there is a threat of easy and unauthorized access to personal information from any place in the data communication system. Such information is scattered into remote locations, controlled under separate auspices, and physically or administratively protected. With a telecommunication network of computer systems, what was previously a laborious job of assembling comprehensive dossiers on individuals may become a simple task. Valuable and sensitive information requires protection against unauthorized disclosure and modification.

Encryption is a tool that may be used in data security applications. It is not a remedy. With improper implementation and use, data encryption may only provide an illusion of security. With inadequate understanding of encryption applications, data encryption could deter the use of other needed protection techniques. However, with proper management controls, adequate implementation specifications, and applicable usage guidelines, data encryption will not only aid in protecting data communication, but will provide protection for many specific data processing applications.

Understanding Data Encryption

Data encryption is a process used to hide the true meaning of data. Encryption is the process of transforming data or clear text copy into an unintelligible form called cipher. Reversing the process of encryption and transforming the cipher back into its original form is called decryption. Encryption and decryption constitute the science of cryptography as it is applied to the modern computer.

Data encryption is achieved through the use of an algorithm that transforms data from its intelligible form to cipher. An algorithm is a set of rules or steps for performing a desired operation. Electronic devices that efficiently perform the mathematical steps of the algorithm specified in the DES are described in these guidelines.

Cryptography (encryption and decryption) has historically been used to protect sensitive information during communication. It can be used for protecting computer data transmitted among terminals and computers or between computers. Data is encrypted before transmission and decrypted after it is received. The algorithm used to decrypt the received cipher must be the inverse of the algorithm used to encrypt the transmitted data. A device used to transmit and receive data contains algorithms for encryption and decryption.

Encryption can be used between data processing machines and data storage devices, such as magnetic tape and magnetic disk. In this application, the data is encrypted before it is written on the storage device and decrypted before it is read. Data is stored in its cipher form and transformed to clear text only when it is to be processed within the computer.

Encryption can be used to authenticate the identities of users, terminals, and computers of a data processing system. Passwords have been used to differentiate between friend and foe during times of war. Knowledge of the secret password was accepted as authenticating the identity of friends. The password was changed for each mission. The DES uses a key, similar to a password, which must be supplied to each group of users of the algorithm. Having the correct key authenticates an individual to a data processing system.

In a similar manner, a terminal or computer may be authenticated as an authorized device of a data processing system. Supplying the correct key to a DES device, when requested by the authorization system, can authenticate a terminal associated with the device. This authorization system may be a special program or a special computer system that has been established to control access to the resources and data of the overall system. The authorization system must be initialized with the authentication keys of all authorized users and devices of the system. Similar challenge-response password systems are currently in use for computer user authentication. When combined with data encryption technology, authorization systems can authenticate the claimed identities of users and devices without compromising the passwords or keys by transmitting them through the system.

The Decision to Use Data Encryption

Data encryption should be used whenever it is the most cost effective method available to protect the confidentiality or integrity of the data. *Confidentiality* relates to the accidental or intentional disclosure of data to an unauthorized individual. *Integrity* relates to data that has not been exposed to accidental or malicious alteration or destruction. Encryption of data prevents unauthorized recipients of the cipher from interpreting its meaning. Encryption can also prevent unauthorized individuals from manipulating the cipher in such a way that the original data is changed in a predetermined manner. Encryption must cost less than the expected loss (risk) that would occur if the protection were not provided, to be effective. Computation or estimation of cost and risk, and the decision to employ cryptographic protection, are management functions of the authority responsible for the data.

Data Encryption Standard

The Data Encryption Standard (DES) is needed to protect sensitive or valuable data within federal or other highly secure computer systems and networks. Data encryption techniques are needed for controlling access to sensitive data in multiuser computer systems, for protecting the integrity of transactions in national and international monetary transfer systems, for disguising sensitive data during transmission, and for authenticating the users and devices of distributed computer systems and networks. Thousands of different encryption algorithms would result in the fundamental incompatibility of data communication equipment. Research and development in cryptographic algorithms are difficult areas; redundant and unusable results often occur. The support of several standards would incur higher costs. The DES provides a basic method for more effective computer utilization and a high level of protection for computer data.

The need to interface with the data processing facilities of federal agencies may make it desirable for private organizations to have and use the DES. Since its adoption as a federal standard, the DES algorithm has been approved as a standard by the American National Standards Institute and recommended for use by the American Bankers Association.

An encryption algorithm must satisfy the following requirements in order to be acceptable as a federal standard:

- It must provide a high level of security.
- It must be completely specified and easy to understand.
- The security provided by the algorithm must not be based upon the secrecy of the algorithm.
- It must be available to all users and suppliers.
- It must be adaptable for use in diverse applications.
- It must be economical to implement in electronic devices and be efficient to use.
- It must be suitable to validation.
- It must be exportable.

The National Bureau of Standards has the responsibility for developing federal information processing standards through Public Law 89-306 and Executive Order 11717. The Institute for Computer Sciences and Technology has the responsibility within the bureau to recommend and coordinate standards and guidelines for improved computer utilization and information processing for the federal government, and to develop the technology needed to support the standard activities. Because of the unavailability of general cryptographic technology outside the national security arena, and because security provisions (including encryption) were needed in unclassified applications involving federal government computer systems, the bureau initiated a computer security program that involved the development of a standard for computer data encryption. Because federal standards impact the private sector, the bureau solicited the interest and cooperation of industry and user communities in this work.

The document discusses the algorithm that satisfied the requirements of a DES. It was developed by IBM, which made the specifications of the algorithm available to the bureau for publication as a Federal Information Processing Standard and provided nondiscriminatory and royalty-free licensing procedures for building electronic devices that implement the algorithm. At the request of the bureau, the National Security Agency conducted an exhaustive technical analysis of the DES. No shortcuts or secret solutions were found and, as a result, the agency confirmed the soundness of the DES's encryption principle and its suitability to protect unclassified data. The bureau published the algorithm as a federal standard, FIPS PUB 46, in January 1977.

How Encryption Reduces Security Threats

Encryption may be implemented in a computer system in order to combat possible threats to the security of computer data. These threats are categorized as *transmission* threats and *storage* threats. Security against these threats is generally termed *communication security* (COMSEC) or *file security* (FILESEC). The DES algorithm can be used in both applications, but the key will be handled differently. The generation, distribution, protection, and destruction of cryptographic keys are referred to as *key management*.

Transmission threats. Encryption can be used to prevent the disclosure of data and to detect the modification of transmitted data. Encryption will combat the threats of accidental or deliberate destruction. Encrypted data can be lost or destroyed as easily as unencrypted data. Adequate backup facilities or copies must be provided to recover from the destruction of either encrypted or unencrypted data. Destruction or loss of the key used to encrypt data is equivalent to the loss or destruction of the data. Threats that are countered with the encryption of transmitted data include spoofing, misrouting, passive wiretapping, and active wiretapping.

Spoofing is the threat of accepting a false claim of identity. Spoofing by a computer system penetrator is a serious threat at many points in a computer system. The computer's data communication system is especially vulnerable to spoofing. The identities of terminals, computers, and users can be simulated so that the receiving device cannot discern a true identity from a false identity. Data encryption can be used for authentication by requiring that a unique encryption key be associated with each identity. Successful communication using this key mutually authenticates the holders of the key (provided that the key has not been compromised) and prevents spoofing. If the key is not known, false messages cannot be correctly generated and entered into the system. Message spoofing is then prevented.

The threat of *misrouting* is directly proportional to the complexity of the communication system and inversely proportional to the reliability of its components. A simple message-indicator scheme, combined with encryption of the routing indicator, may be used to detect misrouting, but prevention can only be accomplished with dedicated lines and permanent connections. In any system (except geographically local systems) the prevention of misrouting is not economically feasible. Data encryption can prevent the unauthorized use of misrouted data, however.

Passive wiretapping is the monitoring of messages during data transmission that can occur along the transmission path in several ways. Wiretapping and radio reception of the transmitted data are the most common methods. The transmission is not delayed or altered, only monitored or copied. This threat is difficult to combat in any way other than physically protecting the transmission path or encrypting the data. Clear text is also vulnerable to monitoring because of radiation, conduction, and acoustic pickup during input and output operations. These threats are prevalent in high-voltage CRT terminals, electrically connected devices, and mechanical printing or punching devices. Encryption protects the clear text from disclosure. The encryption devices should be designed to be an integral part of the original source equipment and the final destination equipment whenever possible. The data encryption devices must be physically protected and designed to minimize electronic emanations.

Active wiretapping occurs when the communication line is broken, a high-speed receive transmitter is installed, and the intercepted data is retransmitted unchanged until a special "looked for" event causes the tapping mechanism to modify the data so false information is accepted as valid. Communication will be slightly delayed while the data is being modified, but this delay is often not detectable because other delays are already in the communication system. Encryption prevents the penetrator from intelligently modifying the cipher so that the decrypted clear text is readable and acceptable. Special precautions must be utilized to prevent the *playback* threat or the *substitution* threat. The playback threat consists of copying a valid encrypted message and playing it back (retransmitting it) to the unsuspecting receiver. If the key has not been changed, the receiver will correctly decrypt the message and may accept it. For certain types of messages (deposits, merchandise orders, etc.), this could have disastrous results. The substitution threat consists of replacing blocks or characters of cipher text with other blocks or characters without deciphering the data or having the key. The perpetrator substitutes the cipher of the known clear text. This can be accomplished in the block mode if each block is totally independent from all others, and no other block or message authentication system is used.

Storage threats.   In addition to combating threats to computer data security during transmission among terminals and computers, the DES may be used effectively for protecting computer data during storage, but the system implementation will be different in the following two cases:

1. In the transmission case, where the cryptographic key must be available at the two participating locations simultaneously and may be destroyed when that transmission is complete.

2. In the storage case, where the key needs to be at one location, but must be retained for reuse when the data is to be retrieved and used. The computer system or the user must be able to provide the key at the appropriate place and at the appropriate time.

Threats that are countered with the encryption of stored data are theft, residue, remanence, addressing failure. Encryption of stored computer data provides protection against the *theft* of data. Data may be stolen from on-line devices (disks, mass storage devices, etc.) by unauthorized access, or from off-line devices (magnetic tape, cards, disk packs, etc.) by physically removing the device and reading it on another computer system. In addition, if there is a threat of a computer data storage facility or a computer center being taken over by force, bulk encryption of all data using a common key that is easily erased from the encryption device effectively renders the data unreadable and unusable by destroying the key. This key must be kept in a physically secure location (safe, etc.) so that it may be reentered into the encryption device when the facility has been made secure again. User-controlled encryption of private data files renders the data unreadable to other system users.

Data that is left on magnetic media and not erased after it is no longer needed is called *residue*. Erasing computer data on magnetic storage media may be a time-consuming process. Overwriting data that is to be discarded in a shared system can use a significant amount of input and output time if done as standard practice. Data recovered by reading discarded data that was not destroyed is considered to be scavenged. If sensitive data is always stored on the media in an encrypted form, tapes and disk packs may be returned to their supplier when no longer needed or the "scratched" data tapes may be reused without erasing. Destroying the key precludes use of the data. System failures during the erasing of magnetic media are no longer a concern if the media are encrypted. Encryption of stored data with the user's private key obviates the need for clearing temporary storage after use.

Remanence is the magnetic flux remaining in a magnetic substance after the magnetic force has been removed. In some magnetic storage media, data stored for long periods of time on the media can remain at a lower signal-intensity level even after the media has been erased. Encryption of all sensitive data stored on such media removes this threat, and such storage media may be released for general usage rather than destroyed. For unclassified computer data, this is a very insignificant threat and encryption would not be justified for this reason alone.

Random-access magnetic storage media have a physical addressing mechanism that positions the data under the reading heads and transfers the data. Software data-access methods generally have a complex data structure associated with the stored data to optimize access to it. Both of these mechanisms have a small, but not zero, probability of *addressing failure*. Encrypting the data by combining the location of the data with the key can prevent accidental reading of the wrong data. Applications of this type in the system will depend greatly on the implementation of the DES device at the proper place in the system architecture.

Use of Cryptography for Security of Computer Data

Encryption transforms data into an unintelligible form, by the use of an algorithm and a key. Encrypted data can be decrypted (returned to its original form) only by using a companion algorithm and either the same key, in the case of a *secret* key system, or a companion key, in the case of a *public* key system. The key is a large secret number that effectively prevents decryption of the data by anyone who does not know the specific key.

Encryption is useful to protect computer data while it is being transferred between people or devices authorized to have the data or while it is inactive in storage. Encryption protects data from unauthorized disclosure, because anyone who does not know the correct key is unable to derive intelligible meaning from the encrypted data. Encryption allows even slight modification of encrypted data to be easily detected, because any modification of the encrypted data will result in gross and unpredictable distortions of the data in its decrypted form. Encryption does not protect the data from destruction; in fact, it increases the chances that the data may be destroyed or unavailable, because if the key is lost, the data encrypted with that key is lost forever.

The applications that need encryption are those that transmit highly confidential data on communication lines. Applications that transmit financial transactions or other critical data may also need encryption if someone is likely to derive enough benefit from modifying the data during transmission to compensate for the risk and the cost of the effort. Encryption of data in storage is an alternative that may be more cost-effective than other storage security controls, especially when appropriate support for encryption is readily available.

Encrypting computer communications. Encryption is the primary control to protect data from the hazards of communication systems. It can be used to forestall the consequences of electronic eavesdropping, intentional modification, misrouting, introduction of spurious messages, spoofing (falsifying the identity of the transmitter), and playback of old messages, and for the authentication of senders and receivers and the protection of acknowledgments that the message was received or not received correctly. The primary difficulties when using encryption for this purpose are to ensure that the encryption does not interfere with communication protocols and to guarantee that the correct key is available to all authorized recipients of a message and to no one else.

Encrypting off-line storage. Encryption of data on tapes and other off-line storage media is an effective way to protect the confidentiality of the data without having to maintain rigorous physical control over the data-storage media. Again, the primary problem is to ensure that the correct key will be available to decrypt the data when it is needed, and that it will not be known to anyone else. In general, the keys should not be stored on the computer because then they would be subject to all the hazards applicable to computer data.

Encrypting on-line files. Because encrypted data cannot be processed until it has been decrypted, encryption of frequently used data will not be efficient unless the encryption is supported by special features in hardware and the operating system.

For encryption of on-line data to be useful, the keys may have to be stored on-line. Even if the keys themselves are always encrypted, except when they are within the encryption device, it is necessary to verify the identity of anyone requesting a key, to determine whether he is authorized to have that key, to document the usage of a key, and to detect any variance in the usage of a key. The primary controls discussed previously will be necessary to protect the keys. Encryption can reduce the scope of the protection problem because it is no longer necessary to ensure rigorous control over those areas of computer storage that contain only encrypted data.

Management considerations. The cost of hardware that implements the encryption algorithm can be expected to decrease rapidly. As more experience is gained in the use of encryption, the cost of planning for its use and of managing the distribution of keys will also decrease. Before hardware implementations of the DES algorithm can be procured for federal use, manufacturers must obtain a certificate of validation for their product from the National Bureau of Standards.

If encryption is to be used at all, it should be used properly. A poorly planned use of encryption or a poor system for managing keys will give a false sense of security.

Cost Considerations

The cost of hardware and software encryption systems varies and is generally dependent on the type of system being protected (microcomputer or mainframe) and the number of secure nodes required in the system.

In a review of encryption system costs, the following should be considered:

- What is the value of the information to be protected?
- How long does it need to be secured (minutes, hours, days, or years)?

- What are the operational and overhead costs associated with a cryptographic system?
  - Installation expenses?
  - Hardware/software costs?
  - Personnel training costs?
  - Cost to change keys?
  - Package maintenance costs?

Cryptographic Hardware

Cryptographic hardware devices are currently available for microcomputers, minicomputers, and mainframe systems. The devices vary in size from the chip level to complete microprocessors. Many computer encryption devices plug into the RS-232-C port.

Cryptographic hardware device features may include the following:

- Operational characteristics that are configurable from the main computer location at any time.
- Dedicated devices—no throughput degradation.
- Security features that render the device inoperable for security breaches.
- On-line checkpoints that force users to periodically respond to prompts in order to maintain link operations.
- Dummy message traffic options for masking other traffic.
- RS-232-C standard interface.
- DES implementation (chip or circuit board).

Cryptographic Software

There are a number of cryptographic software packages on the market today that provide degrees of protection. Some cryptographic software packages encrypt data files for storage and for transmission over communication networks.

Most packages offer cryptographic routines that utilize the DES encryption method, transposition methods, and/or public key encryption. File-compression routines are also offered as part of some of the packages and can compress data storage files from 25 to 80 percent, depending on the package.

Other software package encryption modes include the following:

- *Binary.* Output is a file of randomized bit patterns.
- *EBCDIC.* Output is a file containing a subset of the EBCDIS character set.
- *FIELD.* Output is an exact image of the input file except that selected fields within the record are encrypted.

The U.S. National Bureau of Standards provides a testing facility for the verification of hardware implementation of DES and will certify hardware devices that successfully pass its tests. Software implementations are not currently certifiable, because software can be modified.

Chapter Nine

Audit and Control

Rapid growth of microcomputers has added a new challenge to the auditor's task. As the use of microcomputers increases, the need for control and audit of these computers also increases. The control issues in a microcomputer environment are described, and a detailed step-by-step procedure for auditing microcomputers is provided. The particular issues involved in auditing stand-alone microcomputers, auditing microcomputers used as terminals to mainframes, and auditing microcomputers in a distributed processing environment are reviewed, and checklists are supplied. Checklists are also provided to aid in defining risks and to show how to build an effective audit approach for reviewing specific control issues. The tools and techniques needed to audit a microcomputer environment are described. The concerns involved with data accuracy, data control, and data validation are reviewed.

THE CHALLENGE

A few years ago auditors were wondering how to establish and implement audit controls for the minicomputer. The super minis brought the power of the mainframe to the smaller business and also created enhanced processing in larger organizations through distributed data processing.

Now auditors are faced with a more difficult challenge—the microcomputer. Auditors who are working at establishing controls in the microcomputer area are running into the following problems:

- Microcomputer software packages do not have adequate accounting controls or audit trails.
- The small business with one micro does not have the time or money to spend on audit controls.
- Auditors are now not only faced with what controls to establish in the stand-alone micro environment, but also in the office automation environment of local area networks involving word processing, electronic mail, telemetry, message switching, and graphics.

- Networking exposes a more comprehensive technical threat in communications. Controls need to be established for networks that use cable, fiber optics, CATV, microwave, and satellite communications.
- Fewer people are required to run the micro, and this has resulted in some companies combining job responsibilities and effectively eliminating the separation-of-duties control mechanism.

The rapid growth of microcomputers has added a new challenge to the auditor's task. Most control and audit procedures have been designed for large-scale computers. The auditor attempting to review a microcomputer using the large-computer review methods will find many of the controls not applicable or uneconomical, and many of the audits ineffective.

The microcomputer poses some audit risks not present in a large computer site. For example, vendors normally provide good support for their large computer installations, but vendor support for the microcomputer may be minimal or nonexistent. Therefore, not only have the controls and audit procedures changed, but so have the risks.

The auditor needs to develop an audit approach that addresses the risks and controls of a microcomputer environment, and to use audit tools and techniques designed for that environment.

The audit processes described in this chapter include those for use with stand-alone microcomputers, microcomputers that are being used as terminals (terminal emulation mode), and microcomputers that are part of a distributed network or a distributed system. This chapter also addresses data control and data integrity issues.

AUDITING STAND-ALONE MICROCOMPUTERS

Microcomputers and Control

Many auditors assess a microcomputer site using the same approaches as when auditing larger computers. Unfortunately, these approaches may identify control problems that are not correctable. For example, in a large computer installation, a control principle is "do not let programmers into the computer room or operate the computer." In a microcomputer installation, this is still a good control principle, but not a practical one. Most organizations that use micros to run their business do not have a "data processing" individual. Clerks, or the company's owner, run the computer(s). Usually, no programming is done unless contracted for from an outside software service firm.

The auditor cannot expect the microcomputer site to devote the same amount of resources to the development of control procedures that is expected of a large, central-computer organization. The auditor should not expect to find a standards manual, a detailed systems-development control methodology, or a separate data library.

Situations that were considered low-risk in the large computer site may constitute high risk in the small computer site. For example, the reliability of hardware and software is not as great in the microcomputer as in the large central computer. The large-computer manufacturer can afford to spend the time and resources to develop redundant hardware circuits, controls, and debugging software that, if provided by the manufacturer of the microcomputer, might put the micro manufacturer at a severe competitive price disadvantage.

The auditor needs to reexamine control and audit methods in the microcomputer. Auditors must forget the methods and procedures used in the large-computer installation and redirect their efforts to the risks in the microcomputer realm.

Microcomputer Control Issues

Control issues are threats to the integrity of the microcomputer system. These control issues can be used in establishing the scope of the audit. The issues define the areas of concern to the auditor.

The auditor selects those issues that are to be included in the audit. For example, one of the issues is user satisfaction. An audit may be finance-oriented, and thus would not be concerned about the operational aspects of the microcomputer installation, such as user satisfaction. However, in another audit, the concern that users' needs are not being satisfied may be a major objective.

The auditor must understand the control issues in a microcomputer environment. Once this understanding has been gained, then the auditor can determine the applicability of each control issue to the audit. The identification of the applicable control issues determines the microcomputer-audit scope.

Figure 9–1 summarizes control and audit issues for microcomputers. Subsequent checklists are provided to review the adequacy of control over each of the issues.

The checklists are designed to be answered "yes" or "no." A yes indicates the item of concern has been adequately addressed by the microcomputer installation. A no indicates that further investigation should be undertaken to determine the severity of the concern. A Not Applicable (N/A) column is provided for items on the checklist that are

FIGURE 9-1

Microcomputer Audit and Control Issues

No.	Issue	Description
1.	Systems development	The procedure to develop or acquire applications.
2.	Systems documentation	The formal documentation available explaining what the system does and how it performs its function.
3.	Hardware reliability	The ability of the hardware to process data based upon the hardware specifications.
4.	Software reliability	The ability of the software to process data based upon the software specifications.
5.	Hardware maintenance	The preventive and corrective program to ensure the continued reliability of hardware.
6.	Software maintenance	The preventive and corrective program to ensure the continued operation of the software.
7.	Training	The materials and courses provided to explain how the hardware, software, and application systems function.
8.	Service level	Assurance that the desired level of processing can be sustained.
9.	Standardization	Use of uniform procedures to increase the performance and ease of use in maintenance of the resources.
10.	Access control	Procedures to prevent the unauthorized use of microcomputer resources.
11.	Recovery	The procedures and tools necessary to restore the operation after integrity has been lost.
12.	Audit trails	The records required to reconstruct and substantiate processing.
13.	Cost-effectiveness	The procedures to ensure that the minicomputer operations are beneficial to the organization.
14.	Controlled applications processing	The procedures and measures installed in application systems to ensure the accuracy, completeness, and authorization of data.
15.	Continuity of operations	The ability to maintain operations to meet the needs of the organization.
16.	User satisfaction	Meeting the established requirements of users.

not applicable for the organization being reviewed. A "Comments" column is provided to qualify "yes" answers in which a concern is not completely satisfied and to amplify "no" areas. Comments are helpful in conducting an investigation of the item.

Systems-development control. Millions of dollars were spent during the years in which organizations with large computer installations learned how to build systems properly. This process continues. Many small installations will not take advantage of the time-tested techniques that were developed. Companies that do so can avoid the waste inherent in poor systems development. For example, it has been learned that in designing systems, it is best to first define requirements, then develop system specifications, and then to do the programming and testing. In some microcomputer installations, users begin the system development process by writing programs. These factors are a management concern. The auditor's concern in the developmental process should be primarily directed toward the processing workload as opposed to one-time systems. Those nonfinancial systems, with minimal control needs, do not require a highly structured systems-development approach. The effort required to build well controlled financial systems is worthwhile. The checklist in Figure 9–2 covers some of the considerations in this area.

Systems documentation control. Purchased or developed microcomputer applications may only have minimal documentation. Users developing their own applications frequently feel they do not need documentation. The documentation provided by microcomputer vendors varies significantly, from outstanding to poor. Some microcomputers have excellent, easy-to-read, easy-to-follow documentation, while others provide only the minimal documentation necessary. Lacking adequate documentation, users may not be able to use the system effectively or to modify applications economically. Figure 9–3 covers documentation.

Hardware reliability control. Large computers have extensive redundant circuitry. The hardware is able to check on itself. Many large computers have self-diagnosing circuitry. When problems occur, the computer diagnoses its own problem and takes action accordingly. Minicomputers without some of this diagnostic circuitry may encounter similar problems, but without the self-diagnosing circuitry to notify the operator, the problem is not detected. Figure 9–4 covers hardware reliability.

FIGURE 9–2

Auditing Microcomputers: Systems Development

No.	Item	Yes	No	N/A	Comments
		Response			
1.	Has an approval procedure been established so that management can approve applications before they are started?	—	—	—	
2.	Has an approval procedure been established requiring management approval prior to purchasing computer applications?	—	—	—	
3.	Is the cost/benefit of an application determined prior to commencing the project?	—	—	—	
4.	Is a determination made if an application can be purchased prior to developing an application in-house?	—	—	—	
5.	Before placing an application on the microcomputer, is a determination made that the microcomputer has sufficient capacity to execute the desired function?	—	—	—	
6.	Prior to project approval has it been determined if the proposed microcomputer system function can be performed by another application system in the organization?	—	—	—	
7.	Do computer personnel possess the necessary skills to develop applications for the microcomputer?	—	—	—	
8.	Has a systems-development procedure been established?	—	—	—	
9.	If so, is the complexity of the process related to the importance of the project?	—	—	—	

Software reliability control. The development of high-quality software requires extensive testing. Testing is a costly process, and one that must be perfected by an organization over a period of years. Without this testing, software may occasionally fail or, even worse, produce erroneous results without detection.

FIGURE 9–3

Auditing Microcomputers: Systems Documentation

No.	Item	Response Yes	No	N/A	Comments
1.	Has a minimum level of documentation for microcomputer systems been established?	——	——	——	
2.	Is a minimum level of documentation applied to purchased applications?	——	——	——	
3.	Are operator instructions documented?	——	——	——	
4.	Does documentation exist on how to use the outputs from the application?	——	——	——	
5.	Is there documentation on how to fix a problem in purchased applications?	——	——	——	
6.	Do purchased applications have documentation explaining how to get vendor help?	——	——	——	
7.	Are the application controls documented?	——	——	——	
8.	Is documentation prepared in accordance with the importance of the application to the organization?	——	——	——	

FIGURE 9–4

Auditing Microcomputers: Hardware Reliability

No.	Item	Response Yes	No	N/A	Comments
1.	Does the vendor provide a guarantee of the reliability of the hardware?	——	——	——	
2.	Does the hardware have circuitry to identify hardware problems to the operator?	——	——	——	
3.	Is the organization provided with a manual explaining how to test the reliability of the hardware circuitry?	——	——	——	
4.	Is a log maintained of errors to help track the reliability of the hardware?	——	——	——	
5.	Are procedures established to contact the vendor in the event of hardware problems?	——	——	——	
6.	Is the reliability history of the microcomputer evaluated prior to purchase through reference to publications or a survey of existing users?	——	——	——	

Many microcomputer users rely heavily on vendor-produced system and application software because they lack extensive data processing knowledge. Therefore, when software produces erroneous results, the users may not be able to detect the problem or, if they do, they may be uncertain of the cause and correction. Figure 9–5 covers software reliability.

Hardware maintenance control. Any piece of machinery can fail. When it does, service is needed to restore the hardware to its normal condition. Vendors of microcomputers may or may not service their own computers. In addition, if they service the computer, they may not do it on site. Some vendors may not even have local representatives, and thus a user would be required to ship the computer back to the factory for repair. If the user only has one microcomputer, he can be left

FIGURE 9–5
Auditing Microcomputers: Software Reliability

No.	Item	Yes	No	N/A	Comments
		Response			
1.	Has the degree of reliability desired in the software been determined?	—	—	—	
2.	Have tests been made to determine that the software achieves the predetermined degree of reliability?	—	—	—	
3.	Prior to purchase, have other users of purchased software been contacted to determine the reliability of the software?	—	—	—	
4.	If versions are changed, have backup versions been maintained in case the updated version proves unreliable?	—	—	—	
5.	Do the developers of the in-house software have the necessary skills to develop software?	—	—	—	
6.	Are procedures established on how to test software?	—	—	—	
7.	Are logs maintained on software problems to identify high-problem software?	—	—	—	
8.	Are procedures established on vendor or developer contracts to cope with software problems?	—	—	—	

without computer capacity for a period of many days, weeks, or even months. Figure 9–6 covers hardware maintenance.

Software maintenance control. Software has the same types of problems as hardware. When problems occur, they need to be fixed. In some instances, the microcomputer user may have the source code of the software and, thus, have the opportunity to fix the problem. In other instances, the vendor refuses to release the source code, in which case the vendor must fix the software package.

When the microcomputer user relies upon a software package and it fails, he or she may need it fixed quickly. Minicomputer vendors may not have the staff to fix a software package in a reasonable period of time. In some instances, it may be difficult even to contact the vendor

FIGURE 9–6
Auditing Microcomputers: Hardware Maintenance

No.	Item	Yes	No	N/A	Comments
			Response		
1.	Does the vendor of the hardware offer maintenance service?	___	___	___	
2.	Is the service convenient to obtain?	___	___	___	
3.	Has the maximum permissible downtime been established?	___	___	___	
4.	Can the vendor provide service within the maximum downtime?	___	___	___	
5.	Have procedures been developed on when and how to call vendor maintenance personnel?	___	___	___	
6.	Are microcomputer operators trained in how to perform routine maintenance?	___	___	___	
7.	Has the cost of maintenance been predetermined and budgeted?	___	___	___	
8.	Are logs maintained to show the amount of downtime?	___	___	___	
9.	If downtime is excessive, can a refund or renegotiation of the contract be made with the vendor?	___	___	___	
10.	Are alternative (to manufacturer) services for maintenance available?	___	___	___	

and explain the problem. Many microcomputer users have only minimal data processing skills and thus are handicapped in attempting to identify a problem and the potential cause of that problem. Figure 9–7 covers software maintenance.

Training control. Users in a microcomputer installation need training in the operation of both the hardware and the software. Many microcomputer vendors offer no formal training. Those vendors may or may not supply self-study instructional material to help the user learn to use the hardware and software capabilities.

FIGURE 9–7
Auditing Microcomputers: Software Maintenance

		Response			
No.	Item	Yes	No	N/A	Comments
1.	Does the organization possess the necessary skills to maintain in-house developed software?	___	___	___	
2.	Has a procedure been developed to indicate when maintenance should be performed?	___	___	___	
3.	Do the vendors of purchased software provide maintenance?	___	___	___	
4.	Is vendor maintenance convenient to obtain?	___	___	___	
5.	Has the cost of maintenance been determined?	___	___	___	
6.	Has the maximum desired downtime for software been determined?	___	___	___	
7.	Can the vendor provide maintenance within that downtime period?	___	___	___	
8.	Are logs maintained to show the amount of downtime?	___	___	___	
9.	If downtime is excessive, can a refund or a renegotiation of the contract be made with the vendor?	___	___	___	
10.	If the vendor goes out of business, is source code available for continuing modification of leased software packages?	___	___	___	
11.	If software package vendor goes out of business, are rights of user protected?	___	___	___	

The scope and ease of understanding of these training tools may determine how effectively the microcomputer can be utilized. Poorly explained features may never be used. In addition, users may spend large amounts of time attempting to learn how to use the microcomputer as a result of the inadequate training material available to them. Also, changes and modifications to hardware and software may have no training material accompanying them. Figure 9–8 covers training.

Service-level control. Microcomputers can easily become overloaded. Their capacity is limited, and when the capacity of the system is approached, the service level degrades quickly. Some hardware commands and software capabilities may be inefficient. For example, some of the mathematical functions may take an extensive amount of time to execute. If the users are unaware of these inefficiencies, they

FIGURE 9–8
Auditing Microcomputers: Training

		Response			
No.	*Item*	*Yes*	*No*	*N/A*	*Comments*
1.	Does the vendor provide training classes on how to use the microcomputer?	——	——	——	
2.	Are self-teach training materials available on the use of the microcomputer?	——	——	——	
3.	Are training courses and/or training material available for purchased software application packages?	——	——	——	
4.	Are methods established to train users on in-house-developed applications?	——	——	——	
5.	If a vendor goes out of business, does the organization own the rights to continue teaching courses?	——	——	——	
6.	If the vendor goes out of business, can the organization reproduce copyrighted materials for in-house use?	——	——	——	
7.	Are training materials updated when hardware, software, and in-house-developed applications are updated?	——	——	——	
8.	Is the effort expended on training proportionate to the value of the resource to the organization?	——	——	——	

FIGURE 9–9
Auditing Microcomputers: Service Level

No.	Item	Yes	No	N/A	Comments
			Response		
1.	Are the resources adequate to handle the essential applications?	——	——	——	
2.	Has a procedure been established for prioritizing work when demand exceeds capacity?	——	——	——	
3.	Has a procedure been established for prioritizing work after a computer problem?	——	——	——	
4.	Are service levels monitored to determine when action on the system capacity needs to be taken?	——	——	——	
5.	Is a log maintained of jobs to determine where resources are utilized?	——	——	——	
6.	Are users regularly queried as to their level of satisfaction?	——	——	——	

may use capabilities that require an unreasonable amount of time for execution. Figure 9–9 covers service-level issues.

Standardization control. Standards should exist within a single microcomputer environment and between microcomputer environments in an organization. While it is recognized that a microcomputer installation cannot justify the expenditure of large amounts of resources to develop standards, some minimal standards should be established. For example, access standards should be established.

The long-range direction for microcomputers is to become connected into a network. Without some long-range planning, organizations may acquire a variety of microcomputers that are not compatible. When this happens, data from one computer cannot be readily transmitted or transferred to another computer. Standardization is covered in Figure 9–10.

Access control. Access control is the key control in the microcomputer environment. Restricting usage of the microcomputer resources is the strongest control that can be used. Access controls need to limit access to the physical computer area as well as to the programs and

FIGURE 9–10
Auditing Microcomputers: Standardization

		Response			
No.	Item	Yes	No	N/A	Comments
1.	Does the organization have a procedure to follow in acquiring microcomputer hardware and software?	___	___	___	
2.	Can all the organization's microcomputers communicate?	___	___	___	
3.	Are there certain vendor requirements, such as offering a language like BASIC, that must be met prior to acquiring a microcomputer from that vendor?	___	___	___	
4.	Before it can become operational, does the microcomputer installation require operational programs to meet minimal standards such as preventing one program from destroying the data of another program?	___	___	___	
5.	Are data files adequately labeled so that they can be identified by an application program prior to use?	___	___	___	
6.	Has one individual been appointed to oversee the microcomputer standards?	___	___	___	

data. Physical access controls can be difficult to install in a microcomputer environment. However, low-cost, workable alternatives to a secure computer room are available. The microcomputer can be located on a supervisor's desk so that the supervisor can control physical access to the computer. Another effective method is to make one individual responsible for protecting the computer from unauthorized access.

Restricting access to programs and data may be dependent on the capabilities built into the microcomputer operating system. Some microcomputers have a password system that restricts access to persons with the correct passwords. Although this is normally a single-level control, it is better than no control at all. Access also needs to be restricted to data stored off-site. Organizations store backup data away from the computer to protect the microcomputer site from a disaster. Should fire or other problems occur, the backup data permits the installation to regain operational status quickly. Figure 9–11 covers access.

FIGURE 9–11
Auditing Microcomputers: Access

No.	Item	Response: Yes	No	N/A	Comments
1.	Does the microcomputer operating software include access control?	___	___	___	
2.	Are procedures established to evaluate the access-control features provided by the hardware and software vendors to determine whether or not they should be utilized?	___	___	___	
3.	Is a determination made for both data and programs as to who can have access to those resources?	___	___	___	
4.	Has a determination been made and enforced regarding who can have access to the microcomputer facility?	___	___	___	
5.	Are microcomputer access violations reported to management?	___	___	___	
6.	Are microcomputer security violators punished?	___	___	___	
7.	Have all the economically feasible physical security measures been taken?	___	___	___	
8.	Are microcomputer data processing personnel subject to the same access rules as any other user of the system?	___	___	___	

Recovery control. Recovery is restoring the integrity of computer processing after it has been lost. The data integrity can be lost due to hardware failure, software failure, application system failure, operator error, or physical catastrophe. The problem may come quickly, resulting in a halt to computer operations, or erroneous processing may occur for an extended period of time before it is uncovered.

Recovery is a two-part process. The first part is retaining the necessary data and developing the procedures necessary to recover after a problem. The second part is executing those procedures when required. Many microcomputer operating systems offer limited or no recovery procedures. This can be a problem if the microcomputer has large amounts of data stored on-line. The recovery process is one in which many microcomputer installations are deficient. Most recovery procedures are learned the hard way. The time and effort needed to develop a good recovery procedure is normally time well spent. Figure 9–12 covers recovery.

Audit trail control. Audit trails provide for the reconstruction of single-transaction processing and for the reprocessing of large amounts of data for recovery purposes. Audit trails can be created by the operating system or by application programming.

Large computer installations have operator logs, communication logs, and database system logs. These provide an excellent audit trail for backup and reconstruction purposes. Unfortunately, most microcomputer installations do not have these types of logs.

FIGURE 9–12
Auditing Microcomputers: Recovery

No.	Item	Yes	No	N/A	Comments
			Response		
1.	Has a determination been made regarding which applications need to be recovered after a problem?	___	___	___	
2.	Has a determination been made regarding how quickly each application must be recovered?	___	___	___	
3.	Are resources available to meet the above time constraints?	___	___	___	
4.	Has sufficient backup data been saved to meet the above requirements and time constraints?	___	___	___	
5.	Have recovery procedures been established?	___	___	___	
6.	Have recovery procedures been practiced to determine they are effective?	___	___	___	
7.	Are operating personnel trained in recovery procedures?	___	___	___	
8.	Are recovery procedures documented?	___	___	___	
9.	Have arrangements been made for alternative processing, such as at another microcomputer site, in the event the microcomputer should be down for an extended period of time?	___	___	___	

The need for an audit trail may not be obvious to the minicomputer installation. Many do not have accountants as consultants and, thus, do not recognize the significant role of the audit trail. This, coupled with the minimal or absent audit-trail aids provided by the vendor, can lead to some serious microcomputer processing reconstruction problems. Figure 9–13 covers audit trails.

Cost effectiveness control. Microcomputers should be installed if they are more cost-effective than other processing solutions.

FIGURE 9–13
Auditing Microcomputers: Audit Trail

No.	Item	Yes	No	N/A	Comments
			Response		
1.	Have audit trail requirements been defined for each application?	___	___	___	
2.	Can all financial transactions be traced to their appropriate control totals?	___	___	___	
3.	Can financial control totals be traced downward to all the supporting transactions?	___	___	___	
4.	Have the important transactions been identified?	___	___	___	
5.	Can important transactions be reconstructed if necessary?	___	___	___	
6.	Are procedures established to log operator actions?	___	___	___	
7.	Are procedures established to reconstruct programs if necessary?	___	___	___	
8.	In a communication environment, are procedures established to reconstruct communication processing if necessary?	___	___	___	
9.	In a database environment, have procedures been established to reconstruct database processing if necessary?	___	___	___	
10.	Is the audit-trail information sufficient to support the reconstruction of processing and requirements?	___	___	___	

The determination of this cost-effectiveness requires the organization to determine or estimate both the benefits and the costs of installing a microcomputer. These cost/benefits can then be compared with other processing solutions.

Few microcomputer installations go through a detailed cost/benefit analysis. The reason for this is that the cost of the microcomputer usually does not warrant an extended study. However, when all of the costs are accumulated, organizations may be surprised at the total costs associated with obtaining a microcomputer.

Many organizations estimate that it costs three or four times the cost of the microcomputer to prepare for the installation. These other costs include evaluation and selection of microcomputers, the contractual process, training of employees to use the microcomputer, site preparation, and obtaining additional disks, paper, etc. After these costs have been expended, then additional funds are necessary to obtain or develop application systems.

Microcomputer installations need not go through the same detailed cost analysis performed for the large computer installation. However, the organization should perform a cost/benefit calculation. Without this calculation, many non-cost-effective systems may be installed. Figure 9–14 covers cost-effectiveness.

Controlled applications processing.   One of the major issues is the control within applications processing. Controls are necessary to ensure that transaction processing is accurate, complete, and authorized. Without adequate controls, the integrity of processing cannot be assured.

Control in an application begins when the data is entered. Control assures accuracy of input and processing, integrity of data files, and accuracy and completeness of output reports. In addition, control should prevent improper transactions from being processed.

Controls in financial applications should balance the computer data to externally controlled totals. These external controls provide assurance that the data within the computerized application is adequately controlled. For example, in accounts receivable, the cash applied to the receivables should be reconciled to the cash deposited in the bank. Figure 9–15 covers control within applications processing.

Continuity of operations control.   The microcomputer installation should determine the importance of continuity of operations. Management should decide the number of hours, minutes, or days that the computer can be down without adversely impacting operations. This is

FIGURE 9–14

Auditing Microcomputers: Cost-Effectiveness

No.	Item	Yes	No	N/A	Comments
			Response		
1.	Does management require a cost/benefit study prior to acquiring a microcomputer?	___	___	___	
2.	If so, have those procedures been complied with?	___	___	___	
3.	Do the costs include documentation, training, site preparation, and other costs associated with installing a microcomputer?	___	___	___	
4.	Is a cost/benefit study made, even if performed in a cursory manner, prior to purchasing or installing new applications?	___	___	___	
5.	Are users of the microcomputer aware of the costs associated with using that equipment?	___	___	___	
6.	Are microcomputer users aware of the cost of alternative means of processing?	___	___	___	
7.	Are system applications and reports regularly reviewed to ensure that unneeded or obsolete systems or reports are eliminated?	___	___	___	

the primary decision in determining the procedures installed to ensure continuity of operation.

The microcomputer issues discussed in this chapter include the types of risks faced. Any one of these risks could cause the computer to go down and not be operational for extended periods of time. Once the maximum down period has been determined, the necessary counter-measures can be designed to ensure that operations can continue.

In microcomputer installations, it may be necessary to have two or more computers to ensure continuity of operations. However, this may only be effective against hardware failures and not effective against some of the other risks. The importance of continuity of operations determines the amount of resources expended to ensure that those operations continue. Figure 9–16 covers continuity of operations.

FIGURE 9–15
Auditing Microcomputers: Controlled Applications Processing

		Response			
No.	*Item*	*Yes*	*No*	*N/A*	*Comments*
1.	Are the application risks identified?	——	——	——	
2.	Has the severity of those risks for the microcomputer applications been determined?	——	——	——	
3.	Are controls established to reduce the risks to an agreed-upon level?	——	——	——	
4.	Are control violations documented and reported to management?	——	——	——	
5.	Does management take appropriate action on those control violations?	——	——	——	
6.	Are controls documented?	——	——	——	
7.	Are controls in the operating environment studied before application controls are built?	——	——	——	
8.	Are the controls in purchased applications known?	——	——	——	
9.	Are the controls in purchased applications adequate?	——	——	——	
10.	If controls in purchased applications are inadequate, have steps been taken to supplement those controls?	——	——	——	

User satisfaction control. User satisfaction in a microcomputer installation may be difficult to measure. If users are skilled and microcomputer requirements are established in enough detail so that they are measurable, then user satisfaction can be measured. However, in many microcomputer installations, user expectations have not been defined and, thus, are not measurable.

Prior to approval of the acquisition of a microcomputer, the expectations for that computer should be defined and quantified. The results can then be measured against the requirements to determine achievement. In addition, users should be queried as to whether or not they are achieving their objectives, because requirements change. This may make measurements against initial requirements inappropriate. Figure 9–17 covers user satisfaction.

FIGURE 9–16

Auditing Microcomputers: Continuity of Operations

No.	Item	Yes	No	N/A	Comments
1.	Have the operations needed for conducting the day-to-day work of the organization been identified?	___	___	___	
2.	Are there procedures to ensure that those operations run on a timely basis?	___	___	___	
3.	Have appropriate data been stored off-site to ensure continuity of those operations in the event of a disaster?	___	___	___	
4.	Has sufficient documentation about the microcomputer operation been stored off-site so that processing can be continued in the event of a disaster?	___	___	___	
5.	Has a contingency plan been developed to restore operations in the event of a disaster?	___	___	___	
6.	Has the impact of disasters been identified, and sufficient countermeasures incorporated into the contingency plan to offset that impact?	___	___	___	

FIGURE 9–17

Auditing Microcomputers: User Satisfaction

No.	Item	Yes	No	N/A	Comments
1.	Have the users' requirements been identified and documented?	___	___	___	
2.	Are those requirements measurable?	___	___	___	
3.	Are they measured?	___	___	___	
4.	Have procedures been established to determine whether or not user requirements have been achieved?	___	___	___	
5.	As user requirements are changed, are the methods of measuring user satisfaction changed accordingly?	___	___	___	
6.	Are users periodically interviewed regarding whether or not the computer satisfies their needs?	___	___	___	
7.	Are procedures established to eliminate or change systems that do not satisfy user needs?	___	___	___	

Microcomputer Auditing Problems

The audit methods used in large computer installations are usually not effective in a microcomputer installation because of the characteristics of that installation. The microcomputer poses certain audit problems that may not exist in the larger installations. These problems are discussed below in order to explain to auditors the need for changing their audit approach when reviewing the microcomputer environment.

Risks unknown. Control checklists, audit programs, and risk lists have done much to help the auditor identify the risks in a large computer environment. These are not the same risks or the same severity of risks that exist in a microcomputer environment. It is possible that both management and audit personnel are not aware of the types or severity of risks faced in a microcomputer installation. Therefore, the control and audit effort in those installations may not address the more serious risks.

Audit software packages unavailable. Audit software packages are written for the large computer installation, primarily large IBM and IBM-compatible computers. Rarely will the auditor find an audit software package available for microcomputers.

Multiple vendors. The auditors, both internal and external, may be faced with a variety of microcomputers. It is more difficult for the auditor to justify investing the time and effort needed to understand the characteristics of a microcomputer when the auditor's organization or client may have microcomputers from many vendors.

Lack of internal control review aids. Few checklists, guidelines, and audit programs are written for the microcomputer. Therefore, the auditor may not have guidelines to follow in evaluating internal control.

Unreliable hardware/software. The lack of control circuitry and hardware, and control procedures in testing software, make the operating environment less reliable for a microcomputer than for the large computers. In large computer installations, the auditors are able to devote most of their effort to application auditing. Because of the unreliability of hardware and software in the microcomputer environment, the auditor may have to devote a much larger portion of the audit resources to verifying the hardware/software controls.

Unskilled users.   Auditors in large computer installations may rely upon the skills of the data processing personnel to prevent and detect problems. In many installations, these people have done an exceptionally good job in spite of the lack of control standards. Unskilled users in microcomputer installations may not be aware of the need to control many of the risk situations that are under control in larger installations.

Minimal audit literature.   There is little literature in professional auditing publications on the problems of and solutions to microcomputer audits. Therefore, many auditors are not aware of some of the significant differences between the audits of large computers and microcomputers.

Minimal audit tools and techniques.   Few auditors assess microcomputer installations. Most of the auditing that is performed is done around the computer rather than through reviewing the controls within the computer system. For this reason, audit methods and practices for auditing microcomputers have not been developed, leaving the effort to develop the approach to those few audit groups actively involved in auditing microcomputers.

Lack of minicomputer audit skills.   For all of the above reasons, most auditors lack the skills needed to audit effectively in a microcomputer environment. The solution to these problems is to follow the audit approach recommended in the following section, which is designed to address the control issues in a microcomputer environment.

Microcomputer Audit Approach

The microcomputer audit process presented here provides a step-by-step procedure for auditing a microcomputer installation. The method is similar to that used for any audit situation, but is customized for the microcomputer installation. The balance of this section describes how to execute these audit process steps.

The microcomputer audit process involves five steps, which are shown in Figure 9–18.

Step 1: Determine microcomputer use.   Microcomputers can be used as stand-alone terminals or for distributed processing. In evaluating a microcomputer installation, the auditor must first determine

FIGURE 9–18
Microcomputer Audit Process for Stand-Alone Terminals

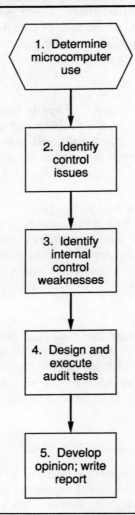

which use is being made of the microcomputer. Although a microcomputer may be used for more than one use, the auditor should determine the dominant use.

The audit process described here is for use with stand-alone microcomputers. If the microcomputer is used merely as a terminal, the auditor should refer to the section later in this chapter that discusses how to audit the terminal in emulation processing mode. If the microcomputer is part of a distributed network, the auditor should refer to a later portion of this chapter that discusses the audit process in a distributed system.

When the microcomputer is used as a stand-alone computer, the remaining four steps are executed. If the microcomputer is used in a distributed network or as a terminal, the auditor should not use the approach outlined in the remainder of this section but, rather, should refer to the appropriate section of this chapter for audit guidance.

Step 2: Identify control issues. Use of the microcomputer poses risks to the organization. These risks can be described as control issues. Sixteen control issues were described earlier in this chapter, and checklists were provided. The auditor must determine which of those issues are enough of a threat to require audit review. If the auditor determines that a control issue, such as hardware maintenance, is not applicable to the organization, then no additional auditing need take place for that potential concern. However, if the auditor determines that hardware maintenance is a control issue that needs to be addressed, then it should be included in the audit program.

Step 3: Identify internal control weaknesses. The auditor must determine whether internal controls are adequate for those control issues included within the audit program. If control weaknesses are detected, then additional auditing must take place to determine whether or not that control weakness could be or is resulting in a loss to the organization.

Step 4: Design and execute audit tests. The auditor conducts tests for two purposes: first, to determine if the identified controls are in place and working; and second, to determine the extent of losses associated with identified control weaknesses. Later in the chapter some of the more common microcomputer audit tools and techniques are described.

Step 5: Develop opinion; write report. The last part of the audit process is to develop an opinion on the adequacy of control and to communicate that opinion to management. Later in this chapter tips and techniques on writing reports for the microcomputer environment are provided.

Reviewing Microcomputer Internal Controls

The system of internal controls should be reviewed periodically. As stated previously, the microcomputer controls will be different from the controls in the large computer installation. The controls reviewed are those designed to reduce risks inherent in previously discussed microcomputer control issues.

Segregation of duties is difficult in a microcomputer installation. The segregation among operations achievable in a large installation is not achievable in a microcomputer installation, because of the small quantity of staff.

Auditors cannot rely heavily on segregation of duties for control in a microcomputer installation. Auditors must rely on other controls and tests in determining the integrity of operations. They may be required to conduct more tests in a microcomputer installation because of this inability to rely on a usually weak system of internal controls.

The types of controls that an auditor might find in lieu of segregation of duties include the following:

- Supervisory review.
- More extensive application controls.
- More independently maintained control totals outside the computer area.
- More frequent audits.

The checklists that were provided in Figures 9–2 through 9–17 have been designed for each of the microcomputer control issues. The auditor must determine which issues are to be reviewed during the audit and select the checklists for those control issues. The issues divide the microcomputer installation into controllable units. Therefore, the issues can be evaluated individually.

Level of control. As you review the internal control questions, you will note that many of the questions are general in scope, in contrast to the specific questions that would be used for a larger installation. The reason for the limited number of questions and the generality of scope is that the auditor must use more discretion in reviewing controls in a microcomputer installation. The auditor should not expect, or recommend, the level of control that exists in a large installation. That level of control would not be cost-effective in a microcomputer installation and may, in fact, make the microcomputer installation unworkable.

Use of the checklist questions must also be tempered by cost-effectiveness criteria. The auditor must take into account the size of the staff as well as the size and number of microcomputers.

The level of controls is also dependent upon the importance of the application to the organization. Less-important applications will have less documentation, fewer controls, etc. The auditor must also weigh the internal control assessment against the importance of the application to the organization.

Microcomputer Audit Testing

The auditor tests for one of the following four reasons:

1. To evaluate the functioning of controls.
2. To identify control weaknesses.
3. To determine the severity of the control weaknesses.
4. To substantiate financial balance.

The control environment in a microcomputer installation may or may not allow the auditor to rely on internal control. The auditor may review the system of control and make the decision that, because of the limited staff, duplication of duties, and ready access to information from many people, the controls cannot be relied upon. In those instances, the auditor will make a decision to perform substantive testing. In other words, the auditor must verify the data in total that is processed by the microcomputer.

If the auditor decides that some, or all, of the system of internal control may be reliable, then control testing can occur. Obviously, this is the more effective audit approach, as lesser amounts of data need to be examined.

Audit testing in a microcomputer installation can be divided into two general categories:

1. Testing when controls are unreliable.
2. Testing when some reliance can be placed upon controls.

The type of tools and techniques used by the auditor to conduct tests will vary, depending upon the category of the audit testing.

Testing when controls are unreliable. The size of the microcomputer, the segregation of duties among the microcomputer staff, and the type of applications run on the microcomputer affect the auditor's decision to rely or not to rely upon controls. When the auditor determines that controls are unreliable, then audit tests must concentrate on the data processed by the computer as opposed to the controls in place in the organization. The audit emphasis in this situation will be on the existence of the items recorded by the computer.

Many auditors approach a microcomputer installation whose controls are unreliable as if it was a manual environment. They ignore the fact that a computer exists and base their audit upon the more traditional evidence. Provided that traditional hard-copy evidence is available, which it is in many microcomputer installations, the auditor can perform an effective substantive audit while ignoring the computer.

Microcomputer installations without the traditional forms of evidence pose a dilemma to the auditor. When electronic evidence is the only evidence available, the auditor will have to request or obtain listings of that evidence. It would be more appropriate for the auditor to control and execute the programs that list the electronic evidence rather than ask the microcomputer operators to perform the task for them. A question of auditor negligence may arise should the auditor opt to audit electronic evidence, but not take the steps necessary to evaluate the population of evidence stored in the microcomputer files.

The microcomputer substantive audit begins with statements showing the data processed by the microcomputer. The content of the statements will reflect the systems processed by the microcomputer. For example, if financial data is processed, then financial statements will be produced. However, if production schedules are created on the microcomputer, then the statements will relate to those schedules.

The methods of audit to be used are similar to those used in any other audit of data. If the auditor needs to analyze and list the data on the computer files, the task can be accomplished by one of the following three methods:

1. *Audit software.* Some audit software is available for microcomputers. However, it is rare, and in many instances the software has been developed by the organization itself. Such software may be found in large organizations that have several microcomputers. The audit software is primarily used to list the evidence included in the data files.

2. *Microcomputer utilities.* Most microcomputers provide utility programs to perform a variety of tasks. Some utilities provide the capability of listing information contained on microcomputer disk files. The capabilities, with the exception of sampling, are similar to those in conventional audit software packages.

3. *Special programming.* The auditor can use one of the languages available on the microcomputer to list the files used by that computer. One of the simpler languages included on many microcomputers is BASIC. Again, this language has the capabilities similar to audit software, with the exception of sampling. However, with data auditing, the auditor normally wants to list all of the file as opposed to sampling from that file.

Evaluating microcomputer internal controls. When the auditor has made a decision that some reliance can be placed on microcomputer controls, then those controls must be tested. The recommended assessment approach is for the auditor to evaluate controls based on the microcomputer control issues described in this se tion. Rarely will the auditor be able to rely upon internal control for all the issues in a microcomputer installation, but he may be able to rely on those controls dealing with certain issues. Many of these issues are operational as opposed to financial and, thus, are more internal-audit-oriented than external. For example, the internal auditor would be concerned with recovery, and, even in a one-person microcomputer installation, the auditor can assess the adequacy of recovery controls. These are normally not people-dependent, but procedurally dependent.

With a limited data processing staff, it may be difficult to assess the reliability of controls that are dependent on the appropriate segregation of people. It may be necessary for the auditor to first assess the severity of the risk before testing the controls. If the risk is minimal, the auditor may not expect or require strong controls. On the other hand, if the risk is large, the auditor may look for strong controls. Both the auditor's test and the recommendations made to management should be based on the severity of the risk.

The recommended testing approach in a microcomputer environment will be based on whether the auditor is testing procedures or the segregation of functions. Both the approach and the testing will vary.

Testing segregation of function controls. The microcomputer control issues that involve the testing of segregation of function are:

- Access control.
- Audit trails.
- Controlled applications.

The types of testing tools that are effective in evaluating the adequacy of control over these factors include the following:

• *Internal control questionnaire.* The use of an internal control questionnaire designed exclusively for the microcomputer environment helps in assessing the adequacy of controls in a microcomputer environment. Note again that internal control questionnaires designed for large-computer installations probably are not effective in a microcomputer environment. These microcomputer internal control checklists should be used as a guide to identify areas for audit probing. They should not be considered complete. The auditor may need to supplement the questionnaires based on responses to questions and areas that are organization-dependent.

• *Control violations testing.* The auditor attempts to accomplish a task by violating the control. For example, if the auditor should not be granted access to a particular resource, the auditor will attempt to obtain that resource to determine whether or not the controls are effective. Control violation tests can be used to test access controls, security procedures, and physical controls.

• *Data file analysis.* Using audit software or microcomputer utilities, the auditor performs an analysis of the microcomputer data. The analysis is performed with the use of audit software and can be a static analysis on data, provide a trend analysis, do comparisons between two files, and so on. The auditor is probing, looking for weaknesses in control.

• *Documentation reviews.* The auditor reviews documentation to determine if controls are adequate for the desired purpose. For example, in determining if internal controls are adequate in purchased applications, the auditor would review the documentation provided by the vendor to determine whether or not the package contained sufficient controls. Documentation reviews can be time-consuming in that the auditor must learn what the application is supposed to accomplish, how the application achieves those objectives, and then whether or not the documented controls satisfy the requirement under review.

• *Interview.* The auditor discusses with one or more individuals an area of audit concern. For example, rather than review documentation to determine whether or not an application is adequately controlled, the auditor may interview the individual responsible for that application. The auditor would ask that individual the same questions that the auditor hopes to answer through a documentation review. However, the auditor should be cautioned that people tend to explain things as they should be happening rather than how they may, in fact, be happening.

• *Manual auditing.* The auditor uses the tools and techniques of the conventional manual audit. These would include vouching, confirmation, and refooting mathematical information. While these procedures do not utilize the power of the computer or address some of the more sophisticated methods of control, they may be effective in a minicomputer environment in which an adequate audit trail exists, and where there is only minimal reliance on electronic evidence and automated controls.

Procedural testing. Procedural testing will evaluate the controls of the following microcomputer control issues:

- Systems development.
- Systems documentation.
- Hardware reliability.
- Software reliability.
- Hardware maintenance.
- Software maintenance.
- Training.
- Service levels.
- Standardization.
- Recoveries.
- Cost-effectiveness.
- Continuity of operations.
- User satisfaction.

The procedural testing relies less heavily on the people-oriented controls and more heavily on the development, implementation, and operation of good methods and procedures of doing work. Thus, the microcomputer with no staff or a very small data processing staff can still be reviewed for the adequacy of its procedures.

In addition to the effective testing techniques and procedures described for testing segregation of functions, the following testing tools can be used:

• *Authoritative source.* The auditor may wish to consult with an authoritative source regarding some aspect of control. For example, if the auditor is concerned about hardware maintenance or hardware reliability, the auditor may wish to refer to some of the updating services that evaluate hardware and software.

• *Disaster testing.* The auditor simulates a disaster to determine if the organization can recoup from that disaster. The types of disasters tested include hardware disaster, operating system disaster, and application system disaster. Normally, the auditor picks a small area and asks the installation manager to recoup without using the on-site documentation, programs, hardware, and data.

• *Observation and investigation.* The auditor may wish to observe and investigate the execution of procedures. Knowing what the procedures are may not determine how those procedures are practiced in the microcomputer installation. Observing and investigating situations to determine that the appropriate procedures were used and are effective will provide the auditor with assurance as to whether or not the procedural controls function properly.

• *Benchmarking.* The auditor may wish to establish, or have users establish, standards of performance. The auditor uses these standards to determine whether the procedures achieve the required or desired level of performance. The actual results are then measured against those benchmark standards. Failure to meet those standards indicates ineffective procedural controls.

Developing Opinion; Writing Report

The last step in a microcomputer audit is to present to management audit findings and recommendations. Management relies on the experience and judgment of the auditor to develop those opinions and recommendations. This part of the process cannot be automated, nor does management want this process to be automated. However, because auditing a microcomputer is different from auditing a large-computer installation, the inclusion of a few tips and techniques on opinions and recommendations might be worthwhile. In drawing conclusions and recommendations about a microcomputer installation, the auditor should do the following:

• *Think microcomputer.* The same type of conclusions and recommendations that may receive good acceptance in a large-computer installation may be viewed as impractical and unworkable in a microcomputer installation. The auditor must place himself/herself in the position of microcomputer management, and then try to evaluate potential conclusions or recommendations to determine if they are meaningful to that installation. For example, the recognition that duties cannot be segregated the same way they are in a large-computer installation is of no value to the microcomputer manager.

• *Subject recommendations to a cost-effectiveness analysis.* The auditor should go through a mini cost/benefit calculation for each recommendation. If the auditor cannot convince himself/herself that the recommendation is cost-effective, it should not be made. If the idea is not cost-effective, the auditor may wish to consider alternative recommendations that are more appropriate in a microcomputer environment.

• *Be future-oriented.* The installation of a microcomputer is normally the first step in a process that evolves and gets bigger over a period of time. The auditor should put findings, conclusions, and recommendations in the context of what that installation might be like in a month, a year, or two years. By this line of thinking, some problems that appear borderline in today's environment could conceivably be quite serious as the installation grows. Unless the auditor takes this into account, some of the recommendations may not be presented in the proper context.

• *Write micro reports.* Audit managers in microcomputer installations do not want extensive audit reports. The installation may be a part-time responsibility for some managers, and to get a 20- to 30-page audit report will create an immediate negative impression. Audit reports in microcomputer installations should be presented in two or three pages. If more information is required it can be presented as an appendix or a supplemental letter.

AUDITING MICROCOMPUTERS USED AS TERMINALS (TERMINAL EMULATION MODE)

Many organizations, in addition to using their microcomputers in a stand-alone and/or distributed processing mode, also make use of the microcomputers as standard terminals in an on-line, real-time mini or mainframe processing environment. Terminal emulation programs can be run on the microcomputer and, in effect, make the microcomputer function like a standard CRT terminal. Most emulation programs offer a variety of CRT terminal-type choices that can be selected by the operator. The main advantage of using microcomputers in a terminal emulation mode is that only one hardware device need be on a person's desk, instead of both a terminal and a microcomputer.

The term *terminal,* when used in the following section, refers to microcomputers being used as terminals under a terminal emulation mode.

Microcomputer Terminal Emulation Mode Control Issues

The objective of identifying control issues for microcomputer terminals is to direct the auditor's effort toward high-risk audit areas. This enables the auditor to take a more systematic approach to the audit of micro-computers being used as computer terminals.

Approaching an audit from the perspective of addressing audit issues provides the following advantages:

- Narrows audit scope to high-risk areas.
- Eliminates unnecessary probing to identify problem areas.
- Differentiates central-computer problems from microcomputer terminal problems.
- Maximizes audit time and resources.

Microcomputer terminal emulation control issues can be categorized as follows:

- Data integrity.
- Microcomputer terminal integrity.
- Access control.
- Continuity of processing.

These four issues are listed and briefly described in Figure 9–19.

Data Integrity

Data is transmitted to and from the computer with computer terminals. All of the input data, and much of the output information, is entered via a computer terminal. The terminal both helps and hinders the accurate and complete entry of data. In addition, data distributed from the computer to the microcomputer terminal can be misused.

FIGURE 9–19
Microcomputer Terminal Emulation Mode: Control Issues

Issue	Concern (Explanation)
Data integrity	Loss of accuracy and/or completeness of data
Terminal integrity	Loss of data integrity due to microcomputer terminal hardware and/or software failure
Access control	Data entry, deletion, or alteration of data by unauthorized sources
Continuity of processing	Inability to recover and/or restart operations after loss of data or processing integrity

Certain controls can significantly increase the integrity of microcomputer terminal-processed data. However, the initiation of those controls is dependent on understanding the conditions that lead to loss of data integrity. The data integrity concerns covered in this control issue are independent of the loss of data integrity due to hardware/software failure and problems with the centralized computer or application.

The conditions that can cause the loss of data integrity during the microcomputer terminal data-entry process include the following:

- Inadequate data-entry instructions.
- Inadequate training of data-entry operators.
- Difficult-to-interpret prompting messages.
- Complex entry procedures.
- Poorly lit or housed microcomputers/terminals.
- Inadequate data-validation routines.

The problems that can cause the loss of data integrity in using information supplied to the computer terminal include the following:

- Inadequately described data (e.g., cryptic titles and headings).
- Inadequate instructions on the use of data.
- Poorly presented data.
- Data not being received on a timely basis.
- Data not directed to the appropriate individual.
- Inadequate capabilities to obtain background and/or additional supporting data.

Normally, in a terminal operation the operator is restricted to predetermined segments of available data. This concept is normally more desirable than distributing reports of several hundred pages. However, the selection of the data, the capabilities to obtain more data, and the explanatory material surrounding the data are important factors in ensuring proper and effective use of the data.

Terminal Integrity

The integrity of the data, from the point of entry to the point where control is transferred to the centralized computer for use by the end recipient, is dependent upon the reliability of the terminal hardware and the strength of the software controls. Some terminals do not have software controls, making data integrity solely dependent upon the hardware controls. In other instances, the software controls may be more valuable in ensuring integrity than the hardware controls.

The control of terminals normally starts with the data input or output through the point where the information enters or leaves the control of the communication package. Normally, there is a communication package that interfaces the microcomputer terminal to the main computer. There may be both a hardware and a software link between the terminal and the communication software package. Frequently, a common carrier, such as the Bell system, is also involved in the link between the terminal and the central computer.

The types of hardware problems that can cause the loss of data integrity include the following:

- Undetected hardware malfunction.
- Inadequate hardware-checking capability.
- Improper interface between the terminal/microcomputer and common carrier.
- Inadequate "hand-shaking" routines between the communication systems and the terminal. (Hand-shaking routines are normally hard-wired circuitry that synchronize transmission between the terminal/microcomputer and the main computer.)
- Improper instructions on the use of the equipment and/or diagnostic error indicators.

The types of problems associated with terminal software that can cause the loss of data integrity include the following:

- Problems in the software logic or inadequate testing.
- Inadequate instructions on the use of software and/or diagnostic messages or indicators.
- Improper interface between the terminal and the communication software package and/or common-carrier requirements.
- Improper interface between software terminal packages, such as a terminal operating system, and the data-entry application.
- Failure to act on a software diagnostic warning message.

Access-Control Integrity

Access control to a computer terminal is a two-tiered security process. The first tier of security is controlling physical access to the terminal. The second tier of security is controlling access to process transactions.

The type of access control used to protect the terminal will be dependent on the location of the terminal and the capabilities and/or damage that can be performed through the terminal. For example, the very nature of the terminal may make physical access restrictions impractical (a bank wants its cash-dispensing terminal within easy access of any depositor). However, in cases where physical access is unrestricted, then transaction access may be very tightly controlled.

Determining the need for and types of access control requires consideration of the following:

- Value of assets accessible by the terminal/microcomputer.
- Capabilities available to the terminal user.
- Physical location of terminal.
- Access restrictions to location where terminal resides.
- Ability of people to manipulate terminal.
- Liquidity and movability of assets controlled through the terminal.

The concerns that an auditor would have regarding accessibility to a microcomputer/terminal include the following:

- Physical destruction to terminal.
- Addition, deletion, or modification to computer records.
- Disclosure of confidential information.
- System shutdown.

An access concern that is not widely publicized but that is extremely dangerous is spoofing. The spoofing concept is designed to obtain passwords or other keys to processing from another terminal user. Under the spoofing concept, the perpetrator requires physical access to the terminal. The perpetrator then opens processing and activates a program that simulates the terminal's security system. The perpetrator then leaves the system awaiting an authorized user to commence operation. The spoofing program leads the regular operator to believe it is a security system and requests from the operator his/her password. Upon receiving the password, the spoofing system stores it in the perpetrator's work area and then logs off the system. The regular operator believes there has been a temporary problem and reactivates the system, at which time the password is reentered and processing occurs. At a later time, the perpetrator can come back to the system and obtain valid passwords, enabling him to perform unauthorized acts.

Continuity of Processing

The ability of the microcomputer terminal to provide continuity of processing is dependent on both the reliability of the hardware and the processing capacity of the system to satisfy user requirements. Should either prove inadequate, users of terminals could be greatly inconvenienced or lose business. For example, when airline reservation systems are down, travelers cannot buy tickets. Being unable to buy from one airline may cause a traveler to purchase a ticket from another airline.

While the continuity-of-processing solution is normally beyond the control of the terminal users, it is a terminal-control issue. While the terminal operations function may not be able to take the full corrective action, it can both identify problems and ensure that the necessary information is available at the terminal site to reconstruct processing in the event of problems. The restart/recover procedures are normally developed in conjunction with the central computer site.

The restart/recovery process is a two-part process. The first part involves retaining the data necessary to reconstruct and/or restart processing in the event of problems. The second part is the development and testing of the procedures necessary to restore integrity after it has been lost.

The concerns that an auditor should have over the ability of a microcomputer operating in emulation mode to recover operations after a problem include the following:

- Incomplete retention of transaction-entry data.
- Inability to retrieve transaction data economically.
- Incomplete or inadequate restart or recovery procedures.
- Personnel inadequately trained in the recovery process.
- Failure to predesignate alternative processing sites or arrange for backup hardware.
- Inadequate manual procedures to continue processing during computer downtime.
- Inadequate manual procedures to capture needed processing data during downtime.

Terminal Audit Risks

A microcomputer used as a terminal, like part of an organization, is but one of the many interrelated pieces that constitute a larger system. However, just as auditors have learned to break financial systems down into their component parts for audit purposes, so must they learn to break down computer systems into their component parts.

As auditors assess the components of financial applications, they allocate their audit efforts according to risk. The higher the risk of a component of a financial application, the greater the amount of audit effort devoted to that component. For example, in accounts receivable, the bad-debt write-off component is a high-risk part of the application and, thus, warrants extensive audit effort. The same logic needs to be applied to computer systems, in which the auditor attempts to assess the degree of risk inherent in terminal operations.

Terminal/Microcomputer Audit Approach

The terminal audit approach is similar to the audit of any other operational functions. What changes are the steps that the auditor needs to perform when computer terminals are involved. The following audit steps highlight the approach to follow when the audit includes computer terminals:

Step 1: Identify computer network. The auditor needs to understand the scope of the computer network. This can best be illustrated in a flowchart. It would show the main computer as the center of the flowchart, with lines connecting the central computer to the terminals/ microcomputers. Both the number of terminals and the organizational unit controlling those terminals should be identified on the flowchart. At the end of this process, the auditor will know the scope of the network and the organization entities accountable for the operation of the network.

Step 2: Identify application systems. Superimposed on the flowchart should be the application systems operational on the network. The application should be categorized wherever practical, such as a billing/invoicing/receivables application, and a color drawn on the flowchart indicating which terminals have access to which application systems. (Obviously, if every terminal can access every application, there is no need to draw application usage on the flowchart.)

Step 3: Identify terminal type. The functioning of the microcomputer should be indicated. Some auditors like to list the specific hardware at each terminal site.

Step 4: Identify terminal risk. The combination of the applications accessible to each microcomputer provides an indication of the risk at each location. This can be indicated on the flowchart or on a separate worksheet. Normally, the categorization of risk into high, medium, and low is sufficient; but if more precision is required, a risk analysis can be used to develop a quantitative annual loss expectation (ALE) for each terminal.

Step 5: Identify terminal controls. The operational controls for each terminal should be identified and indicated on the flowchart. Again, this can be done on a worksheet if the controls are voluminous or the flowchart is cluttered with other information. The controls identified should be both environmental terminal controls, such as password protection, and application controls.

Step 6: Prepare risk/controls matrix. The matrix in Figure 9–20 is designed to show the usefulness of controls, which controls reduce which risks, and whether the risks have been reduced to an acceptable level. The matrix lists the risks down the left-hand column and the controls across the top of the matrix. The auditor may wish to list specific risks of concern within the matrix for each control that reduces a designated risk. One of the following three indications should be given regarding the strength of the control:

H (high) = Very effective control.

M (medium) = Effective control.

L (low) = Control of some effectiveness.

Step 7: Assess adequacy of terminal controls. Using the risk/controls matrix for each terminal, the auditor then assesses the strength of the controls. Horizontally, for each risk, the auditor will have identified the controls that address that risk and the relative strength of the controls. Based on professional judgment, the auditor will then assess whether the totality of the controls is sufficient to reduce the risk to an acceptable level.

The matrix is also valuable in assessing the cost-effectiveness of individual controls. For example, if a particular control appears very effective against numerous risks, the auditor could assume that to be a cost-effective control. On the other hand, if a control exists that is not very effective in reducing many risks, and those risks have a number of stronger controls, the auditor could conclude that the particular control

FIGURE 9–20
Risks/Controls Matrix for Microcomputer Used as a Terminal

Microcomputer Controls								
Terminal Risks								
Data integrity								
Terminal (microcomputer) integrity								
Access control								
Continuity of processing								

of minimal effectiveness may not be cost-effective. At a minimum, the control would warrant additional investigation to evaluate its cost-effectiveness. The matrix also shows risks that appear to be overcontrolled and, in those instances, may actually recommend the reduction of controls.

Step 8: Design and conduct audit tests. Based upon the level of risk, the auditor would conduct tests for the following two purposes:

- To determine that the controls are in place and effective.
- To determine the impact of a control weakness.

The selection and conduct of the tests would follow the same procedures used in conducting any other audit of an automated application. Previous chapters have described the test selection process, as well as the options available for terminal microcomputer testing. Among the tests that should be considered are:

- Computer audit software.
- Integrated test facility.
- Control flowcharting.
- Test data.
- Modeling/simulation.

Step 9: Write and disseminate audit reports. The findings from a terminal audit can impact any or all of the following parties:

- Terminal users.
- Application system analysts/programmers.
- Computer operations.
- Security officer.
- Database administrator.
- Systems programmer.
- Communications officer.
- Common carrier.

This wide diversity of involvement in terminal operations requires that the auditor identify the individual who can take action to correct an identified weakness or implement a recommendation. Frequently, findings are sent to the wrong individual—which either delays implementation of the recommendation or confuses the issue enough so that the recommendation never gets properly implemented.

Frequently, the correction of problems or the implementation of recommendations may require the consensus of several individuals. In these instances, the auditor should act as the catalyst to get the recommendations adopted and implemented. The complexity of some technical operations means that the auditor, as the only individual having direct access to all personnel involved, is the logical candidate to bring together concerned individuals to monitor the correction process.

Data-Entry Terminal Audit Program

Data-entry microcomputers/terminals are in use for a wide variety of applications. Most applications that are operational on a computer could be improved through the use of data-entry microcomputers. The micros permit the more timely entry of data and easy analysis of data stored within the automated application.

The data-entry micros are normally located in non-data-processing areas. Thus, they are used and monitored by people not aware of many of the risks and problems associated with automated systems. Therefore, it is important that the procedures and methods for operation be as simple as possible and that controls exist.

Much of the data-entry usage on micros/terminals is performed with the aid of screens. A screen provides a list of options or aids in entering the data. Therefore, the extent and clarity of the screen becomes important in ensuring the integrity of the entered data.

Figure 9–21 is a checklist of items that need to be addressed in auditing data-entry terminals.

AUDITING DISTRIBUTED PROCESSING SYSTEMS

Data processing professionals have been continually improving the responsiveness of computerized applications to the needs of their users. One way of increasing responsiveness of computerized applications is a distributed data processing system. While few organizations have achieved all the advantages claimed for distributed processing, many are designing applications that utilize distributed concepts.

The growth of microcomputers, minicomputers, low-cost mass storage, and communication lines provides the technology needed for dis-

FIGURE 9-21
Microcomputer Terminal Emulation as Data-Entry Terminal

No.	Item	Yes	No	N/A	Comments
			Response		
1.	Have adequate instructions been provided to individuals using microcomputers as data-entry terminals?	___	___	___	
2.	Have the individuals using the terminals been adequately instructed in those procedures?	___	___	___	
3.	Are procedures designed to identify errors made in data entry?	___	___	___	
4.	Are procedures established to prompt or aid terminal users in entering the correct information?	___	___	___	
5.	Are extensive data-validation routines used to ensure the integrity of the data entered?	___	___	___	
6.	Have transactions been identified with terminals as a method of improving data integrity and access control?	___	___	___	
7.	Do data-entry operators have a formal means to report problems?	___	___	___	
8.	Are data-entry operators advised when the central system is down?	___	___	___	
9.	Are users of data on terminals instructed in the expected reliability of that data?	___	___	___	
10.	Is the performance of the terminal hardware monitored?	___	___	___	
11.	Is the terminal subject to regular preventive maintenance?	___	___	___	
12.	Is the terminal sufficiently sturdy to withstand some physical abuse?	___	___	___	
13.	Does the terminal not display or print entered passwords?	___	___	___	
14.	Is the terminal shut down after a nominal period of no activity?	___	___	___	
15.	Is the terminal shut down after a reasonable number of invalid attempts to use the terminal?	___	___	___	
16.	Does local-site management accept responsibility for proper use of terminals?	___	___	___	

FIGURE 9–21   *(concluded)*

No.	Item	Yes	No	N/A	Comments
17.	Are access violations monitored and reported so that violation profiles can be established?	—	—	—	
18.	Are processing capabilities identified with specific terminals?	—	—	—	
19.	Are terminals located in areas where they are observable by supervision?	—	—	—	
20.	Are individuals held accountable for their terminal usage?	—	—	—	
21.	Can all transaction processing be identified with a specific individual?	—	—	—	
22.	Are procedures established for handling work in the event a terminal is down?	—	—	—	
23.	Are recovery procedures available for data-entry terminals?	—	—	—	
24.	Are recovery procedures periodically practiced for data-entry terminals?	—	—	—	
25.	Are backup copies of transactions entered on terminals maintained for a reasonable length of time?	—	—	—	
26.	Are procedures established on dial-up networks to ensure that the terminal is connected to the proper facility?	—	—	—	
27.	Are error messages identified according to the priority of action that should be taken on those messages?	—	—	—	
28.	Are procedures available for operators to easily correct errors?	—	—	—	
29.	Are operators aware when the central computer fails to accept messages, and the point where the message has been accepted?	—	—	—	
30.	Are backup terminals/micros available in the event the primary data-entry terminal is down for extended periods?	—	—	—	

tributed systems. It appears that the hardware needed for sophisticated distributed systems is available, but the systems analysts and software designers have yet to maximize the use of this hardware for distributed processing. Based on the stated advantages, one can expect many distributed systems to be developed within the next few years.

Auditors need to become involved in the development of this new computer technology. We have learned in the past that systems technology continually outpaces control development. Only by getting auditors involved in the early stages of systems development can an organization be assured that control will receive the proper attention.

The audit of a distributed data system has many similarities to the audit of a computer center. In conducting the audit, the auditor should equate the distributed system with a distributed data center. The distributed system is in effect a distributed computer center. The audit of a distributed system is the audit of the general controls over the processing of the distributed system. However, as with other advanced data processing technology, there is a migration of control from application to environment.

The environmental controls in an advanced data processing environment assume much greater importance than in a batched environment. The review of a distributed data system is primarily a review of environmental controls. The assessment of the environmental controls will affect the review of the controls over the applications operating in a distributed data environment.

This chapter discusses distributed systems from an auditor's perspective. It is important for the auditor to be aware of exactly what is being distributed and to review the "distributed data processing system" in order to learn precisely what is distributed. After this determination, the audit and control problems can be put into the proper perspective.

Characteristics of a Distributed Processing System

The concept of distributed data processing systems implies a decentralized approach to data processing. The distributed concept places computer power where it is most effective in meeting the needs of the user. User responsiveness is a key part of distributed data processing.

There are many different definitions and concepts about what is known as distributed data processing. For example, distributed data processing is completely decentralized. The distributed units have autonomy in processing, just as decentralized organizations have functional autonomy within each decentralized unit. The analogy between a decentralized organization and distributed processing may help illustrate what is meant by distributed systems.

One of the misconceptions about distributed systems is the confusion between on-line applications with microcomputers and a distributed data processing system. In most on-line applications, the processing is not really distributed. The central computer in an on-line application is the master, and the terminals (even if intelligent microcomputers) are slaves to the central computer.

The audit and control problems associated with a decentralized organization are basically the same as those associated with distributed data processing. The autonomy of operation of a decentralized unit creates variations that make both controlling and combining results difficult. There is also the problem of coordinating and directing the decentralized functions toward a common goal. The difference makes coordination and overall direction complex.

We need to examine the characteristics of a distributed system in order to understand the audit and control problems of that system. The characteristics of a distributed system can be divided into five areas, as shown in Figure 9–22.

It would be difficult in today's data processing environment to find many, if any, examples of a distributed system with all five characteristics present. Most distributed systems today incorporate one or two of the distributed characteristics. We will examine each of the characteristics in detail.

Assignable resources. The objective of a distributed data processing system is to be more responsive to user needs. This means being able to apply data processing resources where they are most beneficial to users. Thus, if group A requires extensive data processing resources on day one, the resources should be assigned to group A on that day. When group B needs resources on day two, those same resources should be reassignable to group B.

Being able to reassign resources on a short-term basis provides the necessary flexibility for meeting the data processing resource needs of users. If the need for resources exceeds capacity, the resources must be allocated to the areas with the highest priority. Thus, from an organizational perspective, resources are allocated on the basis of priority of needs, as opposed to ownership of resources.

The method of assigning resources is a mechanism to be solved by data processing personnel. It is immaterial where the resources physically reside, because the location of the resource should be transparent

FIGURE 9–22
Characteristics of a Distributed System from a Data Processing Perspective

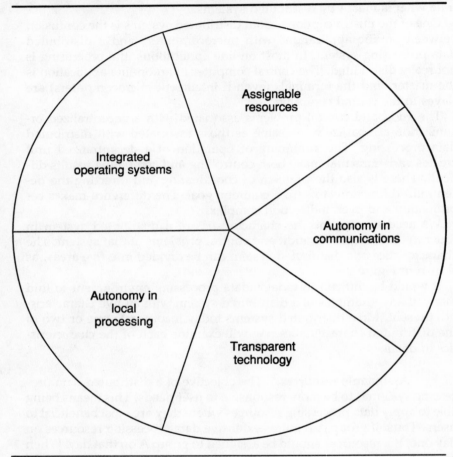

to the user. When one interacts with data processing resources using a terminal, it is immaterial whether the processing capacity is in the next room, a mile away, or 5,000 miles away. The concern is that the capacity is available when needed.

Autonomy in communications.   In an on-line computer operation, communications are directed by the central computer. The terminals or microcomputers are slave to the polling algorithm of this central computer. When the central computer wants to transmit messages to the terminals or microcomputers, it has authority to direct and interrupt terminal processing so that the terminal gets that message. On the other hand, when an on-line terminal wants service from the central computer, it must ask permission first before service is granted.

In a distributed environment, there is no central computer with authority over outlying units. Each distributed processing unit has autonomy in communication. There is no master and slave relationship. Autonomy in communication means that a processing unit cannot force a message on another unit, or vice versa. Each processing unit has autonomy. If a unit desires not to take messages from another distributed unit, it may refuse to do so. A response in that case could be "not available," "delay sending message until tomorrow," and so on. The same relationship occurs when that unit sends a message to another unit. It is a communication system of equals.

Transparent technology. An objective of a distributed system is that the system be transparent to the user. The user should not be aware of, or concerned about, how the distributed system is interconnected. The user should be able to enter a request and have that request satisfied without concern for how it is satisfied.

The distributed system may include multiple microcomputers, multiple physical databases, computing power in many locations, a network of complex communication gear, and a complex operating system. The method of organizing the system and tying that organization together in a cohesive operating unit should not have any effect upon the user's request.

Autonomy in local processing. Each distributed processing unit should have authority to design, implement, and operate its own applications. The information sent to the consolidating system may need to be in a standard format, but the methods by which that information is collected, accumulated, and stored should be under the control of the distributed unit. Local autonomy in processing enables a local unit to select the methods and techniques used in processing. Again, the decentralized concept in running the distributed system is an important part of the process.

Having autonomy in local processing enables the manager to develop applications in a manner that best meets the needs of the users in that processing unit. The hours of processing, the means of interacting with users, and local standards and conventions all come under the autonomy of the local manager. In a situation with local autonomy, the system is free to react quickly to changing needs in the local unit. The local manager can change priorities in the local data processing unit immediately to react to an emergency user need in that unit. With a centrally controlled application, the local manager's requirement would have to be measured against all other requirements before an implementation priority would be determined.

Integrated operating systems. The total distributed network must be tied together by an operating system. However, rather than being like an authoritative operating system of a centralized computer center, the distributed operating system must be more of a negotiator. The integrated operating system of a distributed environment is a coordinating mechanism as opposed to one that directs operations.

True distributed operating systems must have the capabilities of achieving the previously discussed characteristics of a distributed system. In other words, the characteristics of a distributed operating system must include the following:

- The ability to assign resources to meet the current needs of users.
- The ability to control a communication network in which no unit has authority over another unit.
- The ability to tie together all the distributed aspects of a system so that the hardware, software, and application technology is transparent to the user.
- The ability to coordinate multiple distributed processing units in which each has its own autonomy for methods of operation.

At the same time this transparent distributed network is being operated, control must exist over the system, and the system must be auditable.

Audit and Control Concerns of Distributed Processing Systems

Distributed systems are being implemented because they offer advantages over conventional computerized applications. Specifically, they do the following:

- Permit data processing to be more responsive to the needs of the user.
- Reduce the cost of computer processing.
- Provide processing capabilities to users that enable them to be more competitive in performing their functions.

One industry that appears to be moving rapidly toward distributed data processing is financial institutions. The demand for financial institutions to offer distributed services seems to be increasing. The new variety of distributed customer services being offered by financial institutions includes the following:

- Twenty-four hour banking with cash dispensing terminals.
- Electronic transfer of funds between financial institutions.
- Preauthorization for banks to pay certain bills.
- Direct deposit of funds into customer accounts (e.g., automatic deposit of social security and payroll checks).

These services are typical of those that appear to be headed toward distributed data processing systems. Using these as our example, we can begin to see some of the potential control and audit problems. While these problems are not unique to financial institutions, these applications illustrate the concerns.

The control concerns presented by distributed data processing systems include the following:

- The ability of technology to be responsive to the distributed system requirements.
- The ability to coordinate data updates used by several units when the data files are distributed.
- The ability to control updates when many users will be vying for the same data resources at the same time.
- Maintaining the service level required by users.
- Developing accepted priority systems for allocation of resources.
- Maintaining the integrity of software systems in a distributed environment.

The auditing concerns in a distributed data processing system environment include the following:

- Obtaining auditors with sufficient skills to perform effectively in this environment.
- Developing audit tools and techniques that are effective in this environment.
- Having auditors with sufficient experience to be able to evaluate the effectiveness of controls in this environment.
- Recognizing potential control problems in a new technology.

There are no easy answers to these control and audit concerns. The one premise that is indisputable is that unless auditors get involved early, they will not be able to contribute to the success of distributed systems. With each new step in technology, the integrity of the system becomes more dependent on the adequacy of the automated system of controls.

One last concern affects both the control and the audit of the distributed data processing system. Among the desired characteristics of a distributed system is that it should be transparent to the user. In other words, users do not need to know, nor should they care about, the technical aspects of the system. Stated another way, this means that the user does not understand the control implications or the control mechanism for a distributed system. In other technologies, auditors have always counted on heavy user involvement as one of the keys to effective control. This type of control may not be workable in a distributed data processing system. Without user involvement, the auditor may have to play a more dominant role in the development of controls for a distributed system.

Audit Approach

The technology for distributed data processing systems is evolving. Though few auditors are concerned about confronting a full-blown distributed data processing system in the near future, some distributed characteristics are now appearing in computerized applications. The audit approach must be tailored to meet the specifications of the system being audited.

Earlier in this chapter we reviewed the "ideal" distributed data processing system. However, it is recognized that today's technology makes the implementation of such a system impractical. What we are finding in practice are applications that use some of the advantages and objectives of a distributed data processing system. The use of these distributed characteristics has control and audit implications.

What is needed in the audit approach of a distributed system is an assessment of the system being audited versus the "ideal" distributed system. We can do this by looking at the aspects of the system that are distributed. We discussed previously the audit and control concerns of the "ideal" distributed system. The audit and control perspectives cover the same area, but from different viewpoints. For example, having the system transparent from the perspective of the user is a data processing implementation objective. Translated into an auditor's perspective, we see a control concern because the user is not involved in the implementation of the system. We must now look at the distributed system from an auditor's perspective.

An auditor looks at applications, not the characteristics of a technology. Viewing a distributed system from an auditor's perspective, there are five parts of an application operation that can be distributed. These areas are shown in Figure 9–23.

The audit approach for a distributed system is dependent on which of the areas is distributed. Each area will be discussed individually.

FIGURE 9–23
Characteristics of a Distributed System from an Audit Perspective

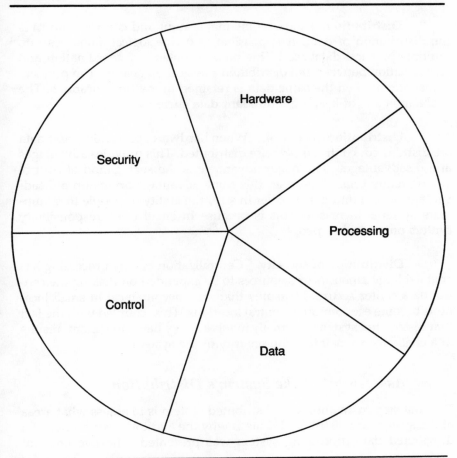

Distribution of hardware. It would be impractical to have a distributed data processing system if hardware was not distributed. Therefore, the first prerequisite of a distributed system is the distribution of hardware such as microcomputers. This poses the potential audit and control problem of having assets and resources distributed at many remote sites.

Distribution of processing. Again, it would be difficult to conceive of a distributed data processing system without distributing processing capabilities. The amount and location of processing capabilities can vary, but processing must be distributed from the central location. The amount of processing distributed determines the degree of control and audit concern.

Distribution of data. One major audit and control concern is the distribution of data. It is possible to divide logical databases into multiple physical databases. This poses problems of coordination and reconciliation between the distributed physical databases. The problem is magnified when the same data is retained in multiple locations. The problem is one of keeping redundant data current.

Distribution of control. When hardware, processing, and data are distributed, control is likewise distributed. This provides advantages and disadvantages. The major advantage is the segregation of control among many units. However, this same advantage brings up a disadvantage: as the unit gets smaller in size, the ability of people to manipulate systems increases. This is because in small units responsibility centers on a few key people.

Distribution of security. Centralization of data processing has enabled large amounts of resources to be expended on making the central data center secure. Measures that are uneconomical in small locations become economical in central locations. This, coupled with the fact that distributed systems normally involve heavy data movement, results in a challenge to maintain the security of the system.

Assessment of the System's Distribution

The first step in an audit of a distributed system is to assess what areas of the system are distributed. This is why the auditor's perspective of a distributed data processing system was presented. The five areas of a distributed system (as seen from an audit perspective) become the tools for measuring the areas and amount of distribution.

These five audit areas will be used as the basis for conducting an audit of a distributed system. However, before beginning the audit, the auditor must first examine the total distributed system and measure the distribution of each area. Once measured, the results of that measurement should be placed on a form such as the one shown in Figure 9–24.

This self-evaluation form on the maturity of distributed systems provides guidance in using the audit program for each of the five audit areas. If a particular area is not distributed, it can be audited in the conventional manner. However, the more that area is distributed, the more need there is to look at it from a new perspective. The new perspective is to examine the distributed area independent of the applications run on the system.

FIGURE 9–24
Self-Evaluation on Distributed Systems' Maturity

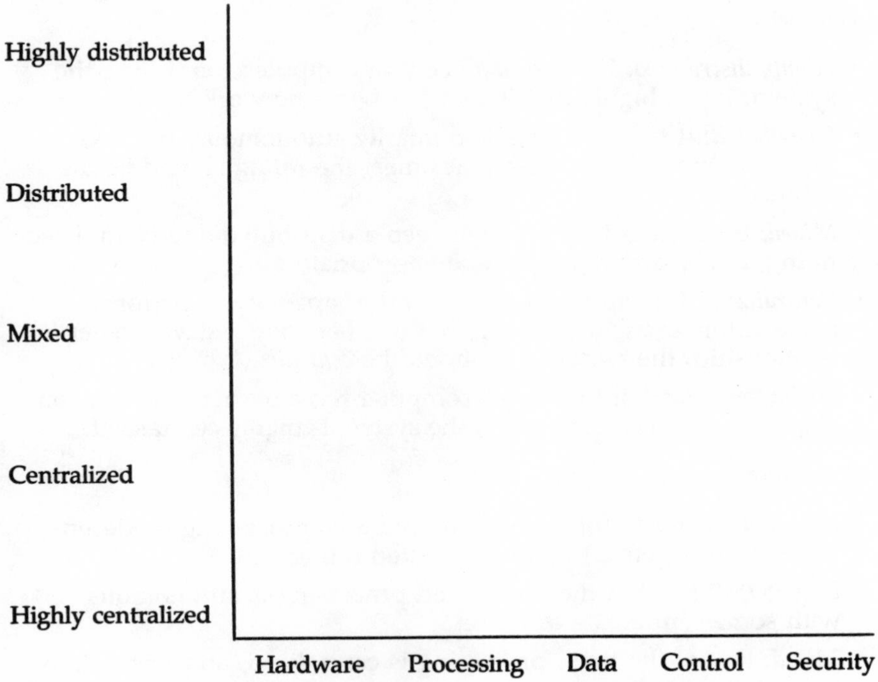

	Hardware	Processing	Data	Control	Security
Highly distributed					
Distributed					
Mixed					
Centralized					
Highly centralized					

The auditor should review each of the five areas and then rate them according to these five categories:

1. *Highly distributed:* Meets the "ideal" distributed system characteristics.
2. *Distributed:* Comes close to the "ideal" characteristics of a distributed system.
3. *Mixed:* Has some of the characteristics of a distributed system and some of the characteristics of a centralized system.
4. *Centralized:* System is basically a centralized system, with a few distributed characteristics.
5. *Highly centralized:* Has practically no characteristics of a distributed system.

The assessment step starts with this process of the auditor rating each of the five areas of a distributed system (i.e., hardware, processing, data, control, and security) according to one of the above five ratings. Each of the five areas will be covered here individually, explaining how to assign a rating. The ratings can be plotted onto Figure 9–24.

Hardware

- *Highly distributed:* If there is no central computer controlling the system, it is a highly distributed hardware network.
- *Distributed:* If the hardware is primarily autonomous, but reverts to a slave/master relationship at times, the rating should be distributed.
- *Mixed:* If the rater is unsure between a distributed and centralized rating, a mixed rating would be appropriate.
- *Centralized:* If microcomputers have the capability to perform some autonomous processing, but it is basically a slave/master relationship, the assessment should be *centralized*.
- *Highly centralized:* If the central computer has a master/slave relationship with the microcomputers, the system is highly centralized.

Processing

- *Highly distributed:* Completely autonomous processing by decentralized units gets a highly distributed rating.
- *Distributed:* Most of the distributed processing is autonomous, with some centralized direction.
- *Mixed:* Part of the time, processing is centralized, and part of the time, distributed.

- *Centralized:* Mostly centralized direction, with the microcomputers performing a few autonomous operations.
- *Highly centralized:* This is centralized processing where the microcomputers perform tasks assigned by the central unit.

Data

- *Highly distributed:* The physical data is under the complete jurisdiction of the remote area.
- *Distributed:* The data is physically located at the remote area, but the central system retains a degree of control over the accuracy and completeness of data.
- *Mixed:* The data is at the remote site, but under the complete control of the central unit.
- *Centralized:* The data is located at the central site, but accessible by the remote area.
- *Highly centralized:* The data is located at the central site and not accessible by the remote area.

Control

- *Highly distributed:* The complete control of the local system resides with the local manager.
- *Distributed:* Control is under the direction of the local manager, but follows central guidelines.
- *Mixed:* Control is performed locally, but ultimate control remains at the central location.
- *Highly centralized:* Both control and operation are run from the central location.

Security

- *Highly distributed:* Security is under the control of the local manager.
- *Distributed:* Security is under the direction of the local manager, but follows central guidelines.
- *Mixed:* Security is under the direction of the local manager, but maintains a close relationship with the central location.
- *Centralized:* Security is under the operation of the central group, but maintains a close relationship with the local manager.
- *Highly centralized:* Security is under the complete control of the centralized group.

From these criteria, the auditor can rate the five areas according to one of the five ratings. This rating will serve three purposes. These are to provide the auditor with:

1. An evaluation of the amount of actual distribution occurring in the computer environment.

2. A prioritization of which distributed systems' characteristics should be audited first; the most highly distributed one being the one audited first.

3. Guidance as to whether the audit should occur remotely or centrally.

The following sections will discuss how to audit each of the five areas.

Auditing Distributed Hardware Concerns

The audit and control concerns of hardware in a distributed system are similar to those in a conventional computer center. The specific concerns center on accountability and compatibility of hardware. The auditor is concerned that there be reasonable accountability for hardware, and that diverse microcomputer hardware equipment does not affect compatibility with other pieces of hardware.

Distributed systems means distributed authority to select hardware designs made specifically for the hardware needs of an operating unit. However, distributed hardware does not mean stand-alone hardware. The equipment selected for a distributed system is a resource of the distributed system. While autonomy exists in satisfying needs of local users, the same cooperative spirit needed to make the distributed systems successful must exist in hardware selection.

The hardware in each part of a distributed system is a system resource. These resources must be assignable to all users of the distributed system. *Assignable* may mean movement of physical hardware, or it may mean assigning the use of the resource to another unit of the distributed system.

The auditor should review the hardware of the distributed system from a perspective of accountability and compatibility. Figure 9–25 provides an audit program for auditing the distributed hardware concerns. In completing the worksheet, the auditor should evaluate the handling of the concern as very adequate, adequate, inadequate, or not applicable. The evaluations have the following meanings:

- *Very adequate:* The implemented controls appear to satisfactorily solve all concerns in a competent manner.

FIGURE 9–25

Distributed Processing Systems Hardware Concerns

		Response			
No.	Item	Very Adequate	Adequate	Inadequate	N/A	Comments
1.	Have the input data requirements been established?	___	___	___	___	
2.	Have provisions been made for backup hardware?	___	___	___	___	
3.	Have hardware performance criteria been established?	___	___	___	___	
4.	Does the microcomputer at the outlying units have the capability to utilize the capacity available to local users?	___	___	___	___	
5.	Have provisions been made for the hardware among the various units to interface properly?	___	___	___	___	
6.	Have plans been made to increase the capacity of the hardware, if the need exists?	___	___	___	___	
7.	Are the hardware control features, such as memory protection, being utilized?	___	___	___	___	

- *Adequate:* The implemented controls are such that any problems occurring as a result of the implementation will not significantly affect the operation.
- *Inadequate:* The concern has not been adequately addressed, or the solution will not eliminate the occurrence of significant problems.
- *Not applicable (N/A):* The item of concern is not applicable to the installation being reviewed.

For concern evaluations of Inadequate or Adequate, where there is some question regarding the adequacy of implementation, the Comments column should contain some explanation of the concern.

At the completion of the review, all concerns rated Inadequate should be pursued, as should Adequate evaluations where a note in the Comments column indicates some special concern. The auditor should make a determination of the seriousness of the item and take whatever action is required.

Auditing Distributed Processing Concerns

Processing in a distributed system involves application programs, the operating system, and the people operating equipment. The combination of the three utilizes the capabilities of the hardware to produce processing results.

In reviewing the processing area of a distributed system, the auditors need to satisfy themselves that the following concerns have been addressed:

- Processing capacity is adequate.
- Processing capacity is assignable.
- People are adequately trained.
- Application systems produce compatible data.
- Adequate planning exists for continued compatible growth.

Figure 9–26 provides a list of items of distributed processing concerns. In reviewing distributed processing, the auditor should evaluate these concerns in the same manner as outlined for Figure 9–25.

Auditing Distributed Data Concerns

One of the major concerns of distributed systems is the distribution of data. In stand-alone systems, data exist in many units of the organization. However, in those instances the data are not shared by multiple users. In a distributed system, data are shared.

With multiple physical databases, the need exists to have common elements in two or more physical databases. Having the same data appear in multiple databases increases the problem of data integrity. Detailed records must be maintained regarding every location of a particular data element. When a change is made in one physical database, it must be made to all databases containing that common data element.

In any database environment, there is the problem of multiple accesses to the same data element at the same time. A major operating

FIGURE 9–26
Distributed Processing Concerns

No.	Item	Very Adequate	Adequate	Inadequate	N/A	Comments
			Response			
1.	Are there agreements between remote distributed processing sites on policies regarding receipt and transmission of communications between the sites?	___	___	___	___	
2.	Have provisions been made for restart and recovery in the event of system failure?	___	___	___	___	
3.	Have documented operating instructions been prepared?	___	___	___	___	
4.	Have documented operating instructions been distributed to all units?	___	___	___	___	
5.	Have operation personnel in all units been instructed on the operating requirements of the distributed system?	___	___	___	___	
6.	Is a message priority structure used to ensure that the most important messages get delivered first?	___	___	___	___	
7.	Is a processing priority structure used to ensure that the most important processing gets accomplished first?	___	___	___	___	
8.	Are all messages received by the remote distributed processing site logged for backup and audit trail purposes?	___	___	___	___	

FIGURE 9–26   *(concluded)*

No.	Item	Very Adequate	Adequate	Inadequate	N/A	Comments
9.	Is the processing documentation up-to-date?	___	___	___	___	
10.	Has provision been made for dynamic load leveling so that the total processing load can be distributed across available computers?	___	___	___	___	
11.	Can the load-leveling procedures move the processing capability to the data?	___	___	___	___	
12.	Can the load-leveling capabilities move the data to the processing capabilities?	___	___	___	___	
13.	Have procedures been developed to handle lockout situations (i.e., user A has record one and is holding it until he gets record two, while user B has record two and is holding it until he gets record one)?	___	___	___	___	
14.	Has a detailed plan been prepared outlining the requirements for the distributed data system?	___	___	___	___	
15.	Have processing performance criteria been established?	___	___	___	___	
16.	Have provisions been made for the software in the various units to interface properly?	___	___	___	___	
17.	Have the output processing requirements been established?	___	___	___	___	

problem in a single database is to lock out secondary accesses to a data element when it is in the process of being updated. Current technology with one database is still struggling with the solution to this problem. If the same element appears in multiple databases, and can be accessed by many users simultaneously, the solution to the lockout problem is magnified.

Another data concern in a distributed environment is data definition. With distributed systems goes a high degree of autonomy. If one unit wants to slightly deviate the definition for its own needs, it may be able to do it. On the other hand, permitting this to happen can cause serious compatibility problems when consolidating data.

Figure 9–27 provides a checklist for reviewing the distributed data concerns. The auditors should satisfy themselves that these concerns have been adequately addressed in the distributed system. The worksheet rating should be performed in accordance with instructions for Figure 9–25.

Auditing Distributed Control Concerns

One of the least recognized concerns of a distributed system is the distribution of control. Studies of control in a data processing environment have previously indicated that too little attention has been addressed to the subject of control in a computerized business environment. Thus, without learning how to fully control a conventional data processing environment, we are moving rapidly into a distributed data processing environment.

There are no standards by which to determine adequacy of controls in a distributed data processing environment. There have not been enough true distributing systems experiencing control failures from which one could draw conclusions. It must be recognized that much of our experience in building adequate controls is obtained from failure to achieve adequacy of control in previous systems.

One of the major control problems in a distributed system is enforcement of standards. When processing units have a high degree of autonomy, issuance of standards from a central location is inconsistent with the distributed objectives. It is difficult to tell a local manager that he or she has authority over a computer operation, and then at the same time describe in detail how that operation is to be run.

Figure 9–28 provides a list of distributed control concerns. This area is one in which the auditor can make the greatest contribution. The previous three areas are ones in which data processing personnel has a solid base on which to enter a new technology. The same is not true in

FIGURE 9–27
Distributed Processing Systems: Distributed Data Concerns

No.	Item	Very Adequate	Adequate	Inadequate	N/A	Comments
		Response				
1.	Is the data stored at one remote distributed processing site backed up in another remote site?	___	___	___	___	
2.	Does each message contain a code identifying the sender?	___	___	___	___	
3.	Does each message contain a code identifying the intended receiver of the message?	___	___	___	___	
4.	Is there a provision to store messages destined for a remote distributed processing site that is out of service?	___	___	___	___	
5.	Do the data rules prohibit any user from redefining data?	___	___	___	___	
6.	Could the data in the distributed databases be combined into a single organization-wide database should the need exist?	___	___	___	___	
7.	Are standard data definitions used in all units?	___	___	___	___	
8.	When common data elements need updating, has provision been made to update all duplicate data elements simultaneously?	___	___	___	___	
9.	Is the data documentation up-to-date?	___	___	___	___	
10.	Is one person accountable for each element of data?	___	___	___	___	

FIGURE 9–28
Distributed Processing Systems: Distributed Control Concerns

No.	Item	Response				
		Very Adequate	Adequate	Inadequate	N/A	Comments
1.	Has a policy been established pertaining to what can and cannot be processed on a distributed data system?	___	___	___	___	
2.	Has a detailed plan been made for implementing a distributed data system?	___	___	___	___	
3.	Has a detailed schedule been established for implementing a distributed data system?	___	___	___	___	
4.	Do all the remote distributed processing sites get together on a regular basis to discuss operating procedures?	___	___	___	___	
5.	Is it forbidden to enter master commands in one remote distributed processing site for execution at another remote distributed processing site?	___	___	___	___	
6.	Has a detailed conversion plan been established for moving to a distributed data system?	___	___	___	___	
7.	Has a detailed plan been established to provide sufficient training for all people involved in a distributed data system?	___	___	___	___	
8.	Have the users established acceptance criteria that must be met before the distributed system goes operational?	___	___	___	___	

FIGURE 9–28 *(continued)*

No.	Item	Very Adequate	Adequate	Inadequate	N/A	Comments
9.	Have procedures been established to monitor system response times?	—	—	—	—	
10.	Has provision been made to monitor the number of times, and the length of time, that system malfunctions occur?	—	—	—	—	
11.	Do all remote distributed processing sites prepare schedules of needs so that the allocation of resources can be equitably distributed?	—	—	—	—	
12.	Is the user at one remote distributed processing site forbidden from overriding the conventions at another remote distributed processing site?	—	—	—	—	
13.	Has one individual (or processing unit) been appointed to control the distributed processing system?	—	—	—	—	
14.	Is the individual in charge of the distributed processing system the only individual able to use system commands affecting more than one site?	—	—	—	—	
15.	Have the system commands affecting more than one site been restricted to one terminal?	—	—	—	—	
16.	Is the system monitored to determine that remote distributed processing sites participate as full partners in the distributed processing system?	—	—	—	—	

FIGURE 9–28 *(concluded)*

No.	Item	Very Adequate	Adequate	Inadequate	N/A	Comments
17.	Are reports maintained on the amount of resources used by each unit in the distributed processing system?	___	___	___	___	
18.	Have all users' needs in the distributed system been equally addressed?	___	___	___	___	
19.	Have cost/benefit analyses been made on the distributed processing concept?	___	___	___	___	
20.	Have post-implementation reviews been made to determine that installation specifications were achieved?	___	___	___	___	
21.	Does the failure of any one unit affect the continued operation of any other unit?	___	___	___	___	
22.	Were other alternatives considered before going to the distributed data systems concept?	___	___	___	___	
23.	Do all remote distributed processing sites obtain regularly scheduled maintenance?	___	___	___	___	
24.	Are outgoing messages verified that they contain a valid destination address?	___	___	___	___	
25.	Do the remote distributed processing sites send copies of control and problem reports to a central site for central review and action?	___	___	___	___	
26.	Has the insurance coverage been adjusted to reflect the increased resources at remote distributed processing sites?	___	___	___	___	

control. The auditor should evaluate the control items in accordance with the rating system provided with Figure 9–25.

Auditing Distributed Security Concerns

Organizations can develop a good security system for assets in a central location. This can be true for data processing as well. When data is stored in central locations, remote facilities are only used for retention of backup information. In a centralized environment, the people with the highest data processing skills are present to oversee security on a daily basis. This has made security an accomplishable task in electronic data processing.

The use of communication lines added a new dimension to security. No longer was the computer room "vault" adequate. Information was passing in and out of the computer room over communication lines on a regular basis. It was now necessary to secure both the communication lines and the computer room.

The advent of distributed data processing systems brings distributed data, hardware, processing, and control. Security must now progress beyond what was expected in on-line applications. Just as we were learning how to secure information over communications lines, technology changes again. The use of cryptography, callback techniques, and other communication control practices have proven that there can be effective controls for safeguarding data over communication lines. These, plus new controls, are needed in a distributed environment.

A "divide and conquer" strategy may prove to be appropriate for distributed data processing systems. No longer can security be concentrated in a central location. As processing is distributed, so must be security. It is not practical to build well-secured computer rooms in a distributed data processing system. One of the main characteristics of distributed systems is the ability to assign resources. This reassignment can mean movement of hardware, processing, and control. One day processing may be heavily concentrated at location A, tomorrow at location B, and the next day at location C. This continually moving concentration of processing and data requires mobile security.

Figure 9–29 provides a list of distributed security concerns. The auditor should evaluate these concerns in accordance with the instructions for Figure 9–25.

In summary, after evaluation of the distributed security concerns, the auditor will have completed the distributed system review. The total review of the five areas must be consolidated to get an overview of the adequacy of control in the distributed system environment. The report

FIGURE 9–29
Distributed Security Concerns

No.	Item	Very Adequate	Adequate	Inadequate	N/A	Comments
			Response			
1.	Where appropriate, have remote distributed processing sites been restricted to authorized applications for that site?	___	___	___	___	
2.	Has a user profile been established to restrict access to individuals authorized to use resources?	___	___	___	___	
3.	Are passwords used to identify users of the distributed systems?	___	___	___	___	
4.	Are remote distributed processing sites in a physically secure location so that only authorized personnel can actually use the equipment?	___	___	___	___	
5.	If lockable keyboards are a feature on the remote microcomputers, is the feature properly utilized?	___	___	___	___	
6.	If sufficient unauthorized accesses are attempted from a remote distributed processing site to data at other sites, is that remote site locked out of the system?	___	___	___	___	
7.	Do microcomputers have a nonprinting feature for use when individuals enter their security passwords?	___	___	___	___	

FIGURE 9–29 *(continued)*

No.	Item	Very Adequate	Adequate	Inadequate	N/A	Comments
8.	If the microcomputer cannot be contained in a physically secure location, has a physical keylock been put on the unit's off/on switch?	___	___	___	___	
9.	Must the remote distributed processing site facilities be opened by a supervisor?	___	___	___	___	
10.	Are remote distributed processing sites locked out of the distributed systems during the hours when they are normally not in operation?	___	___	___	___	
11.	Is the concept of the callback technique used when sensitive data is involved? (When a terminal calls over a common-carrier communication line to another terminal, the second terminal disconnects the connection and calls back to the known location of the first terminal.)	___	___	___	___	
12.	If dial-up telephone numbers are used, are the numbers kept secret?	___	___	___	___	
13.	Have the objectives of security at the remote sites been documented?	___	___	___		
14.	Is security at all the remote distributed processing sites reviewed to ensure consistency in security procedures?	___	___	___		
15.	Is encryption or are secret keys used to protect sensitive data?	___	___	___	___	

FIGURE 9–29 *(concluded)*

No.	Item	Very Adequate	Adequate	Inadequate	N/A	Comments
16.	Are control reports prepared on security violations (including unsuccessful attempts at using passwords)?	___	___	___	___	
17.	Have disaster plans been developed?	___	___	___	___	
18.	Have disaster plans been tested?	___	___	___	___	
19.	Are there procedures on the preferred methods for disposal of sensitive documents at remote distributed processing sites?	___	___	___	___	
20.	Has a security classification been established for sensitive data?	___	___	___	___	
21.	Is the totality of all the data in the system considered when determining the data's security classification?	___	___	___	___	
22.	Is the documentation of security procedures up-to-date?	___	___	___	___	
23.	Are employees having access to sensitive data subject to special controls?	___	___	___	___	
24.	Are all systems commands logged so they can be reviewed by supervision at a later time?	___	___	___	___	
25.	Is there stringent control over the use and storage of circuit-test equipment?	___	___	___	___	

on the review should be prepared in a manner similar to that of a review of the data center. It should be distributed to the appropriate parties.

DATA CONTROL AND INTEGRITY

Data Accuracy

The risk of reliance on a single source of information makes inaccurate data a greater concern. If data is inaccurate, it will be used inaccurately by all applications that use that particular data element. For example, if a product price is wrong, it will result in inaccurate customer billing, inventory value, credits, sales commissions and bonuses, and so on.

It is possible that errors affecting the accuracy of the data will not be detected, because people are not monitoring the data, and details may not be balanced to totals after processing. For example, if an element of information is entered $69 as a detail record, but $89 is added to the control total, that condition will not be detected until a reconciliation has been made. At that point, the cost of correcting the inaccuracy may exceed the value of the error.

The greater accessibility to data increases the possibility of intentional and unintentional manipulation. People interfacing with the computer may change the value of individual records or the values between records, or take small amounts from many records and place them into an account under their control. All these manipulations affect the accuracy of data in the database.

With regard to organizations achieving the data accuracy objectives, the concerns include the following:

- Data is not truncated.
- Data is entered correctly.
- Data is accumulated correctly.
- Data is identifiable to the user.
- Data is not misrepresented through electronic limitations, such as overflow.

Data Control Priorities

Data is complete. The risk associated with incomplete data is increased because of the greater reliance on data as a source of information. In a manual application, if data is incomplete, only a single transaction may be affected. In a computerized environment, every application using the incomplete data is affected.

An incomplete data condition may not be detected until it is too late to take corrective action if the details are not regularly balanced to the totals. If extended periods of time occur between reconciliations, data can be lost, and the cost of searching for the data could exceed its value.

The centralization of data in a computer provides greater accessibility to that data. This greater accessibility provides an opportunity to manipulate the data for the advantage of a particular individual. In this manipulation, data (i.e., organizational assets) can be lost.

In a database environment, data can be lost because of simultaneous updating. Two programs may attempt to update the same element of data simultaneously. Without proper controls, one of the two updates will be lost when the data is returned to the database. Data can also be lost if a pointer chain is broken.

With regard to organizations achieving the data-completeness objectives, the concerns include the following:

- Transactions are not lost.
- All transactions are entered.
- Transactions are entered in the proper accounting period.
- Lost transactions can be identified.
- Detailed records support the control totals.

Data is authorized. The main impact of the computer on the authorization of data is in the changing methods of authorization. The primary control over data authorization has been with the user level, which is not part of the computer environment. This is changing as authorization is being automated. For example, inventory is being automatically replenished.

Because there is greater accessibility to data, the possibility exists that unauthorized data will be entered. Access controls in a computer system can lessen this possibility. The data in most organizations is not equally accessible to all users. Restrictions are imposed for a variety of reasons. Access to raw data is often restricted because interpretation of the raw data cannot be made without specialized knowledge or information that is not stored with the data. Some data is viewed as private and given special protection because the information could be used to the disadvantage of the person or organization. Sometimes aggregated data is viewed as worthy of protection, while the individual components are considered to have no special value. For example, individual sales data may be accorded only minor protection, but total sales figures are severely restricted.

The authority to enter data by means of source transactions or maintenance activities is usually much more controlled than the authority to access it. To protect the organization from defalcation, the authority to enter and access data is enforced in various ways. The ability to change data is often restricted to transactions that automatically provide a complete audit trail. This is analogous to the accounting requirement that no erasures be made in accounting journals. Corrections require an adjusting transaction in the journal of transactions, rather than a simple change to an existing entry.

The authorization of data can be controlled using security profiles of users. These profiles have the capability to control data in the following manners:

- Use (e.g., read-only, update, delete, etc.).
- Control use at field level.
- Limit use by values (e.g., update pay-rate field for fields with a value of up to $199.99).
- Limit rate of change (e.g., change pay-rate field by no more than plus or minus 10%).

With regard to organizations achieving the data authorization objectives, the concerns include the following:

- Improperly authorized data is not accepted.
- Data that is not authorized is not accepted.
- Authorization is verified.
- Practices to avoid proper authorization, such as issuing two small purchase orders rather than one large order, are identified.

Information is timely. Information from application systems should be available at the time of decision or action. The information needs to be available for the appropriate individual at the correct location. Failure to provide information could result in improper decisions or actions.

Timeliness is dependent on the application and type of information. In some applications, information is not critical to the process and, thus, the timely control objective assumes minimal importance. In other applications, such as on-line status systems, actions cannot be taken until the needed information is available.

With regard to organizations achieving the timely objectives, the concerns include the following:

- Information is sent to the right place.
- Information is delivered to the right person.
- Information is delivered on time.
- The needed information is identified.

Results are supportable. The audit trail is a control used for providing evidence for problems that have been detected or for verifying the propriety of processing. If an authorization violation is detected and the audit trail is incomplete, the necessary corrective action may not be ascertainable. Thus, anything that affects the completeness of the audit trail has an effect on the supportability of the results.

An audit trail is adequate if it is complete and if the data needed is easily obtained. The computerized environment has a minor impact on the type of data retained for audit-trail purposes. In practice, the movement to a computerized environment usually increases the amount of data available for audit-trail purposes. This is because the operating environment also retains data that can be used. There is a risk that the audit trail will be split into many segments. One part of the trail is located with all the application data, and the second part is retained in the operating environment as part of the recovery activity. Without proper planning, it may be extremely difficult, and probably impractical, to piece together all the segments of the audit trail. Thus, while the audit-trail data may exist, for practical purposes, the audit trail can be incomplete.

The computer-operating-environment audit trail is often destroyed within a brief period of time because of the extensiveness of the audit trail. Some organizations use a utility program to condense the amount of data retained for audit-trail purposes. Others retain the information only as long as is needed to recover from hardware and software failures. In most organizations, the computer-operating audit-trail information is retained in a time sequence so it can be used to recover operations. This may make it impractical to locate the needed information for the more traditional purposes of substantiating processing.

With regard to organizations achieving the supportable objectives, the concerns include the following:

- Transaction processing can be supported.
- The support is adequate.
- Transactions can be traced to control totals.

- Control totals can be supported by detailed transactions.
- Support information is readily retrievable.

Data Validation

Two problems associated with invalid data need to be addressed:

- Invalid data leads to erroneous outputs and can be the cause of harmful human, social, and economic effects.
- Invalid data can destroy the credibility of the system, demoralize those trying to use it, cause excessive system maintenance costs, and even cause the system to be unavailable or unusable.

Data validation involves the examination of computerized data to determine if it is accurate, complete, consistent, unambiguous, and reasonable. This section gives an overview of the direct methods that can be used to evaluate data in order to identify likely errors. Since these direct-evaluation methods are not able to find all errors, data integrity also depends on the correctness and integrity of all the activities by which the data is collected and processed. Controls must be used in order to prevent subtle errors from being introduced into the data. Data validation is a very basic control, but it should only be expected to detect gross errors. It will not compensate for poor control over other aspects of the applications system.

Data should be validated, first, during data collection and entry, prior to its use by the system, and then continuously, as new data is generated or used during processing.

Errors should be detected and corrected as soon as possible in order to prevent the propagation of invalid data throughout the system and the potential contamination of the system database. Once invalid data has been identified, it must be corrected. The process of correcting errors is itself prone to further errors, and data validation methods should be applied thoroughly during the correction activity.

Input-data verification, consisting of operational procedures to assure that source data is accurately transcribed to machine-readable form, is an important aspect of data validation. It includes manual information handling controls.

Three important measures are consistency and reasonableness checks, validation during data entry, and validation during processing.

Consistency and reasonableness checks. Relationships between data elements that arise from the intended meaning of the data can be used to identify errors in the source data as well as errors in data preparation and processing. Often, past records that are already in automated form can be used to predict probable values for current records. Any major deviation from expected values can be flagged for further investigation. The appropriate checking to identify suspicious values must be defined by those who are familiar with the application and must be included in the application design. It cannot be left to the programmers to determine.

Validation during data entry. Automated editing and validation should be used in both batch and on-line systems. In a batch processing system, validation routines may be run against the input data before it is processed. Validation can occur as each transaction is processed, with transactions that contain errors being recorded on a file for correction at a later time. On-line systems can provide the data entry personnel with immediate validation information so that detected errors can be corrected immediately. In either system, checks that must also use information from the database may not be practical until just before processing.

Three basic techniques for editing and validating data during data entry are the following:

1. Fields can be checked for:

   - Legitimate characters (format checks).
   - Proper sequences with respect to corresponding fields in preceding data records.
   - Reasonableness.
   - Consistency with other fields in the record.
   - Values within specified ranges or limits.
   - Valid items or codes and validity of a self-checking number contained in an extra digit(s) appended to the field.
   - Cryptographic check digits (i.e., data authentication information appended to a field that is a cryptographic function of all the data in the field).

2. Records or transactions can be checked for:

   - Completeness.
   - Consistency of fields in the record with items in previous transactions or with other items in the database.
   - Valid sequences of transactions.

3. A group of records or transactions can be checked by maintaining:

   - Control totals (e.g. batch, hash, amount, document, running).
   - Record/transaction counts.

- Batch-number checks.
- Item/transaction balances.

Validation during processing. Further checking of input data during processing and validation of data that is generated by the application system are essential for assuring data integrity. Many of these techniques are also used by auditors to audit data integrity. All the methods described above for validation of input data can be applied during processing.

Six techniques for validation during processing are as follows:

1. Integrated test facility (ITF). The ITF allows the performance of the application system to be monitored by incorporating dummy master records into the database. Once these records are in place, test transactions that are included with live data can be processed against the dummy records during the normal processing cycle. Processing results of the test transactions can then be compared with predetermined results.

2. System control audit review files (SCARF). Specifically designed tests placed within the application's code are performed on the processed data during normal processing. Some criteria are selected to extract desired records (e.g. processing exceptions, predetermined samples) and to write them onto a file, which can be reviewed at a later time.

3. Tracing. This means following (tracing) specifically marked or tagged transactions as they are processed by the application system. It requires additional application codes and an extra field in the transaction for the tag. During processing, a record or trail is generated for the marked transaction; it can be analyzed to determine if the processing was correct.

4. Sampling techniques. They involve inspecting portions of the data to determine their validity.

5. Run-number controls. They account for each run of an application system against a database. The run number kept in the database and the application program must agree.

6. Reconciliation of control files. Important elements of the database are identified, and a file of transactions is maintained with a running total. Periodically, the old balance (taken from the last reconciliation) is added to the running total and must equal the new balance (taken from the database).

Chapter Ten

Microcomputer Insurance

This chapter discusses some of the elements of microcomputer insurance policies, and a sample policy is provided. These materials are applicable for microcomputer, minicomputer, and mainframe computer operations. A checklist is provided for reviewing the insurance coverage that is described.

BASIC CONSIDERATIONS

A number of insurance companies are now offering specific policies for a firm's microcomputers. Note, however, that firms that already have an existing policy for their mainframe operations may be automatically covered for any micros used in their business.

If you have a microcomputer at home, be aware that your ordinary homeowner's insurance may not cover the computer equipment or software. The standard homeowner's policy is what is known as a "named perils policy"; that is, it will generally cover the contents of your home against specific disasters such as fire, theft, and flood. Homeowner policies were not designed to protect against computer-related problems such as power surges, hardware or software failure, or data losses.

In order to facilitate the claims process, if required, make a detailed list of all computer equipment including, for each component, the following:

- Make.
- Model number.
- Description (printer, monitor, etc.).
- Serial number.
- Date purchased/leased.
- Date installed.
- Replacement cost.
- Actual cash value.

Also include the insurance company's name, contact person and phone number, and policy number. Keep the list in a safe place, possibly a safe-deposit box or at a separate company location.

In general, micro insurance policies cover the following:

- Direct physical loss or damage to your microcomputer system. Media, programs, data, documentation, and source materials that are used to support the system are also covered.

- Accidental erasure or loss of data.

- Dishonest or fraudulent use of the microcomputer system by your employees or outside parties.

- Unusual electrical damage caused by outside problems. These include spikes, brownouts, or power surges that are not covered under normal maintenance contracts.

- Extra expenses incurred to continue your business because of a covered loss.

Premiums are relatively inexpensive; a small outlay can obtain $25,000 in coverage. Deductibles vary.

Figure 10–1 illustrates a sample microcomputer insurance policy, written in easy-to-understand language. Note what this policy will and will not cover. Contact your insurance company for the latest insurance coverage/policy.

INSURANCE COVERAGE CHECKLISTS

Figure 10–2 is a checklist that can be used for reviewing the insurance coverage outlined in this chapter. It is applicable for both microcomputer and mainframe operations. The checklist covers the following areas:

- Data processing equipment.
- Data processing media.
- Extra expenses.
- Business interruption.
- Valuable papers and records.
- Accounts receivable.
- Other insurance considerations.

FIGURE 10-1
Sample Microcomputer Insurance Policy

---

*ACU All Risk Computer Protection**

This agreement is sponsored by the Association of Computer Users Inc. (ACU) and offered through the Data Security Insurance Agency Inc. by the St. Paul Fire and Marine Insurance Company. This agreement is offered to ACU members and nonmembers.

Coverage Summary

Limit of Coverage	$25,000
Deductible	$ 250

What This Agreement Covers

We'll protect you and your business against all risks of:

- Direct physical loss or damage to your small computer system. Media, programs, data, documentation, and source materials which are used to support the system are also covered.
- Accidental erasure or loss of data.
- Dishonest or fraudulent use of the computer system by your employees or outside parties.
- Unusual electrical damage caused by outside problems. These include spikes, brownouts, or power surges that aren't covered under normal maintenance contracts.
- Extra expenses incurred to continue your business because of a covered loss.

We explain what we mean by each of these in the following sections.

Small computer system. We'll cover loss or damage to the small computer system you own, lease or rent from others, or for which you are legally

---

*42189 Ed. 3–82. Printed in U.S.A., Insuring Agreement 32B, Property Coverage.

FIGURE 10–1 *(continued)*

responsible. This system is covered wherever it's located, including while in transit and at temporary locations. However, we won't cover any property you rent or lease to others.

Small computer system means the small computer which is described on the sales, lease, or rental receipt which is attached. This receipt is part of this agreement.

Media. We'll cover loss or damage to the magnetic media which is regularly used with the small computer system. But we won't cover media which can't be replaced with media of the same kind or quality.

Media means materials on which data are recorded, such as magnetic tapes, floppy disks, or hard disks.

Programs. We'll cover loss or damage to programs either purchased or written on a custom basis, which are regularly used with the small computer system.

Data. We'll cover loss or damage to, or accidental erasure of, data stored in the computer system, whether in the memory or on the media.

Data means facts, concepts, or instructions converted to a form usable in your data processing operations. This includes programs, documentation and source materials.

Documentation and source material. We'll cover loss or damage to documentation or source materials which support the small computer system.

Dishonest or fraudulent use of the small computer system. We'll cover loss of money, securities, or other property you own, lease, or rent from others, or for which you are legally responsible, which results from computer theft.

Computer theft means dishonest or fraudulent use of the covered small computer system by your employees or outside persons. This includes:

• Intentional, unauthorized and fraudulent entry of data which creates unauthorized data records; or

• Intentional, unauthorized and fraudulent changes to data on disks, tapes or other media.

Property includes your business proprietary information, such as customer lists, patents, formulas, trade secrets, or other confidential information. But it doesn't include the proprietary information of others.

In order for a claim for loss of proprietary information to be paid, you must:

1. Prove that the proprietary information was taken from you by an employee or an outsider using the covered small computer system.

2. Prove the amount of your loss.

Unusual electrical damage. We'll cover damage to the small computer system, not normally covered by computer maintenance agreements, caused by external electrical problems such as spikes on the line, brownouts, or power surges.

Extra expense. We'll pay necessary extra expenses you have in continuing your business because of a loss covered under this agreement. These include any operating expenses over and above what it would normally cost you to conduct your operations had no loss occurred, such as expense to rent or use another computer system or facility.

FIGURE 10–1 *(continued)*

What We'll Pay

Equipment. We'll pay the actual cost of repairing or replacing the damaged equipment, but we won't pay more than the amount it would cost to repair or replace the lost or destroyed item with property of similar kind and quality.

Data, programs, documentation, and source materials. We'll pay the actual cost of reproducing lost or accidentally erased data, programs, documentation, and source materials provided you actually replace or reproduce them.

Media. We'll pay the cost of replacing lost or damaged media with material of the same kind or quality.

Extra expense. We'll pay extra expenses you incur from the date of your loss for as long as it should reasonably take to resume normal operations. You agree to resume your normal operations as soon as possible. We'll pay the amount you actually spend for expenses, but no more.

Of course, we won't pay more than the limit of coverage for any loss.

Exclusions—Losses We Won't Cover

When we use the word "loss" in this section, we also mean damage.

Mechanical or electrical breakdown. We won't cover loss to the equipment caused by internal mechanical or electrical breakdown, failure, or deficiency in design, specifications, materials, or workmanship. But if fire or explosion results, we'll pay for the loss caused by the fire or explosion.

Corrosion. We won't cover any loss caused by corrosion, rust, or changes in humidity or temperature.

Equipment being repaired or serviced. We won't cover any loss caused by, or that occurs while equipment is being repaired or serviced, unless fire or explosion results. We'll only cover the damage caused by the resulting fire or explosion.

Your dishonesty. We won't cover any dishonesty loss caused by fraud, dishonesty, or a crime committed by you, a partner, your officers, your directors or your trustees. Nor will we cover any loss which doesn't involve the use of the covered small computer system.

Wear—depreciation—deterioration—pests. We won't cover any loss resulting from any of the following causes:

• wear and tear
• depreciation
• gradual deterioration, or
• insect or animal pests like termites or mice

Loss of market. We won't cover any loss caused by loss of market or loss of income.

Construction laws. We won't cover any extra expense loss caused by laws governing the construction, repair or demolition of buildings or other structures.

Strikes. We won't cover any extra expense loss due to delay caused by strikers or anyone else at the site of your damaged business who interfere with your efforts to fix the damage or resume your normal operations.

FIGURE 10–1 *(concluded)*

Investigation expenses. We won't cover expenses incurred by you in establishing the existence of or the amount of any computer theft loss.

Disappearance—inventory. We won't cover computer theft losses for property that just disappears or that you find missing when you take inventory.

War and government seizure. We won't cover any loss caused by: War (declared or undeclared). Invasion. Insurrection. Rebellion. Revolution. Civil war. Or seizure of power. Or anything done to hinder or defend against these actions. We won't cover seizure or destruction of your property under quarantine of customs' regulations, or confiscation by any government or public authority. Nor will we cover illegal transportation or trade.

Nuclear activity. We won't cover any loss caused by nuclear reaction, nuclear radiation, or radioactive contamination. And we don't intend these causes of loss to be considered fire, smoke, explosion, or any other insured peril. But we'll cover direct loss by fire resulting from nuclear reaction, nuclear radiation, or contamination if the loss would otherwise be covered under this agreement.

Limit of Coverage

The limit of coverage is $25,000. This limit is the most we'll pay for all losses no matter how many protected persons are involved or how many claims are made in any one policy period.

Deductible

You'll be responsible for the first $250 of each loss. We'll pay the rest of your covered loss up to the limit of coverage that applies. You agree that any recovery or salvage on a loss will belong to us until the amount we paid has been made up.

Where We Cove,

We cover events that take place in the United States of America, its territories or possessions, Puerto Rico, or Canada.

Other Insurance

Other insurance may be available to cover a loss. If so, we'll pay the amount of your covered loss that's left after the other insurance has been used up, less your deductible. But we won't pay more than the limit of coverage that applies.

Insurance for Your Benefit

This insurance is for your benefit. No third party having temporary possession of your property, such as a transportation company, can benefit directly or indirectly from it.

Expenses for Reducing Loss

When a covered loss occurs, you must do everything possible to protect the property from further damage. Keep a record of your expenses. We'll pay our share of reasonable and necessary expenses incurred to reduce the loss or protect the covered property from further damage. We'll figure our share and your share of these expenses in the same proportion as each of us will benefit from them.

Source: St. Paul Fire and Marine Insurance Co., 1982. Reproduced by permission.

FIGURE 10-2
Insurance Coverage

No.	Item	Yes	No	N/A	Comments
			Response		

Data Processing Equipment

1. Does the company insurance policy cover the damage or destruction of the following equipment, whether the equipment is owned, leased, or rented?
   a. Computer.   ___ ___ ___
   b. Related peripherals.   ___ ___ ___
2. Is supporting equipment covered, including:
   a. office machines?   ___ ___ ___
   b. furniture and fixtures?   ___ ___ ___
   c. forms and forms handling equipment such as decollators and bursters?   ___ ___ ___
3. Are there any policy exclusions in regard to data processing equipment?   ___ ___ ___

Data Processing Media

1. Does the company insurance policy cover the damage or destruction of data processing media, including:
   a. magnetic tapes?   ___ ___ ___
   b. magnetic disks?   ___ ___ ___
   c. magnetic diskettes?   ___ ___ ___
   d. paper tapes?   ___ ___ ___
   e. punch cards?   ___ ___ ___
   f. magnetic drums?   ___ ___ ___
2. Are filing and data-storage cabinets included in the policy coverage?   ___ ___ ___
3. In the event of damage or destruction of data processing media, are reproduction costs covered? (Reproduction costs are costs of the replacement of media after a loss.) These costs include:
   a. original data production costs.   ___ ___ ___
   b. off-site work expenses.   ___ ___ ___
   c. additional payroll expenses.   ___ ___ ___
4. Are there any policy exclusions in regards to data processing media?   ___ ___ ___

FIGURE 10–2 *(continued)*

No.	Item	Yes	No	N/A	Comments
	Extra Expenses				
1.	Does the company insurance policy cover extra expenses, including:				
	a. rental of temporary office space?	___	___	___	
	b. facilities and equipment?	___	___	___	
	c. moving expenses for files and equipment?	___	___	___	
	d. utilities?	___	___	___	
	e. communications equipment?	___	___	___	
	f. temporary construction?	___	___	___	
	g. cleaning and maintenance service?	___	___	___	
2.	Are the following systems covered under the "extra expenses" agreement?				
	a. Air conditioning system?	___	___	___	
	b. Electrical system?	___	___	___	
	c. Water system for water-cooled computers?	___	___	___	
3.	Are there any policy exclusions regarding "extra expenses"?	___	___	___	
	Business Interruption				
1.	Does the insurance policy cover the monetary loss resulting from total or partial suspension of operations due to damage or loss of:				
	a. data processing equipment?	___	___	___	
	b. data processing media?	___	___	___	
	c. related support systems such as air conditioning, electrical, and water?	___	___	___	
2.	Does the policy contain the "measure of recovery" and "resumption of operations" clauses of the agreement?	___	___	___	
3.	Are there any policy exclusions regarding "business interruptions"?	___	___	___	
	Valuable Papers and Records				
1.	Does the insurance policy cover:				
	a. source documents?	___	___	___	
	b. vital records?	___	___	___	
	c. data center documentation?	___	___	___	
2.	Are there any policy exclusions in regard to valuable papers and records?	___	___	___	

FIGURE 10–2 *(concluded)*

No.	Item	Yes	No	N/A	Comments
	Accounts Receivable				
1.	Does the company's insurance policy cover the loss of receivables due to the destruction of accounts-receivable records, if applicable?	___	___	___	
2.	Does the policy also include reimbursement for:				
	a. interest charges on loans?	___	___	___	
	b. collection expenses?	___	___	___	
	c. other miscellaneous expenses for re-establishing records of accounts receivable following loss or damage?	___	___	___	
3.	Are there any policy exclusions in regard to "accounts receivable" records?	___	___	___	
	Other Insurance Considerations				
1.	Does the insurance program consider the following?				
	a. Data center cost.	___	___	___	
	b. Building cost.	___	___	___	
	c. Fire and smoke damage.	___	___	___	
	d. natural disasters.	___	___	___	
	e. water damage.	___	___	___	
	f. power failure.	___	___	___	
	g. computer related crime.	___	___	___	
	h. errors and omissions.	___	___	___	
	i. man-made disasters.	___	___	___	
	j. employee dishonesty.	___	___	___	
	k. bonding.	___	___	___	
	l. third-party liabilities.	___	___	___	
	m. off-site locations.	___	___	___	
	n. automatic insurance.	___	___	___	
	o. "named peril" items. (You must indicate each possible loss by name, such as falling aircraft or construction equipment crashing into the data center.)	___	___	___	
	p. general liability insurance.	___	___	___	
	q. personal inquiry. (To help protect against libel, defamation of character, or invasion of privacy suits.)	___	___	___	
2.	Is the insurance coverage up-to-date with the current hardware configuration and data center and records value?	___	___	___	

Chapter Eleven

Legal Issues and Legislation

Some of the legal issues involved in software protection are briefly outlined in this chapter. These include piracy or unauthorized duplication, copyright, trade secrets, patents, and employee contracts. State and federal computer-related crime laws and legislation are also discussed.

SOFTWARE PROTECTION

Piracy

Piracy (unauthorized duplication) continues to plague software development houses in the United States. One industry executive estimates the revenue lost from the pirating of software products amounts to 30 percent of the annual industry sales. With $16 billion in sales, that is close to $4.8 billion in lost revenue. With industry sales expected to rise to about $20 billion in 1993, lost revenues may reach $6.0 billion.

The federal copyright laws do not act as much of a deterrent. Counterfeiting sound recordings and motion pictures may subject a culprit to a fine of $250,000 and a five-year prison term; duplicating software illegally only results in a $25,000 fine and one year in prison. Also, software-embedded chips (ROMs, RAMs and PROMs) do not seem to qualify for protection under the copyright laws.

In 1982, the U.S. Congress (H.R. 6420) attempted to add some teeth and clarity to the Copyright Act as a further measure of protection, but little has been done since.[1]

---

[1] Jack Bologna, "The Basics of Fraud Prevention," *Corporate Fraud Digest* 1, no. 11 (June 1983), p. 5.

There are four basic means of legal protection available for software package developers:

1. Copyright.
2. Trade secret.
3. Patent.
4. Employee contract.

The software developer has the discretion of using one or more of these areas of law to protect his proprietary assets.

Copyright Law

Copyright Act: The Copyright Act of 1976 is a revision of the Copyright Act of 1909; U.S.C. Title 17 became fully effective on January 1, 1978.

To come under copyright protection, a work must be:

- In the form of a "writing"; that is, fixed in some tangible form from which it can be reproduced.
- A product of original creative authorship.

Interpretations of the new law hold that computer programs or software fall under the copyrightable works category. The definition of "literary works" (Section 101 of the act) refers to works expressed in "words, numbers, or other verbal or numerical symbols of indicia." It should be noted that only the programmer's "literary" expression—that is, the program—would be copyrightable, not his ideas, systems, or other methodology (see Section 102(b) of the act).

The Copyright Act allows a specific program, such as a strategic-planning graphics program, to be copyrighted. However, the *idea* for the program cannot be copyrighted. In summary, the copyright law protects original works of authorship on fixed intangible media of expression from which can be perceived, reproduced or otherwise communicated directly or indirectly, with or without the aid of a machine or device, for a period of more than transitory duration.

The Copyright Act says that the original author of a computer program (the person who writes the program) is the rightful owner of the copyright. However, the exception to this is the employee who writes a program as a part of his/her job. Under this exception, the employer is considered the owner.

The copyright owner has five exclusive rights:

1. Reproduce his own work in copies.
2. Prepare derivative works based on the original.
3. Perform the work publicly.
4. Display the work publicly.
5. Distribute the work to the public.

Rights of the product's user.   When a person buys a copy of the program from a retail store or through a distributor, the purchaser will either own the program or will have the right to use it through a lease arrangement. If the program is owned, the owner has the right to make copies for backup or storage and make modifications to the program in order to make it appropriate for his own use. The owner does not have the right to copy or distribute the program to anyone else or to distribute modified versions of the program. If the program is leased, a license accompanies the program stipulating the rights of the lessor.[2]

Criminal acts.   Under copyright law, there are four kinds of criminal acts:

- Infringement of a "copyright willfully and for the purposes of commercial advantage or private financial gain."
- Intentional fraudulent use of a copyright notice whereby a copyright notice is placed on an article when the defendant knows the notice to be false.
- Fraudulent removal of a copyright notice.
- Knowingly making a false representation in a copyright registration application.

Trade Secrets Law

Technological and business information that is used secretly within an enterprise, which lends a competitive advantage, and which is not known generally by competitors, is legally protectable as a trade secret. Material that is protectable as a trade secret is broad and includes varieties of information for which patent protection is never available. For many types of technological information, such as complex industrial processes and formulas, trade secrets and patents are alternative forms

---

[2] Trudy E. Bell, *Personal Computing*, May 1983, pp. 131–134.

of protection. Other innovative matter, such as computer software and related developments, which may be marginally protectable by patent or copyright, is generally better protected as trade secrets.[3]

Trade secret law has been ruled by the U.S. Supreme Court to be independent of, and complementary with, the patent system. This allows the choice of either seeking patent protection for computer software or retaining the matter as a trade secret. (See *Gottschalk* v. *Benson*, 409 U.S. 63, 1972.)

In asserting trade secret ownership, one "has the burden of establishing that adequate safeguards were taken to protect secrecy."[4] Measures that have met previous legal tests of safeguards include employment agreements and practices of nondisclosure, vendor contracts, and the range of stringent security practices common in protecting classified information.

The body of trade secret laws relevant to computer crime has grown steadily. One of the most prominent cases was *Telex Corporation* v. *IBM* in which IBM recovered $23 million from Telex for theft of IBM product development material. There have been numerous prosecutions for theft of computer programs and software.

Patent Law

It was not until recently that the U.S. Patent Office began issuing patents for software products. A U.S. patent is essentially a contract between the government (the people) and the inventor. The patent gives the inventor a 17-year right to exclude the public from making, using, or selling the invention.

Software patents for program inventions comprise three necessary elements:

1. A body of text or specification that describes the inventor's field and the problem that the invention solves, such as increased processing speed or increased productivity.

2. A set of drawings, flowcharts, program listings, etc., that explain how the invention (program) works.

3. At least one claim, or defining "word picture," that defines exactly what the public is excluded from making.

---

[3] Roger W. Milgrim, "Trends in Trade Secret Litigation," *Assets Protection* 1, no. 1 (Spring 1975), pp. 9–12.

[4] Ibid.

It is important to note that only special features of programs can be patented and not the entire program.

An inventor or owner of a patent may license others to make, use, and sell a patented program invention in return for licensing or royalty fees. Computer hardware usually meets the substantive requirements of the Patent Code (see U.S.C., Title 35—Patents). Patent law covers not only the Code, but interpretations of that code by the federal courts and the regulations and actions of the Patent Office.

Employee Contracts

One way of protecting a business's proprietary information is by legal agreements with the firm's employees. Employee contracts should be structured to explain the company's policy regarding the ownership of proprietary information (trade secrets) or ideas developed in the course of the business, and explain what should happen with that information if an employee leaves to join a competitor. The employee contract can also contain restrictions pertaining directly to company-issued or privately owned microcomputers used on the job.[5]

STATE COMPUTER-RELATED CRIME LAWS AND LEGISLATION

In order to combat the rising computer-related crime rate, authorities at the state and federal levels have been actively pursuing legislation under which to effectively prosecute computer criminals. A list of state laws is presented in Figure 11–1. Contact your state legislator for further information.

---

[5] Trudy E. Bell, "Configure Your Business to Protect Information Assets," *Personal Computing*, July 1983, pp. 133–136.

FIGURE 11-1
State Computer Crime Laws and Legislation

State	Description
Alabama	SB853
Alaska	Sect. 11.46.200 (a) Theft of services
	11.46.484 (a) Criminal mischief—3rd degree
	11.46.740 Criminal use of a computer
	11.46.985 Deceiving a machine
Arizona	Title 13. Ch. 23—Organized Crime and Fraud
	Criminal Code, Computer fraud: classifications 1st and
	Sect. 13.2316 2nd degree
	Penalties:
	1st degree—five years in prison
	2nd degree—1½ years in prison

California

Penal Code, Sect. 502, A1077 (Proposed), A1078, A2551, S2149

HBS-66. Makes it a crime to "intentionally" access or cause to be accessed any computer system or computer network for the purpose of (1) devising or executing any scheme or artifact to defraud or extort or (2) obtaining money, property, or services with false or fraudulent intent, representations, or promises; or to maliciously access, alter, delete, damage, or destroy any computer system, computer network, computer program or data. Penalties: felony punishable by a 16-month to 3-year prison term and/or $2,000–$5,000 fine.

A2551—Anti-Hacker Bill. California legislators have proposed a bill that would assist in the prosecution and conviction of hackers, which is difficult under the state's current computer crime law. Bill 2551 divides system penetrations into two categories: (1) Felonies, including illicit access that ends in malicious systems tampering; (2) Misdemeanors, including unauthorized access to a system with no intent to do damage.

Colorado

Crim. Code 18-5, 5-101 to 18-5.5-102

H.B. 1110. Prohibits knowingly using a computer for fraudulent means; assault or malicious destruction of a computer, its software, or stored data. This bill defines more precisely computer terms including: services including, but not limited to, computer time, data processing, and storage functions. Use: to instruct, communicate with, store data in, retrieve data from or otherwise make use of any resources of a computer system or computer network.

Penalties: Class III misdemeanor—theft under $50—fine of $50–$750 and up to 6 months in jail. Class II misdemeanor—a theft over $50 but under $200—a fine of $250–$1,000 and 3 to 12 months in jail. Class IV felony—theft

FIGURE 11–1 *(continued)*

State	Description
	between $200 and $10,000—a fine of $2,000 to $30,000 and 1 day to 10 years in jail. Class III felony—theft of more than $10,000—5 to 40 years in jail.
Connecticut	Sect. 53 a—250 to 261: Computer-related offenses
Delaware	Title 11, Sect. 931 Definition
	932 Unauthorized access
	933 Theft of computer services
	934 Interruption of computer services
	935 Misuse of computer system information
	936 Destruction of computer equipment
Florida	Chapt. 815 HB 1305
	Prohibits various forms of theft abuses against computer equipment, of a computer, and "whoever willfully, knowingly and without authorization accesses or causes to be accessed any computer, computer system, or computer network." The law is specific about a number of abuses such as destruction of data, disclosure of confidential information, and modification of computer programs.
Georgia	Code 16-9-90 to 16-9-95
Hawaii	Sect. 708-896
Idaho	Chapter 22, Title 18, Sect. 18-2201 and 2202
Illinois	Sect. 15-1, Criminal Code
	Sect. 16-9, Unlawful use of computer
Iowa	Chapter 716A
Kentucky	Sect. 434.840–860
Louisiana	Title 14, Sub-D, Computer-related crime
	Sect. 73.1-5
Maine	Chapt. 15, Title 17-A., Sect. 357—Theft of Services
Maryland	Art. 27, Sect. 146 and Sect. 45A
Massachusetts	Ch266, Sect. 30, HR 4844 (Proposed)
	S240 (Proposed)
	S240 (Proposed), based on recommendations drawn from more than 600 users, computer security experts, educators and legal authorities. There are two categories:
	1st degree computer fraud: "The accessing of any computer system to obtain goods and services illegally or to execute a scheme to defraud." Includes: altering, destroying or preventing access. Penalties: fines up to $20,000. Maximum 5 years in prison.
	2nd degree fraud: targeted toward hackers "assessing a computer system or database without authority." Penalties: fines up to $5,000 in a one-year period.

FIGURE 11–1   *(continued)*

State	Description
	The bill also includes civil provisions that would empower judges to impose injunction on offenders before criminal proceedings are initiated. Those provisions would also make convicted violators liable for triple damages in subsequent civil suits brought by victims. Restitution plan: force offenders to reimburse victims financially or through a work program outlined by a judge.
Michigan	Title 28, 28.5.29 (1), HB 4112 The bill is designed to "prohibit access to computers, computer systems, and computer networks for certain fraudulent purposes; to prohibit intentional and unauthorized access, alteration, damage, and destruction of computers, computer systems, computer networks, computer software programs, and data; and to prescribe penalties." Penalties: a felony is a violation of more than $100 and is punishable by imprisonment for not more than 10 years; or a fine of not more than $5,000, or both.
Minnesota	Sect. 609.87 to 609.89 Enacted 1982 Penalty for damage or theft totaling: $2,500: Penalty: maximum 10 years prison & maximum $50,000 fine. $500–$2500: penalty: 5 years in prison and $5,000 fine. $500: 90 days in jail and $500 fine.
Mississippi	S493 (Proposed)
Missouri	Sect. 569.093 to 569.099
Montana	Sect. 45-2-101, 45-6-310, 45-6-311
Nebraska	L1017 (Proposed)
Nevada	Sect. 205.473 - 477
New Jersey	Chpt. 20, Title 2C Title 2A-sub 6: Computer-related offenses-civil liability
New Mexico	30-16A-1 to 30-16A-4, H.B.S.8. Prohibits misuse of computers, computer fraud (electronic embezzlement of money, property or services), malicious destruction of a computer or its information, and unauthorized computer use. Penalties: misdemeanors to third-degree felony.
New York	A8616 (Proposed) A8617, 8619, 8621, 8647, 8754, S1122, 7356, 7378, A29 (Proposed), H1116, S464
North Carolina	Art. 60, Section 14-453 to 14.454, H. B. S. 397 Prohibits physical damage to and into a computer, altering, damaging or destroying a computer software program, system, or network; verbal or printed communication threats with intent to extort money through a computer network. Penalties: misdemeanor to felony punishment.

FIGURE 11–1   *(concluded)*

State	Description
North Dakota	Century Code, Ch 12.1 - 06.1
Ohio	Sect. 2913.0
Oklahoma	Sect. 1951 - 1956, Title 21
Oregon	SB 149 (Proposed)
Pennsylvania	Title 18, Sect. 3933, Computer Crime Law.
	1. Felony (third degree): For "gaining access to, altering, damaging or destroying any computer, computer system, software, program or database with criminal intent to interrupt the functioning of any organization, to defraud or to steal services or property." Penalties: maximum fine of $15,000 and up to a 7-year prison term.
	2. Misdemeanor (first degree): same as above. However, the perpetrator was not utilizing the technology to commit a more serious crime, such as embezzlement. Penalties: maximum fine of $10,000 and a prison term of up to 5 years.
Rhode Island	Sect. 11-52-1 to 11-52-4, H.B. 5775
	Penalties: a fine of not more than $50,000 or a prison term for not less than two years nor more than four years, or both.
South Carolina	Ch 16, Sect. 16-16-10 to 16-16-40
South Dakota	Ch 43-43B
Tennessee	Criminal Offence Part 14
	Sect. 39-3-1401 to 39-3-1406
Texas	Proposed
Utah	Sect. 76-6-701 to 76-6-704
Virginia	Code of Virginia, Ch 5, Title 18.2
	Sect. 18.2 - 152.1 to 18.2 - 152.14
Washington	Sect. 9A.48.100
Wisconsin	Sect. 943.70
Wyoming	Art.5, Sect. 6-3-501 to 6-3-505

Source: Computer Protection Systems Inc., 5151 State University Drive, Los Angeles, CA 90032.

Chapter Twelve

Disaster Preparedness and Recovery

Disaster-recovery planning and arrangements for contingency backup operation are important. This chapter provides information and procedures for developing the required contingency plans. A checklist is provided to aid in the analysis of the priority of concerns to management. The three levels of security and disaster recovery measures that should be considered in balancing the cost to need are described as mandatory, necessary, and desirable. The practical levels of disaster recovery measures are emphasized. The development, testing, training for, and implementation of an emergency plan are outlined. The routine backup requirements and the controls during time of failure are discussed.

FACING UP TO THE THREAT

A disaster can be defined as an event that is likely to cause significant disruption in an organization's operations for a period of time. The history of data processing reveals many cases of man-made and natural disasters striking companies that were unprepared and unable to cope with the emergency. These companies suffered considerable damage and loss to equipment and facilities; in some cases, there was also loss of life.

Each organization is faced with its own unique threats and vulnerabilities. These threats and vulnerabilities depend largely on the nature of the company's products or services and its geographic location.

Your organization can protect its assets against disaster by planning for disaster or emergencies. The purpose of disaster (and recovery) planning is to ensure against and minimize the loss of human, capital, and information resources of the firm. Timing, organization, and proper execution of defensive efforts are the essence of disaster/recovery planning if you wish to fulfill that purpose. What you do and when and how well you do it are critical factors of success.

No matter how pleasing or positive a process called "change" may be or how unpleasant or negative it may be, we do not like it. Because we resist in a number of different ways this concept called change, from an organizational point of view, a business-not-as-usual concept, we also resist or even deny the need for disaster planning because it represents potential negative change.

Many organizations already prepare for corporate change via strategic planning. It is much easier to digest predicted "positive" changes than the changes that may result from a disaster. Subsequently, what many organizations end up with is the out-of-sight, out-of-mind ostrich approach to disaster planning. Remember, however, that although the ostrich's head may be protected by this approach, other parts of his anatomy may be in a lot of trouble.

So why plan for disaster and for disaster recovery? The answer is that *disaster does happen*, and it does not care if we are prepared for it or not. We must remember that the purpose of disaster/recovery planning is to ensure against and minimize the loss of capital, information, and, most important, the human resources of the firm.

Preparedness

In the disaster-recovery planning context, preparedness emphasizes the qualities of being prepared for any type of disaster or failure that can completely or partially disable a data processing operation, and being prepared to recover completely or partially from the disaster or failure and to continue processing in a total or partial processing mode. The concept of preparedness denotes a need to plan in advance. Disaster planning at the macro level addresses the areas of organizational backup files, documentation, and data and system recovery.

Planning

The primary objective of emergency planning is personnel safety and welfare; secondary objectives include the following:

- Minimizing loss of assets.
- Minimizing business interruption.
- Providing backup facilities and services.

- Providing trained personnel to conduct emergency and recovery operations.

Emergency procedures need to be established for each type of disaster and varied levels of interruptions of service—that is, for short- or long-term interruptions. These time periods must be defined by your company and may vary depending on the type of system or process that could be affected by a disaster.

Planning for data and/or microcomputer system recovery must be done in advance of a disaster occurrence. Planning for data/system recovery is best done in an atmosphere that promotes detailed and total planning rather than the "if you want it bad, you will get it bad" environment usually encountered at the time of a system crash. Planning for recovery at the time of system failure has caused many mistakes to be made; programmers and operators "try" a quick-fix that only degrades the system further. Fortunately, most quick-fixes come out all right, but the firms that teach their personnel the shoot-from-the-hip approach to problem solving usually end up shooting themselves in the foot.

Planning for recovery includes the implementation and placement of data/system recovery methods, procedures, services, products, and equipment. These items generally must be in place and operational prior to the occurrence of a disaster or system failure. It will be of little use to install recovery software that uses logged or journaled entries for its recovery mechanism after an on-line database failure. Such software packages must be operational prior to and during the failure.

The sequential functions of management are said to be (1) planning, (2) organizing, (3) directing, and (4) controlling. The basic purpose of planning, the first step in the management process, is to anticipate future outcomes on the basis of recurring phenomena and to scan the horizon for threats, risks, and opportunities; that is, changes in needs, wants, demands, and desires of customers—trends. The planning process is intended to guarantee organizational survival in a world of uncertainty. So planning is an effort to control what is controllable. For example, while we cannot control the weather, we can control how we respond to climatic conditions to guarantee survival.

While planning is the design of a desired future, our knowledge of the future is not always certain. The degree of certainty we possess about the future then dictates the kind of planning we do. If our knowledge of the future is certain, our planning is done by commitment. If our knowledge is relatively uncertain, we plan by contingency. And if our knowledge of the future is highly uncertain, we do responsiveness planning.

Some aspects of the future are virtually certain. For example, all things tend to wear out or become obsolete over time. So we set up reserves to replace them in the planning process. Some aspects of the future are relatively uncertain. For example, we cannot predict when any discrete event may occur (such as a machine malfunction), but we can determine its probability over time and its cost consequences if we do nothing to prevent it. (Here, preventive maintenance is a form of contingency planning.)

Some aspects of the future are highly uncertain, as, for example, when a natural disaster will occur and what its cost consequences are likely to be. Here, the effort should be directed to responsiveness planning. (How quickly can we respond to minimize the loss? How long will it take to fully recover? How and where do we operate in the interim?)[1]

Reliability

Reliability can be defined both in qualitative and quantitative terms in the area of probabilities. More specifically, microcomputer system reliability can be defined as the probability that the system (hardware and software) will perform its intended function over a specified period of time in the environment specified for its usage.

The required reliability factor for a given system may vary from one organization to another, or from one system to another within an organization, depending upon the specific purpose and requirements for that system. A brief period of downtime may be intolerable for organizations that use the micro to run their daily business activities.

A way of describing reliability of a system (hardware and software) is in quantitative terms relating to the rate of failure. This concept is usually addressed as "mean time between failure" (MTBF). Depending on the organization, the application being processed, and the type of hardware being used, MTBF will have different levels of acceptability. Two failures per day may be completely acceptable for one organization and completely unacceptable for another. Each organization must analyze the cost of system downtime and the effect it has on its operations and its service to the organization's customers or system users.

The primary purpose of disaster planning for microcomputers is the continuity of data processing service. Reliability of hardware and soft-

---

[1] Jack Bologna, *Strategic Planning for Corporate Directors of Security and Risk Management* (Madison, Wisc.: Assets Protection, 1981), pp. 11–12.

ware is a key factor in the preservation of data processing security and data integrity.

Loss Limitation/Degradation Strategies

Loss limitation deals with the ability to limit or contain the amount of loss through hardware, software, and manual methods. The objective of loss limitation in a data processing context is to keep downtime to a minimum. Effective loss limitation depends on early problem detection and prompt corrective action.

Systems that suffer a failure in a loss-limitation structure would either stop processing to avoid further problems or would "fall back" to a less efficient mode, or a degraded mode of operation. Degradation strategies dictate a need to keep the system running even if it means bypassing the faulty portion of the system, such as a faulty printer or an incorrect software application.

Phrases such as "graceful degradation" or "fail softly" are used to describe situations where a failure does occur and the system can be brought down easily instead of just halting or abnormally terminating. Software routines that "close" files in case of system/program failure are examples of the fail softly concept.

MANAGEMENT REQUIREMENTS AND CONSIDERATIONS

The purpose of disaster-recovery planning is to prepare in advance to ensure the continuity of business information if the data processing capability is lost. Thus, disaster-recovery planning is a management, rather than a technical, issue. It deals with the realities of people, organizational relationships, and special interests. Disaster-recovery actions are highly prioritized, and many normal operations are neglected. Management must take the lead and continually access the technical considerations involved as to their utility. Disaster-recovery planning and arrangements for contingency backup operation are just as important, relatively, for microcomputer systems as they are for the larger systems.

Management must realize that there are no entirely secure computers. Many computer operations have fine methods for security in place, and management can be assured that the best possible actions have been taken, but there are always people, electronics, and natural disasters that can suddenly disrupt the operations.

In planning for disaster, management must realistically look at priorities, including the following:

- Legal obligation requirements.
- Cash flow maintenance.
- Customer services.
- Competitive advantages.
- Production and distribution decisions.
- Logistics and operations control.
- Purchasing functions and vendor relationships.
- Ongoing project control.
- Branch or agency communications.
- Personnel and union relations.
- Shareholder and public relations.

Management must assess the importance of the microcomputer system operations to these facets of their business, then decide the type of effort that should be put into the backup of the computer function.

Management must also consider how the microcomputer disaster-recovery plan will interface with existing organizational policies and procedures. There may already be a disaster planning guide for the overall business. In this case, the electronic data processing (EDP) guide should fit into it. Most organizations have plans in place for at least some of the following:

- Fire protection equipment installation and maintenance.
- Emergency fire alarm procedures.
- Fire monitor or instructor training.
- Guard duties, training, and procedures.
- Relationships with external emergency alarm services.
- Relationships with local fire and police departments.
- Bomb-threat procedures.
- Strike or mob-threat procedures.
- Storm-emergency information and restoration plans.
- Emergency control centers.

These are all supportive of EDP recovery, and management must see that the microcomputer plans fit with them.

Priority Concerns of Management

The principal area of concern in disaster recovery operations for most organizations is the safety and well-being of the personnel involved. This concern should remain paramount. The principal business concern is the maintenance of accounting records and customer services. The business-interruption loss must be kept as low as possible, and the required cash flow maintained. Legal and reporting requirements must, of course, be maintained also.

An additional fundamental concern is the protection of facilities, equipment, programs, and supplies. Figure 12–1 is a checklist that expands on these concerns. Management can use it to check the fundamental, minimum requirements of a disaster-recovery plan.

LEVELS OF SECURITY AND DISASTER-RECOVERY MEASURES

A disaster-recovery plan is developed to minimize the costs resulting from losses of, or damages to, the resources or the capabilities of the microcomputers and related services. It is dependent for success on the recognition of the potential consequences of undesirable happenings. There are many resources related to microcomputer system operations. Some particular subset of these is required to support each function that is provided to others in the organization. These resources include people, programs, data, hardware, communications equipment and systems, electrical power, the physical facility and access to it, and even items such as paper forms.

All resources are not equally important, nor are they equally susceptible to harm. The selection of safeguards and the elements of a contingency plan should, therefore, be done with an informed awareness of which system functions are supported by each resource element and of the susceptibility of each element to harm. The cost-effective protection of a microcomputer system operation is thus dependent on the following:

- The importance to the organization of each of the component parts of the computer functions.
- The general probability of something undesirable happening to each of the components.
- The likely results and ramifications of various types of disasters that could occur.

FIGURE 12–1
Priority Concerns of Management

No.	Item	Yes	No	N/A	Comments
		\multicolumn{4}{Response}			

Staff Protection and Actions

1. Have all staff been trained in the fire alarm, bomb threat, and other emergency procedures?
2. Do all staff understand that when the alarm sounds they:
   a. immediately vacate the building?
   b. do not return to pick up items from desks?
   c. report to supervisors at designated points?
3. Do all staff know who to call in times of emergency or where the emergency telephone list is located?
4. Do the disaster-recovery planning teams understand that the protection and safety of people in the area is paramount?
5. Have good management notification procedures been developed for any emergency of any size?

Maintenance of Customer Services and Cash Flow

6. Has management strictly prioritized the most necessary services to be maintained in an emergency?
7. Are all user groups involved in customer services and cash handling working with the plan teams?
8. For on-line customer services, can alternative operations be brought up within 24 hours?
9. Are most cash deposits sent directly to banks and not vulnerable to a disaster in the computer area?
10. Does the organization have plans for controlled public press releases in times of disaster?

FIGURE 12–1 *(continued)*

No.	Item	Yes	No	N/A	Comments

Maintenance of Vital Documents

11. Have the vital documents and records of the organization been thoroughly analyzed and control procedures set up? ___ ___ ___

12. Does the organization use a remote, safe document storage vault? ___ ___ ___

13. Is there use of computer output microfilm/microfiche or the microfilming of documents, and are copies stored in a safe vault? ___ ___ ___

14. Are application and operations documentation of programs handling vital information backed up in safe storage? ___ ___ ___

15. Is the legal department satisfied with the EDP handling of vital documents? ___ ___ ___

Protection of Facilities, Equipment, Programs, and Supplies

16. Are the organization's fire, safety, and engineering people working closely with information services? ___ ___ ___

17. Have the fire and safety systems in the EDP facility area been reviewed by an independent person? ___ ___ ___

18. Have discussions been held with all equipment vendors as to their response to an emergency situation? ___ ___ ___

19. Has there been a recent review as to the documentation level of programs and the existence of updated backup copies of the programs and the documentation? ___ ___ ___

20. Is there a complete listing of all supplies and copies of all forms available in a second site, and are emergency backups of critical forms held in a second site? ___ ___ ___

Backup Arrangements: On-Site

21. Are there contingency plans formalized for these three levels of response to trouble?
    a. Delay and correct situation. ___ ___ ___
    b. Readjust scheduling and use some off-premises equipment. ___ ___ ___
    c. Shift to backup office site. ___ ___ ___

FIGURE 12-1   *(continued)*

No.	Item	Yes	No	N/A	Comments
22.	Is the data-backup library located in a separately locked room or locked cabinet?	___	___	___	
23.	Are critical program and data files identified and backed up to protect specific systems considered vital to the business?	___	___	___	
24.	Are these backup files continually updated?	___	___	___	
25.	Is the use of files continuously logged?	___	___	___	
26.	Are copies of the microcomputer system operating manuals kept in fire-proof storage?	___	___	___	
27.	Is a supply of critical forms kept in a separate building or with the vendor?	___	___	___	
28.	Is a listing of all administrative and technical manuals maintained to assure their identification if lost or stolen?	___	___	___	
29.	Are data programs and system procedures sent for storage in another area?	___	___	___	

Backup Arrangements: Off-Site

No.	Item	Yes	No	N/A	Comments
30.	Have formal reciprocal agreements for backup been made with organizations?	___	___	___	
31.	Do the agreements include specifications as to:				
	a. machine type/model?	___	___	___	
	b. disk units: type and number?	___	___	___	
	c. utilities?	___	___	___	
	d. input procedures?	___	___	___	
	e. available hours for backup processing?	___	___	___	
32.	Does the backup facility keep the prime facility aware of any changes made to either hardware or software?	___	___	___	
33.	If the processor or the resources of the backup facility are less than those of the prime facility, have the program changes been taken into account?	___	___	___	
34.	Does the backup facility itself offer satisfactory security?	___	___	___	

FIGURE 12-1 *(concluded)*

No.	Item	Yes	No	N/A	Comments
35.	Is the backup facility at a reasonable distance?	—	—	—	
36.	Are the available hours for use of the backup system known?	—	—	—	
37.	Is the possible effect on critical schedules known?	—	—	—	
38.	Have the jobs to be operated at the backup site, together with their data on disk, been identified?	—	—	—	
39.	Has a recovery plan been developed with each step assigned to an employee?	—	—	—	
40.	Has the plan been received by the safety department or engineering group, and approved by all involved?	—	—	—	
41.	Has a disaster ever been simulated, with the backup facilities used, as a rehearsal?	—	—	—	

- Preparations that can be made to minimize the chances of disasters, and the costs if they do occur.

Any part of a disaster-recovery plan is overhead cost until it becomes necessary to activate it. It is, therefore, necessary to consider the importance of the resources and services and to justify all the parts of security and disaster-recovery measures by estimating the losses that could occur through lack of these precautions. The combination of initial expenditures and insurance coverage must be balanced against the necessity of the service and the probability of the need of the recovery procedures. There are some actions that are mandatory, however. They must be taken, whatever the cost.

There are three levels of security and disaster-recovery measures that should be considered in balancing cost to need: *mandatory, necessary,* and *desirable.*

There is no absolute scale, and these measures will vary as conditions change. Management must review what is mandatory and necessary for their organization, support those efforts first, and then consider the justification analysis of desirable measures. These measures are outlined below.

Mandatory Measures

Mandatory security and disaster-recovery measures are those related to fire control, alarm systems, evacuation procedures, and other emergency precautions necessary to protect the lives and well-being of people in the area involved. Mandatory measures also include those needed to protect the books of account of the organization and to hold its officers free from legal negligence. The protection must include the assets of the organization as much as possible. The cost of these mandatory measures must be included in the cost of doing business. The items must also be reviewed periodically as to routine operation and adequacy. They should be reviewed with organization counsel.

Necessary Measures

Necessary security and disaster-recovery measures include all reasonable precautions taken to prevent serious disruption of the operation of the organization. This will include selected areas of manufacturing and distribution, engineering and planning, sales and marketing, and employee relations.

The necessity of the measures must be determined by senior management, who should also review their understanding of the need periodically. Since the necessary measures will be included in the base operating cost of the organization, each selected measure must be reviewed as to both degree and speed of emergency backup required.

Desirable Measures

Desirable security and disaster-recovery measures include reasonable precautions taken to prevent real inconvenience or disruption to any area of the organization and to keep the business under smooth control. The cost of some precautions related to personnel is small, but planned action is important to maintain operational efficiency and morale. The cost of other measures, such as arrangements for alternative sites for microcomputer systems and programming personnel and their terminals, may be large. Estimates and plans must be made, however, to allow reasonable and cost-effective management decisions once the extent of a disaster is understood. Many of the microcomputers in an organization will fall into the "desirable measures" category and will not be given priority in disaster recovery planning.

Priorities are as follows:

- The mandatory measures should be implemented as soon as possible.
- The necessary measures should be implemented in time-phased, prioritized order, with a definite plan approved by senior management.
- The desirable measures should be implemented as circumstances allow. Overhead cost is balanced against perceived need and desirability.

Practical Levels of Disaster-Recovery Measures

A disaster-recovery plan should be specific to the organization and tailored to its needs. An off-the-shelf plan is of no use whatsoever at the time of a security event when individuals need to know exactly what their role is and the steps they must take. The presence of a "paper plan" does not in itself provide a disaster-recovery capability. All people in the organization who may be involved in a recovery activity should also be involved in the plan preparation, training, and testing.

The disaster-recovery planning process can take many months and involve a great deal of activity and cost if the full process is carried out in a monolithic way, which would mean the following:

- Review of all data sets and data files.
- Discussion with all users.
- Complete assembly of all documentation.
- Full risk-identification and risk-analysis study.
- Detailed review of ongoing organizational security practices.

Such an approach could be self-defeating as it could be very costly and time-consuming, and management would lose interest in supporting it. It would also put off the installation of mandatory and necessary security measures that are most critical to the operation.

The better approach to disaster planning for microcomputer systems is for a small team to gather under the direction of a supervisor and make a short-term, high-impact plan to get something in place that will handle the most pressing needs and have high visibility. The steps that should be taken are as follows:

1. Assemble all readily available operations and systems documentation, including the vendor material.
2. Assemble the reports of any audits or security studies of related computer functions.

3. Create lists of the operating application systems in the first estimation of the order of priority.

4. Consult with senior management to get its opinions as to the
mandatory and necessary applications in an agreed order of
priority.

5. Determine the minimum configuration on which these mandatory and necessary systems can run and arrange for tests on
backup microcomputers.

6. Determine if these critical systems can be backed up and run
off-site, in an emergency, in the time required.

EMERGENCY PLANNING METHODOLOGY

Because of the possible devastating effect that an emergency could have
on computer operations and personnel, great care must be exercised in
the development of a company's emergency plan. All potential types of
emergencies must be considered, as well as the appropriate defense and
recovery actions that are required to minimize the loss and damage that
could result from each type of emergency.

The following emergency planning methodology will assist you in the
development of your company's "data center" emergency program. The
methodology consists of eight elements. Management approval should
be received upon completion of each element, or phase, of the methodology. This approval process will ensure management's commitment to
the project. It will also provide the important feedback that is necessary
to resolve any development problems as they occur—rather than later
on in the project, when it could be difficult, expensive, and time-
consuming for a redevelopment effort. Figure 12–2 gives an overview of
the eight elements, and a discussion of each follows.

Project Initiation

The objective of this phase of the methodology is to develop the details
of the emergency-planning project in sufficient depth to enable management to make a decision relevant to the needs of an emergency-
planning program. The project initiation phase covers the following
areas:

- Definition of potential data center threats and vulnerabilities, taking into consideration any previous disasters that may have affected the company or nearby geographical areas.

FIGURE 12–2
Emergency Planning Methodology

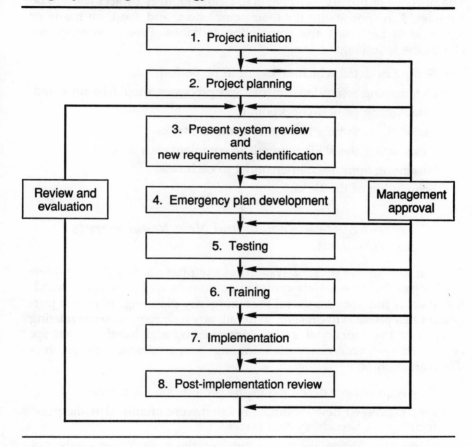

- Establishing the objectives of the project, both in broad terms and specific goals. Consideration should be given to corporate expansion, future needs, new technology, and the social-economic environment.
- Examining the potential benefits of an emergency plan that may be realized by the company and the customer/user. Both economic advantages and unmeasurable advantages should be defined.
- Considering factors relating to time, cost, company policy, federal and state regulations, and any other factors that may enable management to make a decision.

Project Planning

The purpose of project planning is to clearly identify project tasks to be completed, responsibility for their completion, and the time frame or schedule of task start and completion activities. Project planning includes the following:

- Stating in detail which tasks are to be performed.
- Determining what departments and processes should be reviewed.
- Establishing project checkpoints.
- Estimating the time it takes to complete tasks.
- Designating the skills required to complete each task.
- Assigning appropriate personnel to each task.
- Scheduling of the tasks.

Present System Review and New Requirements Identification

The purpose of the present system review phase is to gain an understanding of the current data-center operations as well as an understanding of areas that may be useful for emergency planning. Also, the purpose of this phase is to present, in detail, any new requirements relating to each of the functional areas, departments, and locations that are concerned with emergency planning and preparedness. This involves the evaluation of:

- Any requirement described in the project-initiation phase.
- Any expressed new requirements that were identified while performing the present system review.
- Company policies, insurance considerations, employee safety and welfare considerations, laws and government regulations.

The activities of this phase include the formal identification of the benefits of an emergency-planning program for the company. Any costs associated with new equipment, procedures, etc., are also identified.

The completion of this phase represents a critical management review and approval point in the emergency-planning project methodology. It is at this time that all the areas involved must approve the new requirements as defined and the benefits as identified. One of the major purposes of this phase is to ensure that the company's needs will be satisfied by the emergency plan. What follows is a listing of the areas that need to be studied and reviewed.

Management consideration

General.
Organizational.
Emergency control center.
Training and communications.
Financial.

Threats and vulnerabilities

A list of possible threats and vulnerabilities that your organization may be exposed to.

Insurance

Data processing equipment.
Data processing media.
Extra business.
Business interruption.
Valuable papers and records.
Accounts receivable.
Other insurance considerations.

Personnel

Selection and screening.
General considerations.
Backup personnel.
Employee assistance.
Training.

Documentation

Documentation considerations.

Supplies

General considerations.
Backup site.
Forms handling & security.
• General.
• Shipping.
• Receiving.
• Storage.
• Accountability.
• Rotation.
• Obsolete forms.
Alternative methods of report preparation.

Physical facilities

Physical location.
Construction.
Internal facility.
Housekeeping.

Backup site

Backup site considerations.

Hardware

Hardware considerations.
Support equipment.

Software

Program and operating systems.
Backup.
Databases.

Records

Value of records.
Protection of records.
Off-site storage.

Communications

General considerations.
Hardware.
Software.
Backup.

Utilities & services

Communications utilities.
Data processing services.
Electrical utilities.
Gas utilities.
Maintenance service.
Postal service.
Security services.
Vendor service.
Water utility.
Transportation.

System's customers (users)

General considerations.

Emergency Plan Development

The importance of a well-organized, fully documented emergency plan cannot be overemphasized. Policies and procedures governing the activity prior to, during, and immediately following an emergency should be understood and followed by all employees.

In general, and depending upon your specific disaster-recovery requirements, the emergency plan will cover the following areas:

- Management/administrative.
- Liaison with outside organizations.
- Business continuity.
  - Policy statements.
  - Succession of management.
  - Financial considerations.
  - Emergency policies.
  - Legal considerations.
  - Organizational planning.
  - Personnel.
  - Physical facilities.
- Emergency control center and control teams/assignments.
- Emergency response.
  - Backup facilities.
  - Hardware.
  - Software.
  - Records.
  - Communications.
  - Transportation.
  - Documentation.
  - Supplies.

Testing

Once the company's emergency plan has been developed, it is important to test each of the emergency procedures as thoroughly as possible. Bugs in the plan should be worked out and corrected immediately. Too many times, companies have developed and implemented emergency plans that were not tested. Unfortunately, "live tests" resulting from actual emergency situations have proved to be costly.

A team approach should be used to test the plan. Modular testing should be conducted and the results monitored, taking into consideration each procedure and policy in the emergency plan. Tests of procedures for emergency control center operations, vital records, fire fighting, evacuation, loss control, and other emergencies will ensure that plans are adequate and workable and will, at the same time, provide an opportunity for training data-center personnel.

Training

Appropriate elements of the emergency plan should be communicated to the data-center personnel and related support personnel through the following techniques:

- *Job descriptions.* They should contain a clear explanation of responsibility for emergency and security policies and procedures.
- *Employee orientation sessions.* These should be held for old and new employees.
- *Bulletin boards.* These are for brief, unclassified notices.
- *Posters.* These serve as visual reminders.
- *Company newsletters.* These can contain articles on data-center security and emergency procedures.

Specific training should be conducted in emergency preparedness, emergency response procedures, emergency warning systems, evacuation procedures, emergency control center operations, CPR techniques, fire fighting, first aid, and operations of special communications equipment. It is also important that company policies be established to ensure that management personnel periodically review and understand the emergency plan.

Implementation

Implementation of the emergency plan occurs after the plan has been fully tested and approved by management. Depending on the size and nature of the company, formal implementation may consist of the following:

- Formal company news bulletins to all personnel.
- Notification of only those personnel specifically involved in emergency procedures.
- Formal or informal orientation/training sessions for specific personnel or for all personnel.
- Notification of all outside support agencies that the emergency plan has been implemented.

Post-Implementation Review

In order for the company's emergency plan to be effective, a continuous review and evaluation of the plan is necessary. Changes in personnel, job function, technology, physical-site layout, and the social-economic environment may alter various emergency policies and procedures within the plan. Tests and training drills should be conducted at both scheduled and nonscheduled intervals to test the effectiveness of the emergency plan and the personnel.

DATA AND SYSTEM RECOVERY/RESTART METHODOLOGY

There are a number of methods and procedures that can be used to prepare for system recovery after a disaster, to analyze the extent of the problem, and to take action when systems fail. Some of these are briefly described in this section.

Designing the system for ease of recovery. These systems and techniques are systems management responsibilities and are absolutely basic to the capability of recovering from a disaster.

Establishing a system base for recovery. Many of these are standard control and audit methods and will already be in place in any well-run organization. The procedures that are routinely in use and under control will provide the fundamental information for system and data recovery.

Routine Backup Requirements

Disaster recovery can only be successful if there is a routine backup, at least daily, of the system software, proprietary packages, sensitive or critical programs, and data, and there is a regular testing of hardware and communications backup facilities. Figure 12–3 outlines some of the general areas that will have to be considered.

Specific, detailed plans must be made in all areas. Most of the routine backup of important programs will be done daily. It will be more frequent for on-line systems and databases, if any. It is difficult to generalize about routine system backup because of the great variations possible. A few of the key points are the following:

- Production programs and data files must be protected against change or deletion for audit control and backup.
- Retrieval and access to confidential data files must be restricted.
- The ability to recreate the entire library and to protect programs and job-control streams against loss is critical to successful recovery.
- An index of all documentation and backup material stored off-site should be kept up-to-date for audit purposes. Any additions or deletions should be recorded.

Disaster-recovery systems requirements. The requirements for the disaster recovery of systems principally relate to the capabilities of the personnel and equipment to use the routine backup materials in

FIGURE 12–3
Routine Backup Requirements

Secure Operating System and All Proprietary Software

1. Maintain a central library file of all program products.
2. Routinely dump all necessary software to diskette or tape, and store at a secure site.
3. Use a library management program, if available.

Maintain Adequate File Backup for Application Systems

1. Review all operational systems for adequate backup and documentation.
2. Establish a routine backup schedule for all operational systems.
3. Review file security for all new applications and all modifications.
4. Enforce file security specifications and procedures.
5. Assure that backup files represent the latest data.

Enforce Controlled Library Procedures

1. Confirm procedures and responsibility for all tape and disk handling.
2. Maintain separation of functions in handling data files.
3. Assure that all necessary library files are routinely rotated to a secure site.
4. Duplicate and keep off-site all run books and systems-control programs.
5. Establish procedures for copying tapes, duplicating microfilm, reading cards to tape, or performing other operations necessary to maintain backup files with the latest available data.

Review Backup and Recovery Procedures with the User Departments

1. Determine which files must be backed up.
2. Establish backup responsibility and schedules for each user area.

---

order to reconstruct the data, programs, and conditions of the last successful run before the security event. The systems staff will be the key to a successful recovery because they are in the best position to do the following:

- Determine where the systems were at the time of disaster.
- Reconstruct the data, programs, and conditions.
- Modify the job-control language as necessary.
- Produce a repeated run on the new equipment for audit review.

Disaster-recovery hardware and communications requirements. In addition to the preparation of the disaster-recovery operations procedures, a principal requirement is to have full and detailed documentation stored in a secure site for the following:

- Hardware configurations at the original site and the backup site.
- Communications configurations at the original site and estimated for the backup site.
- Descriptions of all networks and terminals involved, with locations and responsibilities.
- All operating procedures and standards.
- All fire-alarm and emergency systems at both sites.
- Floor plans of both sites.

There is always a problem of keeping such documentation updated. The best solution is to have as much of it as possible, even the equipment configurations, on a programmed documentation system. It is then readily updated at a terminal and is always backed up with the routine system library program.

Figure 12–4 presents a brief overview of the data and system recovery/restart phases. There are seven phases that should be followed to recover from a data or system fault:

1. Preparedness phase.
2. Fault analysis phase.
3. Planning for recovery and restart phase.
4. Recovery phase.
5. Restart phase.
6. Testing phase.
7. Post-recovery/restart monitoring phase.

FIGURE 12–4
Recovery/Restart Phases

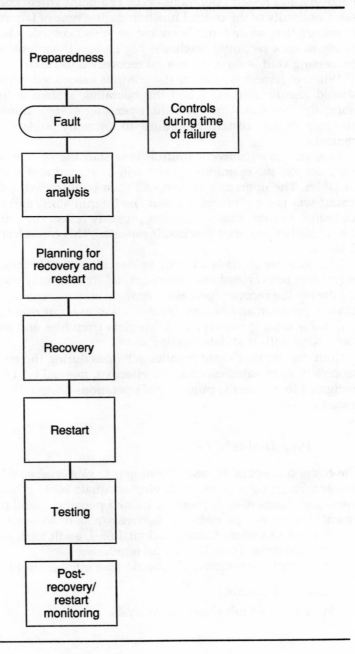

Controls During Time of Failure

Recovery and restart operations occur at a point where control is weakest. Continuity of the control function during time of failure is necessary to ensure that no data has been lost or misprocessed. Also, the opportunity of data security breaches is high when the attention of the data processing staff is directed toward recovery and restart operations.

When a system is started, the controls associated with that system should also be started. When the operating system is in use, this is normally the case. However, the operating system must rely on the integrity of the restart procedure to properly initiate the recovery controls.

One way to circumvent controls is to start the system several times. For example, the operating system will be started and some action will be taken. The operating system will then be restarted, but the second restart will not be informed about the interim start, and thus the logs and other control features will not properly reflect the activities within that unauthorized start process. If repeated, this could lead to a system disaster.

The recovery mode is a highly vulnerable period because the operating system has crashed and, thus, normal controls may not be functioning during the recovery process. Recovery may use special software that enables program and/or data manipulation to occur during recovery. It is possible during recovery to delete data from files and then to restart the system with that data missing.

Controls should closely monitor activities during the restart/recovery process. If automated controls are effective, manual controls should be instigated to ensure the propriety of operations during the recovery and restart processes.

Preparedness Phase

The entire concept of disaster planning is to *plan in advance* for a possible disaster. Preparedness means having adequate backup hardware, software, and database files, properly trained personnel, and properly documented recovery procedures. Recovery/restart software must be in place prior to a system failure, and vital files, audit logs, and programs must be maintained and backed up regularly.

Preparedness considerations should take into account the following:

- Audit and control.
- Vulnerability/fault causation analysis.

- Hardware.
- Software.
- Records: magnetic (database) and manual.
- Communications.
- Documentation.
- Emergency response procedures.
- System's customers (users).

Fault Analysis Phase

Depending on the nature of the fault that caused the disaster, fault analysis may be either simple or extremely difficult, if not almost impossible, as in the case of transient indeterminate faults. A successful fault-analysis phase requires a methodical analysis approach in determining the fault causation. A well-defined approach will channel the analyst's efforts and resources in the right direction. At the same time, it will help eliminate unnecessary and time consuming work.

Some general points to consider during the fault analysis phase are these:

- Be thorough. (Consider all possible situations.)
- Make sure all information is relevant. (The information that is gathered should pertain to the fault analysis.)
- Be accurate. (Frequently test and analyze the information that is being gathered for consistency and accuracy.)
- Make use of fault analysis aids where possible. (This includes methods, techniques, software and equipment.)

It is necessary to address three areas of concern when analyzing system hardware, software, or database faults:

1. *Duration of the fault* (timely analysis):
   - Transient.
   - Permanent.

2. *Fault causation* (loss-cause analysis):
   - Determinant.
   - Indeterminate.

3. *Effect on the system* (damage assessment):
   - Local.
   - Catastrophic.

Planning for Recovery and Restart

In data and system recovery, planning needs to be done on different levels.

1. Macro level: for organizational survival.
2. Micro level: for preparedness—planning in advance for personnel scheduling, backup files, software recovery packages, etc.
3. Micro level: for recovery—at the time of system failure.

At the time of system failure, planning for recovery/restart must be initiated based on the results of the fault analysis.

The planning phase also allows for a time to stop and think—to take a pause from the crisis situation at hand. As indicated earlier, many programmers and operators do not take the time to fully analyze a situation and instead react to data or system failures with the quick fix. This technique frequently degrades the data and system further.

Planning considerations. The following items should be considered when developing a recovery/restart plan:

1. The plan must be flexible. Continued, ongoing planning will be required to maintain control of the recovery/restart process.

2. There may be an extremely large amount of documentation that must be reviewed and controlled.

3. Experts, auditors, computer vendor personnel, etc., may have to be retained to assist in the recovery/restart process.

4. Available EDP information may cover only a short period of time—or may only be available at a specific point in the data processing cycle.

5. Recovery/restart techniques may require that test data, or files, be prepared. Programs may also have to be written.

6. Time for a recovery/restart staff planning conference, to review the fault situation, must be allowed.

7. Plan how to obtain manual and computerized records, and how to copy them if necessary.

8. Plan how to control all recovery/restart operations, both computerized and noncomputerized.

9. Allow time for the analysis of the intersystem processes. (For example, an accounts-payable system transaction may also affect a general-ledger system account.)

10. Changes are usually necessary in a normal business environment and sometimes cannot be avoided. Therefore, the control of change is

extremely important. If the recovery/restart is expected to take an extended period of time, allowance for the following changes may have to be made:

- System design changes.
- Program changes and new programs.
- New equipment.
- Technical upgrades: hardware and software.
- Social changes: laws and regulations.

11. Depending on the nature of the fault and the extent of the disaster, consideration may be given to:

- Halting the system immediately (all processing jobs).
- Suspending processing of only the task/hardware that caused the fault.
- Using a degraded mode of processing.
- Switching to a standby system.
- Switching to a standby subsystem.

12. Establish priorities for what jobs have to be run on a degraded system.

13. Develop alternative restart/recovery strategies and choose the best one.

14. Test the recovery/restart options prior to their actual use.

Planning conference. A planning conference or meeting should be conducted by the chief systems analyst and should include all the restart/recovery staff and other personnel who will be involved with the restart/recovery process. With all of these people meeting in one place, it will be easier to discuss the scope of the restart/recovery as well as any constraints under which the process must operate. Assignments should be made during the conference so that each person knows what job he or she and the other team members are to perform. Additional points to be considered for a planning conference are the following:

1. Review of the reason for the fault and possible corrective actions.

2. Detailed discussion of the recovery/restart plan and of the various applicable planning considerations.

3. Review of potential recovery/restart problems and areas of sensitivity.

4. Review of timing and sequence of the steps of the recovery/restart process and the methods to be used.

5. The degree to which any other agencies or people may be involved in the recovery/restart process, and what their exact role in the process will be.

6. The details of the staff's job duties, and the reporting structure as it relates to the recovery/restart process.

7. Establishment of a central recovery/restart control/command point.

Recovery Phase

Recovery is the process in which operations or data are restored to a point of known integrity after the original integrity of the processing, or data, has been lost. Once the recovery process has been completed, the system can be restarted and normal operations resumed.

Recovery techniques will vary, depending on the hardware and operating system and the nature of the processing, whether it is batch, on-line or a combination of both. The criticality of the system involved dictates the degree of recovery measures implemented.

The following aids can be used to restore the data and system:

- Audit trail.
- Checkpoints.
- Data recovery software.
- File backup.
- File directory recovery.
- Magnetic media recovery software, equipment, and services.
- Reconstruction.
- Recovery/restart software.
- Tape library management systems.
- Vendor-supplied utility recovery program.
- Manual procedures.

Recovery can involve the use of techniques to reconstruct the status of the system as it was immediately prior to its failure. These techniques, if successful, allow for the continuation of processing from the point of failure. The reconstruction of a system's status takes into consideration such options as maintaining a journal or log of:

- Input buffer status.
- Input queues.
- Database record image prior to update.
- Database record image after update.
- Output queues and output buffer.

The recovery process also involves the reconstruction/correction of any data that was lost or damaged.

Restart Phase

Restart is the process of beginning operations at the point where the integrity was known when operations ceased.

The following aids can be used to restart processing in a full or degraded mode of operation:

- Audit trail.
- Checkpoints.
- Data-recovery software.
- Recovery/restart software.
- Manual procedures (reenter data, etc.).

The restart process should be continually monitored to ensure that the restart operations were successful.

Testing Phase

After the recovery and restart processes, testing should be done to determine if (1) cause of the fault has been corrected; (2) recovery process was successful; (3) restart process was successful; and (4) if any damage caused by the fault has been corrected.

Postrecovery/Restart Monitoring

Post-recovery/restart monitoring involves the continual review of the system and the cause element to ensure that the problem has been corrected. It may also involve a review of the preparedness for data and system recovery.

Chapter Thirteen

Baseline Security

The concept of baselines of computer security controls is outlined. A baseline of security controls is a set of generally used controls meeting commonly desired control objectives that should be present in any well-run computer operation. Their justification is derived from common usage and prudent management, rather than from a detailed assessment of vulnerability or risk. Microcomputer baseline security worksheets are provided in this chapter.

EVOLUTION OF THE CONCEPT

The baseline security concept is the result of many years of experience in the field of computer security. Over the years many security checklists, worksheets, and audit guidelines have been established and updated by specialists and practitioners who have researched and implemented computer security in larger organizations. This combined knowledge is now at the level where a standard of security, or baseline, can be developed. This baseline should prove beneficial to all organizations using computers. Security needs specific to a particular organization should be added to the baseline for that organization.

In 1982 the U.S. Department of Justice, Bureau of Justice Statistics, released a manual that presents the baseline concept.[1] (The document was prepared by SRI International under a grant award. Donn B. Parker was the project leader.)

The manual gives a background on the baseline security concept and presents the descriptions and specifications of 82 controls. Some of the

---

[1] *Computer Crime: Computer Security Techniques* (U.S. Department of Justice, Bureau of Justice Statistics. U.S. Government Printing Office: 1982-361-233/1873), pp. 35–36.

following material is extracted from Section IV, "New Computer Security Concepts."

A baseline of security controls is a set of generally used controls meeting commonly desired *control objectives* that should be present in every well-run computer center. The justification for having them is derived from common usage and prudent management rather than from explicit identification of vulnerabilities and reduction of risks.

A control objective is a condition or event that is to be avoided, deterred, detected, prevented, or recovered from. Examples are as follows:

- Avoid violations of laws and regulations.
- Detect unauthorized system use.
- Prevent unauthorized access to sensitive areas.

A control is a policy, method, practice, device, or programmed mechanism to accomplish a control objective. A control has implementation variants that are established in the detailed specifications for the control in a particular case. Baseline controls have never before been identified, and it is not known how many would qualify universally or within any specific organization. However, the baseline concept is now feasible because of the control selection experience gained as the computer security field matures.

A baseline of security does not have to be a rigid, unalterable set of control objectives and their required controls and variants. The purpose of a baseline is to specify a minimum set of controls such that, if a control is omitted, there would be explicit reasons identified for its absence or for why an alternative control is equivalent. If these exceptions from a baseline are acceptable to the authority ultimately responsible for security, the baseline could still be said to be the accepted criterion. In fact, this exception-taking is the process by which baselines evolve.

A universally applicable baseline is improbable. As espoused by different specialists and organizations, baselines may differ. For example, differing baselines may be established by insurance companies, banks, and manufacturers. Baselines for microcomputer security will also differ, depending on how the microcomputer is used within the organization—as a stand-alone, a network node, a terminal (terminal emulation node), or in a micro-to-mainframe capacity. Security experts, auditors, and consultants may have differences of opinion about which controls belong in a baseline. In addition, some controls, and even some control objectives, will become obsolete as technology changes and advances.

MICROCOMPUTER BASELINE SECURITY WORKSHEETS

The following information was derived in part from the aforementioned Department of Justice (DOJ) manual. The worksheets presented in this section contain only a summary description of the information contained in the DOJ manual and have been modified to meet the specific requirements of baseline security for microcomputers.

The baseline security worksheets are for your selection, modification, and use. Each organization is unique and will have some specific baseline requirements that are peculiar to its operations. Space has been allocated on the worksheets for this purpose. After each baseline element, the chapters covering that element appear in parentheses.

FIGURE 13–1

Baseline Security Worksheet for Control Objective 1: Prevent Asset Responsibility Loss

No.	Control/Description	User Notes
1.1	*Assets accountability assignment*	

Specific management and/or microcomputer users are assigned explicit ownership or custodial accountability and usage rights for:
- all data.
- data handling and processing capability.
- controls.
- computer programs.

This can be accomplished by:
- establishing policy.
- establishing meaning of "ownership."
- establishing meaning of "usage."
- establishing meaning of "custodianship."
- requiring that forms be completed and logs be made designating and recording such accountability for data and programs, and copies of them in all locations and for specific times.

(Chapter 2)

| 1.2 | *Data accountability assignment to users* | |

Assign the user responsibility for:
- the accuracy.
- the safekeeping.
- the dissemination of the data the user handles.

(Chapters 2 and 9)

FIGURE 13–1 *(continued)*

No.	Control/Description	User Notes
1.3	*Separation and accountability of EDP functions*	

In many one-user microcomputer environments, separation of duties is impractical, if not impossible. Small organizations may have only one user or operator. In larger organizations, although there may be many microcomputer users, a particular microcomputer may be assigned to a department in which only one person uses it. In these cases separation of EDP functions is usually not required or justified.

However, where possible, separation of EDP functions and separation of standard accounting and sensitive duties should be enforced.

(Chapter 2)

| 1.4 | *Computer security management committee* | |

A high-level management committee can be organized to develop microcomputer security policy and oversee all security of information handling activities.

(Chapter 2)

FIGURE 13–1 *(concluded)*

No.	Control/Description	User Notes
1.5	*Remote-terminal (microcomputer) user's agreement*	

All remote-microcomputer users should be required to sign a user's agreement before they are permitted to use the main-system resources. The agreement should:
- include who shall pay for systems-related expenses.
- identify physical location of microcomputer.
- identify any relocation of micro units.
- establish maintenance and service of equipment.
- assign training of users.
- state hours of usage.
- instruct on further dissemination of information obtained from the system.
- detail proper usage of system.
- assign physical security of micro equipment.
- indicate service-provider rights to deny service and to inspect equipment.
- establish insurance coverage.
- establish liability for losses.

(Chapters 2 and 9)

FIGURE 13–2

Baseline Security Worksheet for Control Objective 2: Prevent Disclosure, Taking, or Unauthorized Use of Documents

No.	Control/Description	User Notes
2.1	*Confirmation of receipt of documents*	
	The confirmation process consists of verification of receipt of documents. Manual and computerized controls should be established to ensure adequate document audit trails so that no documents can be lost in handling.	
	(Chapters 2 and 9)	
2.2	*Discard document destruction*	
	Input/output documents, including human-readable documents or nonerasable computer media (carbon paper, one-time printer ribbons, etc.), should be reviewed for potential loss sensitivity and appropriately destroyed when no longer needed.	
	(Chapters 2 and 9)	

FIGURE 13–2   *(continued)*

No.	*Control/Description*	*User Notes*
2.3	*Proprietary notice printed on documents* Sensitive and valuable documents should have a classification (e.g., "sensitive," "private," "proprietary," "confidential," etc.) or an explicit warning indicating that the information is the property of a certain organization. *(Chapter 11)*	
2.4	*Courier trustworthiness and identification* Couriers are frequently used to distribute computer output reports to computer users. Couriers must be especially trustworthy, have a background investigation, and be bonded. *(Chapter 2)*	

FIGURE 13–2   *(concluded)*

No.	Control/Description	User Notes
2.5	*Keeping security reports confidential*	
	Computer security requires the use and filing of numerous reports, including results of security reviews, audits, exception reports, documentation of loss incidence, documentation of controls, control installation and maintenance, and personnel information. This information should be kept strictly confidential and seen by the appropriate personnel only on a need-to-know basis.	
	(Chapters 2 and 10)	

FIGURE 13–3

Baseline Security Worksheet for Control Objective 3: Prevent Modification, Disclosure, or Unauthorized Use of Obsolete or Incomplete Input/Output Data

No.	Control/Description	User Notes
3.1	*Suppression of incomplete or obsolete data*	
	Dissemination and use of incomplete and obsolete data should be prevented or restricted by directive of the organization.	
	(Chapters 2 and 9)	

FIGURE 13–3   *(concluded)*

No.	Control/Description	User Notes
3.2	*Completion of external input data* If missing essential data is still missing beyond a time limit, take steps to obtain the appropriate data. *(Chapters 2, 7, and 9)*	

FIGURE 13–4

Baseline Security Worksheet for Control Objective 4: Prevent Disclosure or Unauthorized Use of Personal Information

No.	Control/Description	User Notes
4.1	*Personal data input/output inspection* An organization that receives or disseminates databases to or from outside sources should have an input/output control group. Potential privacy and confidentiality problems are then caught before data is made available to outsiders. *(Chapters 2, 6, 7, 9, and 11)*	

FIGURE 13–4   *(concluded)*

No.	Control/Description	User Notes
4.2	*Separation of personal identification data* Databases that identify individuals as well as contain sensitive information about individuals should be separated into a file of personal identifiers and a file of data with an index linking the identifiers with the data. *(Chapters 2 and 7)*	

FIGURE 13–5

Baseline Security Worksheet for Control Objective 5: Avoid Destruction of Assets and Business Interruption

No.	Control/Description	User Notes
5.1	*Physical security perimeter* The physical perimeter within which security is to be maintained, and outside of which little or no control is maintained, should be clearly established. All vital functions should be identified and included within the security perimeter. *(Chapter 5)*	

FIGURE 13–5 *(continued)*

No.	Control/Description	User Notes
5.2	*Placement of equipment and supplies*	
	Equipment, such as telephone switching panels and cables, utilities, and computer devices, and supplies, such as paper, ribbons, and magnetic media, should be placed or stored to ensure their protection from damage. Dust, vibration, chemical effects, fire hazards, and electrical interference are produced by some equipment and supplies, and they should be kept separate from equipment and supplies affected by these phenomena. *(Chapter 5)*	
5.3	*Security for sensitive areas during unattended periods*	
	Sensitive areas during unattended times should be made physically secure. *(Chapter 5)*	

FIGURE 13–5 *(concluded)*

No.	Control/Description	User Notes
5.4	*Areas where smoking and eating are prohibited*	

Smoking and eating are usually not permitted in the larger computer installations. Many microcomputer-using organizations also have established policies on smoking and eating/drinking because of the possible damage that can be caused to the microcomputer equipment.

Establish a policy for smoking, eating, and drinking, with signs and designated areas.

(Chapter 5)

| 5.5 | *Alternative power supply* | |

Determine the need for a power supply independent of the public utility source for uninterrupted power service.

(Chapter 5)

FIGURE 13–6

Baseline Security Worksheet for Control Objective 6: Prevent Human Injuries and Other Damage from Contingencies

No.	Control/Description	User Notes
6.1	*Emergency preparedness* Emergency procedures should be documented and periodically reviewed with occupants of areas requiring emergency action. *(Chapters 2 and 12)*	

FIGURE 13–7

Baseline Security Worksheet for Control Objective 7: Prevent Unauthorized Access to Sensitive Areas

No.	Control/Description	User Notes
7.1	*Minimize traffic and access to work areas* Personnel traffic in areas where microcomputers are located should be minimized and controlled, especially where sensitive information is processed. *(Chapter 5)*	

FIGURE 13–7   *(continued)*

No.	*Control/Description*	*User Notes*

7.2   *Physical-access barriers*

Physical access through a security perimeter from a less sensitive area to a
more sensitive area or between areas
where different privileges apply must be
limited. Controls could include:
• sign-in/out log.
• challenge of unauthorized entry by
  authorized persons.
• challenge access by posted signs.
• mechanically or electrically locked
  doors.
• guards.
• mantrap.
(Chapter 5)

7.3   *Remote microcomputer/terminal physical
security*

Physical-access barriers, accountability
for use, and resistance to visual and
electromagnetic monitoring of terminals
and local communication loops should
be maintained and periodically reviewed.
  Controls include:
  • barriers.
  • usage logging.
  • terminal-locking mechanisms.
  • mechanisms to prevent removal of
    equipment.
(Chapters 4 and 5)

FIGURE 13–7 *(concluded)*

No.	Control/Description	User Notes
7.4	*Universal use of badges*	
	Badges are used to control access to sensitive data processing areas. All persons should be required to wear them. Different-color badges, with photos in some cases, should be used for employees, visitors, vendor representatives, and employees requiring temporary badges. *(Chapter 5)*	
7.5	*Programming-library access control*	
	Computer-program libraries containing listings of programs under development and in production, and associated documentation, should be protected from unauthorized access. *(Chapter 7)*	

FIGURE 13–8

Baseline Security Worksheet for Control Objective 8: Prevent Damage to Equipment

No.	Control/Description	User Notes
8.1	*Electrical equipment protection* Equipment should be protected by mechanisms for power failures or other power problems. *(Chapter 5)*	

FIGURE 13–9

Baseline Security Worksheet for Control Objective 9: Prevent Unauthorized Taking and Facility Damage

No.	Control/Description	User Notes
9.1	*Inspection of incoming/outgoing materials* Certain materials and containers should be inspected, and entry or departure restricted. This measure prevents unnecessary or dangerous materials from entering areas, reduces suspicion of otherwise trusted persons, and reinforces restrictions on unauthorized persons. *(Chapter 5)*	

FIGURE 13–10

Baseline Security Worksheet for Control Objective 10: Prevent Compromise of Data

No.	Control/Description	User Notes
10.1	*Isolation of sensitive computer production jobs* Some production systems, such as those producing negotiable instruments or processing personal information are sufficiently sensitive to potential loss to require special handling. *(Chapters 6, 7, and 9)*	
10.2	*Protection of data used in system testing* In many cases, sensitive data is used for program testing. This data must be controlled and accounted for. *(Chapter 9)*	

FIGURE 13-10   *(continued)*

No.	Control/Description	User Notes
10.3	*Magnetic tape/diskette* Microcomputer centers should have magnetic tape and diskette erasure devices, commonly referred to as degaussers, for the erasure of the contents of the magnetic media. *(Chapters 5, 7, and 9)*	
10.4	*Data classification* Data may be classified at different security levels to produce cost savings and effectiveness of applying controls consistent with various levels of sensitivity of data. When data is classified, it may be identified in two or more levels, often referred to as general information, confidential information, secret data, and other higher levels of classification named according to the functional use of data, such as trade-secret data. *(Chapter 2)*	

FIGURE 13–10 *(concluded)*

No.	Control/Description	User Notes
10.5	*Cryptographic protection* A high level of data communication and storage protection can be obtained by using the Data Encryption Standard (DES). *(Chapters 6 and 8)*	

FIGURE 13–11
Baseline Security Worksheet for Control Objective 11: Prevent Unauthorized Program or Data Modifications

No.	Control/Description	User Notes
11.1	*Correction and maintenance of production system* In many microcomputer environments, especially where custom applications have been programmed, it may be necessary to correct program errors during a production run. Any program changes should be supervised, documented, and tested. *(Chapters 6, 7, and 9)*	

FIGURE 13–11 *(concluded)*

No.	Control/Description	User Notes
11.2	*Limited use of system utility programs*	
	Most microcomputer systems have one or more utility programs capable of overriding all or most computer system and application controls. These programs should be kept on a secured directory or off the system completely. When required, the utility could be transferred to the microcomputer via diskette or communications.	
	(Chapters 6, 7, and 9)	
11.3	*Production program authorized version validation*	
	The authorized versions or copies of production programs, according to identifiers, are checked with a list of authorized copies and changes made to the production programs to determine that the version of a production program to be run is authorized.	
	(Chapters 6 and 9)	

FIGURE 13–12

Baseline Security Worksheet for Control Objective 12: Detect Computer,
Application, and Communications Systems and Operations Failures

No.	Control/Description	User Notes
12.1	*Microcomputer user trouble-calls logging* All calls from users and staff regarding problems with a microcomputer and communications system are logged detailing the caller's name, time, date, and nature of the problem. *(Chapter 9)*	
12.2	*Microcomputer program quality assurance* A testing or quality control group should independently test and examine computer programs and related documentation to ensure integrity of program products. *(Chapter 9)*	

FIGURE 13–12 *(concluded)*

No.	*Control/Description*	*User Notes*
12.3	*Computer program change logs* All changes to microcomputer programs should be logged. The log can be used as a means of ensuring formal approval of changes. *(Chapter 9)*	
12.4	*Exception reporting* Exception reporting on a timely basis should be designed into microcomputer applications to report on any deviation from normal activity that may indicate errors or unauthorized acts. *(Chapter 9)*	

FIGURE 13–13

Baseline Security Worksheet for Control Objective 13: Prevent Interference with Auditing

No.	Control/Description	User Notes
13.1	*Independent control of audit tools* Audit programs, documentation, and test materials should be kept in secure areas by the audit staff. *(Chapter 9)*	
13.2	*Independent microcomputer use by auditors* Audit independence can be considerably enhanced by using a microcomputer not associated with the data processing activities being audited. *(Chapter 9)*	

FIGURE 13–14

Baseline Security Worksheet for Control Objective 14: Prevent Loss,
Modification, Disclosure or Destruction of Data Assets

No.	Control/Description	User Notes
14.1	*Diskette and tape cartridge management avoiding external labels* A magnetic media management system can be used to keep track of all diskettes and cartridges using the media's serial number. *(Chapters 6, 7, and 9)*	
14.2	*Separation of test and production systems* When an organization is large enough to have need for more than one microcomputer, there is distinct advantage to limiting the development and testing to one microcomputer system and the production work to another microcomputer. *(Chapters 6, 7, and 9)*	

FIGURE 13–14   *(continued)*

No.	Control/Description	User Notes
14.3	*Minimizing numbers of copies of sensitive data files and reports* The number of copies of sensitive diskette, cartridge, disk, or paper files should be minimized. Destruction dates should be specified and destruction instructions followed. *(Chapters 6, 7, and 9)*	
14.4	*Data file and program backup* Periodically updated data and program files should be copied and cycled from the immediate site to local and off-site storage areas by file generations (father, grandfather, etc.). Backup should also include documentation such as operating instructions, program specs, and extra computer forms. *(Chapters 6, 7, and 9)*	

FIGURE 13–14 *(continued)*

No.	Control/Description	User Notes
14.5	*Secrecy of data file and program names*	

Names for data files and computer programs are necessary for computer program development and documentation. They are also necessary for job setup and, in some cases, for computer operation. However, file and program names need not be known by those who are in a transaction relationship with the microcomputer system and not concerned with programming of computer applications. Therefore, it is best that users work on their microcomputer's applications through a system of menus. Selection is done by menu item number rather than by program name.

(Chapters 6, 7, and 9)

14.6   *Input data validation*

Validation of all input to a microcomputer system should be performed to help ensure that data is correct and appropriate.

(Chapters 7 and 9)

FIGURE 13–14   *(concluded)*

No.	Control/Description	User Notes
14.7	*Limit transaction privileges from terminals*	

The transactions that a particular use is permitted to initiate are limited. Logs may be kept for all attempts to use an unauthorized system, transaction, or system command. The log can be used to determine who needs training or perhaps disciplinary action.
(Chapters 7 and 9)

14.8   *Microcomputer system password file encryption*

The password file in the computer system contains master copies of passwords to verify correct identification and password input from terminal log-ins. This data file is one of the most sensitive in the entire computer system and, therefore, must be properly protected.

Passwords in the file should be individually encrypted using a one-way encryption, algorithm. When a password is entered, it is immediately encrypted with the same algorithm and compared with the encrypted form of the master password for matching.
(Chapters 6 and 7)

FIGURE 13–15
Baseline Security Worksheet for Control Objective 15: Recover from
Business Interruption

No.	Control/Description	User Notes
15.1	*Contingency recovery equipment replacement* Commitments should be obtained in writing from microcomputer equipment and supply vendors to replace critical equipment and supplies within a specific period of time following a contingency loss. *(Chapter 12)*	
15.2	*Disaster recovery* Every business should have a written disaster recovery plan. *(Chapter 12)*	

FIGURE 13–15   *(concluded)*

No.	Control/Description	User Notes
15.3	*Financial loss contingency and recovery funding* Specialized EDP insurance is available and should be considered when insurance covering other types of losses in a business may not apply. *(Chapter 12)*	

FIGURE 13–16
Baseline Security Worksheet for Control Objective 16: Detect Unauthorized System Use

No.	Control/Description	User Notes
16.1	*Computer system activity records* Most computer systems produce a number of system activity logs, journals, and exception reports. Such recordings should be periodically and selectively examined, both manually and through automated means, looking for key indications of possible unauthorized activities. *(Chapters 6, 7, and 9)*	

FIGURE 13–16   *(concluded)*

No.	Control/Description	User Notes
16.2	*Monitoring microcomputer use* On a random or periodic selective basis, communications between the host computer and remote microcomputers should be monitored. Examine file names and contents. The usage is logged and analyzed to determine that the user is only performing actions that have been explicitly authorized. *(Chapters 6, 7, and 9)*	

FIGURE 13–17
Baseline Security Worksheet for Control Objective 17: Detect Unauthorized Activities of Employees

No.	Control/Description	User Notes
17.1	*Employees' identification on work products* All microcomputer users should have standard identification in the form of official names, numbers, or passwords. This identification is to be entered into all records, data input, and activity logs and journals to identify workers associated with all work products. *(Chapters 6, 7, and 9)*	

FIGURE 13–18

Baseline Security Worksheet for Control Objective 18: Prevent Inadequacy of System Controls

No.	Control/Description	User Notes
18.1	*Assigning responsibility for controls* Certain individuals or departments should be assigned specific responsibility for reviewing and enhancing system and application program controls. The individuals include: • EDP auditor (or internal auditor). • computer security officer(s). • other corporate management. *(Chapter 9)*	
18.2	*Participation of computer users at critical development times* Computer users, including those providing input data and using computer output reports, should supply explicit control requirements to systems analysts and programmers who are designing and developing application systems. Users should continue to monitor the controls after the system has been implemented. *(Chapters 2 and 9)*	

FIGURE 13–18   *(continued)*

No.	Control/Description	User Notes
18.3	*Requirements and specification participation by EDP auditors* EDP auditors should participate in the development of requirements for important applications systems to ensure that the audit requirements in the applications systems are adequate and that adequate controls have been specified. The approval process should include the formalized sign-off of system specifications by the EDP auditors. *(Chapter 9)*	
18.4	*Vendor-supplied program integrity* Many new vendor-supplied computer programs have been developed with control and integrity built into them. Any modifications to these programs will possibly compromise the built-in capabilities. *(Chapter 9)*	

FIGURE 13–18 *(concluded)*

No.	Control/Description	User Notes
18.5	*Technical review of operating system changes* Whenever any change is to be made to the microcomputer operating system programs, a review of the change should be made. The intent is to make sure that the new changes are valuable and will not compromise controls and integrity, have an unanticipated impact on some other part of the system, or interfere excessively with vendor updates. *(Chapters 6 and 9)*	

FIGURE 13–19

Baseline Security Worksheet for Control Objective 19: Avoid Violations of Laws and Regulations

No.	Control/Description	User Notes
19.1	*Compliance with laws and regulations* A statement regarding the new or modified system's compliance with relevant laws and regulations should be provided in requirements and specifications. Direct quotes from laws and regulations regarding EDP security, privacy, copyright, patent, and trade secrets should be included. *(Chapter 11)*	

FIGURE 13–20

Baseline Security Worksheet for Control Objective 20: Prevent Unauthorized Computer Access

No.	Control/Description	User Notes
20.1	*Telephone access universal selection*	

Limiting access to a computer and data files can be an important means of security. A microcomputer interfaced to the dial-up public telephone network is exposed to access from any telephone in the world.

Access controls include:
- password management.
- point-to-point wire or leased line telephone access.
- access-control devices such as dial-back and encryption devices.
- restriction of dial-up activity to certain times of the day.
- file/database security.
- unlisted phone access numbers.

(Chapters 8 and 9)

| 20.2 | *Microcomputer/terminal identifiers* | |

Automatic identification circuits can be installed in, or associated with, microcomputers for identification in host computers. Microcomputer/terminal identifiers are used to indicate whether a particular micro or terminal is permitted to initiate or receive certain transactions.

(Chapters 8 and 9)

FIGURE 13–20   *(continued)*

No.	*Control/Description*	*User Notes*
20.3	*Passwords for microcomputer access* Secret passwords are commonly used for access to microcomputers and from microcomputers used as terminals to host computers (terminal emulation). One way of providing user passwords is via a computerized random number/letter generator and printing directly through sealed envelopes, using the same carbon-paper-in-envelope techniques that are used for many bank cards. The sealed envelopes are delivered directly to the user without the password being seen. *(Chapters 7, 8, and 9)*	
20.4	*Dynamic password change control by user* In some organizations, users are allowed to change their passwords any time once they have logged on to the system. *(Chapters 7, 8, and 9)*	

FIGURE 13–20   *(concluded)*

No.	Control/Description	User Notes
20.5	*Microcomputer/terminal log-in protocol*	
	The protocol for logging into a host computer or microcomputer system from a terminal or another computer system should be designed to reduce unauthorized access. The computer's response to a log-in should provide a minimum of information to avoid providing an unauthorized user with any assistance.	
	(Chapters 7, 8, and 9)	
20.6	*Computer system password file encryption*	
	The password file in the microcomputer system and host computer system contain master copies of passwords to verify correct identification and password input from log-ins. These files should be protected, and passwords in the file should be individually encrypted.	
	(Chapters 7, 8, and 9)	

Chapter Fourteen

Securing the Microcomputer-to-Mainframe Link

The microcomputer-to-mainframe link has had a significant impact on the data processing function. The concept has grown quickly and is having a broad effect on the way people think about personal computers, data processing departments, and office automation. As information processing extends from the central site to remote sites, the challenge of providing security over information and its processes becomes more difficult.

This chapter provides security guidelines for the microcomputer-to-mainframe link, and a program to review the adequacy of current security. The security review program is oriented toward the four microcomputer-to-mainframe link approaches: terminal emulators, database extract and download, link utilities, and embedded links. A fully developed microcomputer-to-mainframe link security program that is based on the practices of several leading corporations is also included in this chapter. The chapter also presents an in-depth review of on-line system security considerations.

THE SCOPE OF THE PROBLEM

When microcomputers are linked to the mainframe, they provide a window of access to centralized resources. Information that was under the full control of the centralized group is now distributed among multiple processing sites. Once the data passes to the microcomputer, the centralized security function loses much of its ability to provide security over that information.

Many of the centralized sites have established a security officer function. Having a single individual accountable for computer security ensures that the function will not be overlooked. However, the security officer function does not have to be a full-time job. It can be part-time or a committee function with the chairperson of the committee being the security officer.

With the need defined and responsibility assigned, security in the central site becomes formalized. Security policies and procedures are developed, then implemented. The result is that security becomes an important part of the central site.

Years ago, the physical layout of the central site was constructed around security requirements. Physical access was normally limited, with procedures in place to challenge unauthorized visitors. Inventories were maintained of data media, and approval documents were needed to possess that media. In addition, many installations used security software packages such as RACF and ACS II. All of the normal accesses to information were secured.

The early introduction of the microcomputer was viewed as an extension of an individual's personal processing. It was not seen to warrant security measures. However, as individuals became more proficient in the use of the microcomputer, they became data starved. Supplying the data needed by individuals necessitated access to the centralized site.

The approaches for accessing central information resources vary, but all pose the same security threat. Information that was protected centrally loses much, if not all, of that protection once it is dispersed to the microcomputer site. The specific security challenges that are incurred when the microcomputer is linked to the mainframe include the following:

1. Information protected in a central site is copied, and when located outside the central site it is without the same security measures.

2. Individuals operating the microcomputer site may not have direction or training on how to provide security at the microcomputer site.

3. Opening access for the microcomputer to the central site may permit the microcomputer user to perform intentional or unintentional unauthorized acts using central facilities.

4. The movement of data is difficult, if not impossible, to control once it is transmitted to the remote site.

5. The microcomputer site may be left unattended and accessible by unauthorized individuals.

6. Information, when no longer useful, may be discarded in a way that allows scavengers to collect and use it in an unauthorized manner.

The problem with security at the microcomputer site that is linked to the mainframe is a recent phenomenon. While some organizations have recognized the seriousness of the problem, others have not. The approaches vary, from centrally imposed security procedures to a loosely worded caution for microcomputer users to be careful.

The challenge of providing good security is difficult for three reasons:

1. There are many methods for linking the microcomputer to the mainframe.

2. Organizational structure in most organizations does not take into consideration any central control over microcomputers in various organizational units.

3. There are few "off-the-shelf" security software procedures and approaches available to assist in providing the needed security.

FOUR APPROACHES TO LINKING MICROCOMPUTERS TO MAINFRAMES

Part of the reason that the microcomputer-to-mainframe link is so complex and confusing is that there are different products that are called micro–mainframe links. They are a diverse lot because the need for these links varies from one user to another; different products serve different needs. Four options are terminal emulators; packages for extracting and downloading information from databases; link utilities that connect software packages onto the mainframe with other software on the micro, regardless of the data environment; and what are called embedded links. The last two items are micro-to-mainframe links that are not sold as individual products, but are a feature of a more comprehensive product.

Terminal Emulators

Terminal emulators are an advanced technological approach for turning a $5,000 hardware cost into an $800 one. They may involve software or a combination of hardware and software. They allow the personal computer to function as an ordinary terminal, and let a user connect to a host computer without having to get another terminal dedicated to that host. They are used to eliminate the need to have a microcomputer- and mainframe-based terminal on the same desk.

This would not be interesting if the micro-to-mainframe link accepted a lot of these products for the file-capture capability. For example, the user logs on with the emulator and initiates a host session with a query language, structures a query, and turns off the file-saver feature. The query is executed and the data that gets down to the micro is saved in a file. As a result, the user can then log off the host, perform processing with this file, and then use it for something to be done on the personal computer such as sort it, put it in a different format, and so forth. Another way this works is to give the ability of creating a file in the microcomputer that is essentially a keystroke file, or a keyboard macro, which can drive the sessions so that if the same kind of inquiry is needed over and over again, it does not have to be rekeyed each time.

The terminal emulator approach has a number of drawbacks (see Figure 14–1). Users who have started out on micros do not know the mainframe environment. They do not know the log-on sequence and what is needed to attach to the particular application. They do not know the query languages that are necessary to get information from the host. And they do not know the names of the files that hold the information

FIGURE 14–1
Problems with Terminal Emulators

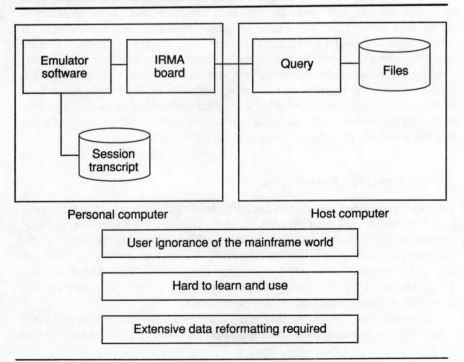

they want. These things are not easy to use or learn for the person who is not well versed in the data processing orientation. Micro users come from a completely different mind-set. There is some resistance and trouble in converting them to users who are proficient on the mainframe.

Even if a user gets this far, there is an extensive data reformatting problem. Once the file in the micro is captured, a lot of work is needed to put it into Lotus or DBase, or any of the other products on the market. To get it into something as rudimentary as the DIF format, a lot of messaging is needed. There is not much available to do this. At most places, people do not know how to do it. It is too time-consuming, and the people who could figure it out do not want to get involved with it on a regular basis.

Database Extract and Download

The database extract and download is perhaps the largest category of micro-to-mainframe link software today. Figure 14–2 shows the personal computer on the left and the host on the right. Software for this product resides on the host and micro, instead of being solely a micro product. The benefit is that the user is insulated from the mess of deal-

FIGURE 14–2
Database Extract and Download

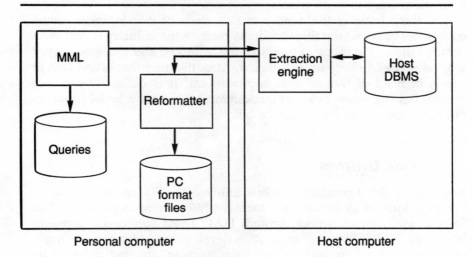

ing with the host computer; the user does not have to know anything about the host. All he or she needs to do is know the password and have his or her micro software initialized by the data processing department or an administrator, so that the idea works properly with the particular host installation. The product has a menu orientation, and the user can view the different data sets that are available with the technical term and an extended English description for each field. Selection is done by moving the cursor around to get the desired data.

These products handle the recording automatically. In some cases, they support only one micro format: for example, it may be tied to a Lotus. In other cases, the user can simply tell the link what micro application is wanted, and the translation is made correctly. The user creates a query on the micro that can be stored. It goes to the micro-to-mainframe control module, which relays it to the host. The host processes that query against data stored on it, packages the output from that process, and relays it back to the micro, where it is reformatted, stored, and filed according to the required format. This is one general approach.

There are about half a dozen variations of some products in this category. Some are batch and some are interactive. With some the user will have to wait overnight for a response, and with others the user will get an instantaneous response. Another key difference is that some are open format and others are closed. Some are proprietary links to specific host database management system packages with specific micro productivity software packages. Understand what you are getting into to make sure that what you are looking at will support the various applications your users want to work with.

The third issue is the quality at this stage of development. Some companies have put out their products because the industry is hot. With some of these, the range of functionality is limited and the speed is not what is needed to keep users satisfied. Also, the friendliness and ease of use is in need of tremendous improvement. It is definitely a caveat emptor (let the buyer beware) marketplace; there are a lot of products out there today that do not fit the bill.

Link Utilities

Another family of products are link utilities (see Figure 14–3). One of the more interesting of these products is a Micro Tempus product called Tempus-Link, which works through HAPI (host application program interface). HAPI allows an application developer to build a micro application and a host application and have them talk to each other. This

FIGURE 14-3
Link Utilities

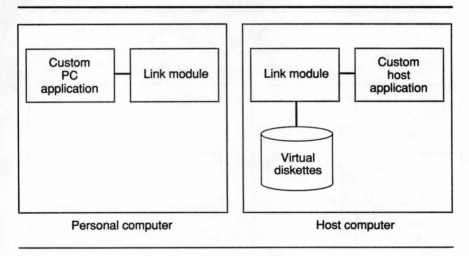

provides a means for the micro to output some data, have it passed up to the host along with the task name or process, and have the host evoke and run a process using the data that is passed up, and then relay its output back to the micro, where the process can repeat if necessary. Ongoing interactive sessions can occur between the micro and the host with no user intervention. This is the essence of the distributed processing architecture that involves hosts and micros. Companies are starting to do things with this. The basic model can be enriched by a number of options, such as building a virtual diskette capability on the host that looks like another floppy drive to the micro user, but is part of the host DASD. By doing that, a host program can automatically provide file information for micro users by dumping it into this diskette, and the user can come and get it anytime he wants to.

Embedded Links

The last approach is embedded links (Figure 14-4). These are links that are not sold as a stand-alone entity. They represent part of the functionality for a more comprehensive product. Embedded links improve the functionality of the product by distributing the processing load appropriately between the microcomputer and the host.

FIGURE 14–4
Embedded Links

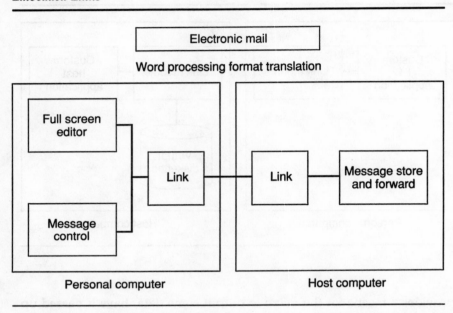

Electronic mail provides one example. With an entirely host-based electronic mail package, a line editor on the host has nowhere near the usability and power of the full-screen editors that come with the good micro word processing packages. The user is connected to the host for the entire session that in a dial-up environment is expensive and could take a large amount of overhead on the CPU, which could be used for other things. Use the power of the micro to get around all of this. A product like this puts a full-screen editor and a piece of control software on the personal computer so that, under micro control, the user formats the message, designates the address, and selects all of the options. Only when that is done is the session with the host established, the message uploaded and then downloaded, and so forth. The usability of the product is increased and the cost associated with it is decreased by taking what used to be a host application and making it a host-micro application.

Some examples of modeling software are EMPIRE (Employee Information Reporting System) and FOCUS. One situation in which a large model might be on the host would be a budget. This capability can be given to the department head to fill in his/her particular budget. This is done by handing out worksheets that someone has to keypunch. Now it can be put on a diskette and allows the user to work it on the diskette, run a sensitivity analysis, and then consolidate the elements. This is an application put in an embedded micro-to-mainframe link as part of the model language.

There are word processing products that allow another movement of an editable document from one company's word processor to another: for example, from NBI to Xerox or Wang. ITI makes a product called Soft-Switch that does this. This product supports MultiMate, and a professional can rough out a document into MultiMate and upload it to the office Wang system, and the secretary can edit it. This also has a micro-to-mainframe link embedded in it so that the micro user can identify the MultiMate document and easily upload it without having to understand telecommunications.

THREE METHODS TO PROVIDE SECURITY

Security procedures for the microcomputer-to-mainframe link normally originate within the central computer site. The central site, having an awareness of the need for security, creates an organizational awareness. This frequently takes place in the form of a memo to, or meeting with, senior management. The result is corporate oversight of the micro-computer-to-mainframe link.

When the microcomputer interacts with the centralized site, existing security procedures adequately deal with normal threats. The micro-computer user acts in the same capacity as any other on-line user and is subject to passwords and other security procedures. The security challenge involves proving security after that interaction has occurred. At this point, the centralized information is located at the microcomputer site and the central security procedures no longer provide security at that site.

Organizations have adopted one of the following three methods for providing the needed security. The first two methods are the most common. This section proposes a third approach. The correct approach can be known only after security has been evaluated and a determination made regarding the magnitude of the security threat:

1. Extend mainframe security procedures.
2. Extend existing security procedures over information stored in the user area.
3. Develop a security approach designed uniquely for the microcomputer-to-mainframe link.

Method 1: Extend Mainframe Security Procedures

If security over the microcomputer-to-mainframe link is administered by the same individual who administers the mainframe security, the mainframe security policy is normally extended to the microcomputer. The mainframe security officer has a large-site orientation and background. This encourages that individual to use the same security practices at the microcomputer site as were used at the mainframe site. The types of security procedures used under this method include the following:

• *Attempts to provide physical security for the microcomputer.* This includes securing the computer to a work area with bolts, alarms that sound if the microcomputer is unplugged, and other approaches attempting to isolate the microcomputer from easy physical removal.

• *Providing locked cabinets for diskettes and supplies.* Microcomputer users are provided secure cabinets to store diskettes, reports, or other documents requiring protection.

• *Controlling physical access to the microcomputer.* Through the use of keys or other mechanisms, limit the usability of the microcomputer to a preselected group of individuals.

• *Acquiring and implementing security software and tools to make access difficult.* This approach tends to treat the microcomputer-to-terminal link as if it was exclusively a terminal emulator. The security practices that were effective at the central site are transferred intact to the remote site. Although customization is needed, the basic approaches are the same: for example, the physical location at the remote site cannot emulate the central site.

Method 2: Extend Existing Security Procedures over Information Stored in the User Area

It is argued that information from the central site has been transmitted to users from the day computers were installed. The information often originates from the user and is processed at the central site, and the reports or other documents are remitted back to the user. These documents are copies of the information contained on computer media at the central site.

By interacting with users, the central site adopts a custodial responsibility. The central site is responsible for data from the time it is given to it from the user until it is returned. To document this custodial responsibility, some centralized sites use transfer documents by which the transfer of responsibility is indicated by signing. For example, before the output reports are given to a user, the individual accepting them signs a document indicating they are received. This avoids the problem of leaving reports at a central location for pickup by users. Without signing, there are often periods where neither the central site nor the user has full custody over the information.

Once the information is turned over to the user, the central site no longer accepts responsibility for that information. Since this process has been occurring for about 30 years, the information now provided on computer media should not change the security concepts.

When this approach is used, no security measures are established for the microcomputer-to-mainframe link. The central site protects itself from access by the microcomputer in the same manner it protects itself in all other processing situations. The security at the microcomputer site is left to the individual at that site. The security is deemed the same over the microcomputer-controlled information as it is for reports, manuals, or other documents containing similar information in the hands of that same individual.

Method 3: Develop a Security Approach Uniquely Designed for the Microcomputer-to-Mainframe Link

This method assumes that there are unique risks to the microcomputer-to-mainframe link. If there are new or increased risks, the same control processes that were used at the central site or at the remote site before the microcomputer-to-mainframe link was instituted will not be effective.

Organizations that review security at the central site are finding that the programs used there are ineffective for the microcomputer-to-mainframe link. Several security reviewers indicate that only about half the items used in a security review at the central site are applicable to the remote site.

The risks that appear to be new or increased when the microcomputer-to-mainframe link is utilized include the following:

- Machine accessibility to information.
- Easy removal of information (it is easier to steal a diskette than a large pile of paper).
- Easy manipulation and analysis of information.
- Removal of information and the processing equipment to an off-site location with less security protection than it had on-site.
- Inadvertent destruction of central resources because of improper controls and training on microcomputer procedures.

SECURITY EVALUATION PROCESS

The review of the microcomputer-to-mainframe security is a three-step process.

Step 1: Identify the organization's approach. The type of security analysis that needs to be performed will vary, based upon the approach used, the terminal emulator posing the least challenge, and the embedded links posing the greatest security challenge. Study the four approaches described earlier (terminal emulators, link utilities, database extract and download, and embedded links) and determine which one(s) are used in the organization.

Step 2: Evaluate the security practices used. Through interviews, investigations, and tests, determine the effectiveness of the security practices that are in place and working. The approach suggested for doing this is an investigative approach. Figures 14–6 through 14–9 are checklists designed to assist in the investigation.

The checklists are designed so that "yes" responses indicate good security practices and "no" responses represent potential security vulnerabilities. The greater the number of "no" responses to the items on the checklist, the greater the security vulnerability. The assessment should be made on the number of "no" responses and the severity of the items.

Step 3: Recommend security improvements. The product of the microcomputer-to-mainframe link security evaluation will first be an opinion regarding the effectiveness of the security (derived from Steps 1 and 2), and then recommendations to eliminate security exposure.

The recommendations should be tailored to the identified security exposures. To assist in developing these recommendations, a security approach for the microcomputer-to-mainframe link is presented later in this chapter. The concepts presented in that section are based on the policies and procedures used by several leading organizations.

Alternatives to different aspects of security are presented so that those most adaptable to the needs of your organization can be selected as models. "Recommended Approaches to Security" following is designed to be used as a reference in developing specific recommendations.

Evaluating Emulator Security

Figure 14–5 is a checklist that contains security items relating to the terminal emulator approach to linking the mainframe to the microcomputer. The items contained in this checklist represent security practices relating to this approach. "Yes" responses indicate good security approaches, while "no" responses represent potential vulnerabilities.

The security assessment checklist also contains a Not Applicable (N/A) column. If the item is not applicable or appropriate to security in your organization, check the "N/A" column. For "no" responses, or items for which you are unsure, a comments column is provided for additional amplification.

Database Extract and Download Security Evaluation

Figure 14–6 provides items that need to be evaluated during a review of the security over the database extract and download approach. This approach is becoming more common. Many organizations have implemented it through an information center in which diskettes of commonly used information are readily available. For example, a diskette containing sales data might be one of the readily available extracts. In other organizations, the needed information is downloaded over communication lines to the microcomputer.

The database extract and download security checklist is designed so that "yes" responses indicate good security procedures and "no" responses represent potential vulnerabilities. The checklist is designed to be used by the security evaluator after investigation has been undertaken. It is good practice to become familiar with the questions, conduct the investigation, and then answer the items on the checklist.

Utility Security Evaluation

Figure 14–7 includes a list of security items to be reviewed with this link approach. As the approaches become more sophisticated, there is greater concern over the security vulnerabilities associated with the link utilities; thus, the security review intensifies.

The checklist is designed so that "yes" responses indicate good link utility security procedures, while "no" responses indicate potential vulnerabilities. As with the other checklists, all items may not be appropri-

FIGURE 14–5
Terminal Emulator Link Security Evaluation

No.	Item	Yes	No	N/A	Comments
			Responses		
1.	Is there a corporate policy on the use of microcomputers?	___	___	___	
2.	As part of that, or a separate policy, is computer security included in the policy?	___	___	___	
3.	Does the computer security policy cover the microcomputer-to-mainframe link?	___	___	___	
4.	Do procedures exist to assist in the implementation of the microcomputer-to-mainframe link security?	___	___	___	
5.	Is an individual responsible for over-seeing the microcomputer-to-mainframe link security?	___	___	___	
6.	Do users of the microcomputer link understand security responsibilities?	___	___	___	
7.	Are users of the microcomputer link trained and/or instructed on how to implement their security responsibilities?	___	___	___	
8.	Is security over the microcomputer link periodically reviewed?	___	___	___	
9.	Has terminal hardware linkage been thoroughly tested?	___	___	___	
10.	Has terminal software linkage been thoroughly tested?	___	___	___	
11.	Is the microcomputer link subject to the central site access procedures?	___	___	___	
12.	Are terminal emulator risks defined?	___	___	___	
13.	Are controls established to reduce the magnitude of unacceptable risks?	___	___	___	
14.	Is the terminal mode subject to all central-site terminal security procedures?	___	___	___	
15.	When information received in the terminal mode is processed using microcomputer programs, are security practices still in effect?	___	___	___	

FIGURE 14–5 *(concluded)*

No.	Item	Yes	No	N/A	Comments
16.	For confidential data, is microcomputer memory cleared after processing is complete?	—	—	—	
17.	Do microcomputer users remove and protect all media used during processing?	—	—	—	
18.	Can only authorized users access the microcomputer when it is used in the terminal emulation mode?	—	—	—	
19.	Are there passwords/codes that identify all terminal users?	—	—	—	
20.	Are terminal user codes matched to the resources that an individual is authorized to access?	—	—	—	
21.	Can the central site positively identify the microcomputer-emulated terminal to ensure that it is communicating with a preauthorized facility (for example, using hang-up and call-back procedures)?	—	—	—	
22.	Will the microcomputer be automatically shut down after a predetermined period of inactivity?	—	—	—	
23.	Is a process established to monitor security over terminal emulation?	—	—	—	
24.	Are potential security violations recorded?	—	—	—	
25.	Are problems quantified and regularly analyzed by the appropriate levels of management?	—	—	—	
26.	Are microcomputers identified and controlled in accordance with the risks they pose as opposed to nonmicrocomputer terminals?	—	—	—	
27.	Is the security at the local site consistent with the importance of the data used there?	—	—	—	

FIGURE 14–6
Database Extract and Download Security Evaluation

No.	Item	Yes	No	N/A	Comments
		Responses			
1.	Is there a corporate policy on the use of microcomputers?	—	—	—	
2.	As part of that, or a separate policy, is computer security included in the policy?	—	—	—	
3.	Does the computer security policy cover the microcomputer-to-mainframe link?	—	—	—	
4.	Do procedures exist to assist in the implementation of the microcomputer-to-mainframe link security?	—	—	—	
5.	Is an individual responsible for overseeing the microcomputer-to-mainframe link security?	—	—	—	
6.	Do users of the microcomputer link understand their security responsibilities?	—	—	—	
7.	Are users of the microcomputer link trained and/or instructed on how to implement their security responsibilities?	—	—	—	
8.	Is security over the microcomputer link periodically reviewed?	—	—	—	
9.	Are databases that can be extracted for microcomputers identified?	—	—	—	
10.	Are the views of the database that can be extracted identified?	—	—	—	
11.	Are the individuals who can receive that information identified?	—	—	—	
12.	Is a matrix prepared that cross-references the views to the authorized individuals?	—	—	—	
13.	Is there a vehicle to enforce that access matrix?	—	—	—	
14.	Are users instructed on how to obtain downloaded database data?	—	—	—	

FIGURE 14–6 *(concluded)*

No.	Item	Yes	No	N/A	Comments
15.	Are users instructed on how to protect the downloaded data?	___	___	___	
16.	Are users instructed on how to destroy the downloaded data?	___	___	___	
17.	Is there a policy stating whether or not downloaded data can be removed from the premises?	___	___	___	
18.	If data is removed from the premises, are records retained of that removal?	___	___	___	
19.	If records are retained, are they periodically reviewed by management?	___	___	___	
20.	If database diskettes are available in an information center, are they protected by the access matrix?	___	___	___	
21.	Is the location of downloaded data known to the central site? (For example, is an inventory maintained?)	___	___	___	
22.	If database data is found to be erroneous, are users of that data appropriately notified?	___	___	___	
23.	Are control totals provided with the downloaded data?	___	___	___	
24.	Is there a method for microcomputer users to report potential security violations?	___	___	___	
25.	Can microcomputer users adequately protect the downloaded data from unauthorized access?	___	___	___	
26.	Will the downloaded data be maintained in a secure location during non-working hours?	___	___	___	
27.	Has the download software been fully tested?	___	___	___	
28.	Are procedures in place to ensure that the database format and the needed micro format are compatible?	___	___	___	
29.	Is the security at the local site consistent with the importance of the data there?	___	___	___	

FIGURE 14–7

Link Utilities Security Evaluation

No.	Item	Yes	No	N/A	Comments
			Responses		
1.	Is there a corporate policy on the use of microcomputers?	—	—	—	
2.	As part of that, or a separate policy, is computer security included in the policy?	—	—	—	
3.	Does the computer security policy cover the microcomputer-to-mainframe link?	—	—	—	
4.	Do procedures exist to assist in the implementation of the microcomputer-to-mainframe link security?	—	—	—	
5.	Is an individual responsible for overseeing the microcomputer-to-mainframe link security?	—	—	—	
6.	Do users of the microcomputer link understand their security responsibilities?	—	—	—	
7.	Are users of the microcomputer link trained and/or instructed in how to implement their security responsibilities?	—	—	—	
8.	Is security over the microcomputer link periodically reviewed?	—	—	—	
9.	Have the link utilities been tested?	—	—	—	
10.	Are the link utilities compatible with central software?	—	—	—	
11.	Are the link utilities compatible with microcomputer software?	—	—	—	
12.	Can the link utilities be identified by source (i.e., microcomputer location)?	—	—	—	
13.	Are the link utilities at the microcomputer site restricted to specific databases?	—	—	—	
14.	Are there procedures to ensure that the link utilities can only access the authorized databases?	—	—	—	
15.	Is there a means to ensure that changes to the central database are appropriately communicated to the link utilities?	—	—	—	
16.	Are there control totals associated with transmitted data to the link utilities?	—	—	—	

FIGURE 14–7   *(concluded)*

No.	Item	Yes	No	N/A	Comments
17.	Are there link utility checkpoints that will stop microcomputer processing when transmissions are incomplete?	___	___	___	
18.	Are link utilities tamperproof?	___	___	___	
19.	Are link utility user exits controlled?	___	___	___	
20.	Are microcomputer users prohibited from modifying link utilities?	___	___	___	
21.	Can link utilities verify the authority of the user to access data controlled by the link utility?	___	___	___	
22.	Will the link utility adequately destroy unwanted data?	___	___	___	
23.	Is the microcomputer user instructed on how to store link utility files?	___	___	___	
24.	Will the data be adequately protected when the primary/authorized users are not at the microcomputer?	___	___	___	
25.	Will link utility programs and data be stored in a secure location during non-working hours?	___	___	___	
26.	Are there procedures to report potential security violations at the microcomputer site?	___	___	___	
27.	Does management regularly review these reported potential violations?	___	___	___	
28.	Are reviews taken to ensure that microcomputer users are reporting potential security violations?	___	___	___	
29.	Are link utility options identified for the potential security risks?	___	___	___	
30.	Have high-risk link utility options been eliminated and/or controlled?	___	___	___	
31.	Can the central site identify unusual processing requests (e.g., data requests during nonworking hours) and cut off those items until their propriety has been verified?	___	___	___	
32.	Is data recoverable in the event of loss of integrity of processing?	___	___	___	
33.	Is security at the local site consistent with the importance of data used at the local site?	___	___	___	

ate to the evaluation. Some of the items from Figures 14–5 and 14–6 may be appropriate to the link utility approach assessment process.

Embedded Links Security Evaluation

Figure 14–8 provides items to be included in the evaluation of the embedded links approach. While few organizations use this approach today, many are considering it. The checklist may prove helpful in establishing the security controls for this approach.

The checklist is designed so that "yes" responses indicate good embedded link security approaches, while "no" responses represent potential vulnerabilities. "No" responses should be documented and investigated. It is poor practice not to indicate the disposition of all "no" responses.

RECOMMENDED APPROACHES TO SECURITY

The implemented microcomputer-to-mainframe link security procedures should be constructed around the following:

- Approach used to link the mainframe to the microcomputer.
- Amount of centralized authority over microcomputer processing, specifically those links of the mainframe.
- Identified microcomputer-to-mainframe link security vulnerabilities.
- Time and resources available to improve security.
- Corporate security policies and approaches.

The three keys to improving security are the following:

1. Establishing security procedures.
2. Administering the security policy.
3. Establishing link security policies.

Each of these three keys is presented below in detail. For each of the key aspects of security, actual corporate documents will be presented to illustrate the concepts.

FIGURE 14–8
Embedded Links Security Evaluation

No.	Item	Yes	No	N/A	Comments
				Responses	
1.	Is there a corporate policy on the use of microcomputers?	—	—	—	
2.	As part of that, or separately, is computer security included in the policy?	—	—	—	
3.	Does the computer security policy cover the microcomputer-to-mainframe link?	—	—	—	
4.	Are there procedures to assist in the implementation of the microcomputer-to-mainframe link security?	—	—	—	
5.	Is an individual responsible to oversee the microcomputer-to-mainframe link security?	—	—	—	
6.	Do users of the microcomputer link understand their security responsibilities?	—	—	—	
7.	Are users of the microcomputer link trained and/or instructed in how to implement their security responsibilities?	—	—	—	
8.	Is security over the microcomputer link periodically reviewed?	—	—	—	
9.	Are the embedded links that will be used identified?	—	—	—	
10.	Are the needs of the microcomputer users for those links identified?	—	—	—	
11.	Has an availability/use matrix been prepared?	—	—	—	
12.	Is the use of the embedded links controlled according to the availability/use matrix?	—	—	—	
13.	Is the use of user exits for embedded links controlled?	—	—	—	
14.	Are the options in embedded links evaluated for their potential security risk?	—	—	—	
15.	Are the high-risk options eliminated or controlled?	—	—	—	
16.	Has the control software been thoroughly debugged?	—	—	—	
17.	Is the control software tamperproof?	—	—	—	
18.	Can the central site detect unusual processing requests (e.g., requests during nonworking hours)?	—	—	—	

FIGURE 14–8 *(concluded)*

No.	Item	Yes	No	N/A	Comments
19.	Are there procedures to control unusual processing requests?	___	___	___	
20.	Are database data available to embedded links controlled?	___	___	___	
21.	Can the host computer control the integrity of data used by the embedded links (e.g., verifying control totals)?	___	___	___	
22.	Can missing data be detected (e.g., control totals incorrect)?	___	___	___	
23.	Are users instructed as to what data can be removed from the premises?	___	___	___	
24.	Are there procedures to inventory or control data removed from the premises?	___	___	___	
25.	Are users instructed in the security policy of the organization?	___	___	___	
26.	Are users given procedures to assess the adequacy of security at their site?	___	___	___	
27.	Is a procedure established for users to report potential security violations?	___	___	___	
28.	Are those procedures followed?	___	___	___	
29.	If so, does management review the reported potential security violations?	___	___	___	
30.	Are there procedures on how to destroy unwanted data?	___	___	___	
31.	Are those procedures consistent with the facilities of the embedded links?	___	___	___	
32.	Are users prohibited from accessing data except through the embedded links?	___	___	___	
33.	Can the host identify the distributed site prior to transmitting/receiving data from that site?	___	___	___	
34.	Are the data attributes at the central site consistent with those needed at the remote site?	___	___	___	
35.	If data attributes are different, can the embedded links compensate for those differences (i.e., reformat data)?	___	___	___	
36.	Is data recoverable in the event of loss of integrity of processing?	___	___	___	
37.	Is security at the local site consistent with the importance of data used at the local site?	___	___	___	

Key 1: Establishing Security Procedures

Policies indicate what is wanted, and procedures explain how to accomplish it. Although the policies should come first, it is the thoroughness of the procedures that determines the effectiveness of the security. The five microcomputer-to-mainframe link security procedures are illustrated in this section as follows:

1. *On-site procedures.* Figure 14–9 deals with the aspects of microcomputer security as they relate to the user protecting his/her microcomputer, related accessories, and supplies.

2. *Personal and off-site procedures.* Figure 14–10 defines company responsibility for personal microcomputers and the security policy when microcomputers are used for business purposes off the premises.

3. *Access to company data and programs procedures.* Figure 14–11 deals with microcomputer access to mainframe programs and data. While directed toward downloading, it is applicable to any link that accesses central information and programs.

4. *Security compliance procedures.* Figure 14–12 has to do with the compliance necessary for corporate security policies and guidelines.

5. *Central support of microcomputer policy.* Figure 14–13 relates to the support to be provided by the central site for the microcomputer user. As links are established, the responsibility for the central site and the microcomputer user need to be clearly established.

Note that these policies, responsibilities, and procedures may not be directly applicable to your organization. They are given as exhibits to follow in developing specific recommendations, and to use, as appropriate, in presenting and supporting those recommendations.

Key 2: Administering the Security Policy

It is important to define responsibility for administering the microcomputer-to-mainframe link security policy. Figure 14–14 establishes the administrator function, and indicates in responsibility number two that the administrator is responsible for ensuring that the security policy is being met. Having this responsibility clearly established is an important step in making good security happen.

FIGURE 14–9
On-Site Microcomputer Security Procedures (for a sample company)

Security

Since the microcomputer is treated as office equipment, the user is solely responsible for the security of the microcomputer and associated hardware. The security issue extends to the software packages used on the microcomputer and the data generated and stored by the user.

Physical

There are only two ways the microcomputer can be made physically secure. One way is to lock it and all the associated equipment (printers, displays, modems, plotters, keyboards, etc.) in a room that has a limited number of keys. The responsibility then falls on the people who have the keys. Another way is to secure the microcomputer to a work surface through a special locking mechanism or with cabling. For other types of locking mechanisms, see the Information Center for further information. If a room cannot be provided or the microcomputer cannot be attached to a desk or table, an alternative solution is to obtain lockable furniture especially made for microcomputers. This type of furniture is available from a variety of office supply companies.

Data Security

Data security encompasses keeping data secure from other users and ensuring that data is not accidentally lost. If all data is on diskettes, then the security problem is a simple one in which you lock the diskettes in a desk or filing cabinet after use. On the other hand, if you are using an IBM PC/XT and storing data on the hard disk, then it is accessible by anyone who knows how to use the machine. Data stored on the hard disk does not go through any encoding scheme, nor does the DOS system program provide any security checking features for people using the microcomputer.

Since diskettes are a magnetic form of storage that is susceptible to damage from a variety of accidents, it is best to make a backup copy of data. To make a copy of the data, use the COPY or DISKCOPY commands as described in the DOS User Manual that is supplied with the DOS diskette. Once the copy has been made, store it in a safe and secure place. Not only does this provide security if data is lost on working diskettes, but a copy of the data is available if the working diskettes are removed from the office. Hard disks are just as susceptible to failure and software problems. On a regular basis do a backup of the hard disk using the DOS BACKUP command. A hard disk contains a large amount of information and will require a large number of diskettes on which to copy. Up to 28 diskettes could be required and they must be formatted using the FORMAT command. Refer to the DOS User Manual for details on BACKUP and FORMAT commands.

In most cases, locking a diskette into a desk or filing cabinet offers security from theft or unauthorized access, but little or no protection against fire. To ensure that data is not lost if a fire occurs at the office, the diskettes should be locked in fireproof safes. Another method is to regularly ship diskettes off-site for storage. If information is lost, the backup diskettes can be retrieved.

FIGURE 14–9 *(concluded)*

Diskettes require special care if they are to give you faithful service. The following rules should be observed when handling and storing data and software package diskettes.

- Do not touch the exposed recording surfaces.
- Protect diskettes from dust by returning them to their envelopes as soon as they are removed from the diskette drive.
- Store frequently used diskettes in their envelopes. Don't lay heavy object on top of them. If they are stood on edge, make sure they aren't bent or sagging.
- Storage temperatures must be between 10° and 50° Celsius.
- Store seldom-used diskettes in storage boxes, away from heat and magnetic field sources such as telephones, dictation equipment, and electronic calculators.
- Because each piece of information occupies a tiny spot on the diskette, small scratches, dust, food, or tobacco particles may make information unusable.

When traveling with diskettes observe the above rules. If going through an airport X-ray scanner, have the diskettes examined separately. The final rule when traveling with diskettes is to ensure that a copy is left at the office in case of an accident.

Another form of security for data on diskettes is the write-protect notch on the right side of the protective cover. After data is entered on the diskette, cover the notch with a tab that was provided with the box of diskettes. The data is still readable but an attempt to write to the diskette will result in an error message. If there is need to write on the diskette again, simply remove the tab.

Software

Almost all software that is used on the microcomputer is licensed. That means that copies of it are not to be made unless there is a specific waiver in the documentation of the software package allowing a user to produce a copy. This also means that if the same software package is to be used on another machine, another copy must be purchased.

Security Agreement

When the department manager signs the equipment acceptance form after the microcomputer is installed, the responsibility for security of the microcomputer, associated equipment, and software is accepted by that person.

Monitoring Responsibility

Internal Audit is authorized to review and comment on department security procedures established for your microcomputer. This includes:

- Physical security (locked up or attached to work surface).
- Matching copies of purchased software to number of machines in the department.
- Checking that the seal placed on the system unit by the Information Center when it was installed is in place.

FIGURE 14–10
Personal and Off-Site Microcomputer Security Procedures

Complete systems, printers, screens, and disk drives are valuable and are relatively easy to take away from offices without detection. Expensive components, such as processor, memory, or peripheral control boards, can be easily removed and are small enough to conceal in a briefcase or pocket. Where possible, microcomputers should be installed in lockable offices; otherwise, the use of security devices, such as anchor pads that lock a microcomputer to a desk surface, are recommended.

Some employees may wish to bring their own microcomputer to use in the office. Where this is considered desirable, employees should be warned that the company cannot accept responsibility for possible damage or theft.

As sophisticated portable microcomputers become available, there may be circumstances where it will be advantageous to allow employees to take systems out of the office on business trips or for use at home. In these cases, measures should be taken to ensure that such equipment is insured while off the premises and that inventory control is maintained. Such use may complicate problems in resolving the issue of ownership of any software developed.

FIGURE 14–11
Procedures for Access to Company Data and Programs

Properly authorized and identified microcomputer users will be allowed access to company data under stringent controls. The individual requesting access and the microcomputer that he/she is operating must first be identified through passwords, ID numbers, etc. for each session. Access to the specific items of data requested by a microcomputer user must have been authorized for that user by the data's owner or the owner's representative. The mainframe computer programs used to gain access to company data on behalf of microcomputer users will be fully under the control of a company data processing organization responsible for the data's integrity and security.

Microcomputer users are allowed to create and modify company data maintained on the mainframe only when their microcomputers are operating as terminals for mainframe computers, using the same programs and controls as for traditional on-line terminals. Such emulation will be done using only company-supported microcomputers and software.

Transfers of data in bulk from mainframes to microcomputer (downloading) will be done by mainframe programs having full controls, and with appropriate capability for selection, summarization, and reformatting. Such data will normally be directed to diskette units within the microcomputer, to be manipulated thereafter by the user. Downloading programs for mainframes and company-supported microcomputers will be written and maintained by company data processing units.

When company-supported microcomputers are used as stand-alone word processing devices, they may send or receive text from other devices, including other microcomputers, by using the company's network of mainframe computers as intermediaries. Special mainframe and microcomputer programs, with full controls, will be written and maintained by data processing for this purpose.

FIGURE 14-12
Security Compliance Procedure

All employees must follow the Corporate Guidelines for Informational Security in protecting information in any form. Access to and use of microcomputers must be controlled so these guidelines are met. Each microcomputer user must have read and signed the Employee Computer Usage Policy.

Information stored on microcomputer machine-readable media (floppy disks, cartridges, tapes, etc.) must be classified, labeled, and handled in accordance with the Corporate Guidelines for Informational Security policy manual. Computer printouts must also be classified, labeled, and handled in accordance with the policy manual.

When the destruction of information on machine-readable magnetic media (tapes, floppy disks, cartridges, etc.) must be accomplished, it must be done by erasing the information. If in doubt about the erasing procedure, get technical help from Information Services.

Each microcomputer administrator must assume responsibility for the protection of information created, stored, or printed on the microcomputer. The administrator of the microcomputer must demonstrate reasonable security before the micro is connected to the computing network.

FIGURE 14-13
Central Support of Microcomputers Policy

The primary support provided for microcomputers will be provided by microcomputer administrators. Information Services will be the backup for the administrators. Information Services may also be contacted for information on microcomputer training courses. However, much of the introduction to microcomputer training for new users will probably be provided by microcomputer administrators, or through the use of self-training tutorials that are available.

The use of standard software throughout the corporation is strongly encouraged. This will make support of software easier and will provide other synergistic benefits. Information Services is the coordinator of this effort. Approved configuration and nonspecialized software will be supported by Information Services.

FIGURE 14-14
Administration of the Microcomputer-to-Mainframe Link

Every microcomputer used must have an administrator. Functional systems managers will assure that each microcomputer in their function has an administrator. The systems managers are responsible for managing the users of microcomputers in their function. The administrators are responsible for the following:

1. Ensuring that users are following the Code of Conduct and copyright laws through training of the users in the Code of Conduct and spot checks on the use of microcomputers.

2. Ensuring that security policy is being met by installing appropriate security software and by performing spot inspections and training of all users in security policy.

3. Handling all routine operational problems with the microcomputer. This includes:

   - Checking out the microcomputer when users have problems and initiating maintenance if it is required.
   - Reordering supplies such as paper, printer ribbons, and floppy disks when necessary to maintain the usability of the microcomputer system.
   - Acting as the local expert on the system. The owner will install and check out all new software and hardware purchased for the microcomputer. The person will also work with Information Services to standardize hardware and software.
   - Maintaining the software for the microcomputer. This includes keeping backup copies of the software for the microcomputer system, ensuring that the software is up-to-date, and keeping documentation up-to-date and available to the users.
   - Training in the use of the microcomputer system for new users. Tutorials will be provided for self-learning.
   - Establishing a system for scheduling and priority of use where there are multiple users of the system.
   - Backup responsibility.

The administrator will have access to more technical help from Information Services for those microcomputers, Displaywriters, and software packages supported by Information Services. Information Services will then work with the vendor directly to handle any problems that cannot be solved by personnel. Many of the above tasks for the microcomputer administrator can be delegated to others, but responsibility for the microcomputers still rests with the microcomputer administrator.

Key 3: Establishing Link Security Policies

Good security procedures require strong senior management support. This support should be based on the intent of management toward security as expressed through policies. It is difficult to implement security procedures from the bottom up, because it requires a coordinated effort to make security work. Management must support this effort through policies and provision of the necessary resources to implement those policies.

Four policies are presented to illustrate needed managerial direction.

1. *Microcomputer policy.* Figure 14–15 outlines the corporate approach to using personal computers. In the implementation section of the policy, it indicates that the users must follow the standards for data security. This policy causes more specific policies and procedures to be developed and implemented.

2. *Security policy.* Figure 14–16 is directed more at the security over the microcomputer (personal computer). It indicates that there will be a microcomputer coordinator (micro coordinator) to oversee microcomputer security. This policy defines several specific security guidelines.

FIGURE 14–15
Microcomputer Policy

Policy

Microcomputing products shall be acquired and utilized in a manner that is cost-effective, secure, and strategic.

Implementation

1. Business Systems shall publish standards for the selection and acquisition of microcomputer hardware and software. All microcomputers must be selected from authorized standards.
2. Managers are responsible for ensuring that sound business cases for acquisition exist, and that anticipated benefits are realized.
3. Business Systems shall provide guidance in the effective use of personal computers, with emphasis on security and backup procedures, documentation, and training. Managers are responsible for ensuring that users receive adequate training.
4. Each user must follow the standards for data security, protection of assets, documentation, and backup.

Objective

The acquisition and use of microcomputing products should make effective use of human, financial, and data resources, while supporting long-term strategies for office automation and computer literacy.

FIGURE 14–16
Security Policy

The security of the hardware and data must be the responsibility of the user who requested the hardware and/or software, and must be in line with the standards as set up by the microcomputer coordinator. Each user location (division, unit, etc.) must set its own policy about taking the hardware off site; however, this is a practice that should be encouraged to provide employees with exposure to microcomputers on their own time.

A control log should be maintained in which users have to sign out all hardware, diskettes, manuals, etc., that are removed from the offices.

In some cases, it may be necessary to lock up all hardware and software after hours to discourage the theft of diskettes and small pieces of hardware.

The data stored on the microcomputers will be "user supplied" as opposed to being extracted from corporate databases. However, the reports generated on the microcomputers may look like corporate reports. It becomes important that all microcomputer reports be identified as such, so there can be no confusion or errors generated by the utilization of microcomputer reports.

Data stored on the microcomputers must be viewed as a corporate resource and treated, where appropriate, with the same level of security and confidentiality as any other corporate data.

When needs and facilities are established to enable microcomputers to access data files on the divisional Wangs or centralized IBM equipment, strict guidelines will have to be established as to what data may be viewed and/or extracted for later use on the microcomputers. However, for the present, there should not be any interfacing allowed between microcomputers and mainframe databases.

---

3. *Security clearance policy.* Figure 14–17 defines who has access to the mainframe computer and how that access is accomplished.

4. *Security self-assessment policy.* Figure 14–18 indicates user responsibility for security. An important part of implementing security policies is periodic self-assessment. This policy defines when and how that self-assessment is to be accomplished.

ON-LINE SYSTEMS SECURITY CONSIDERATIONS

This section is an expansion of the previous section on evaluating emulator security.

Microcomputers used in the on-line terminal emulation mode do not make use of the inherent processing power of the microcomputer. In the

FIGURE 14-17
Security Clearance Policy

Users with the appropriate security clearance will be able to access only copies of company production data that is stored on the mainframe computer. Downloaded information is to be kept on diskettes that are locked up when not in use or on a hard disk that has a security package that restricts access. The resulting hard-copy reports should be locked up when not in use.

All data residing on a mainframe or a microcomputer will have the same standards of security. Those without authorization to production data on the mainframe will not have access to that data or related information on a microcomputer.

FIGURE 14-18
Security Self-Assessment Policy

At least quarterly, each microcomputer user is required to review his/her listings in the company's microcomputer inventory and bring them up to date. In developing programs intended for ongoing use, users are required to follow the corporate standards for microcomputer programming, when such standards have been established. Adherence to the standards for one-time or temporary programs is not required but is encouraged.

When microcomputers are used in ongoing productive applications, the company can be harmed, sometimes significantly, by nonadherence to the rules of effective data processing that have evolved over the years. For such applications, therefore, users and their managements have these responsibilities:

- Protecting appropriate data in microcomputer files from disclosure to or modification by unauthorized individuals. Diskettes containing sensitive information should be locked away when not in use.

- Protecting both data and programs from accidental erasure or other loss. For critical data and programs, remotely stored extra copies will be mandatory.

- Providing for continuity of the application when the current developer and user are not present. Training of a second user is normally required, along with preparation and maintenance of good user manuals and other documentation. User-developed programs must be logical, compartmentalized, and well explained. Such documentation must survive a physical disaster of reasonable size.

All computer programs written by employees using company-owned computer equipment are company property. Individuals leaving the company must return all copies of their programs and documentation to the company.

---

terminal emulation mode, they assume the basic characteristics of a "dumb" terminal.

Throughout this chapter the word *terminal* applies to the microcomputer used in terminal emulation mode.

More information regarding the security and audit of microcomputers in an on-line environment can be found in Chapter 9 and Chapter 13.

Security and Control

On-line application systems present a distinct set of problems related to security and control because of the lack of a hard-copy audit trail, few or no source documents, few off-line checks and balances, a lessening of the traditional separation of duties, and the mechanical means of authorizing transactions. The security of on-line systems is intimately tied to the hardware and software audit controls that are built into the systems. Thus, the security of on-line systems cannot be distinguished, in most respects, from the control of the systems. It is only through proper system design and strong audit controls that the security of on-line systems can be maintained.

On-line application systems can be generally divided into six types, each of which has unique security and control concerns:

1. *Data entry (batch).* Data is recorded at a remote site and then transcribed throughout the day to computer media such as disks, diskettes, or cassette tapes. When the processing at the terminal location has been completed, the data is transmitted as a batch to the host computer. The data may be collected at the central or host location from many terminal locations. All the batches of data transmitted are combined into one large batch and processed by the central computer. For example, take an organization with several outlying sales offices. The remote sales offices take orders and ship products. The information is keyed to a diskette at the sales office and transmitted to the home office in the evening. The central computer located in the home office processes the information to produce overnight billing invoices. The results of the central processing may or may not be transmitted back to the remote terminal location.

2. *Data entry (on-line collection).* On-line data collection is similar to the on-line batch data entry, except that the data is collected by machine and transmitted continually to the home office. There it is batched for processing at a later time. For example, in a payroll data collection system, employees continually punch in and out. The data collection time-keeping device transmits a message that includes employee identification and time to the host computer. A computer can check those transactions immedi-

ately for validity. If a transaction is invalid, according to the computer rules, the transmitter will be so notified. For example, data collection equipment normally has dials that light to indicate whether or not the transaction is acceptable. For unacceptable transactions, the transmitter must reenter the data. As with the batched data-entry system, the processing from on-line data collection equipment is processed at a later time. For example, in the payroll application, the data might be processed weekly when the payroll is prepared.

3. *Remote job entry (RJE)*. Remote job entry permits individuals who are remote from the computer to transmit all the information needed about a job over transmission lines to the computer. The data is batched and sent to the computer for processing whenever computer time becomes available. RJE is commonly used for scientific jobs, repetitive small jobs, and program compilations. Normally, all the data needed to run the job is included with the transmitted data. In many jobs, on-line files are used in conjunction with RJE processing. One example is program compilation using a program library. In order to compile the program, the last process's program source code must be on-line to the computer, prior to running the RJE job, so that it can be modified by RJE-transmitted changes to produce a new compilation. The turnaround time for RJE processing can vary from a few seconds to several hours.

4. *Inquiry.* Inquiry allows a terminal user access to data on-line to the computer. Using inquiry processing, the system user wants immediate access to data contained in an on-line file. For example, in department stores, the sales clerk needs to know if a customer's credit is good before he or she can grant credit to a customer. The sales clerk transmits the customer number to the computer and gets an immediate approval or denial message. Under the inquiry mode of processing, the user is limited to the data currently on-line to the computer. Normally, processing does not occur, but some minor processing is possible. In the department store credit example, the system could add the amount of the proposed purchases to the open balance to see if the total exceeds credit limits before giving a "go" or "no go" on credit approval.

5. *Memo updating.* This mode of processing gives the appearance that computer records are immediately modified using the data entered through a terminal. For example, in an on-line savings and loan system, the savings account balances appear to increase or decrease based on deposit and withdrawals processed through the teller terminal. In actual practice, the transactions are logged. What happens is that a duplicate copy of the savings balances is modified. At the end of the day's transactions, the deposits and withdrawals are run again in a batch mode against the official bank records. The advantage offered by memo

updating is the elimination of control problems associated with destructive updating. In effect, the system is run twice, and the results can be compared.

6. *On-line updating (destructive updating)*. The processing is identical to memo updating, except that the original update is the only update. The transactions are not batched at the end of the day and processed again after normal business hours. The example of the savings and loan on-line teller system previously stated could destructively update the depositor's balance at the time the transaction occurred. The new balance would then become the official bank record. As organizations gain more confidence in their ability to develop well-controlled and auditable on-line applications, they move toward destructively updated files.

Components of Message Transmission

The three components of message transmission are the sender of the message, the method of transmission and the receiver of the message. The message sender is frequently a terminal. The method of transmission includes the modem, transmission facility, and a modem at the other end of the transmission facility. The message receiver may be a computer. There can be many variations of these pieces of hardware in actual practice.

All of these on-line applications use the same methods of transmitting information. The hardware, software, and distances transmitted can vary greatly, but the basic components of message transmission remain the same.

In most on-line systems, the terminal controls the application processing logic. When a message is entered into a terminal, it must contain the parameters needed for processing. Messages can be stand-alone, which means all the information needed to direct the processing is contained in the message, or some of the information can be transmitted during the operator sign-on procedures. The following are the types of information needed to direct processing:

- The computer where processing is to occur.
- The program.
- Master data.
- Security clearance.
- Cryptographic or other code keys needed for translation.

This type of information enables the message-switching unit to route the message to the proper location. Upon receipt of the message-switching, the software makes the necessary routing assignments. It is then transmitted to the central computer through a message-switching system.

The method of transmission is the most technically complex part of the operation. When transmission is made over common-carrier lines (telephone company lines), it becomes necessary to change from the terminal's electronic code structure to the code structure of the common carrier. This code conversion is accomplished using a modem. At the end of the transmission facility, a second modem is required to transcribe from the common carrier's electronic code to the coding system acceptable to the end terminal. Mixing different types of equipment can cause the mechanics of transmission to become extremely complex.

The message-receiving equipment includes the terminal and the modem needed to convert line code to computer code. The data can then enter computer processing from the communication terminal unit, or it can be stored in an off-line storage device to be held until needed by the computer application.

When received by the central computer, the communication-system software performs a series of checks to ascertain whether or not the transmitted information was received correctly. The security software verifies that the sender is authorized to send the message and has the authority to access the programs and data requested. The message is then delivered to the application program through the operating system. The operating system calls the needed application program. If data is needed, the database manager of the system will be called upon to retrieve the desired data.

Security and Control Concerns

Much of the security and control in an on-line application is determined by the features available and used in the total hardware and software systems. The reviewer must have a basic understanding of these systems and their interrelationships to properly evaluate the security and control implications of an on-line application.

Eight security and control concerns can be identified for on-line applications:

1. *Unauthorized system use.* On-line applications are subject to penetration by unauthorized users. Penetration can be used for manipulating data, obtaining data for unauthorized use, or destroying data within the application. Perpetrators look for the weakest control link in the system and enter through that weak link.

2. *Inability to restart.* On-line applications are subject to hardware and software failure. Systems can go down entirely, or in part. When that

happens, service is interrupted to one or all users. Applications should be designed so that, in the event of hardware and software failures, they are able to restart without loss of data in the system up to the point of shutdown. This includes information in the process of being transmitted.

3. *Loss of audit trail.* The application should provide sufficient processing documentation to enable the tracing of transactions from the general ledger backward to inception and vice versa. The amount of documentation provided is a management decision, but it should be sufficient to show who performed what aspect of processing, including authorization of the transaction. In on-line applications, the audit trail must also show terminal users.

4. *Undetected transmission errors.* Hardware and line problems can cause messages to be lost or garbled. The controls present in the hardware and communication software should be sufficient to detect these problems and automatically call for retransmission of messages.

5. *Loss of messages.* Messages can be lost through faulty transmission, shutdown of the system, or application errors. Controls that detect when a message has been lost should be present.

6. *Insufficient documentation.* On-line applications are significantly more complex than batch-oriented applications. This complexity increases the need for documentation of the application. Documentation standards should be established for on-line applications and enforced during the development and enhancement periods.

7. *Undetected software problems.* The number and complexity of software packages add to security problems because it is reasonable to expect that problems will occur in the software packages. Organizations should utilize as many control features as practical in all the software packages so that errors will be detected when they occur.

8. *Inadequate controls.* System designers and programmers may not consider security sufficiently in designing on-line applications. The cost for developing adequate controls is considerable, but the security exposure is also considerable.

On-Line Security Assessment

The assessment of security for an on-line system can be evaluated on the basis of two security attributes. The first attribute is the protection mechanisms put in place to protect the on-line system. The second attribute is the assurance features that measure the reliability of the security protection mechanisms.

Protection mechanisms are specific features intended to establish a high-integrity protection environment to support the stated security policy, either directly by controlling access, or indirectly through various administrative tools. These features include the following:

- *Prevention:* The mechanisms (most software) that are intended to prevent breaches of security, also called enforcement mechanisms. They should be sufficiently powerful, general, and efficient to counter all relevant threats.
- *Detection:* The mechanisms used to detect suspicious events, or to provide a security officer with on-line and off-line security assessment tools. They should permit rapid detection and confinement or error propagation.
- *Authorization:* The mechanisms that authorize accesses and manipulations of a system object to a user or program, including administrative support for them. Authorization *granularity* refers to what level of detail accesses can be controlled. *Policy interface* with authorization mechanisms is the manner in which authorizations are expressed and decided vis-à-vis the stated policy.

Assurance features measure the confidence one has in the security mechanisms. They cover the proper design of the protection mechanisms and the assurance that they operate correctly and reliably in the face of both malicious intent and accident, including failures. These features include the following:

- *Hardware.* Assurance that the security-related hardware operates correctly.
- *Software.* Assurance that a formally stated security policy is supported by the software system design and implementation (software includes relevant firmware; a more detailed matrix would have separate measures for firmware).
- *Development and testing.* Assurance that the system is developed using formal and rigorous controls and standards.
- *Operation and maintenance.* Assurance that the system is operated and maintained to warrant continued confidence in it, even in the face of vendor or user enhancements, modifications, or repairs.

An on-line security evaluator matrix and a worksheet (see Figures 14–19 and 14–20) are provided to measure security using the two attributes (protection mechanisms and assurance features). Instructions on how to use the matrix and worksheet follow the figures.

FIGURE 14–19
Assurance Features and Protection Mechanisms Matrix

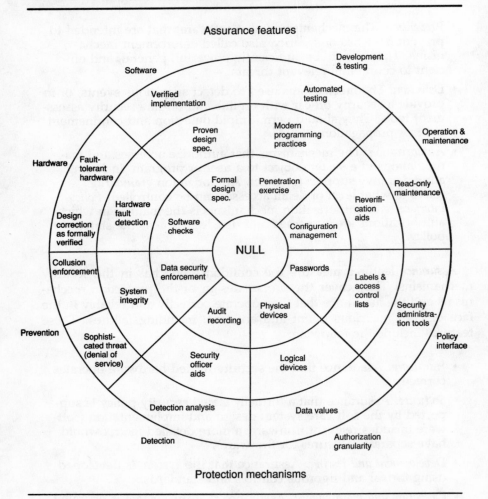

Protection mechanisms

The Assurance Features and Protection Mechanisms Matrix and worksheet are used in the following manner:

1. Evaluate the on-line security for each of the attributes indicated in Figure 14–19. For example, the prevention protective mechanisms are evaluated, followed by the detection protection mechanisms, and so on, until all eight assessment areas are analyzed on the worksheet (Figure 14–20).

FIGURE 14–20

Assurance Features and Protection Mechanisms Worksheet

Item No.	Assessment Area	Security Point Range	Points Assigned	Total Points
1.	*Prevention*			
	a. Null	0	___	
	b. Data security enforcement	1–3	___	
	c System integrity	4–5	___	
	d. Collusion enforcement	6–7	___	
	e. Sophisticated threat	8–9	___	
	Total			___
2.	*Detection*			
	a. Null	0	___	
	b. Audit recording	1–4	___	
	c. Security officer aids	5–7	___	
	d. Detection analysis	8–9	___	
	Total			___
3.	*Authorization granularity*			
	a. Null	0	___	
	b. Physical devices	1–3	___	
	c. Logical devices	4–6	___	
	d. Date values	7–9	___	
	Total			___
4.	*Policy interface*			
	a. Null	0	___	
	b. Passwords	1–2	___	
	c. Labels and access control lists	3–6	___	
	d. Security administration tools	7–9	___	
	Total			___
5.	*Hardware assurance*			
	a. Null	0	___	
	b. Software checks	1	___	
	c. Hardware fault detection	2–3	___	
	d. Hardware design correctness	4–6	___	
	e. Fault-tolerant hardware	7–8	___	
	Total			___

FIGURE 14–20   *(concluded)*

Item No.	Assessment Area	Security Point Range	Points Assigned	Total Points
6.	*Software assurance*			
	a. Null	0	____	
	b. Formal design specifications	1–3	____	
	c. Proven design specifications	4–6	____	
	d. Verified implementation	7–9	____	
	Total			____
7.	*Development and testing assurance*			
	a. Null	0	____	
	b. Penetration exercise	1–2	____	
	c. Modern programming practices	3–5	____	
	d. Automated testing	6–7	____	
	Total			____
8.	*Operation and maintenance assurance*			
	a. Null	0	____	
	b. Configuration management	1–2	____	
	c. Reverification aids	3–4	____	
	d. Read-only memory	5	____	
	Total			____

2. Begin the analysis at the null block on the matrix. A null condition indicates that there are no security measures in that area. Security measures become more sophisticated as the flow moves from the null circle to the most distant circle of the figure.

3. The more sophisticated the security features, the higher the number of security points allocated for each area on the worksheet. For example, a null condition gets zero points, and as the features get more sophisticated a higher number of points is allocated.

4. A score representing the highest number of points for each of the areas should be recorded on the worksheet.

5. The ideal security circle for an on-line system provides an even level of security. For example, null security in one area with a

very high level in another does not provide a good overall security package. Vulnerability tends to occur at the weakest point of a security circle.

Each of the assessment areas, with a brief description of the various levels of security, follows:

1. Prevention.   The levels are as follows:

a. *Null.* System is incapable of enforcing security and integrity principles, either through lack of hardware mechanisms or through lack of software features. **0 points.**

b. *Data security enforcement.* System is intended to be capable of enforcing basic security principles (unauthorized direct access and manipulation) upon individual users attempting (accidentally or maliciously) to directly violate the security policy. The system does not seriously intend to defend against the more advanced forms of indirect programmed attacks. **1–3 points.**

c. *System integrity.* System is intended to be capable of protecting its own integrity against malicious or accidental acts of its users, including secretly programmed attempts to bypass or fool the protection mechanisms. **4–5 points.**

d. *Collusion enforcement.* System is intended to be capable of enforcing data security with two or more users colluding (using covert channels), including the threat of information leakage through implanted software (unintentional downgrading). **6–7 points.**

e. *Sophisticated threat.* System is intended to be capable of enforcing security principles involving sophisticated threats, including the more complex denial of service threats. **8–9 points.**

Note: These last two features are not strictly ordered and are representative of the most sophisticated kinds of mechanisms that can be implemented and the threats they defend against.

The evaluation of the prevention features is based solely on the intent of the mechanism furnished, possibly on their efficiency, but not on how effective they are. That measure is taken under the assurance attributes.

2. Detection.   The levels are as follows:

a. *Null.* System is incapable of detecting misuse (to any great extent) in real-time and has no facility for detecting or assessing damage after an unauthorized penetration. **0 points.**

b. *Audit recording.* System is capable of logging critical security actions in sufficient detail to provide an adequate trace of user and system activities. Measurement of compliance is dependent on the extent of the records and whether or not they are easily directed to a cognizant person for analysis. For example, if the threat is an authorized user turning bad and misusing his legitimate authority, only the owner of a database can help by ascertaining if accesses to it by each person are necessary and proper. It is effective if audit is on a nonmodifiable medium (to prevent after-the-fact tampering). **1–4 points.**

c. *Security officer aids.* These are measures to help the security officer monitor in real-time system activities, even to the extent of transparently watching users' activities. More credit is given if the audit trail is accessible (read-only) to the security officer through a modern database management system with good on-line query capability. **5–7 points.**

d. *Detection analysis.* This enhances on-line security facilities and sophisticated post-analyses to perform history/trend and pattern recognition analysis. **8–9 points.**

Note: The rating of the detection features of a given system will be affected by the prevention rating, because an audit record that is not data-secure might be worthless or misleading.

3. Authorization granularity.   The levels are as follows:

a. *Null.* System is incapable of enforcing access controls. **0 points.**

b. *Physical devices.* System can enforce control over access to physical devices. **1–3 points.**

c. *Logical devices.* System can enforce control over access to logical data structures. Measurements of compliance increases with finer granularity, varying from files to records, or to fields within records. **4–6 points.**

d. *Data values.* System can authorize, based on the value of the data element being accessed, or on the value of some other data element. More credit is given if the system can also perform legality checks (as implied by the security policy), threshold checks, and reasonableness (e.g., type or range) checks. **7–9 points.**

4. Policy interface.   The levels are as follows:

a. *Null.* System has no ability to selectively enforce accesses in accordance with stated policy. **0 points.**

b. *Passwords.* System provides only for passwords as a means of controlling access, either to the system as a whole or to data within it. It is assumed that passwords are always used as the means of authenticating a user on entrance to a system, recognizing that other schemes are possible, and at times are permissible or preferable. **1–2 points.**

c. *Labels and access control lists.* System provides for selective control of access to data based on the specified security properties of data. Whether or not distinction between discretionary controls are expressed would be taken into account in a particular evaluation. **3–6 points.**

d. *Security administration tools.* Appropriate tools are provided to make administration of access control more convenient and subject to audit and automation. Also included in the measurement here is the appropriateness of the division of labor between the user, owner (or custodian) of data, and security officer/administrator. **7–9 points.**

5. Hardware assurance. The levels are as follows:

a. *Null.* System has no facilities for verifying that the hardware is working correctly. **0 points.**

b. *Software checks.* System has software that checks the integrity of the security-related hardware periodically. **1 point.**

c. *Hardware fault detection.* System has hardware that detects an incorrect operation of the security-related hardware. More assurance is achieved if hardware verifies to fail-safe than if hardware fails unpredictably. **2–3 points.**

d. *Hardware design correctness.* Security-related hardware is proven and verified to be correct in operational and degraded environments. **4–6 points.**

e. *Fault-tolerant hardware.* Hardware is designed in accord with high reliability standards akin to those used in deep-space probe missions or nuclear reactor control. It is important if system availability is a major goal for a given system. **7–8 points.**

6. Software assurance. The levels are as follows:

a. *Null.* System where design specification is not formally and rigorously stated and the resulting implementation is developed and tested using traditional testing techniques. **0 points.**

b. *Formal design specifications.* System is specified through a rigorous specification language. The implementation may also be conducted through verifiable procedures, but the design has not been formally proven to be a correct and complete representation of the specification, and the code has not been verified. **1–3 points.**

c. *Proven design specification.* This is system development using provable techniques (assisted by automation) for ensuring the design accurately reflects the design specification. **4–6 points.**

d. *Verified implementation.* The implementation is in principle verifiable (the proper rigor has been taken and proper language used), but it has not been formally verified. **7–9 points.**

7. Development and testing assurance. The levels are as follows:

a. *Null.* System is developed without complying with formal and rigorous controls and standards, and no special attention has been paid to security aspects of the implementation. **0 points.**

b. *Penetration exercise.* System has been subjected to a thorough attempt to penetrate its defenses; any discovered design or implementation weakness or flaws have been corrected, and the process has been repeated until no further flaws are discoverable. **1–2 points.**

c. *Modern programming practices.* System is developed through a carefully controlled and managed implementation process to include software management, structured walk-throughs, top-down programming, and structured programming and testing, and implemented with a modern high-level language. (Structured assembly language, FORTRAN, COBOL, etc., are insufficient.) **3–5 points.**

Note: This feature is sufficiently rich and important as to probably merit its own subevaluation criteria.

d. *Automated testing.* In addition to the above, the system has been tested in a semiautomated way against a test specification proven to be an accurate representation of the design specifications. The test must demonstrate complete implementation of the specification and the validity of all assumptions, not merely that the external interfaces work as intended. **6–7 points.**

8. Operation and maintenance assurance. The levels are as follows:

a. *Null.* No particular attention has been paid to the state of the security aspects of the software after delivery. **0 points.**

b. *Configuration management.* Rigorous controls over the software and hardware configuration are employed after the system is operational, including careful bookkeeping and authorization of changes, with at least a comparison of proposed changes to the security specifications. **1–2 points.**

c. *Reverification aids.* Any changes are reverified with the tools and to the level of formalism used in the design and development process. It is better if automated tools help keep track of what parts of the system need to be reverified for any given design **or** implementation change. Unannounced periodic visits are used to check the system, its controls, and operations. **3–4 points.**

d. *Read-only memory.* Security-relevant trusted software (including all the security kernels) is run from read-only memory, distributed, and controlled by a central authority for a given system. **5 points.**

On-Line Security Controls

It is difficult to perform a competent review of on-line security. The types of security controls that will prevent the casual intruder from penetrating are within the domain of normal reviews. However, controls to prevent the skilled perpetrator from penetrating an application require an equally skilled security evaluator. The following are some of the security and control concerns:

- Unauthorized system user.
- Loss of audit trail.
- Loss of messages.
- Insufficient documentation.
- Undetected software problems.
- Inadequate controls over processing.

On-line applications can be penetrated with highly technical electronic gear. For example, electronic gear can detect the electronic codes being transmitted without being physically connected or located next to the equipment or lines. Most reviewers are not technically qualified to know whether or not the system is adequate to prevent such penetrations.

Most perpetrators seek the easiest method to penetrate a system. In many instances, the weakest link is the terminal operator. Knowing this, the reviewer should look for the weakest security links and concentrate the security review on those weak links. If an in-depth security review is needed, an expert should be retained to conduct the review.

Figure 14–21 provides a checklist of items to be reviewed for the security of on-line applications. These questions are oriented toward the unique security problems of on-line applications.

Environmental Controls

The review of environmental controls will cover supervisory controls related to on-line applications. The environmental controls for on-line data processing operations are those controls that apply to all on-line applications.

The security and control concerns for environmental controls of on-line applications include the following:

- Unauthorized system user.
- Insufficient documentation.
- Undetected software problems.
- Inadequate controls over processing.

The environmental controls set the control atmosphere for other areas of the on-line application. Management can express its interest and intent for control more readily through environmental controls than through the application-oriented controls. It is through the strength and enforcement of environmental controls that management transmits to system designers the importance of building controls into the on-line applications.

Figure 14–22 is a checklist that provides a series of items relating to environmental controls that are generally applicable.

Terminal and Message Controls

The review of the movement of data between the terminal and the main computer requires a high degree of technical competence. It is essential to understand the hardware and software involved in message transmission. Without this understanding, it is almost impossible to perform this part of the review.

In reviewing the controls over terminals and messages, the following security concerns are present. These are operational problems that can result in loss of security control:

- Inability to restart.
- Undetected transmission errors.

FIGURE 14-21
General Security Controls

No.	Item	Yes	No	N/A	Comments
			Responses		
1.	Does the system periodically reverify that an authorized operator is still at the terminal?	___	___	___	
2.	Are additional security or approval codes, beyond those required to gain access to the system, required for entering critical data elements, like changing credit limits?	___	___	___	
3.	Is the responsibility for establishing or changing identification and/or security codes isolated and segregated from the normal operation in the terminal?	___	___	___	
4.	If a terminal does not send or receive a message for a predetermined number of minutes, is that terminal deactivated?	___	___	___	
5.	Is the number of individuals who can use supervisory codes restricted?	___	___	___	
6.	Is the number of terminals that can use supervisory codes restricted?	___	___	___	
7.	Are sensitive/critical commands restricted to one master input terminal on the system?	___	___	___	
8.	Are checks made on personnel having access to critical information?	___	___	___	
9.	Are the organization's personnel-security policies documented?	___	___	___	
10.	Are personnel adequately instructed in security procedures?	___	___	___	
11.	Are all personnel involved in using the system advised of security procedures?	___	___	___	
12.	Are communication and application programs for key applications stored in protected areas?	___	___	___	
13.	Are console logs reviewed regularly to determine if improper use of the system has occurred?	___	___	___	
14.	If message-switching devices are used, is adequate security maintained over those switching areas?	___	___	___	

FIGURE 14–21 *(concluded)*

No.	Item	Yes	No	N/A	Comments
15.	Are phone numbers changed frequently on dial-up lines?	___	___	___	
16.	Are efforts made to keep phone numbers confidential?	___	___	___	
17.	On dial-in calls for on-line applications, does the system disconnect and automatically call back to the location requesting service?	___	___	___	
18.	If a terminal is brought down by the system, is the polling list automatically reconfigured to delete that terminal?	___	___	___	
19.	Is password protection used?	___	___	___	
20.	Does the system have a message intercept for inoperable terminals or invalid addresses?	___	___	___	
21.	Is it possible to log all security violations?	___	___	___	
22.	Are security codes deleted when an individual operator changes jobs or terminates with the organization?	___	___	___	
23.	Is adequate documentation maintained on security procedures?	___	___	___	
24.	Does each terminal have a unique terminal identification code that is checked by the computer?	___	___	___	
25.	If a terminal has a lockable keyboard, is the feature used?	___	___	___	
26.	Is a nonprinting feature used when the operator keys in identification codes?	___	___	___	
27.	Is cryptography used on highly secure data?	___	___	___	
28.	If the terminal has a physical lock, is the feature used?	___	___	___	
29.	Are restricted terminals kept in a physically secure location?	___	___	___	
30.	Does each user of the terminal have a unique identification code?	___	___	___	
31.	Are users instructed on how to keep their identification code secure?	___	___	___	
32.	Are identification codes changed frequently?	___	___	___	
33.	Will the terminal automatically lock up after a reasonable number of attempts to access the system have been logged, even if by an authorized user?	___	___	___	
34.	Are terminals restricted access to certain systems, where appropriate?	___	___	___	

FIGURE 14–22
Environmental Controls

No.	Item	Yes	No	N/A	Comments
			Responses		
1.	Does the user of the on-line application assume responsibility for the accuracy and completeness of the data processed by the application?	___	___	___	
2.	Can one individual be held responsible for each area of the on-line application (terminals, programs, etc.)?	___	___	___	
3.	Are different on-line systems compared to determine which has the best overall transmission accuracy? (This can be used as a means of improving overall transmission efficiency.)	___	___	___	
4.	Does management review all abnormal terminal activities (error messages, excessive terminal shutdowns, etc.)?	___	___	___	
5.	Does management take strong corrective action when security violations are noted?	___	___	___	
6.	Is the history log used to analyze the effectiveness of the system?	___	___	___	
7.	Are the personnel operating the system capable of fulfilling the responsibilities assigned to them?	___	___	___	
8.	Are the remote terminals used enough to justify their existence?	___	___	___	
9.	Are line-usage records maintained for control purposes?	___	___	___	
10.	Are records maintained on transmission-error rates for control purposes?	___	___	___	
11.	Is maintenance regularly scheduled?	___	___	___	
12.	Are the best block sizes determined for transmission to reduce transmission errors?	___	___	___	
13.	Has a maximum error rate been specified, which if exceeded will cause the system to shut down?	___	___	___	
14.	Are the terminals located in an area that provides adequate light, proper temperature, etc., for the operators?	___	___	___	

FIGURE 14–22   *(concluded)*

No.	Item	Yes	No	N/A	Comments
15.	Do the systems provide a reasonable response time (1–4 seconds) so that the system can be operated at top efficiency?	___	___	___	
16.	Are terminals situated so that activity at the terminal is visible to management?	___	___	___	
17.	Are working conditions assessed to reduce the turnover of personnel involved with on-line applications to acceptable levels?	___	___	___	
18.	Are all interested parties advised of critical information whenever deemed necessary?	___	___	___	
19.	Have adequate operator manuals been provided for each user of a terminal?	___	___	___	
20.	Is the audit trail sufficient to satisfy Internal Revenue Service requirements?	___	___	___	

- Loss of messages.
- Insufficient documentation.
- Inadequate control over processing.

Figure 14–23 is a checklist that must be adapted to the type of terminal and lines utilized by the on-line application. The more complex the terminal and line structure, the more intense the questioning should become regarding the items in the checklist.

Application Controls

The application programs must retain responsibility for the accurate, secure, and complete processing of data. However, the application does not have responsibility for messages that are not received, or are received containing garbled or inaccurate information. The terminal and message controls are responsible for delivering all the messages correctly to the applications program.

On-line applications need to guard against garbled or inaccurate information. The more controls over transmission, the greater the proba-

FIGURE 14–23

Terminal and Message Controls

No.	Item	Yes	No	N/A	Comments
			Responses		
1.	Are terminal operators sufficiently trained on the use of the terminal?	___	___	___	
2.	Is sufficient time provided for terminal operators to receive adequate training for the applications they interface?	___	___	___	
3.	Are there restart points in long message transmissions so that the operator does not have to reenter an entire message if the operator makes an error?	___	___	___	
4.	Can terminal operators backspace to correct an error?	___	___	___	
5.	Can the terminal operators erase messages and restart to eliminate errors?	___	___	___	
6.	Do terminal locations without intelligent terminals keep control logs over transmitted data?	___	___	___	
7.	Does the network have a predetermined polling list to limit terminals to ones authorized at that point in time?	___	___	___	
8.	Is it possible to bring terminals up and down during normal system operations?	___	___	___	
9.	Does the equipment have sufficient automatic error checking routines?	___	___	___	
10.	Are remote terminals able to operate off-line in case the line or central CPU is down?	___	___	___	

bility of accurate and complete processing. For example, if messages are prenumbered, the application can check the accuracy of messages received.

In security considerations, there is a close interrelationship between message controls and application controls. Many of the controls within the messages are verified by the application. It is for this reason that the terminal and message controls should be reviewed prior to a review of the application controls.

The security and control concerns associated with reviewing application controls are the following:

- Loss of audit trail.
- Insufficient documentation.
- Inadequate controls.

Figure 14–24 is a checklist of those concerns.

Recovery Controls

The importance of quick recovery to security depends on the type of application. The more closely the application is interwoven into the day-to-day processing of the organization, the more critical are the recovery controls used to restart the system. The recovery controls include the ability to restart the system and the ability to continue capturing transactions while the on-line application is down. Security violations can occur more readily during down-time with uncontrolled restarts.

Alternative processing capabilities (backup) are an essential part of a successful on-line application. The organization's on-line application may be shut down for short periods of time without affecting the application, but alternative processing plans should be developed for long-term shutdowns. In an on-line system, a viable backup alternative must be put into operation within minutes after the main system is shut down if security is to be maintained.

The following are security and control concerns associated with recovery:

- Inability to restart under control.
- Loss of audit trail.
- Insufficient documentation.
- Inadequate control over processing.

Complexity of the recovery routines will be dependent on the completeness of the application controls and the terminal and message controls. The more controls available in the application and the terminal, the easier it is to recover from a shutdown.

One of the most complex aspects of recovery is recovering of messages in queue awaiting processing, or recovery of messages being transmitted when the shutdown occurs. The reviewer must verify that these messages will not be lost. Ideally, the hardware and software will control the in-process messages, but this must be verified through review.

Figure 14–25 provides items to review relative to recovery controls. Again, there must be a good understanding of the characteristics of

FIGURE 14-24
Application Controls

No.	Item	Yes	No	N/A	Comments
			Responses		
1.	Is an audit-trail logging facility maintained by or for the application to assist in reconstruction of data files?	___	___	___	
2.	Is it possible to trace the terminal user or origin?	___	___	___	
3.	Are messages date and time stamped for logging purposes?	___	___	___	
4.	Are messages balanced daily to each terminal in the system? (This is used to account for lost messages.)	___	___	___	
5.	For applications that update files, does the system protect against concurrent file updates? (Does initial access of a record lock that record so that additional accesses cannot be made until current processing is complete?)	___	___	___	
6.	Is the system able to handle the user demand during peak activity?	___	___	___	
7.	Is it possible to take appropriate follow-up action on all error messages?	___	___	___	
8.	Are error messages coded according to urgency of action, so that the serious errors are handled first?	___	___	___	
9.	Is a priority system established so that critical messages can be delivered or processed on time?	___	___	___	
10.	Are changes to the application system thoroughly tested before being placed into production?	___	___	___	
11.	Are all errors logged?	___	___	___	
12.	Is sufficient application documentation maintained on the terminal operations?	___	___	___	

communication systems to appreciate the problems associated with recovery. The reviewer must adjust the responses to recovery items based on the complexity of the on-line applications and the adequacy of controls in the application, terminal, and message areas.

FIGURE 14-25
Recovery Controls

No.	Item	Yes	No	N/A	Comments
		responses			

No.	Item	Yes	No	N/A	Comments
1.	If a peripheral device (disk drive, etc.) should fail, is the system able to switch the file to another device?	____	____	____	
2.	If a program should fail, can the message causing the failure be logged first, then deleted, and the program restarted?	____	____	____	
3.	Does the system contain a history log?	____	____	____	
4.	If so, does it include the following?				
	• Hardware failure messages.	____	____	____	
	• Terminal failure messages.	____	____	____	
	• Terminal start-up.	____	____	____	
	• Terminal shutdown.	____	____	____	
	• All input communication messages.	____	____	____	
	• All output communication messages.	____	____	____	
	• Unusual occurrences.	____	____	____	
	• Error messages.	____	____	____	
5.	Are changes to the operating and communication software packages adequately tested before being implemented?	____	____	____	
6.	On restart, are controls sufficient to verify that no messages were lost during shutdown?	____	____	____	
7.	Is an audible alarm available to signal when data error rates get too high?	____	____	____	
8.	Are all retransmissions logged?	____	____	____	
9.	Does the system have the ability to shut down parts of the system without bringing the entire system completely down?	____	____	____	
10.	Is an alternative source of power available for terminals?	____	____	____	
11.	Is adequate documentation maintained on recovery procedures?	____	____	____	
12.	Is adequate documentation maintained on restart procedures?	____	____	____	
13.	Do modems have front panel lights to indicate if the line is working properly?	____	____	____	

FIGURE 14–25 *(concluded)*

No.	Item	Yes	No	N/A	Comments
14.	Are backup modems available for critical applications?	___	___	___	
15.	Are alternative lines available for critical operations?	___	___	___	
16.	Are alternative procedures developed for short-term shutdowns?	___	___	___	
17.	Are alternative procedures developed for long-term shutdowns?	___	___	___	
18.	Have alternative procedures been tested to determine if they work?	___	___	___	
19.	Is maintenance readily available when and if needed?	___	___	___	

Chapter Fifteen

Some Final Thoughts

Most businesses are just beginning to address the microcomputer security issue. Financial institutions and airlines have already had to face the issue. In their businesses, disruption of microcomputer services can be devastating. In the industrialized world of the 1990s, virtually every company in existence and every human being alive will be impacted by microcomputers. Companies that have not taken the microcomputer security issue to heart yet will be forced to do so.

Security awareness continues to increase steadily. Hardly a day goes by without some news story appearing that contains some element of computer security. Floods, earthquakes, and natural disasters continue to occur. The impact they have on computers and telecommunications almost always makes the headlines. We have recently seen software problems totally disrupt airline services. We have seen hackers tried and convicted for computer crimes. Incidents of computer fraud are growing and will likely continue to do so as more and more dollar transactions pass over telecommunications links. There is no question that all of this will continue at an ever-accelerating rate. The concern already felt deeply by financial institutions will spread to all of industry. The potential risk is too high and the probability, over time, is too great for any prudent management to ignore.

It is likely that expenditures for computer security and related products during the last two years have exceeded those of all prior times. This has occurred in spite of the difficult economic times faced by most companies in the early 1990s. As the economy recovers this trend will accelerate.

TRENDS IN MICROCOMPUTER SECURITY AND RELATED ELEMENTS

This section is not intended to be a treatise on the future, but simply to highlight trends that will have an impact on microcomputer security in light of some of the key future expectations for areas that will affect microcomputer security.

416

Business Trends

Penetration of microcomputers in business will continue to increase in virtually every company regardless of size. The degree of company dependence on microcomputers will continue to increase until microcomputers are as vital to companies' existence as electricity.

Many companies will not take the necessary security precautions so you can expect to see a continuance of computer horror stories. The wise and prudent managers will take note and implement a microcomputer security plan. The foolish will continue to assume it can only happen to someone else—until after disaster strikes. At this point they too will get serious about security.

Criminal Activities

It is estimated that only 15 percent of white collar criminals are convicted. *Crime pays.* There is no reason to be optimistic about the future here. The decline in company loyalty to the employee and vice versa, as well as the callous manner in which some companies handle layoffs and downsizing, will generate animosity toward organizations. There already have been a number of cases where disgruntled employees have set software bombs and committed other malicious actions to be implemented upon their dismissal. The business climate of the '90s may result in an increase in this type of activity.

On the other hand, terrorism and the more violent crimes aimed at companies probably will not increase on a broad scale. Most occurrences would be on the local level because of some mass dissatisfaction, such as a strike, that has gotten out of hand.

Hardware Trends

"Faster" should not result in increased security problems, but "bigger" definitely will. "The bigger the tanker, the bigger the spill." Microcomputer CPU size only becomes more of a problem as it handles larger and more complex applications. Disk drive capacity, on the other hand, will continue to increase, and the security problems, especially as they relate to backup and restore, will also increase. Better, faster, and more secure methods must come into play in this area. Gigabyte 3.5-inch removable disks and magnetic tape are the most likely candidates to improve this situation. Many users who should already be using existing tape backup systems are ignoring the capability. Large-capacity single systems or servers will need to have high-speed, high-density tape backup capability. Adequate procedures for handling these processes must also be put in place.

As memories get larger and larger, the loss of what is currently being held in memory can become a problem and necessitate a great deal of rework. A loss of 16M RAM of current work can be painful. Memory backup via a magnetic drum or other media may become a requirement.

Software Trends

Hardware technology will continue to lead software in the 90s. Do not expect any magic potion in the software arena. Complexity breeds errors and problems. Software, it seems, is destined to give us a series of baby steps in terms of becoming more simple and easier to use. There will continue to be single outstanding packages. Virus-detection systems and password-protection systems will improve. Communications software should see some major improvements, but lack of standards and the "too many cooks" syndrome will likely spoil this stew as it will continue to plague the overall microcomputer system usability issue. Many different things from many different places, all built with minimal to no standards, will seldom play like a finely tuned orchestra that practices and plays together all the time. Until we get smart enough to solve this problem, poor use of the technology and inadvertent errors will prevail.

Database Trends

Databases may be the most fertile field for improvement in the '90s. "Bigger and faster" can definitely help us here in terms of both ease of use and capability. Expect to see some major improvements that will aid microcomputer security. Microcomputer database software that greatly facilitates backup and recovery as well as the off-site storage of critical files, comparable to what is becoming available on the mainframe, should migrate to the microcomputer.

The gigabyte removable 3.5-inch disks will make it easy to lock up files, and databases can be designed to make use of this capability.

Telecommunications Trends

The 1990s will be a time of "networked enterprises" and "client servers." These will add complications to the security issue. In fact, by the end of the decade, it seems inconceivable that there will be any stand-alone microcomputers. Cables, fibers, WANs, LANs, minisatellite transmitter-receivers, and no telling what else will provide convenient and very inexpensive access to the world of networks. Certainly every company and most homes will have broadband capability. Security measures to prevent unauthorized use of signals will greatly improve. It is impossible to prevent access to signals that are floating around in the air, but tapping fibers and other kinds of cables without detection can be made very difficult or impossible. Microcomputer telecommunication servers that can be locked in a closet where they will function without intervention will be the normal mode for companies of any size. This will significantly improve the reliability and security of this telecommunications element.

The caveat here is that there will be no end of "things" that you can have sent to your computer over the network. This in and of itself is fertile ground for viruses, software containing major errors, databases full of inaccurate information, and most every kind of abuse and misinformation known to man.

Who is going to control this? And how? An interesting question!

WHAT TO DO NEXT

If you are trying to decide what your next step should be in developing or updating your microcomputer security strategy, try the following scenario.

Overall Assessment

Before launching any security endeavor, you need to step back and make an overall assessment of your situation. You need to determine in broad terms the following:

- Where am I?
- Where do I want to go?
- What are the steps, in priority sequence, that will get me there?

Impact Analysis

If you have not done one or if it is out of date, a current business *impact analysis* should be done. Expending manpower and money on security is always painful, and there always seems to be a shortage of both. Therefore, you must determine the impact of losses on the various areas of the business from your microcomputer systems if you are going to expend these resources in an intelligent manner. The impact analysis will help you prioritize your security efforts so you will get the most value for your investment.

Determining Vulnerabilities

Which security problems are most likely to occur to your system? What is the likelihood that each will happen to you?

If your microcomputer system is located on the top of Pikes Peak, you are not very vulnerable to floods since the last one that hit that location occurred thousands of years ago in the days of Noah. Obviously, you would not want to expend effort in this direction. Conversely, if power and telecommunications frequently failed on the top of Pikes Peak, and if the outages had an adverse effect on your system, these could be your most vulnerable spot.

A second element of vulnerability would be to determine which portions of your microcomputer system would be adversely impacted by such an occurrence. It may be hardware, software, databases, communications, personnel, or something else.

Chapter Two dealt with this whole area in great detail, so the point here is that you must determine your weakest points and address them first.

Examine Alternative Solutions

In examining the alternative solutions, the permutations and combinations may quickly give you an overwhelming number of possible solutions. In most cases, a number of the solutions will be obviously flawed and need not be pursued. Even so, you will probably need to use your microcomputer to assist in the quantification and analysis of the possible alternative solutions.

Determine Optimum Solution

There may be a large number of solution candidates. The analysis made in the previous step should enable you to pick the best candidates for a more detailed analysis. The detailed analysis should enable you to pick the best solution(s) and also to determine the priority sequence for proceeding through the implementation phase.

Proceed with the Implementation

Implementation of a microcomputer security plan cannot be done on a time-available or part-time basis. It simply will not happen. If it is not going to be done in a timely, competent manner such that it can be tested, maintained, and communicated to and utilized by the people for whom it is intended, *forget it;* don't waste your time or theirs. Use the *prayer solution* (i.e., pray that nothing happens) or buy a lot of business interruption insurance.

In most cases, the project need not be a huge effort. It is often amazing what can be accomplished by a dedicated one- or two-person team that is knowledgeable and competent. Whatever is done, *implementation of your microcomputer security plan should be set up and managed like any other project.*

Ongoing Support, Testing, and Maintenance

Unfortunately, a microcomputer security plan is another one of those areas that you cannot do once and then walk away from. It requires support, administration, testing, and maintenance on an ongoing basis. Expect it.

Just handling investigation of security violations and the administration of a password system may require several people in a large corporation. This is not to say that the persons responsible for administering passwords cannot also do other jobs—but someone must be responsible for it, be trained for it, given time to do it, and so on.

WHEN WILL TECHNOLOGY SOLVE THE PROBLEM?

Will there ever be a time when microcomputer security ceases to be an issue? Microcomputer security will cease to be an issue when there are no natural disasters, there is no crime nor criminals, and there are no ignorant and incompetent people.

The Ultimate Secure System

It would probably be possible to design and implement a nearly foolproof system. But remember this saying: "It is difficult to make something foolproof because fools are so ingenious." Furthermore, such a system would probably be so unwieldy and cumbersome that the people who are supposed to be using the system would be unable to do so. You could build a house so secure that it could hardly be breached by anything short of a nuclear bomb, but who would want to live in it?

All of this is not to discourage or depress you regarding the matter of managing microcomputer security, but to say:

- *It must be part of business as usual.*
- *It must be institutionalized.*
- *It must be part of the cost of doing business.*

Index

Also of interest to you from Business One Irwin . . .

EVERYONE'S SUPPORT SYSTEMS
A Complete Guide to Effective Decision Making Using Microcomputers
Dr. Robert S. Snoyer and Glenn A. Fischer, Editors. Co-published by
Chantico Publishing Co., Inc./Business One Irwin

Offers proven methods to build management and support systems that empower employees and support management decision making at all levels. You'll discover practical ways for your design system to monitor business needs, analyze trends, and save time in planning. Also includes methods to resolve issues concerning data management, security, and information delivery. (400 pages)
ISBN: 1-55623-874-6

SPECTACULAR COMPUTER CRIMES
What They Are and How They Cost American Business Half a Billion Dollars a Year!
Buck BloomBecker

Based on more than 10 years of research and interviews with hundreds of criminals, victims, and security professionals, this thought-provoking book is an insider's look at the vulnerabilities of computer and communication technologies and the people who exploit them. Through this lively and sometimes humorous collection of 18 computer crime stories, you'll discover methods to use laws, ethics, technology, and common sense to fight computer crime. (242 pages)
ISBN: 1-55623-256-X

THE COMPUTER VIRUS DESK REFERENCE
Christopher V. Feudo

Guard against destructive computer viruses that waste your time and cripple your productivity! This book lists and examines more than 700 disassembled viruses and their characteristics, structures, and attack mechanisms so you can better defend against their effects. (672 pages)
ISBN: 1-55623-755-3

THE HIGH-TECHNOLOGY EDITORIAL GUIDE AND STYLEBOOK
1991 Edition, PC and Macintosh Versions
Lewis Perdue

"UNIX" or "Unix"? "Desk-top" or "desktop" publishing? "DESQview" or Desqview"? If your written communications must include computer terminology and references, you'll need this one-stop source for locating the correct usage of the latest technological terms. This easy-to-use, comprehensive guide—filled with contemporary buzz words, acronyms, and definitions—lends to consistent, effective writing and communications. Includes a user-friendly disk that can be loaded into your word processing program's spellchecker. (194 pages, paper)
ISBN: 1-55623-531-3 (PC version)
        1-55623-530-5 (Macintosh version)